Economic Miracle Market South Korea

Dieter K. Schneidewind

Economic Miracle Market South Korea

A Blueprint for Economic Growth in Developing Nations

Springer

Dieter K. Schneidewind
Faculty of Economic Science:
International Management
and Communication
Justus Liebig University Giessen
Giessen
Germany

ISBN 978-981-10-0613-5 ISBN 978-981-10-0615-9 (eBook)
DOI 10.1007/978-981-10-0615-9

Library of Congress Control Number: 2016932330

Printed on acid-free paper

This Springer imprint is published by SpringerNature
The registered company is Springer Science+Business Media Singapore Pte Ltd.

Register of a Few Korean Expressions

aigu, aiju	An expression of surprise, or astonishment
amhaeng eosa	Secret supervisor of the king
Arirang	Popular song; also name of many institutions
baedal	Distribution system
Baekje	Old kingdom
baksu	Shaman
borigogae	Permanent poverty, period of poverty
Bueyo	Historical place in Korea
bujang	Head of department
buk	North
bulgogi	Grilled meat
chaebol	Economic conglomeration
chaengi	Narrow-minded specialist
chajang	Manager, below head of department
Choson	Old name for Korea
Daehan Minguk	Official name of South Korea
daejeonggyo	Male, macho behavior
daekgeul	Chatting on the Internet
do	Province
donghak	Eastern teaching; term for revolutionaries
eum	Yin (female)
galbi	Meat dish
gibun	Feeling; mental state
gimchi	Fermented side dish
gisaeng	Traditional, high-class restaurant
Goguryeo	Old Korea, including Manchuria
gokkam	Persimmon
Goryeo	Old Korea
gu	City district
gukhoe	National assembly

gun	County
gwajang	Head of a unit
gyejang	Team leader
Gyeongbok	Royal palace at Seoul
haenyeo	Female mussel diver
hagwon	Cramming school
Han	Term for "Korean"
hanbok	Cloth for Korean women
hanguel	Korean alphabet
hanja	Chinese pictograms
hansik	Korean food
hoejang	Chairman
hwangje	Emperor
ingan	Seal for real estate transactions
inhwa	Human harmony
isa daeu	Manager, above department head
jeonmu	Senior board member
jigwon	Qualified employee
jikgu-jok	Web user
jolbu	Newly rich woman
Joseon	Name of dynasty, also for Korea
keyul	Name for a modern chaebol
kkangpae	Type of gangster organization
makgolli	Rice liquor
meot	Cool, relaxed, elegant
mudang	Female shaman
nam	South
nunchi	Empathy
perioe	Korean toothpaste brand
pojangmacha	Fast food cart
ppalli ppalli	Hurry up
pungsu	Feng shui
saemaul undong	The new village movement
sahwa	Literal purges in Korea
sajang	President
samguk	Three kingdoms
samguk sagi	The annals of the three kingdoms
samguk yusa	Testimonials of the three kingdoms
samgyeopsal	Pork belly
samil undong	Independence movement
sanmu	Board member
seonsaengnim	Master
Shilla	Old kingdom

si	City
si sang pil bol	With the carrot and the stick
siksa	Meal
Sirhak	Teaching of practical learning
songbang	Business branches
taekbae	Delivery to target
ulzzang (eoljiang)	Divine beauty
waegu	Japanese pirates
yang	Yang (male)
ye	Moral standard, law
eosin	Goddess
Yi	Dynasty (1392–1907)

Preface

During the time of my educational upbringing, as well as in my business life, I have been associated with Germany in manifold ways. Therefore, I am delighted that Prof. Schneidewind has ventured on writing a book on my homeland, which sheds light on various features of my fellow citizens, the national economy, and the business management of our rapidly growing state.

In the 1970s of the proceeding century, my own enterprise, the Dong-A Pharmaceutical Co., Ltd., collaborated on a license base with the German business group of Wella. This relation turned into a joint venture, which developed quickly to the market leadership in its specific market segment in Korea and almost immediately produced positive figures. Later, Wella took over our capital shares. The cooperation was always based on mutual trust, and all the numerous prevailing difficulties were smoothly cleared upon in fruitful dialogues. Both, Dr. Schneidewind, who served as an executive board member of his German headquarter and who had formerly worked for a long period of time in Asia, and Mr. Nolden, his managing director in Korea, who commanded a fluency in Korean language and was well associated with our country, showed great understanding of my homeland and its inhabitants.

International business is always accompanied by frictions and unforeseen events, for which textbooks do hardly provide solutions. However, if the investor shows understanding for the chosen guest country and with patient cooperation on both sides, a successful business relation is, in general, possible.

Besides the business activities, we enjoyed to foster harmonious and amicable relations, which also contributed to a personal and cultural enrichment for both sides. Even though our business relation ended years ago, we still meet occasionally and I appreciate that Dr. Schneidewind has even widened his interest in my home country and, by now, has even moved to Seoul. It was a particular pleasure to read his book manuscript. I cordially thank him for the excellent research work on my country, which I greatly admire and assess. There is still a shortage of published papers on Korea and her business environment. Using the title *Economic Miracle Market South Korea*, Dr. Schneidewind's work has not only shed light on economic facts but also shed light on the Korean history, culture, and society. Some representations are new and highly interesting not only for me but also for most Koreans. Korea investigated from the point of view of a foreigner offers a new, refreshing perspective. Therefore, I sincerely wish the submitted book project the well-deserved success![1]

Kang Shin-ho

[1]A curriculum vitae of Dr. Kang is attached at the end of the book

Acknowledgements

First of all, I would like to thank Mr. Detlef Nolden, for his extensive, invaluable help when writing the manuscript and later supervising it. For many weeks, we have worked together in Zwingenberg, my former residence in Germany, as well as in his residence in Witten at that time. Mr. Nolden graduated from the Ruhr University Bochum with a master degree in Korean sciences and also studied economics in Bochum. Later, he was a temporary student at the University of Boston and at INSEAD. He worked 19 years for Wella in Korea, the last six years as CEO of the local daughter company. Today, he lives with his Korean wife at the lovely Baldeneysee in the vicinity of Essen/Germany.

I owe a sincere "thank you" to the former chairman of the Federation of Korean Industries, Dr. Shin Ho Kang.[2] He wrote the preface to this book and encouraged me to write a volume on some aspects of Korea. My gratitude goes to a friend of Dr. Kang, Prof. Dr. Chongkoi Choi, Emeritus of the Seoul National University, who went through the complete text and provided some inputs and replenishments.

I dedicate this monograph of an East Asian country also to my academic tutors, Prof. Dr. Dres. h.c. Willy Kraus, formerly lecturing on the subject of Economic Development and Economy of East Asia at the Ruhr University Bochum and also Prof. Dr. Ehrenfried Pausenberger, formerly lecturing on the subject of International Business Administration at the Justus Liebig University of Giessen. Both always showed a keen interest in the development of the Asian Pacific area and frequently traveled there.

[2]Dr. Shin Ho Kang was twice chairman of the Federation of Korean Industries and is the managing owner of the leading pharmaceutical manufacturer in Korea since 1967, Dong-A Pharmaceuticals. He formerly served as an advisor of external economic relations to a Korean president. At a conference of German business leaders and scholars in Berlin, he scintillated with a lecture given in German. He proves his vitality at a rather advanced age by learning the Chinese language and also still plays many rounds of golf. He is the coeditor of a dictionary of Korean–Chinese–Japanese–English. In his home country, he is highly respected because of his always modest behavior and his social engagement. This gentleman delivered the following curriculum vitae, which is not at all a typical for a top representative of the Korean business society (selection).

Last but not the least, I thank my wife, Choi Khum-hee, a master graduate of political economics of the Waseda University of Tokyo, for interpreting services on frequent journeys to Korea and her translation of important literature; occasionally, she gave also valuable suggestions to some topics.

Contents

About the Author

Dieter K. Schneidewind (born 1935 in Bochum, Ruhr Area, Germany) is an acknowledged expert of economy and society of East Asia and Southeast Asia. In more than twenty years as a member of the Executive Board and later of the Supervisory Board of Wella AG, he gained solid international management experiences. Prior to that, he founded the biggest daughter company of the Wella Group and headed it for nearly ten years, while, at the same time, he worked at the helm of the Asia-Pacific region. During this time, he founded more than fifteen daughter companies in the Asia-Pacific region; those companies are in Japan, South Korea, and People's Republic of China. Together with the Suisse Schindler AG, the latter company was the first establishment of a business enterprise for production and sales in China with a foreign participation after 1949. After his service period in Tokyo, he was appointed Executive Board member of the German head office and in his later years served as a member of the Supervisory Board. Prior to his dispatch by Wella headquarters to Japan, the author acquired business administration qualifications in central divisions of the international corporation of the Siemens AG at Erlangen and Munich.

Schneidewind graduated from the mathematical and natural science Graf Engelbert Gymnasium in Bochum. Afterward, he graduated in business administration as a student trainee at the Albertus Magnus University of Koln. In 1962, he was awarded a doctorate (Dr. rer. pol.) in social psychology at the same university under the tutorship of the renowned Prof. Rene Koenig. Horst Albach appointed him to the board of editors of the distinguished economic periodical ZfB (Zeitschrift fuer Betriebswirtschaft) and he served also ten years on the board of the Schmalenbach-Gesellschaft fuer Betriebswirtschaft, a supreme German society for business administration. Calls to other committees followed.

The Ruhr University Bochum appointed him in 1979 as a lecturer for the subject of "Economy and Society of East Asia", a position that he kept for twenty-two years. After seven years of weekly lecturing, the state of North Rhine-Westphalia appointed him as an extraordinary professor (Univ. Hon. Prof.). He further taught for another eleven years at the Justus Liebig University Giessen on the subject of "International Marketing," after the state of Hesse had awarded him a second professorship. Schneidewind lectured also for six years at the University of Duisburg on the subject of "Business Administration in Japan." Other teaching appointments on the subject of "Economical and Social Matters of East Asia" led him to the Technical University of Dresden, the Phillip University of Marburg and the ETH Zurich (each for one year); he also taught regularly at INSEAD Fontainebleu and the WHU Koblenz (both private institutions for advanced studies).

The author wrote three volumes on management in Japan and one volume for business expatriates in Korea and edited with A. Toepfer the anthology "Der asiatisch-pazifische Raum" (the Asian Pacific Region). Another twenty contributions for anthologies and encyclopedias focused on the subject of global marketing and international business administration. He currently lives in Seoul, in the heart of the region he was always profoundly interested in.

Seoul, May 2015

Chapter 1
Introduction and Previous Visits to Seoul

1.1 Preliminary Remarks

The former center of economic activities on the globe, which (from a Western point of view) had turned from the Mediterranean Sea to the Atlantic, moved in more recent decades toward the shores of the Pacific Ocean. The states on the Western coasts of the Pacific display an enormous industrial development. For a long time, Japan was the second most powerful economic power of the world, but lost this position to China a few years ago. It will probably further lose its current position as the third economic power to India in the near future. From a qualitative point of view, Taiwan and South Korea have developed remarkably. The latter advanced to become number seven in the international ranking as both an exporting as well as importing nation. After centuries of isolation, South Korea has effectively advanced into the realm of the great industrial nations. Samsung Electronics as well as Hyundai Motors belongs to the world's top enterprises in their respective fields of business. In nine different branches of global industries, Korean companies are ranked within the top ten on sales: smartphones, home appliances, shipbuilding, semiconductors, automobiles, steel, auto parts, shipping, and communication. Furthermore, Seoul is increasingly becoming attractive for investors and salesmen from all over the world.

The Great Korean scholar Yi Hwang (1501–1570), better known as Toegye, uttered that the truth should not be sought for in grey theories, but would more likely be found in the advance of daily life. This saying is a very suitable motto for South Korea today.

South Koreans call their country "Daehan Minguk" (Land of the People of the Great Han). The North names itself "Choson Minchuchuui Inmin Konghwaguk," which translates as "The Democratic People's Republic Choson", Choson (Joseon) being an old name for Korea. Its national flag shows a red star in a white field against a red background. The status symbol of democratic South Korea is the

D.K. Schneidewind, *Economic Miracle Market South Korea*,
DOI 10.1007/978-981-10-0615-9_1

prominent Yin and Yang image, which is also part of the national colors. By incorporating this symbol, Korea admits to the cosmological principles of old China. Within this context, Yang stands for the masculine and is considered as bright and strong and turned toward the sky, whereas Yin (in Korean *eum*) stands for the female and is considered as dark, pliable and turned toward the earth. The national flag of South Korea is likely the only one in the world featuring philosophical principles.

Indeed, Koreans live with these contrasts symbolized by the flag. However, they understand them as complementary—a general attitude of East Asian cultures in general and of Korea in particular. South Korea as a nation has replaced its traditional social and economic patterns by industrial and capitalistic structures within only a few decades [1]. Indicatively the *mugunghwa*, which belongs to the family of hibiscus flowers, is the national flower, as it is associated with a strong will for survival. The magpie (*kkachi*) is the most popular bird in the country, since it is believed to deliver good news.

Of all important industrial countries—South Korea belongs to the so-called G-20 Nations—and despite the fact that South Korea is internationally admired for technological achievements as well as for its old history and culture, it is one of the least known and even well-educated personalities do know very little about its geography, history, and culture. The nation is further unique in many respects: Korea has developed an own written language, *hangeul*, which is not used in any other country. New Year is celebrated like in China according to the lunar calendar at the end of January or beginning of February, whereas the business year in South Korea begins with the first of January—as in the Western world.

Many people associate "Korea" with the ferocious Korean War or the ongoing division of the nation into a southern and a northern part with its numerous conflicts. Meanwhile, manifold progresses of South Korea in the material as well as immaterial fields continue to impresses the world. The Olympic Games in 1988, the Soccer World Cup (jointly with Japan) in 2002, as well as the accomplishments of the G-20 Summit in November 2010, and the World Expo 2012 at Jeoju all contributed to the fact that South Korea could rid itself of the image of a poor and unimportant nation.

The Academy of Korean Studies in Seoul goes to great lengths in order to internationally improve the reputation of the country. Closely scrutinizing more than 1100 books, many of the school textbooks, the academy was shocked to encounter quite crude misconceptions. For instance, a survey revealed that the people of Kazakhstan believe that South Korea is still ruled by a military dictatorship, while the Indians dated the Korean separation prior to 1945, and in Great Britain many are of the opinion that the country still receives developmental aid. Mexican texts rule that Korea has no world cultural heritage sites albeit the fact that there are indeed more than nine world cultural heritage sites in Korea. Chileans are told that there are famines in South Korea as of today; in Paraguay, it is understood that Japan and Korea have been former Portuguese colonies. Finally, it is common belief that Chinese is the prevailing language of the peninsula [2].

Even Henry Kissinger's recent book on China [3] reflects the assertion that Japan imposed tributes on various kingdoms of the Korean territory. Indeed, Japanese annals mention that a small principality (called Shiraki) on the southern Korean shore asked Japan to protect it from northern powers and in turn delivered presents and tributes to Sujin-Tenno (32 B.C.). The widow of Chuai-Tenno, the courageous Jingu Kogo, herself lead an invasion force to Shiraki (202 A.C.) and returned only after being promised tributes. Due to this connection between the Korean peninsula and Japan, a large part of the Chinese civilization was subsequently transferred into the Japanese archipelago. Starting with Ojin-Tenno (270–310 A.D.), punitive expeditions to Korean shores took place throughout the centuries and were later repeated by Nintoku-Tenno (311–399) and in the mid-fifth century. When the Japanese endeavored to turn Shiraki into a Japanese province, renaming it Kudara, the Koreans drove the Japanese ultimately out of the country with the help of Chinese forces. In the south, a small Korean state (called Gaya or Minama) existed for a while under Japanese protection. But in later years, the Japanese influence in these areas diminished as well. No Korean tributes to Japan can be traced in later years and certainly not since medieval times.

A great number of Chinese and Korean people migrated to contemporary Japanese territory approximately between 200 B.C. and 400 A.D. At this time, a Korean or Japanese state did not exist. Instead, numerous ministates existed, most of them ruled by Chinese state philosophies. All these ministates paid tributes to the Chinese court. The territory Wa (Yamato) of the mythical empress Jingu Kogo (Himiko) was comprised of areas in Western Japan as well as in the southern Korean peninsula. The Chinese court recognized Himiko as the ruler of these areas and considered her to be their loyal vassal. This empress was later deleted from the official historical annals of Japan, as she was woman and emperors were traditionally male.

In contrast to the southern kingdoms, the powerful state of northern Goguryo remained completely independent. Hence, the old Japanese claim of Japanese supremacy over Korea has to be dismissed. Taking the fact into consideration that Korea paid tributes to China at a time when Middle Europe belonged to the Roman Empire, only China could claim a supremacy over Korea. Within this context, Paul [4] speaks of a Chinese–Korean cultural environment. Applying the Confucian term of loyalty, only the early kingdoms of Shilla and Baekche were ruled by the imperial system of Yamato (the core of the later Japanese imperium), a fact that was reason enough for Japan to claim hegemony over all of Korea, at least until WW II [5].

It is very likely that literary assistants of Kissinger have studied the book *The Making of the Modern Japan* by Marius B. Jansen and have incorrectly quoted from it [6]. Jansen reported that a Dutch missionary observed at the beginning of the eighteenth century in Nagasaki that some Japanese "celebrated a victory over the Koreans whose country they had converted into a tributary nation" [7]. Yet, prior to this, Jansen described that the Japanese invasion of Korea in 1597 had ended with an obscure escape of the Japanese warriors. "After their disastrous adventure in Korea," it took twelve years, with the Treaty of Kiyu, before Japan was allowed to trade again with Korea "and the trade was strictly restricted to the vicinity of Busan." This example shows how sometimes historic truth seems to be utterly distorted. Obviously, some authors in different countries have not followed the developments in Korea or they simply did not care to adjust their outdated and erroneous views. The Koreans themselves, however, have become quite self-confident and sometimes start to look down on the "lazy Japanese" or "technically backward Europeans." When in the summer of 2010, the North Korean national soccer player Tese, who grew up in Japan, joined a German national league (*Bundesliga*) team, he voiced his opinion on German toilets, which he considered residual. The upper middle class in South Korea uses a toilet also as bidet, and its seat can be comfortably warmed up, while soft music conceals indiscreet noises. Advanced toilet designs even deal with the medical examination of ones urine and feces. Meanwhile, flat screens and luxurious Korean electronic devices are being appreciated all over the world, and more recently, motorcars from Korean factories start conquering the world markets. Furthermore, German and Japanese shipbuilders know just too well who took away new orders from their dockyards. Construction companies globally hit on Korean competitors when trying to get orders in advanced projects of high rising buildings, complex civil engineering, and plant installations—and this competition is by no means settled as a matter of pricing.

In 1945, South Korea had a population of 16 million which sky-rocked to 50 million at the end of 2013 due to a sheer monstrous growth of its population. This is especially remarkable as millions of people have emigrated from the country between 1953 and to the mid-1960s. This migration to other countries can be related first and foremost to the tremendous birth rate over several decades. Yet, the number hardly decreased as many people escaped from North Korea or have returned from Japan and Russia to their home country. All these new citizens needed food, housing, education, and above all strived for a job. Additionally, the enormous money spent on the national defense, in the face of a highly armed Northern army, absorbed a large part of the national budget. This herculean mission was managed by the nation, while at the same time, the standard of living increased steadily and significantly. Whereas the term "reconstruction" is used in the case of Japan and Western Germany post-World War II, Korea completely established itself almost from scratch, turning from an agrarian state into an industrial nation.

Indeed, although the term "Economic Wonderland" is frequently misused, it really applies to South Korea. When German travelers passed Korea while riding the Trans-Siberian railway from Europe to Japan between 1925 and 1935, they reported that they had seen incredible poverty in wretched villages. Ragged figures with emotionless faces flanked the rails, and not even a flash of hope for a better future could be recognized in their stern appearances. After the Great Pacific War, the country encountered cruel internal blows. There was no initial help, neither by the USA nor by impoverished China or thoroughly beaten Japan. The Soviet Union occupied Northern Korea, but their interest was merely to erect a Communist state under its guidance. For this purpose, they only invested into arming that country. Modest advances in the North as well as in the South were thoroughly repressed by the dreadful Korean War. The country was literally flattened and had to pay an enormous blood toll. Subsequently, the misery of the nation could hardly be compared to even the worst situations in the least developed parts of the world, for instance, in African countries or Bangladesh. More than 150,000 children were released for adoption into foreign countries. Until today, children remain very scarce in South Korea.

The enormous tenacity of the inhabitants, as well as their acknowledged desire for self-improvement and their pride in a rich cultural inheritance, contributed to the incredible growth of the country. The international market further proved to be most favorable for Korea, especially with the opening of many foreign markets—in particular the US market—and an unprecedented growth of the global economy. Whereas all these factors were also applicable to the North, they did not have a dictator like Pak Chung-hee, who concentrated the national energies and profited from the rich experiences of excellent, local dynamic entrepreneurs, who commanded giant industrial conglomerates, and the singular Korean *chaebol*. They paved the way for a capitalistic economic growth and brought about "the miracle at the river Han." Pascha [8] written that "all this would be possible by temporary increasing gross investments to one third of the GNP" and a propensity to export from a gaunt 4 % around 1960 to over 50 % in 2013 (Fig. 1.1).

Fig. 1.1 The Lotte World Tower in Seoul, the highest building of Asia east of the Gulf

Thus, South Korea proves to be a magnificent model for developing countries. This, however, would presuppose hard working and well-educated elites in such countries with a patriotic mind, who are not looking for the acquired wealth by strenuous efforts of more developed nations. They would have to develop a population willing to acquire knowledge and to work hard and efficiently. At the same time, an increasingly wealthy Korea has to take care that its people do not start to look for social favors which are only thought for people undeservedly in need.

North Korea, on the other hand, offers only a story of failure. Despite the fact that it had a favorable starting point as it has inherited a versatile industry and owns almost all mineral reserves of the peninsula, the situation has drastically worsened for North Korea, as it lacked the right mind-set and business acumen to achieve wealth. The energies of the proud inhabitants, who are indeed willing to work, were directed to military tasks, prestigious projects, and outdated technologies, while education was severely restricted.

The founder of North Korea, Kim Il-sung, took pride in being the founder of the *Juche*-philosophy, which advocates national independence and economic autarky. While independence is significant for the dignity of a country, economic autarky is a coffin lid and being cut off from global developments proved to be a big mistake. The idea behind the economic seclusion of North Korea was to avoid becoming dependent from the USA, the most hated enemy of Kim Il-sung. Approximately 90 % of the population pays a bitter price for this policy, living in poor circumstances and two million even starving to death. Only about 10 % of the population is well-to-do and lives in the clean city of Pyongyang. Most of these families are related to military and political functionaries or belong to the small elite of different specialists, especially in the field of technology.

Given this situation, the "sword of Damocles" is hanging over both states South Korea and North Korea. Yet, most likely, it will not drop because of the military strength of the USA and the self-possession of China. However, due to stubborn discussion partners on both sides, reconciliation is also unlikely in the foreseeable future. The North asks for unreasonable preconditions, while many residents from the South are afraid of a decreased standard of living, a consequence they had observed within the course of the German reunion.

Nevertheless, South Korea is an amazing example of democratization. It evolved from a long military dictatorship through free elections between 1985 and 1995 into a democratic state with a free market system. Furthermore, the development of industrial structures from a deeply embedded agrarian mentality is exemplary. Moreover, the integration of Korean institutions into international organizations as well as a global acknowledgement and acceptance of South Korea is particularly encouraging. It seems that Korea is more flexible in this respect than Japan, which opens up much more hesitantly and is more concerned that its supposed uniqueness could be endangered.

In order to reach a wider audience, a rather relaxed writing style is utilized for this book, thus renouncing an austere scientific form. This monograph aims to offer a vivid portrayal of the country for readers who are vocationally engaged with Korea or who live in Korea as expatriates. When someone moves into a new, unfamiliar environment, empathy is required in order to live comfortably in these new circumstances. In this particular case, empathy refers to the ability to see oneself in the situation of another person. Moving to another culture such as Korea necessitates a minimum knowledge of the circumstances and the mind-set of native Koreans living in Korea in order to be able to adapt to the environment. As an East Asian culture, Korea has very different historical roots and a prevailing mind-set that differs significantly from the Western tradition. Although the West and Korea are moving closer toward each other, especially in the field of technology, an amalgamation cannot be seen for the near future. Furthermore, if the West and Korea should intermix one day, this process will not be one sided.

Last but not least, this book further addresses all readers who are intellectually concerned with and interested in this country. The main intention of this volume is to present simple aspects of socioeconomical relevance, the business structures, market developments, and the art of business management. Besides some books from Europe, the majority of monographs focusing on Korea are published in the USA. They are usually well researched and frequently written by academic scholars or journalists with an ethnic Korean background. The best contributions to Korean Studies in the English language, however, are produced by Korean institutions and their specialized scholars. There are further important contributions in Japanese and Russian. Whether and to what extend there are any Chinese books that focus on Korea is unknown to the author of this book.

Initially, a portrayal of historical events or a description of the land and people was not part of the manuscript. However, after consulting Korean business experts, it was revealed that it is hardly possible to gain an understanding of the economic and social behavior of Korean people without a historical, cultural, and social background. This is particularly relevant in the field of marketing in which concerned managers have to keep an attentive eye on the sociopsychological structure of individuals and their social surroundings.

Like in many other nations, Korean people demonstrate a prototypical behavior within the masses. Nevertheless, as individuals they behave distinctly unique and thus their behavior cannot be generalized. The swarm behavior of former times has given away to a more group-oriented attitude or is even about to turn into an expressively individual behavior.

Almost all of South Korea is open to technological progress and always turns swiftly to new scientific processes and product developments as well as to international patterns of life. The intelligent and vivacious inhabitants seem to have arrived at a healthy balance between consumption and saving, while never completely renouncing their traditional patterns of life. While older Koreans have strived for a long time for their own national identity, the younger generation of today shows a strong self-determination not overshadowed by any old complexes.

Finally, with respect to the economic reports of this volume, attention should be drawn to the fact that nowadays all currency parities are subject to strong variations. All conversions of the Korean Won (KRW) hereinafter are based on a rate of 1050 Won to one US dollar as of spring 2014.

1.2 Notes on the Transcription of the Written Korean Language

A very special subject is the transcription, especially of Korean proper names, into the Roman alphabet. In this respect, Koreans face a twofold difficulty: First, the Korean alphabet, the *hangeul*, in many instances lacks a matching phonetic symbol for a specific letter of another language and vice versa. Second, in almost all languages, they might learn an "i" is an "i" as originally pronounced in Latin; but in English it is an "ai." This is why many methods for the transcriptions of geographical or personal names have been developed in the last 130 years. Many of these methods differ significantly. The former way of spelling the island of Tschedschu, for example, has changed from "Cheju" into "Jeju." In general, the transcription system of McCune and Reischauer [9] has been adopted and is also the base of the new transcription system (revised Romanization). It is not easy for people, who have not learned the Korean language thoroughly to pronounce the endless words correctly. The main street in northern Seoul, for instance, is subtitled on the street sign as "Cheonggyecheonno."

When reading old books or maps, the reader will be exposed to a confusing variety of different ways of notations. In this monograph, the new, official notation is chosen although occasionally the old version is used, in particular when the person in question chose this spelling for his name cards or if the spelling prevails in historical books. The first president after the Second World War, I, Man Sung, preferred to spell his name "Syngman Rhee." This spelling is also used in historical volumes. Yet, nowadays he is spelled "I Man-sung." President Pak, Chung Hee is known as General Park and nowadays spelled "Pak Chung-hee."

Furthermore, a transcription is often complicated as all vowels sound more or less similar to non-native speakers of Korean. Most Europeans cannot recognize whether a sound is pronounced as an "O" or a "U"; the latter sound being somewhat opalescent. The same is true for all but a few consonants. It is further quite irritating that Koreans usually cannot discern between "W," "P," and "B," between "L" and "R," between "T" and "D," between "G" and "K"; while sometimes "N" changes into "R." A really sharp "T" it is pronounced as "TT." An intermediate sound between "G" and "W" is quite interesting and happens to appear in the Turkish language as well. A matter of curiosity to foreigners is a written sign in *hangeul* that looks like a small "o" and for which there does not exist any Roman letter. If this sign exists in a syllable in front of a vocal, it can be neglected; if it is placed at the end of a syllable, it sounds like "ng."

Generally, spoken Korean frequently sounds emphatic or emotional. Whereas a Western TV anchorman speaks rather slowly and distinguished, his Korean counterpart tends to rattle machinegun-like in a passionate manner, even if he has to announce only trivial issues. This behavior can be attributed to the fact that almost all young men have to serve for quite a long time in the army and are used to short, sharp sentences and keep this habit after their military service. Any conversation, in which objective opinions are exchanged, might end in a dramatic dialogue with raised voices.

In particular, women use a mode of conversation that sounds extremely plaintive, fervent, and occasionally even whiney. The latter tone is possibly a result of thousands of years of subordination. Almost all women are able to express themselves at an incredible speed. Feelings of surprise or consternation are expressed by a lengthened "aigu" or "aijuu."

A fundamental problem caused by the differences between Western languages, and the Korean articulation can be found in the postal service. Whereas the author never encountered problems with the deliveries of letters to and from Singapore or Japan to Europe, in Korea letters might take weeks or months. Sometimes, the mail never arrives due to the difficulties that addresses written in Roman letters cause for officials, especially when the handwriting of the sender is rather cursory.

Quite a few foreigners believe that Korean and Japanese people are much alike. Although they are indeed geographically located quite close to each other, in fact they are fundamentally different in almost all other respects. Korean and Japanese ways of thinking, behaving, and acting differ significantly. Both countries have used Chinese characters for a long time, though they have simplified them to a great degree in Japan and to a much lesser degree in Korea. Furthermore, they have developed phonetic descriptions, but the Japanese *hiragana* (for Japanese words) and *kana* (for foreign words) are syllables, whereas the Korean *hangeul* system is based on letters, which are grouped as syllables, thus combining the advantages of both linguistic systems. Additionally, Koreans have their own calendar as their history dates much further back than the history of Japan. Currently, South Korea lives in the year 4349 after the accession of the throne of its legendary mythical ruler Dangun, who supposedly has established the city of Pyongyang. North Korea, however, lives in 2014 in the year 105, a calculation that is based on the year of birth of Kim Il-sung, who is not only the founder of North Korea but also the founder of the state ideology *Juche*. This ideology emphasizes the self-reliance of the North Korean state and the self-preservation of its popular masses. The fatal history of Choi Seung-hee elucidates the complex and painful history of Korea.

1.3 The Fate of the Danseuse Choi Seung-hee

The difficult curriculum vitae of the danseuse Choi Seung-hee (Choi, Song Hee) shows how much past generations had to struggle for their identity. She was born into a *yangban* family during the Japanese colonization (1911) and, throughout her life, only wished to be a perfect artist. Choi was considered to be one of the most gifted artists of the century, and her ingenious talent was quickly recognized by the Japanese. Hence, she was sent to Japan for a thorough education and handed to outstanding female dancing teachers, who helped her to develop into a world-class star. Under her new name Sai, Koki she enthralled her audience not only in Japan but also in the USA, South America, and Europe. Besides her dancing skills, she showed a great ability as a vocalist as well. She very much wanted to stay in New

York; however, she had to return to Japan where she witnessed the outbreak of the Great Pacific War. Like other Japanese artists, she was used to entertain the armed forces. During one of her assignments in China, she came in touch with the great tradition of the Beijing opera and discovered other East Asian genres, which she wanted to combine with her amalgam of Korean, Japanese, and other international styles of dancing. Yet, this caused political conflicts because she was supposed to appear as a pure Japanese artist representing old Japanese traditions.

After the end of World War II, Choi Seung-hee returned to her home country. She volunteered to help setting up an academy of dancing. However, she was rejected due to her collaboration with the former Japanese occupation forces. Annoyed by the narrow-mindedness, especially of politicians who had returned from exile in the USA, she moved to North Korea, where she was highly welcomed by Kim Il-sung, who, at that time, was very much concerned about the general reputation of his country. Choi Seung-hee successfully established a dancing academy in Pyeongyang and performed on stages in the Soviet Union and other socialistic countries where she was enthusiastically celebrated. This attracted the attention of Beijing and she was invited to set up a dance academy there as well. She happily followed this invitation as she believed to be finally able to realize her old dream to integrate Chinese artistic elements into her repertoire. Nevertheless, North Korea quickly developed into a functionary system of politicians, who were first-and-foremost anxious to consolidate their dictatorial power after the Korean War. Although the artist would have liked to stay longer if not forever, in Beijing, she was ordered to return to North Korea.

Subsequently, Choi Seung-hee had to turn back to the traditional Korean art of dancing and was asked to develop specific group choreographies. This led to disagreements with the North Korean government about diverging opinions concerning artistic tastes. Finally, after a last performance around 1966, she disappeared from the public. Allegedly, together with her husband, she fell victim to one of the frequent purges of the regime, being accused to have attempted to escape to China. Choi Seung-hee's life constitutes a flagrant example of a tragic human fate in the younger history of Korea.

1.4 Earlier Visits to Seoul

I only vaguely remember my first short visit to South Korea in the late summer of 1969. This visit turned out to be not very amusing. Visibly armed soldiers in the dark airport of Gimpo (currently the city airport of Seoul) stared forcibly into my eyes, passed on my traveling documents, and thoroughly inspected my small luggage as I flew in from Tokyo.

In a rather run down taxi, I finally arrived on a bumpy road at my shabby hotel in the old city center. The lobby was dark and the room to which I was guided looked untidy. Nothing really invited a prolonged stay. On the streets, sturdily clothed men roamed the streets, while women could only be seen occasionally.

From 12 p.m., there was a curfew until 4 a.m. in the early morning. Major strategic points such as crossroads, interchanges, large bridges, and railway stations were blocked by barricades and guarded by heavily armed soldiers.

Wandering into the shops of the neighborhood, I did not find any attractive merchandise. This reminded me of the gray and wretched cities of the Ruhr-Area in Germany during the time right after World War II. Only one shop that was tailoring suits for men attracted my interest. Probably, there was a demand for this type of attire for local as well as visiting businessmen. This proved true for the Japanese, German, and Australian technicians, who poured into the country to help construct modern steel mills in the southern parts of the peninsula.

When visiting Seoul for a second time in early winter 1970, it was cold and showery. In walking distance of what is today the ground of the palace-like Lotte department store, I negotiated in a dark and cold shack with an antique dealer on some very reasonably priced pieces of celadon ware. A carbide lamp spent only dim light, and my eyes were irritated by the pungent smoke of a coal-fired oven in the corner, so that I postponed any decision to acquire some bowels or plates. With a high-necked collar, I struggled back through the drizzle to the nearby Chosun Hotel, which was recommended by the Tokyo travel office as the best hotel available in Seoul. Heavy coal fumes from low-rising chimneys hung over an only badly lid city center. Relieved, I took seat at the noble bar of the hotel in order to warm up. Although my desire for a "very dry Martini" could not be met, finally a good Johnny Walker Black was poured into my glass.

Suddenly, two young women at the bar introduced themselves as high school graduates. In a good command of English, they gave an earnest and account of the miserable circumstances of their families with half a dozen children. Unobtrusively, they would show their gratitude for a hot bath and a back passage. It was not long before they turned politely to the few other commercial travelers from the USA, Japan, and Europe. Back in my room, I looked down from the 9th floor at gloomy alleys. Rundown trucks transported big black lumps of coal from an obscure backyard. The road was littered with sooty bits of black junk.

Neatly dressed in a dark-blue suit and an immaculate white shirt, I went down to the lobby, where a neatly dressed driver of a prospective business friend was already waiting. Because I had forgotten to pack neckties, I had bought one in the basement of the hotel. The necktie was of unusual colors in unusual tones of green, yellow, and violet. However, it only costed a dollar a piece. In this attire, I was taken to an exotic *gisaeng* house to enjoy a classic *gisaeng* party, which was extremely popular in higher business circles of that time. It was only many years later that I learned that these parties did not represent at all the traditional events of the past but were only a loose interpretation of those events.

Almost every evening we were hosted in similar hospitable localities with delicious Korean food and sturdy drinks. In a half reclining position, we were treated with delicacies on silver chopsticks directly to our mouth. The lovely hostesses were clad in the traditional *hanbok*, a colorful, bell-shaped dress coming down to the feet and held with a ribbon at the height of the breasts. When we left the places in our black Sedans, we saw the unadorned poverty of the neighborhood.

The conversation always revolved around the almost fanatic will of the South Koreans to build up their country. The attention of the guest was drawn to the fact that signs of improvement could already be seen almost everywhere. It was acknowledged that the North Koreans were still quite ahead; however, it was stressed that in less than five years, South Korea would reach their level only to excel it afterward. In North Korea, life would be much easier than in China in the north, which was their protecting power. They explained that north of the bordering rivers Yalu and Tumen, in between the two countries, it was pitch-dark in China, whereas south of the border, in North Korea there were many brightly illuminated places. This was possible due to generous oil dispatches from the Soviet Union.

Twenty-seven years and almost as many trips to South Korea later, the Westin-Chosun Hotel as it is called today, has been renovated at great expenses. Although many five-star hotels have been opened over the years in Seoul, the Chosun still remains a noble address. The price of a glass of beer has climbed to 14 dollars, and the lobby is frequently crowded by noisy Chinese traveling groups. A glance out of the room window reveals glittering facades and roaring traffic outside.

Gisaeng parties do rarely exist nowadays. They have become prohibitively expensive as the rent for shops and localities have increased tremendously. Furthermore, there are scarcely any young women available, who are eager to earn their money in dubious places. Celadon porcelain is now only offered in the shopping malls of great hotels and costs a fortune.

Today, pretty young ladies dressed according to the latest fashion trends set by Armani or Gucci, for instance, are walking on adventurously high heels into the luxurious boutiques of Myeong, Apgujeong, or Cheongdam. With dignity and elegance, they confidently cross the roads and plazas. Some families in Seoul or Busan reside in apartments of a few thousand square feet, which were designed and planned by renowned Italian or French designers. These apartments are equipped with the latest gadgets of the Korean electronic industry as well as ridiculously expensive Bulthaupt or Miele kitchens. In the noble restaurants of the Shilla Hotel, dainty customers prefer a Dom Pérignon over a middle-class Moët and Chandon when choosing their Champagne brand. Indifferently, they look at some Westerners, who haul their luggage in their mean outfits and who look forward to a cool beer afterward.

In the posh quarters of Seoul, people are well established and not many thoughts are lost on their neighbors north of the 38th parallel. Meanwhile, in North Korea, the lights have turned out, while at the same time, north of the river Yalu broad beams of light have unfurled in Chinese territories. The well-to-do citizens of Seoul indulge in a rather carefree life and an ever-growing class of affluent people propagates a naive belief in an ever-growing progress, whereas responsible politicians are deeply concerned about the future of the country. Indeed, representatives of six states, namely China, the USA, Japan, Russia, and both Koreas, are taking pains to attain a denuclearization of Northern Korea in order to control one of the most dangerous powder barrels of the globe.

In the fall of 2010, even more exquisitely dressed ladies with stunning makeup and the by-now common aesthetic surgeries walk through the upper-level quarters not only of Seoul, but also of many other areas of the country. In the spacious lobby of the Lotte Hotel, seemingly half of the world has a sense of well-being. The cool, elegant, and long-legged ladies of the reception in the club lounge of the New Wing look as if they have stepped out of movie posters. Chinese groups have disappeared from the neighboring Chosun Hotel. Instead, huge, dark Sedans are passing and a cabinet minister heads for lunch, accompanied by half a dozen rather young confidents, among them several women. They enjoy the menu as well as the view of the traditionally arranged garden. The Chosun has become a venue for exclusive and noble parties.

We visited an attractive spot for tourists at the southerly island of Jeju, which is crowded by masses flocking out of numerous tourist buses. We arrived with a taxi and had trouble finding another taxi when we wanted to leave. Several young, smiling police officers asked us about our problem and finally invited us, without hesitation, into their patrolling car and gave us a lift to our next destination, a huge classical temple, which was erected only a few years ago.

Just a few days before, an old temple gateway had been removed from the mountains to a new location on the east side of the plaza in front of the city hall. Not only in Seoul, but in many parts of the country, traditional shrines, gateways, and occasionally whole fortresses are being restored. Of course, nobody wants to re-erect old Korea; however, it is important to respectfully remember its glorious cultural past. In Japan, we cannot observe similar activities in the countryside and only a few places of interest to international tourists are re-established.

The Japanese youth looks much to America and are less interested in the history of their remarkable country. But they like Korean pop music and take any chance to fly in for shopping, preferably to Seoul. Here, they can purchase everything that is also well displayed at Tokyo's expansive shopping district Ginza. Yet, due to the strength of the yen, they can purchase these items to what seem "reasonable" prices for them.

Western visitors, however, hardly consider the *haut couture* purses and garments in Korean shops a cheap bargain. Nevertheless, they travel in an ever-increasing number to South Korea, whereas the figures for Japanese tourists are recently decreasing because of the devaluation of the yen. Japanese tourists are increasingly replaced by Chinese travelers, who find Seoul cheaper than Shanghai. Most visitors immigrate through the bright and modern Incheon airport (55 km west of Seoul). Formalities are usually quickly completed and travelers find themselves only three quarters of an hour later checking into one of the luxury hotels either in the old city center or the modern Gangnam. The taxi driver, however, might tell tourists about his poor living standard and will appreciate a generous rounding up of the transportation fare.

When vacationing only for a few days, foreign visitors will usually feel quite happy and comfortable—almost like at home. Nevertheless, when staying for a longer period of time, life in South Korea can become rather complex. Korea has a very old tradition of life patterns, and these are only Western on the surface. During its first years while establishing itself in China, the Deutsche Bank employed a German sinologist as local head. When asked about this proceeding, Mr. Burgard, the board member responsible for human resources, answered with a smile that it would be easier to turn a sinologist into a banker than a banker into a specialist of the Chinese language, culture, and social affairs. The same might apply for long-term residents in Korea as well!

I admire Korea's culture, I sympathize with the politically divided country, and I like its friendly, open-minded people with their warm hospitality. Recently, I decided to live with my Korean wife in Seoul. Nevertheless, I am a scholar and therefore obliged to academic sincerity. My Korean readers will hopefully not mind if they occasionally feel uncomfortable with my observations. This book should not be understood as a criticism of Taehan Minguk. It rather seeks to reflect observations from an outside perspective and present them to expatriates, who might have problems orientating themselves when arriving in South Korea. I do apologize if I should hurt any feelings of my friendly Korean hosts. I tried to refrain from political matters as much as possible, as I am not an expert within this complicated field. Nevertheless, I take the full responsibility for the content of this work.

Literature

1. Hart D (2003) From tradition to consumption: construction of a capitalistic culture in South Korea, 2nd edn, Seoul
2. Daily JA (2009) Foreign textbooks print blunders about Korea, edition from 13 Oct 2009
3. Paul G (1993) Philosophie in Japan. Muenchen, p 42
4. Paul G (1993) Philosophie in Japan. Muenchen, p 47/48
5. Kissinger H (2011) China. Cambridge/London, p 92
6. Jansen MB (2000) The making of the modern Japan. Cambridge/London, pp 72 and 69
7. Pascha W (2005) Suedkoreas Wirtschaft. In: Kern T, Koellner P (Eds) Suedkorea und Nordkorea. Frankfurt/New York, p 87
8. McCune G, Reischauer E (1939) The Romanization of the Korean Language. University of California

Chapter 2
The Historical Development of Korea

2.1 Prehistory

Formerly, Korea controlled a wide territory, which extended from the Manchurian north to the Pacific Ocean in the south. The present states of North and South Korea cover each, only 20 % of their former territory. The other 60 % stretch from the north of the rivers Yalu (Amnokgang) and Tumen (Dumangang) up to behind Harbin, the capital of the recent Chinese province of Heilongjiang. This Chinese province, together with the provinces of Yilin and Liaoning, comprises the area of Manchuria as of today. Mongol tribes and the Manchus conquered this vast region in the past. Today, approximately more than two million ethnic Koreans still live in this area. These people speak the Korean language but are Chinese according to their passport. Some of them have settled in this area for a very long time, whereas others resettled during the Japanese colonial period.

Ancient Chinese sources refer to the Koreans as Tung-i, settling not only on the Korean peninsula and Manchuria but also on the coast of Eastern China, from where they had been expelled by the Chinese people of Chou and migrated to what is today Korea. The history of this vast area in which the Korean language is spoken is shrouded in the dark for a time span of about 1000 years (2100 B.C.–1122 B.C.). It was ruled in the very north by the kingdoms of Bueyo and the neighboring Go-Joseon, which according to the tradition was founded by Gija, an overthrown prince of the Chinese Shang empire, and comprised of the territory of the recent province of Liaotung, while the powerful state of Goguryeo existed at the center of the peninsula. The area further to the south, roughly 150 km south of the river Han, was ruled by anarchy as numerous clan leaders permanently fought each other.

These Korean states were relentlessly beset from the north by pursuing tribes of Mongolic or Tunguse origin. Additionally, around the turn of the millennium (B.C.), Chinese forces pressed forward, longing for eastward expansion. From

D.K. Schneidewind, *Economic Miracle Market South Korea*,
DOI 10.1007/978-981-10-0615-9_2

650 B.C. onward, Go-Joseon is mentioned in Chinese annals—in fact, the complete prehistory of Korea, until the turn of the next millennium, is only preserved in Chinese records. These Chinese records mention people clothed in white garments on the Korean peninsula, whom they called Han. Consequently, they called the whole territory Han territory. Today's official name of South Korea, "Daehan Minguk" is derived from this original name. Frequently, one hears or reads about the "Country of the Morning Calm," although this designation does by no means match the eventful history or the hectic daily routine of South Korea. The Mongolians call South Korea "Solongo" which means "the country of the rainbow."

Many culturally advanced nations are considered to have a "dual nature." This is also ascribed to Koreans and can be related to their descent. Their Mongolian heritage can be traced back to nomadic cattle-rising tribes. Later, immigrants from China introduced an agrarian culture and brought influences from the Southern Seas, thus establishing the vocation of fishing. These different styles of living developed different kinds of sociopsychological behaviors.

The Korean themselves probably descended from Siberia from around the area of Lake Baikal. Their predominantly Mongolian physiognomy reminds of their origin, even when they are mixed with physical characteristics of Tungusic people. After 1100 B.C., many people from the south of China immigrated to Korea, either as administrative officers or as spouses of noble Koreans. These people often exhibit fine body structures and round eyes. Furthermore, some Malay people entered the southern part of the peninsula, and traces of ethnic groups from the Pacific can be found as well.

The modern Korean language is related to Mongolian, Tungusian, as well as Turkish dialects. Moreover, within the scope of the linguistic group of the Ural-Altaic tongues, it is cognate with the languages of Finland and Hungary. Korean grammar is the same as Japanese grammar; however, the genuine vocabulary is entirely different from that. Nevertheless, there exist many loanwords from the Japanese language, which have lately been adopted by Koreans.

Some archaeological discoveries suggest that human beings have been around in Korea since Paleolithic times approximately 700,000 years ago. Yet, a proof of an existing civilization of the *homo sapiens sapiens* is dated back to a Neolithic time of not earlier than 20,000 B.C. Hence, there was also a period of time (about 20,000 and 10,000 years B.C.) when a land connection to China, Taiwan, and Japan was existent. "The discovery of rice seeds dating back 15,000 years from the middle region of Korea suggests that agriculture began in prehistoric times" [1]. Around 8000 B.C., the art of pottery was developed.

Starting in 3000 B.C., there are mythical legends about rulers of Mongolian origin in Northern Korea. According to one of these legends, the deity Hwan-in sent his son Hwan-ung to earth. His offspring Dangun from the holy mountains close to Pyongyang is supposed to have ascended to the throne on August 15, 2333 B. C. This date is a national holiday in both of the Koreas until today. The city of Liaoyang in what is nowadays Manchuria is assumed to have been the first capital of the country, before the capital was removed to Pyongyang. The story of Dangun is widely considered fiction by contemporary scholars, although it remains an official version in North Korea. Consequently, North Korea has established the tomb of Dangun as its national symbol.

In ancient Chinese records, Korean settlements east of the Chinese borders were described as lands of mountain men with virtues and propriety, which would translate today into the term "seonbi." Because this scenery is supposed to be set in the Taebaek Mountains east of Pyongyang, the regime of North Korea and part of the population take pride in calling themselves the purest race in the world with the highest morals.

2.2 The Kingdom of Goguryeo

The ever-growing empire of Goguryeo absorbed the territory of Go-Joseon, which had developed at the beginning of the Iron Age. The river Liao formed the Western border. Goguryeo further pushed aggressively forward to the north and occupied the area around Bueyo from where many people eventually fled to the south. Thus, the upper course of the river Songhua (Sungari in Russian) became the northern border. Later, two more powerful states formed in the south: Baekche in the southwest and Shilla in the southeast. The term "Three Kingdoms" (Samguk in Korean) is based on these three states. Baekche took in many people from the former Bueyo and established its new capital Wiryeseong in what is today the southeast of Seoul. The capital was walled by earthen ramparts called *Mongchon Toseong*, which are still visible nowadays in the close vicinity of the Olympic Park. Much later, the kingdom of Baekche moved 130 miles further south and established the capital of Bueyo (Puyo) on the banks of the river Geum.

Time and again, Chinese rulers tried to annex the Korean territory. The great emperor Wu Di who reigned from 156 to 102 B.C. invaded and subjugated the peninsula, and China obtained its largest territorial extension in Korea from the south of the river Han in the east to the valley of Ferghana in the west. A commandery was established at Lelang (Changhae) to rule the territory. However, only a few years later, it was already abandoned in 126 B.C. and this territorial acquisition turned out not to be a consistent conquest. Nevertheless, some local Chinese enclaves existed for some 300–400 years. Only in the early Manchu period, did the Chinese empire achieve a comparable territorial expansion.

Around 612, a huge army of the Chinese Sui Dynasty (supposedly more than one million men) invaded the Goguryeo territory. King Yeongyang entrusted his field marshal Eulji Mundeok with the defense of the country. This famous general enticed the enemy, who by far surpassed him in the number of warriors, into a partisan war. The Sui forces had to split up into groups to follow their rivals, who operated in split-up units all over the country. When the Koreans suddenly amassed to a bigger unit, the enemy attacked them with a huge army of over 300,000 men. General Eulji Mundeok had erected a dam across the river Salsu (nowadays Chongchon in North Korea), which was destroyed when the adversaries moved closer. A large number of enemies drowned, and the others were massacred by Eulji's troops in a sudden attack during the following chaos. It is reported that all but 2000 foreign warriors lost their lives. The rest of the Sui army turned back to China. The loss suffered at the river Salsu was so disastrous that the complete dynasty under the famous emperor Yangdi (who erected the grand channel between Hangzhou and Beijing) was shattered and soon replaced by the Tang Dynasty. This heroic battle belongs to one the three highlights in the Korean military annals. Until today, the second highest distinction for military personal is called the "Order of Eulji."

Korean historical sources are much younger than Chinese sources and have a rather mythical character than being based on scientific facts. Korean historical sources are the *Samguk Sagi* (Annals of the Three Kingdoms) of the early historian Kim Pu-sik (1145 A.D.) and the *Samguk Yusa* (The Accounts of the Three Kingdoms) of the monk Iryeon (around 1280 A.D.). Both sources are not primary sources but are based on former oral and written traditions as well as old reports. They contain a lot of legendary material and are considered to be commissioned works to legitimate the Goryeo Dynasty. The authors date the foundation of Shilla to 57 B.C. and of Baekche to 18 B.C. Both countries were dominated by powerful clans, with the Kim clan ruling the area around Shilla. These time periods were dominated by war cries and until today serve as sources of numerous daily historical series on Korean television.

2.3 The Southern Kingdoms of Baekche and Shilla

The kingdom of Baekche aggressively pursued the extension of its territory and attacked northern Goguryeo as well as its eastern neighbor Shilla. Fighting against Goguryeo, Baekche allied with Japanese troops. In this context, one has to remember that large parts of the Japanese upper class once consisted of immigrated Koreans, in particular people from Baekche. When Goguryeo powerfully advanced to the south, Baekche and Shilla united to fight them off. The battles between these three countries devastated huge parts of the nation. In the end, Shilla called on troops of the Tang Dynasty, which landed at the mouth of the river Geum in the Baekche territory. The combined efforts of the three forces ultimately defeated Goguryeo in 668 A.D. Afterward, the Shilla warriors expelled the Chinese, who had intended to settle in Baekche. In the same year, Shilla united the complete Korean peninsula under its authority. Gyeongju (Kyongju) was established as the capital of Korea and became the only capital in the history of the country located in its southern part (668–918).

The remains of the defeated, formerly the Tang forces, escaped to the north of the country into the vicinity of Pyongyang. There, they were attacked by Goguryeo's troops, who had survived the fights against Shilla and its allies and had been forced out of the country. Naturally, the Chinese were enraged by their Korean experiences and, as revenge, punished the citizens of Pyongyang, abducting more than 200,000 inhabitants into slavery in China. Until today, this incident is not forgotten in Korea. The rest of the Goguryeo troops, mainly from the upper classes of their society, united with a particular tribe of the Tunguse people and founded the new kingdom of Balhae (Bohai in Chinese) north of the river Tumen in 699. It lasted until their subjugation in 927 by the Mongolian Khitan tribe. This signified the loss of almost 60 % of the Korean territory.

What remained of the Three Kingdoms was called Tongil Shilla and started to recover from the devastations of the wars. This country was strongly shaped by Buddhism. Its capital Gyeongju (nearly 400 km southeast of today's Seoul) turned into a flourishing center of economy and culture. The city was square-shaped, following the example of the former Chinese capital Chang'an (today Xian), and there were privately as well as publicly owned magnificent buildings. The administration was organized following the Chinese model, and upper-class citizens used Chinese characters (*hanja* in Korean) to write their names. In order to enter the civil service, examinations according to the qualifications of the Chinese mandarin were mandatory. This was meaningful to shape self-assured personalities; however, it did not help to bring the technology and economy, on which the power of a country is based, forward.

Shilla was a considerable naval power and traded with China and Japan. Joe writes that "the national energy which was released after the efforts of war was as it seems concentrated into trade activities across the seas of Northeast-Asia" [2]. Indeed, Korean ports in the south had a leading role in shipbuilding that they retained for a long time.

Ambitious and greedy aristocrats pursued separatist tendencies at the beginning of the tenth century, and in the end, Gyeongju was no longer able to control them sufficiently. Insurrections and small wars paralyzed the country. Interestingly, a small state called Gaya that was traditionally controlled by the Japanese existed between Baekche and Shilla on the southern shores. In times of trouble, it took the opportunity to fight for its own interests.

2.4 The Kingdom of Goryeo

A new kingdom, succeeding Goguryeo, emerged in the northern part of Korea. After numerous battles, Wang, Geon, a high-ranking aristocrat from the center of Korea, gained power over almost all of Korea. Renamed Taejo, he ascended the throne of the new empire of Goryeo (Koryo) in 918 A.D. The name "Korea," which was commonly used thereafter in other countries, is derived from the name of this country. King Taejo established his new capital in the city of Gaesong (about 30 miles northwest of Seoul, in what is today North Korea). His aim was to create a powerful united Korea under a central authority. He skillfully won over old lords and succeeded to revive agriculture, manufacturing, and trade in this country.

At this time, only Baekche und Shilla continued to exist outside Goryeo. Yet, the state of Shilla comprised only of a little more than the city of Gyeongju. The city was eventually raided by Baekche, and the once flourishing metropolis was entirely destroyed, marking the end of the kingdom of Shilla. Afterward, in 936, King Taejo managed to subdue Baekche, thus reuniting a large part of Korea.

After this achievement, Taejo transferred the government seat from Gaesong back to the old capital of Pyongyang. However, his aim to extend the borders of the empire further to the north failed, and his successors were also not able to achieve this aim. Instead, the northern empire attacked Goryeo to annex the complete southern area down to Pyongyang. The time between 993 and 1019 was marked by a permanent state of war between Goryeo and the state of the Khitan in the north.

In 1019, the Khitan once again tried to invade Goryeo and General Gam Gan-chan became a national hero after defeating Khitan's large army. He used old tactics from the Goguryeo period, and after damming up the Samgyo River, he destroyed a quarter of the Mongolian troops by flooding them when they tried to cross the riverbed. In spite of this attack, the weakened enemy marched forward to Gaesong, but was relentlessly attacked and ultimately destroyed by the cavalry of Gam Gan-chan. The Khitan army left the country and never returned. This event entered the national annals as the "Battle of Guju."

From this time, the kingdom flourished and experienced a former unknown prosperity. The foundation for this prosperity was laid by King Seonjong (982–997), when he succeeded to control the aristocracy, further stabilized the economy, and established a government administration, again, mainly based on Chinese patterns. Under the rule of the Goryeo sovereignty, the country experienced one of its best periods in history.

An ever-increasing arrogance of civil servants, particularly toward the military, caused an impetuous and very bloody insurrection 1170 that was followed by numerous other *coup d'états*, which, however, always honored the status of the king. Finally, the Choi family obtained the power and founded a military regime with a valiant army, thus rendering the family much more powerful than the reigning king. It was only after 1220 that civil servants regained power, as the military did not prove capable of concerning administrative work.

Starting from 1231, Goryeo suffered again a series of attacks from the Mongols, this time under the command of the successors of Dschengis Khan. They devastated extensive parts of the country and destroyed a substantial quantity of irreplaceable cultural assets, and the very last traces of the former capital of Gyeongju were finally exterminated in 1235. Yet, the intruders were quite surprised of the strong resistance they met, even though the capital of Pyongyang had to be finally abandoned. The court flew to the lush green island of Gangwha (about 30 miles west of Seoul) and moved the seat of the government to the city of the same name. As the tribes of the steppes lacked any maritime experience, they did not dare to chase the fugitives across the water. The civilian elite around the king pledged for an arrangement with the Mongols, whereas the military preferred to resist the invaders. Finally, the royalists were successful, and King Wonjong was the first Korean ruler to leave the country in 1264 for Beijing (at that time Cambaluc), where he met the Great Khan Kubilai to negotiate a mild form of subjugation. He succeeded, because the Mongols did not strive for a permanent conquest and were only interested in gold and beautiful women. The group of military men disapproved the course of events and occupied several islands at the Western front of the peninsula, among them the big semitropical volcanic island of Jeju in the very south of the country. Kubilai Khan, however, recognized the strategic importance of the island and seized it. From Jeju-do, he was able to control the Sung Dynasty of nearby China as well as Japan, which he intended to subdue. For this purpose, he forced Goryeo to build more than thousand ships, which they had to equip. Additionally, Goryeo was ordered to provide a huge number of soldiers and helpers for the planned invasion of Japan. In 1274 and 1281, colossal fleets attacked the island of Kyushu. The Japanese samurai offered stubborn resistance and were twice lucky enough that violent typhoons shattered the ships of the enemies.

In 1294, Kubilai Khan passed away, and subsequently, the power of the Mongols started to crumble. In China, the Ming Dynasty took over in 1368. Starting in 1352, King Gongmin ruled Goryeo; he reconstructed the old constitution and dispensed it from Mongolic influences. In 1356, his army advanced to the north and reconquered old territories up to the river Liao, thus almost completely retrieving the former territory of the Goguryeo empire.

Meanwhile, forces of the Ming defeated the northern Mongols and afterward started to quarrel with Goryeo over the territories north of the river Yalu. The Goryeo General Yi Song-gye advanced to the north and conquered the former capital of Liaoyang. When the armies of the Ming threatened to launch a counterattack, Yi Song-gye was supposed to stop them with Goryeo's finest armed forces. However, the general was very concerned about the enormous strength of the enemy and, additionally, due to the bad weather, decided to retreat. He further turned against his own king, who resided in the capital of Gaesong, and took over the executive power. This surprising incident altered the real politics of Korean history and heralded the decline of the Goryeo dynasty.

A bizarre historical episode at the end of the Goryeo period was the surprise attack of Japanese pirates at the coasts of Korea as well as Taiwan and South China. During the reign of King U (1375–1388), alone 378 raids were registered. Those buccaneers (*waegu*) ravaged and ransacked Korean settlements and disappeared quickly with their loot. Their base of operations was the Japanese island of Tsushima, located only 25 miles east of Busan. The government tried to negotiate with Japanese officials to find a solution to end these criminal actions. However, because of severe disorders in Japan at that time, there were no officials capable of acting. Indeed, the economic desolation in Japan prompted merchants with a spirit of adventure as well as desperate bandits to pillage foreign shores.

The raids caused tremendous material damage to the empire of the Goryeo and were also a military threat for the armies fighting under heavy losses in the north against Chinese and Mongolian invaders. Korean soldiers were familiar with the effects of gunpowder from former combats with the Chinese and learned to produce gunpowder themselves. Subsequently, ships, which could carry small cannons, were built to attack the pirates. About 500 vessels of the Japanese pirates were sunk, and ultimately, in 1389, their base Tsushima was captured. Afterward, the shores of Korea enjoyed a rather secure time of peace.

2.5 The Founding of the Yi Dynasty and the Kingdom of Joseon

Four years after his coup d'état, General Yi Song-gye usurped the throne in 1392 and thus brought about the downfall of the Goryeo Dynasty after 475 years of its existence. He founded the Yi Dynasty, which ceased to exist only in 1907 with the abdication of King Gojong. The newly established kingdom called itself Joseon (Choson) and was ruled successively by 27 kings. As an advocate of realism, Yi Song-gye resumed negotiations with the overpowering Ming empire, which resulted in a formal sovereignty of China over Korea that ended in 1894 with the Japanese becoming more influential. The new state border, which remains valid to date, was defined using the course of the rivers Amnokgang (Yalu) and Dumangang (Tumen).

Following the example of China, Yi Song-gye introduced a rigorous style of Confucianism, which soon penetrated many aspects of life in Korea, as "Korea's policy, political structures, social ways of thinking and institutions as well as with regard to cultural, intellectual and economical conduct; eventually Korea became more Confucian minded than the Confucian China" [3].

The new king with the postmortem name of Taejo removed the capital of his empire to Hanyang, which is today Seoul. The new capital was erected according to geomantic principles, after the layout of the Chinese capital of Chang'an. The Gyeongbok palace, in the northern part of the city, was built just at the feet of the stately Bugak Mountains and Hanyang ended in the south at the Han River. Only the heart of the city was surrounded by a city wall, but left parts of the metropolis outside of its protection. Recently, approx. 70 % of the old city walls have been reconstructed. There were four main town gates, which derived their name from the four points of the compass. The *Nandaemun* (Southgate) and the *Dongdaemun* (Eastgate) are still well preserved and respectively authentically reconstructed. The distance between these two gates is about 3 miles. The Southgate and the Northgate (called *Ganghwamun*) were separated by a distance of roughly 1.3 miles. The small Cheonggyecheon River ran through the center of this area. The *yangban* families lived in the north as well as in the south of this region, while the east was reserved for middle-ranking military officials. Likewise, middle-ranking officials of the administration lived in the west as well as in the center. At the main road, which still today leads from the Gyeongbok palace to the south and to the river Han, merchants were permitted to go after their business.

Besides the capital, there existed four other cities with a privileged status: Gongju, Jeonju, Yeonheung, and Pyongyang. In addition, 20 prefectures were established, which were organized into 82 counties with 175 districts. The *yangban* class was entrusted with the administration of these corporate bodies. Like the mandarin in China, the *yangban* had to qualify through tough civil examinations for these public offices. Nevertheless, these positions were—unlike in China—reserved exclusively for the nobility, in fact only for families from the southern and Western provinces. Usually, these families possessed a considerable amount of real estate properties and their main pursuit was the exploitation of the lower classes.

In 1398, bloody feuds erupted within the royal family, leading King Taejo to abdicate and to retire into a monstery. Eventually, his son I Bang-won rose to power and stabilized the Yi Dynasty under the name of Taejong. The new king fought against Buddhism and enforced severe Confucian rules. He also established a privy council in counterbalance to the absolute power of the court and established a sewage system in the city of Seoul. When he retired due to his old age, he instituted one of his sons as the new king and entered into history as "Sejong the Great." This magnificent person ruled 31 years until 1450, and this period is considered the most brilliant epoch of Korean history. Today, a golden sculpture of King Sejong boasts in Seoul on the main road south of the Gyeongbok palace, which also carries his name: Sejong-no.

2.6 King Sejong the Great

King Sejong surrounded himself with young scholarly talents from different fields such as arts, literature, natural sciences, civil engineering, agronomy, astronomy, meteorology, cartography, and administration. Under the king's guidance, Joseon flourished. Sejong himself presided over a group of people, who developed a Korean alphabet, called *hangeul*, with twenty-eight letters (today reduced to twenty-four). These letters were grouped into syllables and thus could be quickly grasped. Possibly, this is the most intelligent system of written language worldwide. The complicated Chinese characters remained for the upper classes and scholars. Until today, they are used by a small elite minority. For the ordinary people, the invention of *hangeul* opened new possibilities concerning their education.

The art of printing by using movable metal letters was invented in Korea as early as in 1377–78 years before Johannes Gutenberg of Mainz in Germany printed a copy of the Bible with movable letters. In 1377, Buddhist analects of the monk Baegung were printed in two volumes, still using Chinese characters (*hanja*) in a temple in the town of Cheongju. This work, called Jikji, was acquired by a French diplomat in Seoul under obscure circumstances at the end of the nineteenth century. The remains are still preserved in the Bibliotèque Nationale de France in Paris, though a French president promised once its restitution to the Korean government.

The development of *hangeul* and the invention of printing with movable letters lead to a wide distribution of textbooks. Three hundred years prior to the French, a compilation of the entire knowledge of that time was compiled in a 112-volume encyclopedia. Furthermore, a medical textbook was produced by dozens of therapeutic practitioners. In 264 volumes, this textbook included all officially known medical treatments in East Asia at that time. Another manual from 1433 comprised 959 diagnoses, almost 11,000 remedies, and about 1500 instructions for the practice of acupuncture.

After the "Golden Age" under Sejong the Great, bloody power struggles erupted between high-ranking bureaucrats, foes of the royal family, and scholars, all of them defending different doctrines around 1450. Those who had the upper hand liquidated their adversaries. These cruel purges entered into history as the infamous *sahwa* (Literati purges). The strong principles of a fundamentalist Confucianism did not allow peaceful discussions or compromises, let alone appeasements. Instead, a compromise was considered dishonorable and a shame. This ideology still continues to determine the behavior of several elder Koreans up to the present.

2.7 Aggressions of the Manchu and the Japanese

Toward the end of this historically weak period, the kingdom of Joseon was invaded twice (1592 and 1597) by 150,000 Japanese warriors, led by their famous shogun Hideyoshi. They had planned to subdue Joseon in the passing, while marching on into China which they wanted to conquer, thereby completely misjudging the existing power relations. The Japanese advanced to Pyongyang, but were slowly worn out by the tenacious Korean resistance and by the beginning of winter and consequently harsh weather conditions.

Behind the front on the southern shores, the ingenious Admiral Yi Sun-shin ordered ships to be constructed that resembled turtles. These ships had rounded decks, which were covered with metal sheets, thus withstanding spears and, more importantly, burning torches. They further sported iron spikes that made it hard to board the ships. Admiral Yi cut off the supply line of the Japanese and sunk more than half of their ships as the Japanese were unaware of the treacherous waters of the southern coast. Besides the great victories of Salsu (612) and Guju (1019), this naval battle of Hansando (1592) is the third event every Korean school-age child is proud of until today. The great Japanese Admiral Togo, Heihachiro, who became immortal after the victorious naval battle of Tsushima, was named the "Nelson of Japan" (Togo studied seafaring for seven years in England and on British ships) by British journalists. Togo conceded that he could be perhaps compared to the great Horatio Nelson, but that he could not at all be compared to Korea‘s brilliant Admiral Yi Sun-shin.

Ultimately, a huge Chinese army rushed to the aid of Korea, and the Japanese had to flee the country. Montanus [4] wrote in 1669: "They had been forced to a non-respectable peace and had to renounce all their conquests in Korea." When Hideyoshi passed away in 1598, the Japanese samurai abandoned any further plans to invade the Korean peninsula. However, the retreating soldiers left ravaged fields and destroyed irrigation systems, as well as villages and cities shattered to pieces, pillaged temples, shrines, and palaces behind.

To Western nations, Korea was unknown for a long time. Seafaring Arabic merchants had contact with the Shilla kingdom and already visited the early Hanyang (later Seoul) in the ninth century. The first report on the hermit kingdom was produced by a Portuguese who lived in Japan [5] and probably gained his knowledge from a Catholic priest, who was in the entourage of shogun Hideyoshi, thus supposedly being the first European in Korea. Efforts to land on the shores of Korea were always thwarted. In 1653, shipwrecked Dutch sailors set foot on Korean soil on the island of Jeju. Until their escape thirteen years later, they were forced into a form of slavery. Their bookkeeper, Hamel [6], later wrote an interesting book on their adventures and encounters with Korean people. Until 1882, entering Korea was illegal and subject to the death penalty for foreigners.

Only a few decades after the Japanese invasion, a new powerful Manchu empire developed in the north of the country. The empire strived to expand into all directions. In order to be able to focus on its mission to challenge the Chinese Ming Dynasty, it initially attacked Korea and turned it into a vassal state. The Manchu collected enormous contributions and took many hostages. This time, the northern territories of Korea were lost once and forever.

After the invasions by the Japanese and Manchu, a powerless state remained in which hundreds of thousands of citizens fell victim to famine. The country slightly recovered under the moderate kings in succession. Meanwhile, the Manchu had overpowered the Ming Dynasty in China and ruled the country as the Ching Dynasty, thereby alleviating the pressure on Joseon. Yet, all small economical progresses were set back due to the quick population growth. Furthermore, the continuous murderous internal disputes between rivaling political cliques were further obstacles to a healthy development and hence can be considered a basic evil of Korean history.

2.8 The Self-isolation of Joseon

Its neighbors haunted Korea for centuries, and hence, the nation was very exhausted by all the attacks. As it was generally accepted belief that all evil came from the outside, it is not surprising that Joseon decided to isolate the country. For about 200 years, it became notoriously known as the "Hermit Kingdom," which rigorously refused any contact with the outside world, even prohibiting the cultivation of potatoes from the New World, America. Particularly, Confucian scholars were convinced that all foreign thoughts and ideas would be pernicious for the national mind-set of Joseon. As a result of this seclusion, the country fell back behind the international progress. This proved to be especially fateful for the technological and economic progress of the country. Also, the geographic isolation of the country located outside the common shipping route as well as the small interest of foreign traders in it, because of the lack of attractive minerals, contributed to Joseon remaining rather unnoticed. The mistake of isolating a country was repeated over the last decades by North Korea; there, however, the self-preservation of the regime was considered more important than the prosperity of its citizens.

In 1864, King Daewon-gun came into power. He knew that only an economically strong country could survive the impending times of change. Daewon-gun fought the notorious corruption of the country with an iron fist and cut down privileges of the yangban in the countryside. He further invested and financially strengthened the military defense force of his kingdom. Many astute Koreans started to propagate "practical learning" (*sirhak*) instead of the prevailing academic tenets of Confucianism with their inherent social statics. This contributed to a steady recovery of the country. Moreover, Daewon-gun wanted to increase the national self-esteem by restoring traditional temples and palaces; the Gyeongbok palace in the north of Seoul was in ruins since the Japanese invasion of 1592 and needed to be restored. Of course, these projects devoured enormous financial means. Thus, the king drastically increased the taxes, a measure from which the population suffered significantly.

The monarch was extremely suspicious of the Meiji Reformation of his Japanese neighbors. He detested their sweeping Westernization and had a hunch that Japan's growing strength might on day turn against Korea.

2.9 The Arrival of Aliens

Since the beginning of the nineteenth century, alien ships appeared in an ever-increasing number on the shores of Joseon and demanded the opening of the harbors of the "Hermit Kingdom." The government reacted reluctantly as it was afraid of the "bad influences of the barbarians." American warships forced open some Japanese harbors in 1854, and British contemporaries had proceeded similarly with Chinese harbors earlier in 1840. The Koreans disdained both Japan and China for their weakness and were alarmed by the bellicose actions of the British in the Opium War (1840–1842). Soon Korea itself became a target of rapacious foreign powers.

The Russian empire in her relentless longing for the east had invaded Manchuria and had snatched away the Liaotung peninsula from the Chinese. There, on the east coast of the Yellow Sea, the Russians set up their only two ice-free harbors in the Far East: Port Arthur (today Dalian) and Vladivostok in the east, close to the Korean border. Both harbors became bases for marine forces. In 1864, Russian soldiers crossed the border river Tumen to Korea.

By the middle of the century, Catholic French missionaries as well as local believers were executed, many of whom had to endure cruel torture. As a consequence, although France was not a very ecclesiastical nation at that time, a French marine squad attacked the island of Ganghwa in the northwest of Seoul. Nevertheless, the French march to the capital had to be stopped due to the stubborn resistance of the Koreans and the plan to conquer Seoul was finally relinquished. [Royal annals, which were ravished at Gangwha, were returned to Korea as late as of April 24, 2011.] After this attack, the Koreans fortified Gangwha as well as the harbor of Chemulpo (today Incheon) about 30 km south of it.

In 1866, two US-American ships penetrated Korean waters close to Pyongyang. The first ship ran aground and the shipwreck was disassembled by the local residents and the crew was set free unharmed. However, the second ship was seized, completely destroyed, and the entire crew was killed. [The former North Korean dictator Kim Il-sung assured that his grandfather was part of these patriotic deeds.] Five years later, Americans embarked on a huge punitive expedition and the defending forces of Gangwha were eradicated by means of firepower. The forward march to the capital failed, as the Americans met the same fanatic resistance that the French had already experienced five years before. The fleet of Admiral Rodgers hovered three more long weeks at the mouth of the river Han in the northwest of Gangwha, before they left disappointed for their base in China.

The new Meiji government of Japan (in office since 1868) demanded an opening of the Korean ports. This request was immediately rejected by the arch-Confucian officials of Joseon. Around 1875, in order to investigate the situation of the coastlines, Japanese warships secretly sailed into Korean waters around the mouth of the river Han. Instead of withdrawing from the warning shots of the Koreans, they attacked Incheon and landed on Gangwha and killed the defenders. When retreating to Nagasaki, they raided the coastal region around Busan, hence foreboding the events to come.

Starting in 1873, King Gojong ruled Korea with his powerful wife Queen Min, who had pursued the expulsion of his predecessor King Daewon-gun. Against a strong opposition of many bureaucrats, Gojong finally followed the advice of several foresighted men to open the country to foreign powers. In the long run, they argued it would be impossible to resist their military power. Even more, there was too much to learn from them, and smartly handled, Korea could only profit from an active foreign trade.

2.10 The Opening of the Ports to Foreign Powers

The Japanese were the first who were permitted in the Treaty of Ganghwa to open a legation in Seoul. They further obtained the right for their ships to enter the ports of Incheon and Busan as well as Wonsan (today in North Korea). They were also entitled to some special privileges that were also granted to Western nations by China and Japan. All this was achieved by the Japanese by massively threatening Korea with gunboats in the waters around Gangwha Island. Nahm [7] wrote that the Japanese were "demonstrating the speed with which the Japanese were learning the imperialistic tactics of the Western nations."

After various fruitless efforts, the USA finally negotiated the Treaty of Chemulpo in 1882. In this treaty, not only trade relations were agreed upon, but also exterritorial rights to foreigners. The latter point was a thorn in the flesh of conservative officials, and the treaties with Western powers were considered very imbalanced. Shortly thereafter, treaties of "Amity and Commerce" were signed with Great Britain and Germany in 1883 and in 1884 with Italy and Russia. These treaties were subsequently followed by a treaty with France in 1886. At this time, there was no agreement with China, since the court in Beijing was unwilling to waive the traditional privileges of receiving tributes from Korea.

2.11 Chinese, Japanese, and Russian Interests in Conflict

In July 1892, members of military units, who had not received their pay for more than a year, started a mutiny. The old king Daewon-gun took this opportunity to regain control over the country, while Queen Min had to flee the palace in disguise. During this time, anti-Japanese riots erupted in Seoul during which a couple of Japanese civilians, as well as military persons, were murdered. An envoy managed to flee and returned some months later with a detachment of soldiers and demanded a huge amount of money to compensate for the losses they met. The amount was paid to them.

Realizing what had happened in Seoul, the Chinese decided to send a military unit. The rioters were liquidated and Daewon-gun was taken captive and sent to China and the former Chinese control over the Korean government was re-established. King Gojong and Queen Min returned to the Gyeongbok palace. General Yuan Shih-Kai was promoted and became commander of the Korean army. The Chinese further dispatched two advisors with the status of vice ministers of the foreign office to the new government. The Koreans had to acknowledge that they lacked any knowledge of how to deal with international affairs. One of the advisors, Ma Chien-Chung, was also advisor to the state council, whereas the other advisor, the German Paul Georg von Moellendorff, was to oversee the port authorities and the maritime custom services.

Expeditions to the USA and Japan made the Koreans aware of how backward their country really was. A group of people aimed to modernize Korea in the fields of agriculture, commerce, and industry as well as concerning military affairs and further advocated independence from China. However, they faced strong resistance from a conservative faction around Queen Min. When they felt personally threatened, this group staged a revolt with the support of some members of the Japanese legation. In history books, this incident is called the "Gapshin Incident" (1884). The Korean progressives established a new administration in order to implement political, economic, and cultural reforms. Yet, Chinese troops crushed this movement. Once more, Japanese citizens were killed and their legation was burned down. Only a few Korean modernizers managed to escape with their Japanese friends to Japan.

Only one month later, accompanied by two infantry battalions, Japan's foreign minister Inoue, Kaoru travelled to Korea. He forced the Korean government to pay high compensations for the Japanese lives lost and the Japanese property damaged. A few months later, China and Japan concluded an agreement at Tientsin in which they agreed to completely withdraw their military personnel from Korea. The Japanese abided the agreement and pulled out their troops. Only a few guards remained in order to protect the legation. China, however, stationed about 2000 soldiers, disguised as merchants or policemen, in the country.

In respect of these events, von Moellendorff suggested an agreement between China, Japan, and Russia, which was supposed to guarantee Korean safety and integrity. However, none of the three nations showed a particular interest in this proposal. Von Moellendorff was afraid that China would not be able to assure the sovereignty of Korea in the long run and believed that Russia could take a neutralizing role. The strategic idea was to free Korea from its sandwich position between Japan and China. He suggested to the Tsarist empire to lease an ice-free port on the Geomun islands, located 30 km south of the Korean peninsula, between Vladivostok and South China.

When the British government learned about this idea, they strongly opposed the expansion of the Russian influence in the Far East. Thus, in April 1885, they occupied the islands without any prior notice to Seoul. This was much to the consent of Japan, which was afraid of a growing Russian interest in Korea.

The Chinese emperor had entrusted Li, Hung Chang (Li Hongzhong), a leading Chinese politician and military man, to handle the affairs in Korea. Li considered himself "King of Korea" and forced the British out of the Geomun islands, assuring them that the Russians would not take over. Li was opposed to any independence of Korea and did not show an interest in its neutralization. Instead, he increased the Chinese domination over the country, since he was afraid that the Japanese wanted to annex Korea. Von Moellendorff was in an unfortunate situation, maneuvering between all these antagonistic interests. Li, Hung Chang finally sent the German back to China and replaced him with Owen N. Denny, who had formerly served as a consul general of the USA in China. At this time, the USA were not prepared to play a significant role in Korea.

The dissatisfaction of many Koreans concerning their status as a Chinese protectorate caused riots in Seoul, and Chinese shops were burned to the ground. Japan was similarly unhappy with the situation, as its trade with Korea was increasingly replaced by trade with the Chinese. Basically, Japan considered Korea, controlled by an unfriendly power, as "a dagger pointed at the heart of Japan."

The weak government in Seoul was highly indebted abroad. Only an increase of taxes enabled Korea to comply its obligations. Particularly in the southwest of the country, farmers, miners, and fishermen bitterly opposed such a tax increase and flocked together to found the so-called Donghak Movement (eastern doctrines). The movement demanded the abolition of the *yangban* class, the end of slavery, and the expulsion of all foreigners. When the leaders were finally executed, severe revolts, which the government in Seoul could not handle, occurred. Thus, the government asked Chinese troops for help.

As a counter-reaction, Japanese troops landed at Incheon, seized Seoul, and occupied the Gyeongbok palace. First, the followers of the Donghak Movement were eliminated before the Chinese were defeated in a big battle near Pyongyang. Subsequently, the victorious Japanese crossed the river Yalu and invaded Manchuria, and the important harbor of Port Arthur was captured. The beaten Chinese were demanded to agree to the bitter Treaty of Shimonoseki (1895). This treaty forced them to acknowledge the independence of Korea, and China had to cede Taiwan to the Japanese empire. Furthermore, they had to pay high reparations and were forced to lend the peninsula of Liaotung to the victors for twenty-five years. As a consequence, Japanese exports to China quickly increased to 90.9 % [8].

Japan took control of the Korean government, which first worked smoothly. However, the Japanese authority soon dwindled away, mainly due to two events. First, Russia, with its old interests in the peninsula of Liaotung, demanded to nullify the lease agreement between China and Japan. Shortly after the Treaty of Shimonoseki, Russia allied with France and Germany and confronted the imperial state with the so-called triple intervention. In view of this overwhelming power, the Japanese had to give in. Three years later, Russia itself signed a contract with China to lease the peninsula. Japan considerably lost reputation in the Far East.

Secondly, being an old friend of China, the old intriguer Queen Min had always been in favor of the Russians over the Japanese. At the dawn of October 8, 1885, a group of Japanese men, together with several Korean collaborators, stormed the Gyeongbok palace, murdered the queen, poured kerosene over her body, and burned her remains. King Gojong and the crown prince were arrested and a new prime minister was immediately installed, who assembled a cabinet that was considered to be Japanese-minded.

This monstrous crime caused turmoil among infuriated Koreans. King Gojong, who had usually displayed a rather ambiguous position in political affairs, started to take the reigns of government more firmly. Queen Min was honored with a state burial, and Koreans who had participated in her assassination were executed. Russian-friendly advisors once more gained influence in the court. The king pushed reforms forward energetically, and thus, the Chinese calendar was replaced by the Gregorian calendar. Moreover, modern elementary schools, as well as compulsory vaccination, and an efficient postal system were introduced. The king demanded the abolition of the traditional long hair and set an example by cutting off his own long hair. These changes upset Confucian traditionalists, who started insurrections and murdered high-ranking civil servants.

The king felt increasingly surrounded by traitors and rumors spread that the Japanese wanted to dismiss the ruler. King Gojong and his son disguised themselves as women and entered a sedan chair, which was carried by loyal followers to the Russian legation, where he stayed for about a year. Meanwhile, the infuriated mob had killed all cabinet ministers, who did not flee to Japan. The Russian influence in Korea increased rapidly, and the Japanese tried to seek an understanding with Russia. They negotiated the return of the king into the palace. The number of troops was reduced for both the Russians and the Japanese, and equal troop sizes were ascertained for both parties. Whereas the Russians were supposed to take care of the protection of the Gyongbok palace and the government, the Japanese employed their troops to protect their own settlements in the country. In reality, they jointly gained control over Korea and it was their aim to banish China from the peninsula. At the suggestion of the Japanese king, Gojong assumed the title of *hwangje* (emperor), the first in Korean history, and renamed the country Daehan Jeguk. This act was supposed to weaken further Chinese claims on Korea.

Russia dispatched military instructors to establish a modest Korean army. Concessions were issued to Russian, American, British, and German companies to exploit mineral resources such as iron ore, coal, gold, silver, copper, and tungsten. Railway concessions were authorized to Americans, Russians, and French. Despite earlier negotiations, Japan was excluded from these rights. Nevertheless, some Americans and French later sold their interests to the Japanese.

Young Korean reformers were annoyed by the "Westerners" increasingly dealing with Korean affairs. In February 1898, they established an "Independence Club." The later South Korean Prime Minister Syngman Rhee and the naturalized American So Chae-pil (Philip Jaisohn) were, among others, prominent members of this club which used the slogan "Korea for the Koreans." The club advocated a modernization of the country by investing into the infrastructure, liberating women from their domestic sphere, establishing progressive schools, and stopping to issue concessions to foreigners. Since the conservative bureaucrats surrounding Gojong detested liberal reforms, they pressured him to close the club in October/November 1898. At the turn of the century, the country was economically and morally exhausted. Corruption was rampant, and taxes increased permanently. Riots erupted and thousands of Koreans immigrated to Hawaii. The government was not able to continue the organization of a powerful army. As Nahm [9] phrased it: "The twilight of the Yi dynasty was at hand."

Over the years, the rivalry between Japan and Russia intensified. When Russia tried to establish naval bases in the south of Korea or aimed to purchase land around the river Yalu and, above all, occupied Manchuria, Japan considered to start a war with their major enemy in the Far East. On February 8, 1904, they attacked the Russian fleet in Port Arthur (which was later seized by Japan with great casualties). One day after the attack on Port Arthur, the Japanese landed at Incheon, and soon, the citizens of Seoul heard the roar of cannons. Russia lost three warships in the following naval battle. The next day, despite the frequently affirmed neutrality of Korea, the Japanese marched into Seoul and, in a *coup de main*, started the colonization of the Korean peninsula.

Facing these difficulties, Emperor Gojong asked the USA for help. Yet, President Theodore Roosevelt signaled to the Japanese that he would not intervene if Japan ceased its interests in the Philippines, in which both nations had been interested so far. After achieving consent with the Americans, Japan did not waste any time and immediately gained control over the police force of Korea, its postal as well as telephone services, and its custom services. The Daichi Bank started to function as Korea's central bank. The state of Korea had to formally approve its status as a Japanese protectorate.

Japan then invaded Manchuria and promptly collided with Russian interests. The great Imperial Russian Navy, the second largest of its time, was supposed to free the troops in the Far East; however, it was devastatingly beaten in the naval battle of Tsushima on May 27, 1905, under the command of Admiral Togo. This event signified an important turning point in modern world history, as it was the first time that a non-Western power defeated its rival in a significant military struggle. For the Russians, the game in Korea was over, a fact that was sealed with the Treaty of Portsmouth in August 1905.

2.12 Japan Settles in Korea

The later prime minister of Japan, Hirobumi Itoh, travelled to Korea and proclaimed that no foreign power should ever again settle in this country [10]. A so-called governor general (*tokanfu*) assumed control of the country. He took over the foreign affairs of Korea as well as the power of judiciary, while the national army was dissolved. A merely symbolical role was assigned to the Korean emperor, who now represented the government of Tokyo. Consequently, Gojong was replaced by his son, who was married to a Japanese lady.

After a sequence of riots, in which about 18,000 patriots lost their lives, Japan formally annexed Korea on August 27, 1910. The annexation was euphemistically called "fusion." 14.7 million Koreans became secondary Japanese citizens, called "senjin," hence being differentiated from genuine Japanese citizens called "naichijin." All Korean citizens became subject to Japanese laws, and the local Korean press was severely censored. The country was renamed "Choson," and Seoul had to change its name to "Keijo."

Officially, the use of the Korean language and teaching Korean history were prohibited. Furthermore, everybody had to assume a Japanese family name. Even worshipping Shinto shrines became compulsory for the former Korean citizens. These drastic measures aimed at assimilating Korea completely into the Japanese empire. Human as well as material resources of Korea were supposed to be of use for Japan. Forty percent of the farmland was nationalized and distributed to an increasing number of Japanese farmers. Factories were erected mainly in the northern part of the country, which was rich in resources. Korea was about to become the basis for the Japanese conquest of Northeast Asia. In pursuit of this goal, Japan marched into Manchuria and later established the vassal state of Manchukuo.

Striving for independence, many bloody attacks were attempted, but were always brutally suppressed by the occupation force, which rigorously enforced police regulations. Under such control, the Korean people were barely able to breathe. However, in Tokyo, leading politicians did by no means share the same opinion on how rigidly the Koreans had to be governed. One politician, who advocated more sensitive proceedings in Korea, was Itoh, Hirobumi. Ironically, it was him who later fell victim to a Korean freedom fighter's attempt on his life. In 1919, US President Wilson promulgated the message of sovereign rights of nations. This led Korean patriots to demonstrate peacefully for facilitations. This movement (*samil undong*) started at the Tapgol Park in Seoul and it was the first time in Korean history that great parts of the population testified to a national feeling. Nevertheless, the occupants reacted with severe harshness and thousands of protesters were shot down and condemned by the panicking authorities. Leaders who survived fled to foreign countries.

Far away in Tokyo, the Japanese government finally recognized the discontent of their "new subjects." Therefore, captives were pardoned, and the income of the native population was improved. Many were admitted to lower and middle positions in the administration. The Korean population welcomed the improvement of the infrastructure, the abolition of feudalism, the modernization of agriculture, and a reforestation program for the rather bare hills of the country. The Japanese also established an efficient financial system and laid the cornerstone for a capitalist structure of the country. Yet, they did not allow local entrepreneurs to participate in this process.

The continuously flashing aspiration of Korean people for independence as well as the military aggressiveness of the Japanese against its neighbors led to another period of stern oppression. With the entry of the USA into WW II, the Japanese were forced to activate all their strength in the Far East. The Korean population started to suffer from hunger as food supplies had to be discharged to famish Japan. Hundreds of thousands of Koreans were forced into military service and into enforced labor. A huge number of women and girls were compelled to serve as prostitutes for Japanese soldiers and were heinously called "comfort women." By the end of the war, Korea was an exhausted and drained nation knocked to the ground. Finally, all Koreans, no matter whether they lived in their home country or in Japan, lost their Japanese passports.

Leading heads of the resistance had fled persecution by emigration. Syngman Rhee escaped to Shanghai as early as in 1912, where he founded an exile government, which was later first relocated to Hawaii and then to California. In 1922, he served Korean interests as a delegate of the League of Nations in Geneva without having any significant impact. On this occasion, he met his later wife, an Austrian lady, working as a secretary for the organization.

Throughout the period of Japanese occupation, there had been strong resistance in the country in which politicians, students, Christian leaders, farmers, workers, and entrepreneurs participated. Thousands of active members of the resistance lost their lives; another hundreds of thousands languished in prisons. Within the resistance, particularly leftist and communist-oriented groups stood out. The Marxist–communist cadres were on the one hand very patriotic and active, but on the other hand, they were often hopelessly estranged. One of the many groups served in the liberation army of Mao Ze Dong in the Chinese province of Yennan and founded a Korean independence party under their leader Kim Won-bong. A young man, named Kim Il-sung, who later turned to the Soviet army, worked in this environment. From the east of Siberia, he organized partisan attacks against the Japanese in Manchukuo and the northeastern part of Korea.

In the Treaty of Cairo (1943), Roosevelt, Churchill, and Chiang, Kai-Check had agreed that Korea should become free and independent in due course of time. Stalin approved of this decision soon afterward at the conference of Teheran. At the Yalta Conference (February 1945), the Allied Powers made efforts to convince the Soviet Union to enter war in the Far East as they overestimated the strength of the Japanese forces. In return, the USA agreed to a Russian occupation zone north of the 38th parallel, whereas the USA would occupy the territory south of this border.

Two days after the Americans dropped the first atomic bomb on Hiroshima on August 6, 1945, the Russians declared war on Japan, although Russia had already promised America to enter war in East Asia in October 1943 [11]. On August 10, 1945, Russia marched into North Korea and crushed Japanese troops there. It was not until September 8 that American forces led by General Hodge landed in Southern Korea where they did not meet any military resistance.

2.13 Paving the Way for the Division of Korea

In the interim period between the Japanese surrender and the entry of the Allied Forces, the Japanese Governor Endo, Ryusaku asked the socialist underground fighter Yo Un-hyong to arrange a provisional government for all of Korea. Yo formed a government unit, in which all diverse movements of the country participated, except for an extreme right wing moment, which was excluded. The absent Syngman Rhee was summoned as the first president, and Yo Un-hyong was appointed his deputy. However, the decision of the Allies to officially divide Korea into two occupation zones hit the unprepared country like lightning on September 2, 1945.

After thirty-five years of Japanese suppression, now even two occupation forces would govern the tormented country. Instead of President Wilson's proclaimed sovereign rights of every nation, only the "right of the victors" ruled, even though the Russians can hardly be called "victors" after letting the Americans do all the work over three years and only engaging for three days into the war in East Asia. A clever Stalin could certainly only laugh at his bigheaded ally.

Unlike the USA, Russia was well informed about Korea and many Korean officers served in its army. Meanwhile, local administration units had established themselves, which were approved by the occupation forces under their control. The Russians changed the educational system, printed new money, and relocated several manufacturing plants to the Soviet Union. Hundreds of thousands of North Koreans fled head over heels to the south.

Kim Il-sung served as one of the officers in the Soviet army and was on very good terms with the occupants, who introduced him as a national hero and made sure that he was appointed first secretary of the Communist Party of Korea. He immediately started to designate like-minded people to important public positions. This met strong opposition from patriotic students as well as workers and resulted in many fights, which lasted for many months and in which many patriots were killed. Together with the overpowering Soviet troops, the resistance was finally broken and another hundreds of thousands of people escaped to the South.

From the very beginning of the occupation, the USSR had the goal to establish a socialist state in North Korea. They started with similar reprisals as the Japanese during their occupation and soon were unpopular with the population. Kim Il-sung, who spoke Mandarin and only broken Russian, was appointed president of a newly established administration authority under the patronage of the occupation army. Simultaneously, he served as vice chairman of the newly founded socialist labor party of North Korea, which considered itself the equivalent of the South Korean labor party in Seoul. Kim Il-sung quickly became the most powerful man in North Korea and who fought against anyone who was not of his opinion—no matter whether his opponents were nationalists or communists. The Russians, preparing their later retreat from the country, organized between 1946 and 1948 the North Korean People's Army. From its very beginning, it consisted of professional soldiers and civilians returning from China, Manchuria, and Siberia as well as of young soldiers who had been recruited from towns and villages of the country. The new army was continuously strengthened and supplied by the Soviet Union with tanks and fighter planes.

The Soviet occupation forces soon established a "planned economy," which was supposed to bring the evils of a capitalistic economy to an end. A reasonable part of this was an agricultural reform, which initially distributed land to 725,000 households. South Korea was included in these plans, as it was assumed that the two Korean nations would be reunited in the near future. In general, Kim Il-sung was a fervent nationalist for whom the communist system was only a means of total control of power. Until today, the Northern Regime aspires to a reunion, yet only under the premises of a "completion of the great socialist revolution." This premise indicates that the socialist military cadres strive to perpetuate their power under all and any circumstances.

The US-Americans went to South Korea without having definitely agreed on a plan and did not know much about the history, culture, and language of Korea. One month after his arrival, General Hodge demanded to speak to the provisional Korean government. He told then the vice president Yo Un-hyong that he was not willing to acknowledge his government, while the appointed new president Syngman Rhee had still not arrived in Korea. Hodge tried to govern the country with several Japanese administrative officers, who had remained in the country. This new order was, however, boycotted by the already established administrative committees of the new government.

The supreme commander of East Asia, General Douglas Mc Arthur, was suspicious of the revolutionary potential of Southern Korea and therefore had ordered the establishment of an austere military rule. The Americans had been welcomed enthusiastically as the real liberators from the Japanese yoke. However, they did not reciprocate this respect and indeed regarded the local people as unrefined and backward. This turned the initially positive Korean public opinion into antipathy toward their rescuers. The USA brought Dr. Syngman Rhee (whose real name was I Sung-man) back to South Korea—not as the appointed president but as an independent patriotic politician. Rhee was considered a national hero and was widely respected in the population. Prudently, he refrained from collaborating with all agitating parties of the country and, from the beginning, took a hard position against the North.

On instigation of the USA, the UN stepped into the Korean situation and called upon a national congress that was to work toward the unification of the two Korean nations. Kim Il-sung immediately agreed, whereas the political forces of the South remained suspicious and renounced participation. Eventually, the

Americans introduced a global anticommunist containment strategy with the so-called Truman Doctrine, which demanded strictly democratic elections and the right of self-determination of nations. Thus, the Northern Regime ceased to be a potential partner for unification.

"Whereas the system of the North got the bearings partly by the Stalinist systems of East-Europe in the South, a curious synthesis of Confucian paternalism and the elements of Western democracy took place" [12].

2.14 The First Republic (1948–1960)

Under the supervision of the UN, the first free elections in the history of Korea were held in May 1948. An astounding 95 % of the entire population participated in the election. The supporters of Syngman Rhee obtained 54 % of the seats in the new national assembly, which subsequently voted for him with an overwhelming majority to become the new president of the state. The first republic of South Korea was born. Shortly thereafter, the new state was recognized by the USA. Soon afterward, the Americans pulled off their troops and left behind a country dominated by social chaos, which was politically unstable and economically bankrupt.

The North did not respect this development and invited the new republic to the city of Haeju to discuss the foundation of a joint state. The south did not accept this invitation. The Northern government proceeded on its own and called on general elections for the whole country. Officially, 99.9 % in the North voted in favor of the "Supreme National Assembly," which declared that the South had voted in "secret elections" with 77.2 % for its approval. The Supreme National Assembly elected Kim Il-sung as new prime minister. South Korea was simply considered the Southern part of the new Northern administration. The Soviet Union soon recognized the state of North Korea, and henceforth, a real division of Korea was fixed indeed.

Not all people in South Korea were happy about this development and, inflamed by Northern agitators, a communist rebellion erupted on the island of Jeju. The rebellion was subjugated, and approximately 30,000 inhabitants of the island were killed in this process. Subsequently, communist and socialist forces contrived a huge insurrection in the Jeolla province with Gwangju as a center. They were joined by more than 200,000 students, workers, common citizens, and even soldiers. South Korean elite troopers and paratroopers defeated this uprising and prevented the outbreak of a civil war. A bloody witch hunt followed and traced infiltrated cadres from the North in the entire country, cruelly chasing and eliminated them. These events constitute a dark chapter in the history of South Korea. However, the country indeed could have turned into a communist community, thus inviting the North to intervene.

In contrast to the Americans, the Soviets took care of the consolidation of the Northern State. Though Seoul remained the factious capital of Korea, Pyongyang was established as the provisional capital of North Korea, where the new central government resided. It obtained a special status, and the six provinces of North Hamgeyong, South Hamgeyong, North Pyong-an, South Pyong-an, Hwang-hae, and Gangwon were controlled by it.

The "Supreme People's Assembly" was elected by all citizens eighteen and older for a period of four years. It had a council of twenty-three members, and its chairman was simultaneously head of state, a rather formal position. All twenty-three members belonged to the Workers' Party. The council handled all draft legislations and regulations between the sessions of the "Supreme People's Assembly." However, it had no legislative power, because all laws were drafted within the Central Committee, which has the ultimate power in the country. Kim Il-sung served as the general secretary of the Workers' Party and was appointed prime minister of the cabinet. He further served as the supreme commander of the army. The party and the military have always been closely interwoven. Yet, recently it seems that military personnel have taken over, after some powerful politicians were promoted to high military ranks. Civilian counterparts in office play a merely symbolic role. The principle task of the Korean People's Army was the defense of the principles of Marxism–Leninism in the sense of a self-sacrificing spirit. The interests of individuals had to stand back in favor of the interests of the community. Under Kim Il-sung, the Northern state was centered on the Kim family, and consequently, his son became his successor. With the appointment of Kim Jong-un however, the leadership seems to have ultimately turned into a pluralistic group governing that uses "the great leader" more as a symbolic figure for its authorization.

The border between the two states was initially not hermetically closed. The North, for instance, supplied the South with electricity, whereas the South provided the North with food. The UN had urged the former allies to withdraw their troops. In December 1948, the Soviets started to retreat and the Americans followed in May 1949. However, the USA left a small military contingent in the south of the country.

Patriotic leaders, who by all means wanted to achieve unification, presided over both Korean nations. Syngman Rhee expressed his strong will to get to the North by political means. Kim Il-sung referred to a peaceful reunion and suggested mixed election committees. At the same time, he tried to persuade Stalin to attack South Korea. He was very annoyed that the UN was not likely to acknowledge his state and regarded South Korea as the only legitimate representation of Korea.

Considerable parts of the population of the South sympathized with the Northern Regime, and complete units of the southern defense forces deserted to the North. Kim infiltrated South Korea with a significant number of guerilla fighters, who were dispatched to the southern provinces of North Jolla and South Gyeongsang. The long and partially rugged coastlines of these provinces enabled a secret landing of troop carriers. The guerilla fighters united with local communist partisans. Yet, all these underground fighters were wiped out by the South Korean army until April 1950.

2.15 The Korean War

Kim Il-sung had to realize that he did not achieve anything with guerilla tactics. He was indirectly encouraged to act more aggressively when the American Secretary of State Dean Acheson announced that South Korea was not their first defense priority. With the tacit approval of Stalin and the moral support of Mao (both, however, withholding their own forces), strong North Korean troop detachments attacked the South in the morning of Sunday, June 25, 1950. A weak South Korean army was no match for them and they quickly conquered the whole country, except the bridgehead of Busan in the utmost southeast of the country as well as a tiny mountainous enclave near Daegu.

The USA, on its global crusade against communism, was very alarmed. The UN also demanded the aggressors to retreat behind the 38th parallel, a demand that was declined by North Korea. As a result, the USA established a military alliance, which was joined by fifteen other states. General Mc Arthur was appointed as supreme commander of this alliance. Besides the South Korean troops, the USA provided the majority of the fighting troops with Great Britain, Australia, and Turkey also contributing substantial support.

In a most surprising move, Mc Arthur landed his troops in the back of the enemy at Incheon. Because of the extraordinary strong tidal currents, a landing at this place had been considered impossible. But with great spirits and proficient amphibious vessels, Mc Arthur succeeded in this daring move. Already on September 15, Seoul was reconquered, and five weeks later, Pyongyang was captured. The allied troops faced the Chinese border across the river Yalu another five weeks later. The American air force had a great share in this military achievement by rigorously bombing irrigation systems and pouring napalm over the northern cities.

China was highly alarmed by the sudden appearance of American troops at its border. It had formerly issued a warning that China would engage in the fighting, if other troops than South Korean troops would pass the 38th parallel. However, the Americans did not take this warning seriously. Mao Ze Dong initially dispatched an army of approximately 250,000 "volunteers," thus avoiding an official declaration of war to the USA. They crossed the Yalu with an overwhelming force and advanced to the south and conquered Seoul. During this time, McArthur was pondering to make use of the atomic bomb, which would have provoked an extension of the war to the People's Republic of China, in order to force a final victory. Meanwhile, the number of Chinese combatants had massively increased. The estimates vary considerably between 600,000 and three million in total. President Truman dismissed General McArthur, and even though the Allied Forces reconquered Seoul with considerable effort, here, the war ended in a stalemate which lasts until today.

Russia and the USA showed discernment in this state of affairs and, on a proposal of the deputy foreign minister of the Soviet Union, Adam Malik, entered armistice negotiations in the city of Gaesong. Yet, the North and their Chinese supporters did not want to give in. Time and again, they plotted skirmishes which were, respectively, countered by cruel American air strikes. Only after the death of Stalin in March 1953 did the UN convince Kim Il-sung and his ally to yield. However, he demanded that all prisoners of war were to be released before any discussions. To his surprise, more than half of the Chinese and North Korean men refused to return. On the Chinese side, mainly troops of the former Kuomintang army wanted to go to Taiwan. Kim Il-sung used this fact to stop the negotiations. However, the Soviets and Americans pressed for a ceasefire which was agreed upon in July 1953 in Panmunjeom. This armistice was nullified by North Korea in spring 2013, and ever since, the two Korean states are contractually at war again.

A new border of 150 miles, which was very similar to the old border, was agreed upon. North Korea won a piece of land in the west which includes the old capital of Gaesong. South Korea gained the territory around Gansong, an idyllic landscape at the seaside. According to this arrangement, the areas of both states remained almost exactly the same as prior to the war. The USA regained its former sympathies from the Korean population due to its self-sacrificing engagement (its casualties numbered over 155,000 men, among whom 37,000 died). The other allied countries are highly respected in South Korea until today as well.

Both sides suffered high causalities including dead, wounded, and missing soldiers. However, the combined losses of the allies with around 430,000 soldiers were significantly smaller than those of their enemies with approximately 1,400,000. Both capitals, Seoul as well as Pyongyang, were completely destroyed. The Americans lost more than 3000 airplanes. The war lasted three years, almost as long as the war against Japan and Germany. Both Koreas remained independent though thoroughly paralyzed. Kim Il-sung lost his face, yet prevented any upraise by installing a stern dictatorship and eliminating all his adversaries by accusing them that they had wrongly assured him that the citizens of the south would take his side in case of a northern attack.

In the years after the Korean War, the Americans acted very kindly toward South Korea. They transferred more than a billion dollars of subsidies and helped with peremptory orders against Japan when it came to questions of fishing rights, reciprocal demands of property rights, and the repatriation of Koreans, who had been forced to work in Japan. The indirect winner of the war, however, was Japan as the important geostrategical position of the country with its mighty industrial center was proven to the USA and the world. Moreover, the Japanese industry made huge profits supplying the Allied Forces fighting in Korea.

Syngman Rhee was disappointed by the Americans, because they had practically remained at the old border in the north. As he was inclined to military adventures, some US generals considered his expulsion. Since 1948, Rhee had continuously served as the chief of the state. His vice president and the prime minister had been degraded to executive officers, and particularly, those who had collaborated with the Japanese had been discharged, regardless of their abilities. Rhee indeed behaved like a dictator.

Rhee seemed to be unpopular throughout the country and even the national assembly criticized his policies. Despite this fact, his Liberal Party won the elections in May 1954 with a clear majority and Rhee was reelected as president. Afterward, he behaved even more dictatorial in the fashion of feudal kings of bygone centuries. Rhee showed a fanatic anticommunist stance and refused all discussions concerning a rapprochement with North Korea. Within the Republic, he used intrigues to secure his power and turned South Korea into a state under police surveillance.

During the spring of 1960, unrests spread from the southern port city of Masan, which were likely to turn into a rebellion against the government of Syngman Rhee. This rebellion spread to Seoul, where students of the Korea University (one of the three elite universities of the country) marched in a huge crowd to the palace of the president. There, the police started shooting at the demonstrators, killed hundreds, and wounded many more. At this point, the USA dropped Rhee because of his nerve-racking constipation. He had not contributed much to improve the catastrophic situation of the national economy after the war. A large part of the substantial American subsidies had trickled away in corrupt government apparatus. All sides demanded Rhee's resignation, and after he had to recognize that the military forces sympathized with the masses, he agreed to retreat. At the end of April 1960, Rhee quit his services and went to the Hawaiian Islands into exile. Thus, it can be said that "Syngman Rhee, who started as a revolutionary was himself overturned by a revolution" [13].

2.16 The Second Republic (1969–1961)

In May 1960, free democratic elections were quickly held. The Democratic Party received a huge majority in the lower house, which later elected Yun Po-sun as president and Jang Myon as prime minister. As in former times of Syngman Rhee, the lower house and the upper house were supported by the old social stratum of landowners, civil servants, scholars, and influential businessmen. The new leaders had the reputation of being prudent. Almost all of them had studied at Japanese colleges and universities.

At all times, one of the three main diseases of the Korean society was, besides corruption and nepotism, factionalism. Discord also prevailed in the ruling Democratic Party. Generally, the new leaders were perceived as too intellectual and mild. Both the freedom of speech and freedom of press were misused. The rate of criminality increased, the black market flourished, and gangs roamed the streets, while the police was incapable of controlling the social chaos. Wild demonstrations occurred and trade unions, split up into 821 units with only 375,000 members, fostered further unrests. Many people did not understand that a democracy is not a treasury for self-service. The extreme leftist socialist cadres, aided by North Korean support, wanted to turn the situation into their advantage and called on subversion. Altogether, the Second Republic was in disarray and dangerously insecure.

2.17 The Third Republic (1961–1972)

In May 1961, a military coup took place. Its initial purpose was the purge of corrupt generals, who interfered in political affairs. Under General Chang To-yong, a military revolutionary committee was founded. The intellectual leadership, however, remained with major General Pak Chung-hee (who was later always called Park by international media). He proclaimed a nationwide anticommunist program, a moral renewal of the country, and the establishment of a sustainable economic growth in favor of the population, which was still living in poverty. Furthermore, the generals required a development toward a real democratic republic. After achieving all these objectives, they wanted to return to their barracks. The USA was initially very concerned by the military coup, but ultimately they had no objection and refrained from any intervention.

The revolutionary committee was renamed into the Supreme Council for National Reconstruction. Afterward, the junta suspended the constitution, dissolved the national assembly, decreed a stern censorship of the media, and prohibited all political activities as well as student demonstrations. By keeping the old president of the Republic, Yun Po-sun in his official position, a democratic semblance was kept. Soon after his predecessor had been arrested and sentenced to death, General Pak Chung-hee took the chair of the Supreme Council for National Reconstruction. Nevertheless, his predecessor was later pardoned and permitted to seek exile in the USA.

Park soon bustled with activity; he took care of the challenging issue of normalizing the relations to Korea's arch-enemy Japan, which he needed badly for economic assistance. He travelled to the USA and received 415 million dollar of economic aid, allocated over several years with declining installments. He established a First Five Year Plan and taken office with the slogan to achieve "the miracle of the Han River." Actually, indications of an improvement of the economic situation of the country could be observed quite soon.

After a purge, in which 2600 politicians of the opposition were prohibited to be politically active for six years, a new constitution was adapted in a public ballot with 78.8 % of the votes. The legislative system with upper house and lower house was abandoned, and the position of the president was enforced: He obtained the right to appoint and dismiss the prime minister, a function that was abolished four years later anyway. Park himself took charge of the position as an officiating president. In 1962, the members of the junta quit the military service and Park put himself up for the election of the president of the Republic as one of the five candidates. He won the election by a small margin with 42.6 %, whereas the former President Yun Po-sun received 41.2 % of the votes. Two months later, the Third Republic was inaugurated and the civil order reestablished. Pak Chung-hee prepared the nation for a period of "sweat, blood, and hard labor."

This nation, however, was practically destitute. The Japanese government had stated on July 1961 [14] that it would be impossible for South Korea to develop a prosperous, self-sustained economy for seven reasons: (1) overpopulation,

(2) lack of any natural resources, (3) an undeveloped industry, (4) heavy military burdens, (5) lack of capital, (6) less developed political skills, and (7) lack of administrative experiences. Consequently, Park asked Tokyo in vain for financial aid. Meanwhile, Washington, D.C. had become suspicious because of the antidemocratic government of the former military rulers. But to enhance his five-year plan and to be able to build factories for exports, Park very urgently needed capital. In January 2010, the Korean television revealed that Park had paid a desperate visit to Bonn, Germany, during this time. The official reason for his visit was an adjustment for roughly 7000 coalminers and approximately 11,000 nurses, who worked in Germany as temporary immigrant workers. Park and his attendants were great admirers of the former German virtues of diligence and parsimony as well as of their modest way of life.

Furthermore, both countries were linked by the same fate of the separation of their nations. Ludwig Erhard, the German chancellor at that time, sympathized with the South Korean population, which endured starvation and great economic misery. He yielded a capital aid of 18 million dollars and mobilized a syndicate of five German enterprises in order to lend another 26.3 million dollars. Additionally, the West German government granted a deficiency guarantee for exports of German companies to Korea for another 20 million dollars [15]. With this knock-on financing, which was very scanty by today's standards, President Park started the following Korean export miracle. One member of his team later wrote that: "The importance of these loans cannot be underestimated. More to the point, the help which Korea secured from West Germany at this time when Seoul was desperately trying to establish a 5-year economic plan in order to develop its economy, but found itself increasingly isolated from the international community, can be likened to a general suddenly being granted thousands of troops and horses with which to go into battle" [16].

Despite considerable economical advances, the first administration period of Park was characterized by unrest and many demonstrations. Nevertheless, in 1966, the president succeeded in achieving an adjustment with Japan and also to exchange ambassadors with the neighboring country. Prior to this, the foreign minister of Japan had expressed his regret about the "unhappy events of the past."

Differently from his predecessor Syngman Rhee, Park cooperated flexibly and successfully with the USA and President Johnson visited Seoul in the fall of 1966 as a token of the renewed partnership between their countries. Likewise Seoul managed to break out of its isolation with other states. Meanwhile, Korea had succeeded to build a growing export industry that was energetically struggling for international sales and reached 13 % of the GNP in a short time. With a growing internationalization, South Korea attracted a lot of international capital, which was so badly needed for its further growth.

Park, who was the chairman of the Democratic Republican Party (DRP), was supported by this party in the elections of May 1967. He ran against his old foe Yun Po-sun, who was the chairman of the New Democratic Party (NDP). Park again received a majority by ballots and this time 51.4 versus 40.9 %. Immediately after his reelection, Park sought to modify the constitution, which provided only for one reelection of the president. He achieved his goal when the National Assembly agreed to his proposal with 2/3 of its votes on October 1969.

Although Korea continued to develop economically, Park's reelection in April 1971 turned out to become much more difficult than expected. He gained 53.2 % of the votes, yet a young opposition leader, Kim Dae-jung, obtained 45.3 %. The DRP was accused to have falsified the election process. Kim had proven leadership qualities and, furthermore, had suggested appealing social reforms. He even had dared to boldly advocate diplomatic relations to some communist states. The new administration period of Park started with rough student demonstrations and labor unrest. The always virulent centrifugal vigor in Korea came forth very strongly. On December 6, 1971, Park declared a state of emergency and expanded his competences, which were only legalized afterward. Moreover, ten months later, he dissolved the national assembly and declared martial law. Park gave two reasons for his actions: First, the further economic development of the country required an austere leadership; second, in impending negotiations with North Korea in the future, it would be necessary to negotiate from a position of absolute personal strength.

2.18 The Fourth Republic (1972–1980)

A public referendum, which was held in October 1972, received the approval of 91.9 % of all registered voters. Subsequently, it established a new constitution (Yushin reform), which gave the president almost dictatorial power. A newly established National Conference for Unification was established and elected Park at the end of December 1972 with almost 100 % for a new term of six years as president. The Fourth Republic was born. Under his autocratic regime, the world of business witnessed a tremendous economic growth, called the "miracle of the Han River" (this will be elaborated on later).

The president was always alert with respect to his political foes. Particularly, Kim Dae-jung had frequently opposed him and was ultimately forced to escape to the USA. He was kidnapped by the South Korean secret service in a hotel during a journey to Tokyo and was later put on trial in Seoul, where he was sentenced to a long term in prison.

Pak Chung-hee always strived for a strong state and a powerful administration. He advocated a type of democracy, which would first and foremost benefit the country, and he regarded an independent judiciary as not conducive. Over the years, economic success with growth rates above 8–11 % legitimated his view. From the beginning, he favored to assemble big conglomerates (the *chaebol*), as only they were able to finance significant technological developments and could assert themselves in a global competition. The positive results of stern fiscal policies were channeled into the *chaebol* and enabled their expansion, which was further propelled by licenses in their favor. The complete system led to an oligopolistic and monopolistic structure of the entire national economy. Throughout all these years, South Korea turned from an agricultural into an industrial state. The income of the lower and middle classes increased considerably, however, not at the same pace as the total economic development of the industry.

Juergen Kleiner, the former German ambassador to South Korea and professor at Boston University, portrays [17] Pak Chung-hee as an ardent patriot and not at all as a concealed despot. According to him, Park always interceded modestly and incorruptibly for the common good. At any time, his foremost precept was efficiency, and when he encountered bureaucratic obstacles or factional feuds, he tore them down in a non-democratic fashion. With respect to inter-Korean relations, he was absolutely determined to achieve a peaceful unification. Park was generally interested in a relaxation of tensions both locally and internationally. He took much care to establish a commission to coordinate the problems between the North and the South. Despite his sound political behavior, Park was never popular with the public, probably because he lacked a charming and colorful character. This led to several assassination attempts; during one of which, his wife lost her life.

Starting in 1973, North Korea increasingly caused tensions on the peninsula, which were, however, attenuated by phases of conciliatory politics. Negative highlights of this period were naval skirmishes with the North Korean navy in as well as outside of the relevant territorial waters. Another flurry in South Korea was caused by the discovery of numerous deep tunnels, which led from the North, below the demarcation line, deeply into the South. These tunnels were suitable to infiltrate spies, propaganda material, and even troop contingents. Furthermore, a unit of North Korean soldiers, who were disguised as South Korean troops, tried to kill Pak Chung-hee in his official residence. They were detected only thousand yards from their target and completely destroyed. Reportedly, Kim Il-sung admired Park and he was the only South Korean politician whom he respected candidly.

Public demonstrations of politicians, leaders of the two Christian denominations, students and their professors, as well as other people all over the country caused harsh reactions of the Park regime. Within this tense situation on October 26, 1979, the president was shot to death by the chief of his own secret service at dinner party in the Blue House.

Afterward, the nation seemed to tumble into chaos. The population was shaken with precariousness, and their anxiety was heightened by the oil crisis at the same time, which triggered tremendous price increases. The experienced politician Choi Kyu-ha was soon elected as new president and promised to institute an orderly situation at the parliament until the end of the year. For the moment, peace was established. Nevertheless, behind the scenes, Chun Doo-hwan developed into a forceful political power.

Annoyed by intriguing scrambles, violent student demonstrations erupted again, strongly opposing a new military dictatorship, and were supported by socialist forces in the background. In Gwangju, the capital of the Jeolla Province in the southwest of the country, the situation turned once more into an armed revolt. The demonstrators overwhelmed the police and carried off numerous weapons. Parachutists of the regular National Forces brought this rebellion to a bloody end and hundreds of rebels died. General Chun Doo-hwan was mainly responsible for the relentless stance of the military that did not allow any compromise. In Seoul, participants of the assassination of Pak Chung-hee were sentenced to death and hanged. General Major Chun Doo-hwan took over as the chairman of the National Security Committee. He proclaimed a new democratic Korea as a welfare state.

2.19 The Fifth Republic (1980–1987)

Only two weeks after President Choi Kyu-ha had resigned from his office in August 1980, he was replaced by Chun Doo-hwan. The new president appointed a purely civilian cabinet and promised to lift martial law as soon as the political situation stabilized. The shocking revolt of Gwangju still prevailed in the minds of politically responsible personalities. Kim Dae-jung was found guilty of participating in the violent revolt in Gwangju and was sentenced to death.

In October 1980, the ratification of a new constitution became subject of a public ballot. An amazing 95.5 % of the enfranchised Korean citizens took part in the ballot, thereby proving their democratic awareness. The new constitution was approved by 91.6 % of the voters, which marked the beginning of the Fifth Republic. In February 1981, a new National Conference for Unification was elected with 78.1 % of almost 20 million voters. As was to be expected, this board elected Chun Doo-hwan for a term of seven years as president. On this occasion, the South Korean government granted an amnesty which freed 5200 detainees from prison and the death sentence of Kim Dae-jung was also turned into a sentence of life imprisonment.

The 51-year-old Chun appointed almost exclusively 40- to 50-year-old persons to important positions of his administration with the intention to have the country managed by a new generation. At the beginning of 1982, the midnight curfew, which had been introduced 36 years ago, was abolished. Furthermore, a monthly alarm, during which suddenly sirens rang and everybody had to take cover, even leaving the car on a highway, was put to an end.

Chun Doo-hwan basically followed the government style of his predecessor. Consequently, the economy flourished and continued to grow, and South Korea entered the circle of economically developed nations. However, as Chun displayed an authoritarian style of leadership like Pak Chung-hee, he provoked strong oppositional forces and led to fierce demonstrations. Students still remained a very agitated part of society. Finally, Kim Dae-jung was released into exile to the USA, and his comrade in arms, Kim Young-sam, took the leadership of the opposition. The public opinion concerning Chun was quite mixed. On the one hand, he was backed by the military and therefore served as a guarantor of security against North Korea. At the same time, he was equally considered the anchorman of the growing economic strength, which improved the international image of Korea. He further managed to bring the Summer Olympic Games to Seoul and successfully prevented that Pyongyang became a cohosting country. During Chun's term of office, universal suffrage was introduced for the first time in Korean history, thus allowing women to exercise their right to vote in public ballots.

Despite these positive actions, the president was very unpopular, especially among women. He was hated by students as an authoritarian, and both male and female students had mothers, who found him thoroughly distasteful. Chun was a realistic politician and recognized his rather negative image. For this reason, he suggested General Major Roh Dae-woo as presidential candidate for the forthcoming term of office, starting in 1988. He won the election with only 37 % of the votes casted. At the opening ceremony of the 1988 Olympic Games in Seoul, Roh as a president of the Republic and Chun as an elder statesmen sat together in the gallery.

2.20 The Sixth Republic (from February 1988)

Roh Dae-woo ran in his election campaign against three opponents: (1) the actual opposition leader Kim Young-sam, (2) the former opposition leader Kim Dae-young, who was allowed to come back from his exile in the USA, and (3) Kim Jung-pil, a former prime minister in the Pak Chung-hee administration (altogether called the "Three Kim"). The outcome of the election was very close. Kim Young-sam got 28 % and Kim Dae-young 27 % of the votes, respectively. The rivalry of these two men rendered the triumph of Roh Dae-woo. As usual in Korea, the opposition was split into several camps. Roh was peacefully inaugurated in February 1988 and he started his term (1988–1993) traditionally with a great act of grace. Under his rule, the economy continued to grow significantly and foreign businessmen hurried to Seoul in order to sign business contracts, to found enterprises, and to negotiate license agreements.

Many middle-class citizens demanded a real democracy in the preparation of the Olympic Games. Since the eyes of the world were directed to the Olympic Games, the government could not intervene severely. However, after the election, Roh reduced the enormous police pressure and abolished torture, and freedom of opinion became a common right of South Korean citizens. Roh was not really successful in ending the prevailing corruption. Their fatal consequences became visible in the 1990s: Thousands of apartments became uninhabitable, the Seongsu bridge over the Han River collapsed, and the Sampoong departmental store came down. In all cases, an insufficient execution of the construction work was determined as a reason.

The new constitution of October 1987 was the most liberal one so far in Korean history. It provided safeguards against military rule and official abuse of human rights. The presidential term of office was limited to five years, and a reelection became impossible. The president further lost his right to dissolve the national assembly. Roh was considered as much more friendly, relaxed, and forthcoming by the people than his predecessor. However, his military background was disliked, and Roh saw no chance for another military candidate and retired according to the constitutional law after five years of service. This time, the opposition forces agreed in appointing a candidate for the office of president: Kim Young-sam, who represented a moderate course in contrast to the more leftist Kim Dae-young.

Kim Young-sam won the 1992 election and took the office at the beginning of 1993. He was qualified for this position due to his management abilities and his sincere character. Kim navigated a midway course. Although he lacked the charm of a strong man, he was quite popular with a great number of the female voters. He also started his term of office with an act of grace. It was reported that seventy-year-old politicians, who had been imprisoned for unbelievable 37 years, were released in the city of Daejon.

The economy continued to grow significantly under Kim Young-sam. Yet, when the personal wealth increased above a certain minimum, people started to become increasingly dissatisfied—a phenomenon that can always be observed in countries with an accelerating affluence. The quicker the material wealth of a nation increases, the more the people cannot follow the pace and are left behind. This is partly because some people are more diligent and intelligent than others and partly because many citizens suffer from unfortunate circumstances in life. In the 1990s, the income disparities became more visible and people were envious of those who had considerably higher incomes. Therefore, fierce demonstrations and violent incidents occurred time and again under Kim Young-sam. These were usually led by students and trade unions as many of them immediately wanted higher incomes, regardless of their own abilities and qualifications.

A common anger developed against those who were doing better. This frenzy was mainly related to the widespread corruption, which is a traditional problem in the Korean society. It can be frequently observed among relatives of high dignitaries. As the British journalist Breen has remarked: "From the top, corruption has flowed downstream, like a lazy river of filth, leaving its scum everywhere" [18]. Politicians, ministers, high-ranking militaries, judges, top managers, and even university professors were equally entangled in corruption. Kim Young-sam vehemently attacked this deplorable state of affairs. Yet, it was impossible to please everyone involved—neither those who were entangled in the schemes, nor those affected and unhappy about Kim Young-sam's measures, which were not radical enough for them. However, the political culture among younger people improved for a certain time.

Kim Young-sam did not like the division of his fellow countrymen and thus did not immediately take action against some of the most prominent perpetrators. But then, it was revealed that Roh Dae-woo disposed of assets of more than 650 million dollars and that his predecessor, Chun Doo-hwan, had amassed probably even more. These sums were mainly "donations" of the *chaebol* leaders. The president had no choice but to prosecute both. As both former presidents were also charged with the previous massacres of Gwangju, they had to expect severe punishments. Chun Doo-hwan was sentenced to death, and Roh Dae-woo was convicted to 22.5 years in prison. Both decisions were later converted into a life sentence and, respectively, 17 years in prison. On occasion of his retirement from office, Kim Young-sam pardoned both culprits in 1997/98.

The former President Chun declared that he was "penniless" after he and his clan had paid back large parts of the illegally gained fortune. Their real estate, at least objects which could be identified as theirs, as well as pieces of art, was sold at auctions. However, he still owes the state a big sum of money; but the whereabouts of his remaining riches are unknown and he walks free.

During the anticorruption campaigns, many members of the president's own family were prosecuted and severely punished. The same was true for numerous of his acquaintances among politicians, bankers, and managers. Kim Young-sam's period of office was, in general, quite successful. He supported an increased international opening of South Korea and advocated a peaceful development of both Koreas, side by side, until the North would hopefully be convinced of the better system of the South. Kim Young-sam stood for a less strict Confucianism in human relations and promoted the legal equality of women. He was also in favor of US-American forces remaining in the country as long as the threat of the northern neighbor continued.

However, the ever emotional Koreans were spellbound by their former powerful leaders such as Pak Chung-hee, wanted a stronger personality at the head of the state, and did not appreciate Kim Young-sam's differentiated conduct of affairs. Although he had the seat of the Japanese colonial government (*jungangcheong*) demolished under great applause of the Koreans, he did not appear charismatic enough. At the end of his period, he did not deal very successfully with the upcoming financial crisis and further seemed physically shake as well.

At the end of 1997, the passionate Democrat Kim Dae-jung was elected as new president and determinedly started discussions with North Korea. Initially, he made significant progress with his new "Sunshine Policy" and received the Nobel Peace Prize in 2000. In July 2000, the first meeting between the highest authorities of both states had taken place; Kim Dae-young and Kim Jong-il, the son of Kim Il-sung (who had passed away in 1994), had met in Pyongyang. Afterward, the relationship between these two states, as well as between North Korea and some Western countries, relaxed to a certain degree. The South Korean administration was largely exchanged after the elections, thus following the model of the American presidential elections. Immediately after taking office, this new administration started sweeping reforms. According to Yi [19], the following topics were the main issues:

1. Principle of customer priority,
2. Entrepreneurial government management,
3. Flexible and transparent administration.

The introduction of these new principles made the whole governing system more efficient than before, and despite an environment that was turning more complex and difficult (Asia Crisis of 1999), respectable economical results could be achieved rather quickly.

2.21 The Financial Crisis as a Turning Point

At the beginning of his term, President Kim Dae-jung started to work with high pressure to fight the financial crisis and accomplished a couple of reforms. He succeeded in bringing the country back to the path of economic growth. The banking system was modernized, the large conglomerations were tightened, the labor market was made more flexible, and, above all, the general accounting system was made more transparent. Nevertheless, numerous mistakes reoccurred, for instance, the high debts of Korean enterprises abroad, the high overall public debt, and the excessively speculative real estate market.

At the end of his term in office, Kim Dae-jung's reputation declined dramatically. Ultimately, the stubborn North Korean government was a hard nut to crack for the president, his reform of the South Korean administration did not go on as fast as he had hoped, and for many citizens, the dream of home ownership became unaffordable.

The self-educated legal expert Roh Moo-hyun, who became a lawyer without having studied at a university, which is hardly possible in South Korea, won the next election convincingly. He was especially supported by the young citizens, and his election campaign was backed by heavily using modern means of communication such as the Internet. During his five-year term from 2003 to the end of 2007, he stood above all for social justice. For instance, he imposed high taxes on second residential premises, a measure that was much hated by the well-to-do classes and which had subduing effects on the Korean construction boom.

Roh Moo-hyun approached the North with patience and many concessions, but did not show the benevolence and political naivety of his predecessor in face of the North Korean negotiation partners, who were ever pleading for favors. Roh agitated close to socialism but had always the prosperity of his country in mind rather than political dodges. His slogan "Dynamic Korea, hub of East Asia" was quite popular. The idea behind this slogan was that Korea is located almost at the center of Northeast Asia and ranks among the strong economic powers. The new airport at Incheon (55 km west of Seoul) was supposed to serve as a turntable between Shanghai, Tokyo, and Vladivostok. At its opening ceremony, the airport was considered to be the most modern aerodrome in the world. In order to reinforce this idea, South Korea needed to be distinctly international. However, its population has only been hesitantly moving into this direction. Moreover, China was not much in favor of this idea and preferred to settle its logistic affairs directly with Japan or Eastern Siberia. The idea of a "New Singapore" was not very realistic given these circumstances.

2.22 Consolidation Under President Lee Myung-bak

During the new elections at the end of 2007, the adherents of Roh were overthrown by the dynamic, former mayor of Seoul Lee Myung-bak, who made his entry into the "Blue House" (*Cheong Wa Dae*, the official residence of the president). As a convinced liberal politician, he turned the wheel and, for instance, abolished the taxes on second homes. Single-handed, he agreed on the import of US-American beef and thus annoyed the local industry. Lee sided with the USA, which was not very popular in South Korea despite the fact that the country owed them their independence and security. The USA had initiated strict measures against North Korea, and Lee followed their stance by initially refusing any type of concession to the hermit country.

Lee was nicknamed "the bulldozer" and takes pride in a masculine image. Readily, he issued the story that already as a student of the Korea University, he had preferred "*makgeolli,*" an indigenous drink, to all other potions, which were considered more refined liquors.

The mind-set of Lee is very much influenced by the real estate and construction industry. Even though real estate prices declined in London, New York, and Tokyo, he tried very hard to preserve the exorbitant prices, especially in the upper price segment of the real estate market. This was not only due to the interests of his clientele in the construction industry, but because he worried that the light framework of the financial industry of the Republic would crumble, if a global economic and financial crisis struck. As approximately 50 % of the GNP is exported, the country is extremely vulnerable with respect to the stability of the global markets. Since 21 % of the total export value goes to China, South Korea is especially dependent on this country.

On April 2009, scandalous news of the former President Roh Moo-hyun disillusioned the Korean people. The moderate socialist, who had always referred to his simple background and modesty, was tried as his family was accused to have concealed several million dollars of bribes on accounts in Hong Kong and the Virgin Islands. Compared to the enormous assets of his predecessors Chun Doo-hwan and Roh Dae-woo, these amounts were rather small. However, Roh committed suicide by jumping from a cliff. Although he himself did not likely take any advantages, the former president took the responsibility for his family members, who had enriched themselves in the shadow of his authority. The disappointment about this politician was so great, because he was supposed to become a role model for a clean policy. The trust in politicians decreased virtually to zero in South Korea. The political class is only credited with preventing risks of war so far.

Throughout the history of Korea, it is remarkable that this country officially has never attacked a foreign enemy. The successful attack on the Japanese in Kyushu at the end of the ninth century was declared an act of piracy. North Korea refers to its attack on the South in June 1950 as "an interior affair," whereas South Korea comments sophistically on her engagement in Vietnam with 50,000 soldiers that one has not declared war, but had only aided a comrade in arms. It is still important to recognize that the modern South Korean constitution stipulates that a reunion of the country should only be strived for with peaceful means.

Today, South Koreans enjoy the increasing respect of their country all over the world. The Korean compatriot Ban Gi-mun (Ban, Ki-Moon) became the general secretary of the UN, and a Korean-born citizen of the USA, Jim Yong Kim, was appointed the president of the World Bank. The country belongs to the illustrious circle of the G-20. In December 2010, the G-20 summit was held in Seoul and presided by Lee Myung-bak. The 2018 Winter Olympic Games will take place in Pyeongchang, 180 km southeast of Seoul. Slight symptoms of a hubris are unfolding and occasionally people sneer at the lazy and decadent Japanese and Europeans. In the following closing remarks, the author will briefly outline a further positive development of the country.

South Korea is governed by the first female ruler in its history since February 2013. Pak Guen-hee is the daughter of the earlier president Pak Chung-hee. Her parents were both assassinated. During her first year in office, she had to fight off the shadow of her dictatorial father. So far, she has not left big footprints in modern Korean history. However, she governs firmly and resolutely with female dignity.

On the other side of the DMZ (demilitarized zone), North Korea attracts attention only by economical bottlenecks, violations of human rights, and emotional saber rattling.

For further reading concerning the history of Korea, the author recommends the excellent publication of the Austrian professor for international politics, Gottfried Karl Kinderman: "Der Aufstieg Koreas in der Weltpolitik" (The Ascent of Korea in World Politics) [20].

Another gem of literature on Korea is the book "Im Lande der Morgenstille" (In the Land of Morning Calm) [21] of the German Archabbot of St. Ottilien, Norbert Weber. In 1911, Weber went on a long journey to several Catholic mission houses in Korea. The country had been annexed by Japan only one year before, and because of the assimilation policy of the occupants, Weber was afraid the Korean culture would completely vanish in the course of the time. Therefore, he vividly described and richly illustrated everything he observed and studied in the country. After WW I, in 1923, he visited Korea for a second time and produced a black-and-white film, also entitled "In the Land of Morning Calm," with the endeavor to preserve the rich cultural heritage of the country for later generations. This film is accessible on YouTube [22].

Literature

1. Ham D-J et al (2011) Understanding Korean history, Paju-si/Seoul, p 4
2. Joe WJ (1972) Traditional Korea—a cultural history, Seoul, p 149
3. Nahm, AC (1988) Korea—tradition and transformation, Elizabeth (NJ)/Seoul, p 95
4. Montanus A (1669) Remarkable addresses from the East-India company of the united provinces to the emperor of Japan. London 1670 (originally Amsterdam 1669), p 17
5. Schwade, A (1962) Die Beschreibung Koreas durch Luis Frois (ca. 1594) In: Kuhl M, Sasse W (eds) Bruno Lewin zu Ehren seines 65. Geburtstags, Bd. III Korea; Bochum, S. 259–262
6. Hamel H (1668) Verhaal van het vergaan het jacht de Sperwer. Amsterdam
7. Nahm AC cit, p 152
8. Sohn P, Chol Choon K, Yi-sup H (1970) The history of Korea. Seoul, p 213
9. Nahm AC cit, p 201
10. Rutt R (1972) James Scarth Gale and his history of the Korean people. Seoul, p 318

11. Kraus W (1979) Wirtschaftliche Entwicklung und sozialer Wandel in der Volksrepublik China. Berlin, Heidelberg, p 20
12. Kindermann G-K (2005) Der Aufstieg Koreas in der Weltpolitik. Muenchen, p 379
13. Kleiner J (1980) Korea—Betrachtungen ueber ein fernliegendes Land. Frankfurt, p 191
14. Won-chol O (2009) The Korea story. Seoul, p 68
15. Auswaertiges Amt (1961) Deutsch-Koreanisches Protokoll ueber wirtschaftliche und technische Zusammenarbeit. Archiv Nr. 3; Bonn, 13. Dezember, S 3–9
16. Won-Chol O cit. above, p 83
17. Kleiner J cit. above, S 237–238
18. Breen, M (2004) The Koreans—who they are, what they want, where their future lies, rev. Edition, New York, p 238
19. Yi I-S (2001) Mid-term evaluation. In: Korean National commission for UNESCO, The Korean economy—reflections on the New Millenium, Seoul, p 348
20. Kindermann G-K, cit. above
21. Weber N (1915) Im Lande der Morgenstille. Reiseerinnerungen an Korea, Muenchen
22. Weber N In the land of morning calm. https://www.youtube.com/watch?v=VBv-_wDA4hw

Chapter 3
The Country and Its People

The following chapter opens with a short description of the geographical situation of South Korea and its influence on the economic development of the country. Afterward, the author gives a broad outline of the sociopsychological structure of the society in the south of the peninsula. Finally, a draft of the public governmental organization is presented. This chapter should provide a concise introduction for those who have a private or business-related interest in the country no matter if they stay at home, travel to South Korea, or even live and work there for a shorter or longer period of time.

3.1 South Korea—Geography and Climate

The Korean peninsula is basically situated in the northeast of Asia and borders Manchuria with its harsh climate, which transforms into the vastness of Siberia further north. To the West, China is only a forty-minute flight away and the Pacific Ocean stretches over an area of several thousand miles in the south. In the east, Japan can be reached within a few hours by boat. The cities of Busan (in the southeast of Korea) and Kita-Kyushu (on the Japanese Western island of Kyushu) are only separated by the Korea Strait (Chosen Kaikyo) and roughly 150 miles of water. Actually, South Korea is more an island than a peninsula, as all land lines to the north are rigorously cut off.

A traveler can hardly see any differences between the beautiful landscapes of Japan and Korea. At former geological periods, Japan had separated from the Asian continent and still continues to sink into the trenches of the Pacific Ocean. These tectonic movements cause earthquakes and volcanic eruptions in Japan.

Thus, tourists feel much safer in skyscrapers in Seoul and Busan than in Tokyo and Osaka. In 2010, however, newspapers voiced their concern that most high-rise

D.K. Schneidewind, *Economic Miracle Market South Korea*,
DOI 10.1007/978-981-10-0615-9_3

buildings in Seoul and Busan are not being build earthquake-proof and reminded their readers that earthquakes could indeed occur in Korea in the future. Yet, only about 200 light earthquakes have been registered in Korea since 2002, 48 of which were slightly stronger and occurred at the southern coasts of the peninsula [1]. The number of earthquakes with a magnitude above 4.5 on the Richter scale has, however, increased in the last two decades. Seven of such earthquakes have shaken the Western coast of South Korea, the last one with a magnitude of 5.1 on April 1st 2014. This quake was still clearly felt in Seoul as well. The Hallasan volcano on the rocky island of Jeju is 1950 m high and thus the highest mountain in South Korea. Its last eruption was recorded in 1007.

The scenic beauty of Japan is well known, but the same cannot be said about the attractive landscapes of Korea, which are undoubtedly comparable to those in Japan. The Koreans sincerely love their "Land of the Morning Calm" rightly advertise its scenic highlights. Small and large buses offer well-occupied tours, for instance, to the island of Ganghwa west of Seoul, the enchanting groups of islands in the southwest and in the south of the country, the maritime nature conservations with their rare flora and fauna, as well to the breathtaking river valleys and steep coasts in the east. Further attractions are the stunning red autumn leaves of the Seoraksan and the lovely landscape of Gansong at the east coast, close to North Korea and the so-called DMZ.

It is surprising that for a long time, South Korea kept a passive attitude toward international tourism. It is only recently that an extensive program was started to open up the country for foreign tourists, inviting them to visit the "Land of the Morning Calm" and familiarize them with its cultural highlights.

The Korean peninsula passes from north–northwest to south–south east and covers 85,000 square miles. For comparison, Great Britain covers an area of 94,000 square miles and Texas of 269,000 square miles. South Korea as the subject of this work is as big as Portugal and covers slightly more than 38,000 square miles of land.

In the east of South Korea, mountains fold up to 5200 ft, the center of the country is predominantly hilly, and in the west, hills alternate with alluvial plains. 70 % of the land is mountainous and difficult to use for agricultural purposes. There is virtually no point in South Korea, from which one could not see mountains.

Approximately in the center of the country, the mountain chain of Soebaksan (highest elevation: Jirisan with 5840 ft) extend from the southwest to the northeast. Historically, this mountain range served as a barrier between the central and the southern regions of the country. In the east, it meets the middle of the Taebaek mountain range, which extends along the eastern coast in northern direction. Its character is determined by rugged granite altitudes, deep canyons, and roaring waterfalls. The fertile Nakdong plain is located south of the junction of the mountain ranges, in the area of the Nakdong River, which later flows into the East Sea (internationally known as the Sea of Japan) close to the city of Busan. Besides these two dominating mountain ranges, there exists a range of hills north of Seoul, rising up to 3350 ft in the north–northeast and meets the Taebaek mountain range in its further course. This range of hills is densely wooded and located close to the border between North and South Korea.

The Han River (Hangang) in the north is one of South Koreas longest rivers. After a 320-mile journey, it flows into the sea north of the island of Ganghwa and serves as a natural border to North Korea. The stream has its source in the Taebaek range and flows—with some sharp bends—westwards. The Bukhangang, a tributary to the Hangang can be found east of Seoul. It originates in North Korea and crosses the "impermeable border." One of the bizarre episodes, which keep reoccurring between South and North Korea, is linked to this tributary. In the 1980s, North Korea dammed the Bukhangang with a huge dike, the Imnam Dam. This construction immediately caused anxieties among the South Korean population, which believed that the dam could be used as a weapon by blowing it up and thus causing a catastrophic flooding of Seoul. Consequently, in 2006, South Korea built a 1830-ft-long so-called Peace Dam on their side. The Peace Dam has the exclusively preventive function to stave off a possible flooding by the North Korea.

Another important river in South Korea is the 325-miles-long Naktonggang, which originates not very far from the Hangang. It flows briefly into the west and then turns abruptly to the southeast. Whereas the Hangang empties into the Yellow Sea, the Naktonggang flows into the southern part of the East Sea. Both rivers are not navigable for larger ships. Like all other rivers of the country, their water levels are quite unstable and dependent on seasonal weather conditions. The capital, Seoul, is situated at the Han River and the second largest city, Busan, is adjacent to the Naktong River. Other historical cities such as Buyeo (Puyo) or Pyeongyang were river-port towns as well. In former times, the rivers permitted a supply of goods and the transportation of persons with flat-bottomed vessels.

The steep east coast is not suitable to build larger ports. However, in the southeast there is the important port city of Busan, located in the south are Masan, Tongyeong, and Jeoju, and in the west Mokpo, Gunsan, and the very busy Incheon. A glance at the map clearly shows that Korea is facing China, which had a great cultural impact on Korea. For centuries, these two nations had strong economic ties before Japan replaced China in modern times. Currently, however, China has surpassed Japan again with respect to exports to South Korea, while the Korean export to China is three times higher than its exports to Japan.

Seoul is located south of the 38th parallel, which means it is roughly on the same latitude as Palermo in Sicily or Richmond in Virginia. Therefore, the city has a rather subtropical climate during the hot and humid summer. During winter, influenced by the huge Asian landmass, it is usually dry and often bitterly cold in the city. Further south, especially at the ocean shores, the temperatures remain much warmer than in the north and often two rice harvests a year are not unusual. The island of Jeju on the 33rd parallel already reminds a little of the South Seas, but has also experienced cold snaps as there are no mountain ranges from the west to the east to protect the island from rough northerly storms in winter.

3.2 Architectural Features

Traditional Korean houses were originally built of wood and later by using bricks. Since former times, these houses include a floor heating system (*ondul*), which uses the exhaust air of cooking ovens. The flooring is commonly covered with lacquered paper on which one lies comfortably cool in summer and pleasantly warm in winter due to the warmth that comes from below. These houses are significantly different from traditional Japanese houses, which are usually built of wood and a mortar mesh because of the dormant danger of earthquakes. Thus, traditional Japanese houses are often quite cold in winter as this method of building is more suitable for the warmer southwestern regions of Japan. However, what both cultures have in common until today is the fact that residences should by no means be entered with shoes.

Concrete is the preferred building material today. Private, single-family houses are only rarely built. Most people live in apartments inside buildings with four to forty floors. The usual residential living space per capita is considerably larger than in Japan or China, though there are huge differences between the working-class and upper-class citizens. The population density is 1290 people per square mile in South Korea and 830 people per square mile in Japan. However, in Japan the population is more concentrated in a few areas than in Korea.

Moreover, in Japan, especially older people prefer to live in small cozy rooms, whereas Koreans tend to prefer larger living spaces. Furthermore, Koreans often own massive furniture, while Japanese people tend to stow their belongings behind build-in cupboards, partly also as a precautionary measure against the frequent earthquakes. Therefore, different geological conditions determine different structural sceneries with regard to the residential premises in suburbs and on the countryside. Yet, in the province of Jeolla-nam in the southwest of the country, there exist old houses, which resemble houses in Japan. It is no coincidence that a large number of people immigrated to Japan around 400 A.D.

Today, the large urban cities of both countries look very similar and compete in building the highest skyscrapers. Elevated road constructions and breathtaking bridges can be seen on both sides of the East Sea.

3.3 Country of Tunnels

For years, there exists a project to build a 125-mile-long tunnel beneath the sea between Busan and the Japanese island of Kyushu. Because of the constant risk of earthquakes, it is a very risky construction project, does not have a commercial agenda, but is meant to contribute to a policy of appeasement between the two nations, which have disliked each other for centuries. Whereas the older generation of Koreans and Japanese still turn away from each other, the younger generation is much more open-minded on both sides. Unfortunately, most recently, nationalistic groups are emerging both in Korea and Japan. However, the tunnel project has hardly progressed in decades due its enormous expenses. The same is also true for other visions such as an undersea tunnel between China and South Korea or a plan to connect the peninsula with the big island of Jeju in the south.

Inside South Korea, there exist hundreds of tunnels, amounting to more than 440 miles, for railways and roads. There are many short-distance tunnels in Seoul as the metropolis is built on a hilly territory. The construction of the first major road tunnel in the center of northern Seoul underneath Namsan Mountain already started in 1969. The purpose of this tunnel was to also serve as a shelter for 350,000 citizens in case of a North Korean attack. Today, there are two more tunnels that lead through this mountain. Many tunnels were built for the highways traversing the divides of the Taebaeksan and Soebaeksan. Recently, its expertise in building tunnels bestows Korean civil engineering companies with numerous contracts to construct tunnels all over the world.

Additionally, many tunnels were dug from north to south underneath the DMZ by the Chinese and North Koreans for military purposes and to infiltrate troops, spies, and propaganda material. Sometimes, these tunnels reach up to 16 miles into the South Korean territory. According to newspaper reports (JoongAng Daily from October 13th 2009), the tunnels amount to a total length of nearly 200 miles.

Some experts, familiar with the infrastructure of North Korea, refer to the country as a "Swiss cheese" as it is assumed to be completely undermined by caves and tunnels. In times of war, almost all important arms, machines, supplies as well as people in leading positions could find shelter underground and thus significantly reducing the effectiveness of airstrikes. This is a lesson that the communist country learned from the absolute dominance of the American Air Force during the Korean War.

3.4 Nutritional Basis

In general, all essential products can be produced in abundance in Korea. Various regions provide distinct specialties. Based on agriculture and simple products made from natural materials, Korea was able to maintain an autarkical economy.

Due to its long seacoast, similar to Japan, fishing and gathering crustaceans, mussels, and seaweed constitutes the food base of Korea. Both countries have exploited their fishing grounds to certain extent and are now sending their fishing fleets to other fishing areas, which leads to several incidents. Korean fishermen sometimes encounter resistance from their Japanese colleagues and even more often from Chinese or North Korean fishermen. Sometimes, these struggles with Chinese fishing boats in Korean waters have the character of naval battles. Korean fishermen are also not welcome off the Spanish and South American coasts.

Seafood is very popular in Korea and many dishes including fish are always available. At the southern shores of the country, women (*haenyo*) still dive for mussels, crabs, and lobsters. Although this task is very daring and dangerous, in comparison with shell divers overseas, they are quite underpaid in Korea.

Further inland, fishing in the numerous small rivers and lakes is a very popular sport, which is emphasized by the fact that there is a specific television channel that exclusively focuses on this sport. Small and big games are rare and limited to ducks, hares, and wild boars. As some environmentalists lament, there are almost no small animals in the forests, a fact that can be explained with the Korean insatiable demand for meat of any type. The formerly omnipresent tiger was completely exterminated. In the last years, there has been a steady increase of hog fattening, breeding poultry, and horned cattle as well as sheep and goats and—to a smaller extend—horses.

As in many Asian countries, rice is a staple food in Korea as well. Thus, the cultivation of wet rice occupies large areas of the plains and river valleys. The glittering water surfaces of freshly sowed fields, the light-green paddy fields with young rice that turn yellow once the rice is harvested dominate large parts of the valleys. Since rice cultivation is conducted sequentially, the paddies are often located close to each other. Rain and warm summer weather are ideal conditions and enable up to two harvests a year. Thus, late or lacking rainfalls sometimes entail significant crop failures.

In January, 2010, local media services reported that the popularity of rice as a staple food would decline; the per capita consumption of 136 kg in 1970 had dramatically dropped to 74 kg in 2009. Meanwhile, the number has further decreased, which causes a serious problem for the agricultural producers. Therefore, the government asks the food industry to develop new rice-based products. The sales volumes of rice have further decreased during President Lee Myung-bak's term of office as he has interrupted the free support programs for North Korea, until the country would make serious efforts for a nuclear disarmament. Much to the discontent of other rice-exporting countries, an export to South Korea was not possible until 2014. Ever since, the import was liberated but is charged with high custom duties.

Another important staple food are noodles in multiple variations as well as other pasta products. Noodle soups are frequently consumed in Korea and the typical slurping and smacking of lips, which accompanies the consumption of these favored dishes, can be heard almost everywhere. Although a favorite during lunchtime, noodle soups are available throughout the day and also at night. Soups in a great variety of flavors including with fish, crabs, meat, and vegetables are very popular in day-to-day life, especially when in a hurry. These soups are preferably rich in content and heavily seasoned. Numerous ordinary restaurants and snack bars offer these dishes almost around the clock.

During fall, a substantial amount of wheat and barley are harvested in the sunny areas of central and southern Korea. Until it was revealed that imported products would be much cheaper, South Korea was a self-supporter concerning grain. Buckwheat and millet are grown in Korea as well. Potatoes and soybeans are further staple foods. As Koreans in general and Korean women in particular are almost obsessed with consuming vegetables, several vegetables such as Chinese cabbage, white cabbage, green salads, radishes, cucumber, beans, avocados, onions, and mushrooms are locally cultivated. Since many Koreans believe that vegetables are vital for their health, one can see that vegetables are grown in every available small plot of land, not only in the countryside but also in big cities, where they are planted in between small houses, at roadsides, at temporary building sites, and even on cultural properties. An old Chinese proverb claims that food and medicine have the same source—a saying that is obviously taken seriously by many Koreans.

The cultivation of fruits in Korea is also noteworthy. Apples are the most harvested fruits, followed by oranges and large amounts of peaches, pears, grapes, strawberries, plums, and *gokkam* (persimmons) as well as melons and pumpkins. Driving through the countryside, besides rice patties, ginseng fields covered with black plastic attract attention. Since many Koreans like hot dishes, we find huge fields of red and green pepper, chili, garlic, ginger, and sesame. In particular, in the southwest of the country, we also find tobacco and tea plantations. Another specialty in the southwest is the cultivation of mulberry trees, which serve silkworm production and thus the production of silk. Occasionally, silkworms are also roasted and consumed as titbits.

From 1980 to 2001, the total tonnage of crop production has increased from approximately 11 million tons to more than 20 million tons, which is due to the enormous increase of the population during this time.

The distribution of the following farm products is summarized as follows (Table 3.1).

Rice is still a very important staple food, but its significance is decreasing, and a substantial proportion of it is traditionally shipped to Japan. The enormous consumption of cabbage and radishes can be explained by their use as ingredients for kimchi, which is so much loved by most Koreans. Grains as well as soybeans are imported in increasing quantities (USA, Brazil). The production of fruits has also increased. The huge increase of "other" food (table) is caused to a large extent by the growing use of green houses and includes mainly avocados, cucumbers, water melons, and strawberries among others.

Concerning livestock and poultry, the figure of production of beef remained relatively stable with 1.36 million head and 1.40 million head between 1980 and 2001. But the number of dairy cattle increased from 0.18 million head to 0.55 million head. The production of hogs increased dramatically from 1.78 million head to 8.72 head, whereas the number of chicken more than doubled in that period from 40.13 million units to 102.39 million units [3] (Table 3.2).

A total of 40 % of the consumed food is produced at home, while 30 % of the meals are consumed in restaurants and snack bars, whereas another 30 % are takeouts or home deliveries. In particular, modern households are likely to avoid the complicated preparation of meals unless a housekeeper is employed, which is still customary in upper-middle- and upper-class families.

Excellent and diverse food is part of Korea's national characteristic, except for the working class. Meals (*siksa*) in general and dinner in particular are considered daily highlights. In particular, in the countryside—where frugality was formerly the rule rather than the exception—one is amazed by the varied and refined meals that are served nowadays. Because the preparation of these meals is often time-consuming, they are frequently prepared by neighborhood groups. Within these groups, the men are responsible for the supply and the women prepare the ingredients. The subsequent cooking or boiling procedure is conducted together.

Table 3.1 Development of farm products in Korea

	1980 [2]		2001 [3]	
	In thousand tons	%	In thousand tons	%
Rice	3550	312	5515	278
Cabbage	3113	274	3041	152
Radishes	1973	174	1732	87
Grain	906	8	272	13
Onions	454	4	1074	54
Apples	410	36	404	2
Pears	60	0.5	417	21
Potatoes	342	3	205	1
Soybeans	216	1.9	140	0.7
Peaches	89	0.8	166	0.9
Grapes	57	0.5	454	2.3
Oranges	161	1.4	645	3.2
Others	32	0.3	5.935	29.6
Total	11,363	100	20,000	100

Source: Handbooks of Korea 1982 and 2003

Table 3.2 Livestock and poultry

	1980 [3] in 1,000 heads	2001 [3] in 1,000 heads
Beef Cattle	1,361	1,046
Dairy Cattle	180	548
Hogs	1,780	8,720
Chicken	40,130	102,393

Vegetables and Fruits are found in volumes from 1982, and 2004, whereas Livestock and Poultry are jointly handled in a volume from 2004.

The center of most meals is often a rich soup. On special occasions, *Bulgogi* (beef, grilled on hot grates) or *Galbi* (spiced grilled ribs), as well as roasted or steamed crabs and lobster (the latter mainly imported from North Korea and Siberia) are enjoyed. These culinary highlights are served together with sheer endless small side dishes (*panchan*). Thus, when six guests are served, there are usually more than seventy small bowls on the table, which compose an attractive and colorful scenery. "Spicy, fiery, earthy, cool Korean food is diverse and provocative. Its bold and subtle tastes, textures, and aromas are sure to elicit comments, sighs, and even tears at every meal" [4]. Presently, there are efforts to spread Korean food (*hansik*) abroad. This would be an interesting enrichment of international menus.

When eating out in a restaurant, Koreans are sometimes quite impatient. That is why they are used to being served the first appetizers shortly after being seated and while the orders are taken. In less than 10 min, the dishes are delivered. On almost every table—except at expensive restaurants—there is a bell or electric signaler, which is immediately used when the waiting time is deemed too long by the guests. Complaints of the usually pretentious guests are voiced loudly and crudely.

The waiters and waitresses behave patiently, indulgent, and always friendly as the guest is king.

Korean chopsticks are not easy to handle, because they are made of metal and have a rectangular shape. They are quite suited for the Korean food and allow picking up vegetables especially well. Scissors are used at meals to cut noodles, meat, crustaceans, or vegetables into pieces—a rather unique Korean custom.

When dining together, the group of customers serves each other with especially delicious delicacies and loud toasts can be heard when the glasses are refilled. In contrast to the rich selection of dishes, the selection of drinks is rather limited and usually reduced to local beers and liquors made from rice, herbs, or roots. The local wines are only palatable when upgraded with imported wines, usually from South America. In particular, Korean women enjoy wines, particularly those imported from famous vineyards in Europe or California. In international hotels, high-class restaurants, and bars, the internationally most famous brands of liquor are of course available for the connoisseur. However, the consumption of these brands is overall rather limited in this country. Korea is famous as a land of heavy drinking; but because of the increasing number of people who drive a car, drinking habits have changed in general. The drinking habits of upper-class and younger people as well as the consumption of alcohol in restaurants have visibly decreased in recent times. Furthermore, in restaurants, the prices of alcoholic beverages are rather high when compared to the prices of food.

3.5 Western Clothing

From ancient times until the second half of the twentieth century, almost everyone in Korea wore prevalently white garments. In recent times, however, colorful Western clothes are most frequently worn. Businessmen in their offices and salesmen on their job always wear white shirts, dark suits, and elegant neckties and their shoes are always bright and shiny. In all bigger buildings, there is a shoe polisher in the basement. Such a shoeshine service is also offered in many railway and subway stations.

Until a few decades ago, according to the season, the suits were thicker and warmer in winter and rather thin and almost transparent during summer. But due to the improved heating system for the cold season and air-conditioning in the course of the hot summer weeks, today people have a general tendency to wear a light and comfortable apparel throughout the year. A famous proverb in Korea says that one harmonizes best with old friends, whereas clothes should be always new.

The fashion for women is more distinct. Most women try to follow the latest international fashion trends; Koreans are in general fond of novelties. Also, a notable local fashion industry has developed, which is becoming successful overseas as well. Accordingly, a wide range of colors, patterns, and fabrics are worn in the streets of Seoul. The majority of women wear pants in winter and skirts and hot pants during the summer months. In general, the fashion is distinctly female.

Footwear is particularly elegant and depending on the age, usually high heels with daring heels are preferred by young ladies. Jewelry is amply worn in Korea. Some of the jewelry is of high value and some are of more decorative character, depending on the age, income, and preferred individual lifestyle.

A dignified public appearance and good manners are very significant in Korea and shabby or even middle-class apparel has to be avoided by all means in public. Fortunately, there are numerous, rather inexpensive dry-cleaning outlets. Class consciousness is much more distinct in Korea than in Europe or North America.

Factory workers often wear simple, coarse Western outfits, which sometimes look rather poor. This applies also to the attire in the countryside and in fishing villages. Women, on the other hand, often prefer the simple, traditional, and convenient *hanbok*. The younger generation, however, is increasingly oriented to Western clothing styles.

Originally, Korea had a rigid dress code, which depended on gender, social status, age, and also the occasion. A wide white garment that was hold together by a string was the most common cloth. For more festive occasions, and if affordable, men preferred dark gray clothing, while women turned to bright colors. The clothes had to be comfortable in the first place. In particular, for women, who were frequently pregnant, the *hanbok* was a perfect dress.

Women wore rich headdresses and men preferred to wear a dark hat. All shoes, for both men and women, were boat-shaped. Yet, the material used for the shoes differed considerably, depending on their price. The same applied to clothes which, depending on the status of the owner or the occasion, was either made of silk, cotton, or hemp. Wool was hardly ever utilized as it is an animal product and thus could not be used according to the beliefs of Buddhism.

3.6 Traditional Manual Skills

Koreans have an excellent reputation with respect to their manual skills. This certainly proofed to be useful during the industrialization of the country. After a reunion of the two countries—provided there will be qualified investments into the training of the workforce—North Korea should quickly reach the level of the south. Yet, besides the manual skills, the mind-set concerning the quality of the produced commodities has to be developed in order to meet the high international standards. This situation can be compared to the situation in China, where during the strict Communist rule, the consciousness for sincere quality was lost, while the economy was dominated by Communism and where it took a long time until this awareness could be partly re-established.

International comparisons for various crafts, ranging from wood processing, welding, and precision engineering to cooking and hairdressing, position South Korean always at the forefront. The relevant skills are visible in the arts and crafts, where Korea maintains a very high level. Above all, Korean porcelain and ceramics manufacturing is admired in the world. This tradition is traced back to its roots in China and was later passed on to Japan.

Originally, Mongolian horsemen forced their way into the Korean territory (around 400 A.D.) before they invaded Japan, where they assimilated. Later, many Korean skilled laborers immigrated to Japan, fleeing a Mongolian invasion (after 1231) and finally many qualified craftsmen were abducted to Japan in the aftermath of the two invasions of Hideyoshi Toyotomi. This is why the production of chinaware and ceramics bear many resemblances in these two countries, although they both foster their own artistic elements.

The US Americans John C. and Alan Covell observe in their popular scientific book [5] that there exist giant mounts (called *kofun*) in Japan, which indeed resemble the burial places of Mongolian–Korean rulers. When one of them was opened, it displayed artistic productions of bronze and ceramic, horse's bridles made of silver and carved Buddha statues, which showed a distinct Mongolian character. Most of these tumuli have not been officially unearthed until today.

For a long time, the Korean peninsula played a significant role as a bridge between China and Japan. During this time, Japan as well as Korea gained much knowledge from the so-called Middle Kingdom. However, in recent times, China has imported not only sophisticated products but also ample technical know-how from Japan. Today, such a knowledge transfer happens without the traditional intermediary role of Korea. This bridging function was pursued by the southwestern part of Korea, the historical realm of Baekche, and not by Shilla, which is situated much closer to Japan. In the contemporary Jeolla provinces, many houses bear resemblance to the houses of well-situated families in eastern Japan, which reminds of the historical emigration of numerous evacuees from southwestern Korea to the eastern neighboring country.

3.7 Linguistic Challenges and Attitudes Toward Foreign Countries

The majority of older Koreans speak Japanese, which was their first language during colonial times. Younger people, however, generally do not speak Japanese and learn English instead. However, despite an enormous expenditure of time and energy, the results of their English language proficiency often remain rather modest. This can be possibly explained by the Korean alphabet, *hangeul*, which is phonetically detrimental to a correct pronunciation of foreign languages, particularly with respect to English words. For instance, a simple word like "paper" written in *hangeul* can be read as bapa, papa, paba, papal, papar, and bavar, respectively.

Additionally, there are cultural obstacles. When addressing another person, Koreans can choose between five out of six different kinds of honorific expressions, depending on the social status of both partners. That is why Koreans sometimes stuck in a conversation when they try to determine how to correctly address the other person.

The Korean press issues daily newspapers in English. Although not all citizens can read them, younger people are able to read English. The majority of bankers or international businessmen speak English fluently. The same applies to people who have lived for a while in the USA or another English-speaking country. Likewise, there are Koreans who live in various parts of the world, who are fluent in the language of their guest country, may it be French, Spanish, German, or any other language. However, when living in Korea it is hard to get around without a certain qualification in Korean.

A shrinking minority of the intellectual upper classes is still capable to master the Chinese language including the Chinese characters (*hanja*). This qualifies them to read Chinese books and newspapers, which are still edited in a limited number in Korea. For hundreds of years, Korean literature was written in Chinese. However, the knowledge of Chinese characters is generally limited to the use in calendars or maps and to some extent to surnames in Korea. Being able to read these characters further allows access to Japanese writings as well.

Other languages such as Spanish, Russian, Portuguese, Arabic, French, or German are not of great importance in Korea. Nevertheless, translations of literature or specific professional text written in these languages are quite popular. On the other hand, translations of periodicals or newspapers are generally limited to Anglo-Saxon editions.

In the centuries before its opening, Korea was decidedly xenophobic. Foreigners were not permitted to enter the country, and it did not strive for contacts with foreign countries at all. As of today, South Koreans display an interested and friendly attitude toward people from other nations. Big events like the Olympic Games (1988) and the Soccer World Cup (2004) bear witness of this change.

However, concerning international sport competitions or any other competitions in general, patriotic ambitions hardly have any limitations and other contestants are just seen as enemies. This kind of national egoism strongly prevails as well in economic affairs. Whereas in most nations common citizens are scarcely interested in economic statistics and international comparisons, Koreans frequently become enthusiastic when a newspaper reports that "Hyundai has defeated General Motors in producing a car which runs 10 miles with a liter of gasoline instead of 9 miles." Until the end of the millennium, nowhere in Asia was it more difficult (except in India) to establish an international joint-venture—let alone to build a company completely owned by foreigners—than in Korea.

Though Korean companies, in which are usually Korean employees hold the most important positions, can be found anywhere in the world, most Koreans do not like to work overseas for many years. The main reason for this is that his family cannot accompany him, because his children would quickly fall behind in learning when attending foreign schools. Additionally, the employer himself would lose his affiliation within the social cobwebs of his company.

Whereas 13 % of Korean exports are directed to the USA, where they flood the markets with electronic devices and motorcars, hysteric mass demonstrations took place in autumn 2008 when President Lee Myung-bak had agreed in Washington on the import of bigger quantities of beef to South Korea. Many Koreans have not yet accepted the idea that globalization is a bipartite process. The Anglo-Saxon conception of "fair" can hardly be translated into the Korean language and its connotation stands more for debility than for the expression of a noble attitude.

Throughout the very long history of Korea, it was essential for families, clans, regions, dukedoms, and the nation as such to prevail on others. This situation barely left space for abstract rules and laws. The nation has still to digest a long tradition of internal authoritarian rule as well as repressions from evil neighbors. Wittvogel [6] elaborates on the fact that in East Asia the individual despots existed alongside a tyranny of a "mighty hydraulic bureaucracy" as a dominating class. In countries cultivating wet rice, the organization and control of the dike maintenance led to a central execution of power. This was valid for Korea as well, which developed the feudalistic class of *yangban*, which disdained the ordinary people who had to take to all means to secure their necessaries of life. Besides occasional unrests, permanent actions of partisans existed, which were executed from pledged cliques on a regional scale. On both sides, survival was much more important than following chivalrous rules, as pardon was almost never granted from either side.

The majority of blue-collar workers still consider foreign powers as feudalistic, exploiting forces that should be resisted. This is particularly true for cities in the south of the peninsula, which are time and again disturbed by unrests. Within the history of the country, foreigners always came to either take or demand something from Korea. Today, not far from the center of Seoul in the district of Yongsan—formerly occupied by Japanese garrisons—is taken by the US-American military. From this extensive fenced off area, soldiers have access to the city and its amusement centers, which occasionally leads to incidents with usually emotional results. The common citizens of Seoul have no permission to enter this enclave. For many years, it has been announced that this camp—to which the South Korean population owes its freedom—will be removed to the southern countryside or even to the Pacific island of Guam. But the regular menaces of North Korea bring about that a respective decision is time and again postponed, most likely until 2025.

Off and on leftist groups demand the withdrawal of the American troops and intellectually narrow-minded people are prone to emotional activities. Presently, there are only 28,000 US-American soldiers stationed in the country. According to official statements [7], the South Korean army disposes of 691,000 soldiers, whereas North Korea commands an army of 1,117,000 soldiers. The share of the official defense budget amounts actually to 24 % of the GNP in North Korea and 7 % in South Korea.

The government takes great pains to develop a "healthy nationalism" for all citizens. All over the country old buildings are restored, ancient fortifications and gates are reconstructed, and occasionally complete shrines and temples are relocated from the mountains into towns. Furthermore, on holidays—and daily in Seoul in front of the palaces of Gyeongbok and Deoksu—impressive processions with historically authentic robes and weapons are being staged. Koreans are aware of both their long history and outstanding cultural achievements and take pride in them.

Besides the settled mode of life and the organization of affairs of rice farmers, there are still instincts alive that can be traced back to the nomadic horsemen of Mongolian times. It is fascinating how quickly and frequently families change their homes and move from rural areas into cities and move from one urban district to another, when it appears opportune. In periods of bitter poverty, millions of Koreans have emigrated to overseas countries such as Canada, the USA (particularly to Hawaii and California), Japan, Arabic countries, or even to the German Ruhr Area. Whereas families usually stayed and women married and assimilated well, men often suffered from the alien surroundings and missed their habitual kimchi consumption, tempting them to return to their country of origin. Many Koreans in overseas states have observed with astonishment the incredible change to the better in their home country. But the astronomically skyrocketed prices for houses and apartments in Seoul or Busan discourage them from returning home.

North Korea takes special care to preserve old national characteristics and abhors modern Western fashions. This explains why Pyeongyang often mischievously offends international rules as it wants to repel any alien influences and interference. To them, the USA symbolizes all Western evils and consequently are hated with a vengeance. North Korea feels frequently challenged, unendingly tantalized, and sometimes even betrayed by the Americans. Not only in the north do many Koreans believe that the USA and also Japan are not honestly interested in a reunification of the nation and its independence. On the contrary, it is suspected that these countries might be afraid of such an event as a new state would not only count for 75 million citizens, with another 5 million Koreans who live in foreign countries today, who could return. The new state would have a mighty army as well as a nuclear striking capacity. Even worse, it would become a direct neighbor of China and probably lean on the country, not only geographically.

The daily newspaper *The Korean Herald* from September 24, 2014, used the alarming headline "Foreign population reaches all-time high" to report on the presently 1.71 million foreigners who are living in the country. They make 3.42 % of the total Korean population. This is far from a foreignization, especially when according to the newspaper 579,000 Chinese are of ethnic Korean origin, adding to another 137,000 American citizens who also have Korean roots. Deducting these 716,000 persons, the rate of foreigners would shrink to a mere 2 %.

3.8 The Exceptional Position of the South

Seoul is considered the center of the country, whereas all provinces are deemed to different degrees secondary. In particular, the south is looked at as less competent and reliable. Particularly, the outer islands are considered as inferior.

The south has always held an exceptional position in the history of the country. The men of the northern territories usually felt that they were destined to rule the entire country. They believed that the people from the south were less disciplined and chaotic, while they had been ever since neighbors of the culturally advanced Chinese and the powerful Mongols. According to this logic, they believed to provide better statesmanship and to incorporate military virtues. Consequently, the power centers in the early history of Korea were situated in contemporary Manchuria and in the northern parts of Korea with the Han River as the approximate southern dividing line.

Former capitals such as Pyeongyang and Gaesong were located north of the 38th parallel or like Ganghwa (temporary capital) and Hanyang (Seoul) only slightly south of it. Gyeongju is a remarkable exception. It served as the center of the Shilla–Imperium (57 B.C. to 935 A.D) as the capital for the United Korea from the seventh to the ninth century A.D.

The North Koreans resisted the Japanese occupation more tenaciously than their southern brothers. Thus, according to North Korean despots, it is North Korea's destiny to lead the complete nation. However, millions of the most educated people withdrew from Communism and settled in the south, preferably close to Seoul. Today, we find numerous people in the government and the administration of the industry of North Korean offspring, or who were born in North Korea. Among the seven high-ranking economic advisors of President Park, four people were from the north.

The mountain range of the Taebaek in the south constituted a formidable barrier for traffic in former times. Nowadays, it is easily passed by modern highways and by a number of long tunnels. This mountain range stretches from the southwest to the northeast, roughly from Gwangju across Jinan to Gumi. Its summits reach heights of up to 6000 ft and are densely wooded. This topography made any connection to the north, or the process of a creation of larger political units, quite difficult in the past.

Scott [8] describes in a remarkable book that men had always the endeavor to avoid the grip of central powers, which are likely to procure them for taxation and military service. Therefore, important states were preferably established at plain places, with fresh water, natural traffic routes, and on pastures which permitted the cultivation of grain as well as stock farming. Only there did settlements grow, which permitted the rule of individuals over many.

However, establishing modern means of traffic and communication made it increasingly difficult to escape the central grip. Scott gives the example of the people of the Southeast Asian mountains (Myanmar, Thailand, Laos, and Vietnam), where a great number of different ethnic groups still tries to escape from stately authorities. The Bedouins of Yemen or the Pashtuns in Afghanistan defend their independence until today, entrenched in pathless territories behind rugged mountains. Centuries ago, the situation was similar in the south of South Korea, where the people did not want to join other political systems. They offered resistance and sometimes raided northerly territories and, with the Shilla–Imperium, set up even ruled the whole country.

In the southern states of Shilla and Baekje, sometimes there was more trade with Japan than with the north of the common peninsula. Today, the south is naturally part of the state, yet the territory of the former Jeolla province (now divided into the provinces of Jeolla-buk and Jeolla-nam) still likes to accentuate its self-reliance. The great insurrections of the second half of the twentieth century happened predominantly in the south of the country, for instance in Masan, Jinju, Jeju, or Gwangju. Consistently, these areas have been generally excluded from the benedictions of the development of an infrastructure by the central government. Nevertheless, President Park provided for some exceptions as he feared the proximity of the northern neighbor. He established important new industries in the southeast and south of the country such as steel mills in Pohang; petrochemicals, heavy industry, and shipbuilding in Ulsan; heavy industry in Changwon; and petrochemicals in Yeosu. In particular, the heavy and chemical industry was designed to build a capable domestic defense industry at the back of the country.

Apart from this program, which has national priority, the south is steadily catching up and the structure of the country becomes increasingly coherent. In particular, the Expo 2012 in Yeosu mobilized enormous national funds to improve the infrastructure of the southern regions.

As a result of both the geographical as well as political isolation over long periods of time, the Korean people are certainly among the most homogenous in the world. Additionally, the constraint to hold its own stand against the threat of foreign intruders welded the people together. The official historical account emphasizes the homogeneity of nation, whereas the population cherishes its local and regional peculiarities just as the people in Texas or Vermont celebrate their regional identity.

The last three presidents before Lee Myung-bak came from the south of the country and represented a more or less left-oriented, socialistic policy with a thorough skepticism toward the unwanted concomitant symptoms of the recent wave of globalization. Despite the fact that many of their followers did not share their opinion, they could still count on their loyalty and their votes as they come from the same region.

3.9 Modern Trends and Changes

A provincial mind-set and Confucian convictions are no longer dominant among young people in South Korea. For example, in the past, the deceased were buried in a crouched position in the countryside, preferably on one's own field or in a forest fringe under a small grass hill. On special holidays, but at least once or twice a year, the family gathered around the grave hill in order to feast with the dead. They consumed food that they brought along and to drank to his or her health. If the deceased was a smoker, sometimes even cigarettes were lit for them.

With an increasing number of city dwellers, giant graveyards quite far away from the gates of the towns were established with thousands of unadorned grave hills up high into the mountains. Small picnics are still common with conservative families, however, those who think highly of their clan own a valuable tombstone with the names of the closest family members engraved into it. This tombstone is firmly fixed in front of the little mound. Visits of the grave are accompanied by love, reverence, respect and also fear, because according to Shamanistic beliefs the ghosts of the departed continue to live for a very long time and can cause trouble if they are not satisfied. Within the Confucian tradition, cremating the dead was considered undignified and prevented a transition into the world of spirits as the remains of the body could not be buried completely.

On February 1, 2010, The *Korea Times* published the results of an Internet survey among the Korean population, which showed that 92 % of the asked people would want to be cremated instead of being buried traditionally. Hardly anything else can make the change in the preferred values of present-day Koreans more visible. This result signifies a complete withdrawal from former Confucian convictions. Accordingly, the tense generational conflicts in many families that fluctuate between Confucian doctrines and a liberal, modern lifestyle are depicted in numerous television dramas.

Today, the parks in and around Seoul are full of young couples that are not shy to show their mutual affection, something that was unheard of only a few decades ago. In the vicinity of trendy shopping passages or plush hotels, many young ladies and girls can be seen wearing miniskirts—and to a lesser degree hot pants—which end only a few centimeters below decent bounds. Even during a snowstorm, one can occasionally see young women walking around in short open fur jackets and not buttoned blouses. The often thin long legs are only covered in black tights and light footwear is worn. Obviously, women want to look attractive at any price. However, as almost all them are dressed in black clothes, wear high heels, have dyed hair, and ghost-like white faces, they all almost look the same.

In the vibrant centers of Seoul, especially south of the River Han, one feels like being in one of the modern cities such as Los Angeles, Singapore, or Sydney. Only the relatively small population prevents South Korea from becoming a modern industrial power. The high level of education among the population under fifty, the modern infrastructure, and its leading role in the communication industry provide all suppositions for the development of a mighty technological empire. A symbiosis with as a late possibility to turn into a modern industrial power. The People's Republic of China seems to look systematically for such a development and has recently helped South Korea to overcome the current global economic crisis better than other countries.

If China could obtain the position of the USA in South Korea, the days of the northern regime would certainly be counted and a reunification could happen quickly. Of course, many South Koreans would be concerned about the concessions that the Chinese had to make to their longtime protégés. If China would further gather strength, it is even possible that the USA would find an agreement with the new superpower for a worldwide partnership to control the globe. In that case, a withdrawal of American troops from the peninsula would not be inconceivable. However, Japan would vehemently oppose such an arrangement. Although most Koreans sympathize more with the Chinese than with the Americans or Japanese, there would still be doubts about economic advantages and disadvantages. Yet, South Korea has already become the preferred touristic target of Chinese people (42 % of all foreign visitors in South Korea are Chinese) and vice versa.

Another big change in the mind-set of the people becomes evident in the dramatically dropped birthrate of the nation. As of today, every woman gives birth to 1.2 children, which means that from 2030 on the population will start to shrink considerably. In view of a baby boom in the 1980s, birth control was strongly propagated and especially the army encouraged sterilizations. Thus, the average age of the population is still quite low and we see mainly people aged 20 to 45 on the streets. Older people are only rarely seen in public. They are even discouraged to visit some coffee shops because they are suspected to sit there for 3 h over a cup of coffee. Furthermore, some coffee shop owners are concerned that they might discourage younger consumers to enter the store when sitting at the windows.

The young generation seems to be extremely Westernized. Their lifestyle is completely different from that of their parents. On the contrary, they behave like teens and tweens in New York, London, or Munich. But there are some differences as their apparel is much more elegant than that of their contemporaries in San Francisco or Paris. To be sure, there are fast food chains such as Mc Donald's, Pizza Hut, and Starbucks in South Korea, but young Koreans still cherish traditional Korean dishes and most of them are in favor of *kimchi*. Regarding music, local rhythms and melodies clearly prevail. Older and younger Koreans enjoy traditional songs called *kayo,* and with regard to popular music, the so-called *Gangnam Style* has recently enraptured not only fans in China and Japan but also in Europe and the Americas.

Governmental institutions as well as parents are obsessed with the education of their children and take great pains to ensure a proper command of the English language. However, the efforts of the offspring seem to be rather small. In the past, the older generation dreamed to study in the USA or to even get American citizenship. However, today, after decades of emigration to North America the trend is reversed by now. Life appears more comfortable in the "Land of the Morning Calm," even though the chances of a business career in the USA have clearly improved.

In general, young Koreans study very hard. In contrast to former times, everybody has the chance to climb up the social ladder by merit and by virtues. Koreans firmly believe in their chances to enjoy a comfortable life as a result of their investment in their education. This has led to an unprecedented rivalry between 90 % of the students since only 10 % will be able to obtain a desirable position. This causes considerable frustration and depression among the numerous unlucky ones. Despite the relatively high standard of living, a common dissatisfaction prevails in the country. Yet, some 10 % of the population lives in poverty. This applies to older people and those without a formal or professional education. Only 25 years ago, nearly 75 % of Koreans considered themselves middle class; meanwhile, the GNP per capita has increased from 5000 dollar to 26,000 dollar in average. But in 2013, only 20.2 % considered themselves to be part of the middle class. This shows how dramatically the demanding attitudes have increased (The Korea Herald, Oct. 28, 2014). Frustrated, people look at those ten thousands who became rich in short time. These people do not realize that the times have changed and growth in Korea is levelling out as in Germany or Japan some decades ago. *The Korean Herald* warned that "Politicians in rival parties should cooperate in working out a balanced and comprehensive set of policies to prevent Korean society from being torn apart."

An old idiom says "five Koreans, six opinions" which indicates that there are various opinions and quite different social drifts in the Korean population. These opinions depend on the social status, the religion, and the geographical region one belongs to. However, most people are of one opinion when it comes to the interest of the home country, which is defended without compromises. When the emotional temperament of Koreans is aroused, it can easily tide over rational reflections.

Slavery was abolished as late as in 1894. Until then, an astonishing 60 % of the population was registered as slaves (*nobi*) and not as citizens. They were either owned by government, the *yangban* class, military leaders, or wealthy townsmen. A modest middle class was comprised of farmers, soldiers, and merchants. The *yangban*, a kind of scholarly aristocracy, were entrusted with the duties of superior government officers. But they did not care for the well-being of the citizens confided to them. On the contrary, they only cared for their own affluence. In particular, in the later years of the Yi Dynasty (1725 A.D.), the so-called *sedo*-system allowed them to exploit the citizens by participating in trading and financial transactions and by inventing ever-new duties. The *yangban* did not like to walk, to do useful work, and to get dirty hands. Even today, a status-conscious man might be despised if he works in his own garden, papers the walls of his home, or drives a car. His wife is likely to employ personnel for cooking, grocery shopping, and house cleaning. Here, residues of an old consciousness of feudalism can still be recognized.

In Korea, elders, high militaries, religious leaders, the old upper class of feudalism, as well as academic achievements are very much respected. However, above all, the new plutocracy is admired and people admire "success" which is unanimously equated with financial fortunes.

Within this context, the automobile serves as the absolute status symbol of modern Korean city dwellers. A few years ago, we observed that less than 10 % of all cars in the streets of Seoul or Busan were small cars, whereas in parking lots of supermarkets in Europe, more than 50 % of the automobiles would pass as small cars. Only later did we learn that even cars with modest motor capacities were provided with big bodyworks in Korea. In the general view, the ideal car is big and black. Nowadays, however, some people have recognized that smaller cars are easier to drive in crowded cities and can be parked much more comfortably. Nevertheless, the great number of bulky station wagons, which seem better suited for the Australian outback or the Canadian wilderness, in Korean cities is surprising.

One has to understand that whereas, for example, a French person perceives a car only as a means of transport from point A to point B, most Korean car owners take loving care of their vehicles. One takes pride in always having ones car in a neat, clean condition and becomes furious when someone dares to touch it. A few years ago, a policeman in Seoul shot four people when they slightly scratched his car while parking in a narrow lot. In the garages of luxury apartment towers in Seoul, one finds the most expensive models of the motorcar industry ranging from Maybach, Rolls Royce, Bentley, Phaeton, relatively few Cadillacs, Buicks, and Chevrolets to Lamborghinis, Ferraris, Maserati, and the like. They are very often only driven once every three months outside of the garage. The owners of penthouses sometimes own up to ten vehicles. Sports cars such as Porsches or Aston

Martins are not too frequently seen on the road. The same is true for coupes with two doors, as they indicate that no driver is driving the car. Nevertheless, there are always some young enthusiasts who like to drive these cars.

People with an allegedly high standing drive a Mercedes S-Class, a higher powered BMW, an Audi, or a Porsche Cayenne. A Jaguar, Bentley, or Lexus are also high on esteem, yet many prefer the local Hyundai Equus because of the reliable service, especially in rural areas. All these cars are completely overpowered for Korea, which has a general speed limitation of 70 mph. Only the prominence of the motorcar as an important status symbol can explain the success of the big and expensive sedan. The combined market share of Hyundai and Kia exceeds 70 %. Some Koreans explain that they buy foreign cars only because they want to own something, which distinguishes them from others.

In contrast to other countries, we do not find a noteworthy used car market in Korea. The local motor car industry abhors sales of old cars and has set up a system to sell almost all used vehicles to China, Russia, or some Southeast Asian countries. As rumor has it, the purchase of a used car is a great safety risk, since all original parts of the car are likely to have been replaced by fake parts for export.

The motorization of the Korean population continues, but still a person driving a car often feels superior to the pedestrian and pays little attention to him. Whereas politeness dominates personal encounters and people tend to be helpful when meeting them, the automobile rather encourages egoism. When driving in Seoul, people drive recklessly while public places are egoistically turned into parking lots, and drivers stop their car on busy lanes to load or unload their vehicle without any regard concerning the other road users. Officially, one has to drive on the right side, but this rule is hardly ever followed. From a technical point of view, Koreans are very skilled drivers and almost everybody is knowledgeable about the various types of cars and international brands.

In particular, taxi drivers seem to be unconcerned when it comes to traffic rules; they rush either with high speed through a town or sneak along to fetch customers, thus disturbing a regular traffic flow. Often the drivers are already 12 h on duty, listen to music, some of them even watch the news on a little TV screen while driving. They constantly operate the navigation system, enjoy their soft drinks and coffee, smoke, or look out for clients—all at the same time. It might irritate Americans or Europeans when a Korean client does enter the first taxi in a long queue, but rather a taxi that is close to him—even it is the last one in the line. Ambulance cars and even police cars rarely get a free passage in a thick traffic jam. We observed an ambulance car with flashing blue lights on near the Korean Exchange Bank in Seoul, which after 40 min and half a mile still was stuck next to our taxi.

In general, Koreans are not aggressive toward other people. However, everybody wants to "get along" and earn as much money as possible—an attitude that is somehow respected by everybody. Fairness does not mean anything under these circumstances. Thus, it is not surprising that people in Korea squeeze into means of public transport, into elevators and through doors into concert halls and department stores. Even as a pedestrian, one follows a straight course and only reluctantly gives way to other advancing persons. However, the behavior of younger Koreans is about to change and people start to line up on subway platforms and bus stops, hence acquiring more gentle manners.

Whereas the motorcar is worshiped and always spic and span, one can find backyards with a lot of rubbish, just a little bit away from the center of big cities. Even the facade of a Samsung dealer's building is visibly crumbling and holes are not plastered, while rusty wires and pipes are winding up. At the roadside, trees planted for environmental reasons are occasionally misused to hang up tools or tires. Generally, small repairs on windows, doors, etc., are neglected for practical reasons. A few years ago, pavements and public places were littered with cigarette butts. Fortunately, this has almost completely stopped due to the general prohibition of smoking in public as well as the decreasing number of smokers in Korea.

Like in the USA, performance is important in South Korea. Everybody is proud of his achievements and does not attempt to downplay or hide them, as in Northern Europe or Japan. On the contrary, conspicuous consumption plays a significant role in the country. In the eyes of a traditional British gentleman, the boundaries of good taste are often touched or even exceeded. For example, there is a high-class apartment building in the Hannamdong district in Seoul which is named "Richensia." Luxurious apartments with acquisition prices between three and seven million dollars are available, especially in the Gangnam area of Seoul, where it is important to have a prestigious address. The owners of such an apartment try to keep unwanted have-nots out of sight.

Of course North Korea is hated for its troublemaking and aggressive attitudes; but it is even more unpopular in South Korea since they do not like the idea of equalization. Those who have studied harder or have worked more diligently than others claim to have the right to live a better life than others.

3.10 Development into a Social Welfare State

A social network does already exist in South Korea and although it provides far more than governments of less developed countries, it is still in need of improvement in the eyes of Northern European states for instance. With respect to the health insurance, however, Korea is rather exemplary. It requires only a monthly payment of $35 for an unemployed person, the socially weakest member of society.

For working citizens, the compulsory health insurance amounts to 5.1 % of their total income. The employer pays 50 % and the insurance covers the medical support for the whole family. Depending on his income, the fee for those who are self-employed starts with $150 and increases constantly. On average, it amounts to $300 per month per family. Yet, to keep the population health conscious, 20 % of the medical expenditures have to be paid by the policyholders themselves. With regard to these relatively low expenses, medical care in South Korea is situated at an astonishingly high level. The big hospitals have large specialized divisions of physicians, who are usually long-term employees with good incomes. In general, these physicians have qualifications from high-ranking universities and most have studied abroad, mainly in the USA. There are also resident doctors. If somebody requires a treatment or special medication, it has to be paid for immediately using cash or credit card.

Most Koreans do not understand some Europeans criticizing the "two-tire health system" that supposedly exists in South Korea as it is evident for them that in the entire course of life, some people live, eat, sleep, and travel better than others. Nevertheless, people with a higher income have to join the compulsory state insurance and in case of entrepreneurs, freelance professionals, and other income categories, the public health departments stipulate monthly charges by two criteria: Their home address and their vehicle class. These people have to bear up to 60 % of their medical expenditures by themselves. This Korean system is considered almost ideal in many countries, whereas most European systems are based on quasi-Communist extravagances.

Pension insurance, based on capital cover, exists since 1988. The monthly pensions, however, do not cover the expenses for the vast majority, especially elderly people, who are consequently forced to work until they die. On the one hand, the situation improves with growing incomes but on the other hand, in a few decades, there will be many pensioners and only a few working people who can replenish the funds.

Generally speaking, the Korean Social Security System could serve as a model for many other countries. It is structured as follows:

- Social Insurance
  - Health Insurance,
  - Pension Insurance,
  - Unemployment Insurance,
  - Occupational Disability Cover.
- Public Support
  - Assurance of a minimum living standard and
  - Assurance of a basic medical support.
- Social Charity System
  - Help for elderly people (nursing, free public transportation),
  - Care for disabled persons,
  - Support for needy children,
  - Assistance for menaced women,
  - Care for psychiatric emergencies.

Despite all these provisions, a part of the population lives at the subsistence level or even below it; some of them not even being responsible for their misery. The recent unemployment rate of 3.5 % comprises of agricultural seasonal laborers, those who were fired because their positions became obsolete, professionally unqualified people, antisocials, and criminals. The miserable minority as well as the swiftly decreasing number of middle-class people look at the immensely rich upper class, which often obtained its fortune by inheritance or marriage and some of the misery-ridden people might be inclined toward revolutionary changes. Social unrest seems possible at any time. The government is aware of this situation and provides two countermeasures: First, the social budget will be increased, without a tax hike, which means that the national debt will increase. Second, nationalism is stimulated and directed against the North Koreans and Japanese, while radical leftists also show an adverse attitude toward Americans. However, xenophobia does not exist in Korea in general.

In summary, South Korea basically is a developed social state, which avoids exaggerations and leaves sufficient incitements to propel private initiatives. Of course, there is still room to further improve the social system. Nevertheless, these improvements should be brought about without further increasing the debt burden of public funds. In the field of politics, the conservative and left-winged forces are roughly in balance. An extreme drift to either side would be most undesirable.

3.11 The Family

The family is considered a safe haven among Koreans of all different social groups. Although the state has established an extended system of social privileges, people do not really trust the state to be a solicitous father and selfless benefactor. This might be a result of the past harsh period of military dictatorship and the existence of the influential KCIA, which was South Korea's feared secret service.

The state does not endow marriages, it only registers them if requested by a couple going to be married and if the legal requirements are met. Likewise it only registers a divorce when the couple expresses to divorce after an amicable agreement. The latter practice is common among younger Koreans, though it is still disapproved by the older generation.

When the great majority of the Koreans still lived in the countryside, usually three generations lived together under one roof, often including single aunts and uncles. Today, most people live in apartments in skyscrapers located in cities. These apartments do not provide much space because of the high rents charged per square foot. Thus, they only house nuclear families and sometimes one widowed parent. It is rather uncommon that the parents live together with their grown-up children. However, within such arrangements, the wife often suffers from great anxiety if she lives together with her mother-in-law, who in Korea tend to terrorize their daughter in law.

The name of the father, who is considered the patriarch, is used as the family name for all children. In more than 50 % of all cases, the family name is Kim, Bak (Park), Lee (Yi, Li, Ii, I, Rhee), Choi, Chang, Song (Sung), or Kang. Reportedly, there exist only 250 family names in Korea. The wife does not take on the name of her husband after marriage and keeps her own family name. Consequently, one cannot recognize by name whether a couple is married or not.

The Chinese recognized already in former times that Koreans were not only "white-clad people" but also "ceremonial folks." Until today, this sense for formalities and exquisite politeness prevails in Korea. Even family members and close relatives are subject to strict rules. Younger children do not address their elder sisters and brothers with their given names but use respectful terms such as "older sister" or "older brother"; these terms, again, differ depending on whether they are used by girls or boys. Boys call their older sister "*nu nim*" and their younger sister = "*nu-i tong-saeng.*" Girls call their older sister "*on-ni*" and their younger sister "*tong-saeng.*" Things become even more complicated with in-laws. For example, a younger brother's wife is called "*kye-su,*" the wife's older sister is called "*cho-hyong.*" Honorific addresses are used throughout the entire life, even if both partners are already in the 1980s. Names are considered private property and cannot be randomly used by foreigners to address a person. Preferably, one does not use names in general and first names in particular, when addressing a person in Korea. Instead, a more general address such as *sonsaeng* (teacher, master, senior) is more appropriate.

Children usually get double first names such as Byung-do (boy) or Bo-won (girl). Like the surnames, there are not too many different given names as supposedly auspicious Chinese characters chosen to spell names. Female names usually allude to pearls, silk, or a scent and are supposed to refer to the beauty of a person, the status of a princess or anything else considered feminine and attractive. Names for boys are traditionally connected to success, a long life, glamour, fame, or something similar. Nevertheless, many boys carry names with female connotations and vice versa. To further reduce the number of available names, family names can be used as given names as well and the other way around. It is considered good style in Korea if even in families with nine children (regardless if they are girls or boys), the second given name is the same for all, for example, Lee Sun-hee, Lee Kang-hee, Lee Ok-hee, Lee Hong-hee. Preferably, one does not use names in general and first names in particular, when addressing a person in Korea. Instead, a more general address such as *sonsaeng* (teacher, master, senior) is more appropriate.

Because some smart Koreans want to save their individuality when translating their names into Roman letters, they choose variations, which in the case of the surname "Ro," for example, might be read on a business card as Rho, Roo, Lo, Loo, Loh, Lho, or even No. In general, all names are treated with high respect. Everybody always carries name cards, which are exchanged on any feasible occasion, using polite and respectful gestures. Consequently, they are supposed to be carefully saved. As a common practice, name cards indicate the employer and the relevant title within the company. Academic titles are used as well, however, to a lesser degree. Westerners are well advised to use names as little as possible as it is very likely to make mistakes leading to awkward situations or making others feel uncomfortable. In particular, when it comes to indications of relatives, the Korean language turns out to be full of obstacles for non-native speakers.

In a traditional family, the family life is focused on the education of the children. After the rent for the flat, the biggest share of the family budget is dedicated to the education of the next generation. This obliges the children to respect and obey their parents, sometimes also contributing to their livelihood once their parents turn old.

Whereas in the past the marriages of their children have been generally managed by the parents and relatives, or even more frequently by professional matchmakers, today most people choose their future partner themselves—except for members of upper-class families concerned about their wealth, who prefer to marry among their own class. The old custom of rich men to keep concubines—often even in the same household with his wife—is dying out. Also, a wife is no longer dismissed if she fails to give birth. In recent times, marriages with one child or without any children are more often the rule rather than an exception.

Usually, the housewife supervises the family budget and takes a leading role inside the house. The husband solely represents the family to the outside. His wife owes respect to him and, above all others, to her parents-in-law. In particular, the mother-in-law is feared and sometimes even hated by young wives as she is very often recklessly utilized by her. This is a favorite subject in soap operas, which are watched in the evening.

The home of a family is their very private retreat and foreigners are rarely invited. All members of the family usually roam around in very informal outfits, often in their nightgowns. Each person entering a private house or apartment immediately takes his shoes off. To enter a house or apartment with shoes is considered as unhygienic and strange as going to bed with shoes.

The common Korean is highly emotional. That is why quarrels among spouses and/or their children are not unusual. These quarrels are loud and passionate. Yet to the amazement of foreign observers, everything is forgiven and forgotten the next day. Extreme fights frequently coupled with intense emotions sometimes lead to self-mutilations or even suicides, which then—of course—cannot be reversed.

Relatives of big families or clans are keen to be constantly in touch, even if they are separated by long distances. Apart from personal encounters, Koreans communicate vividly with all modern means of communication like mobile phones, faxes, e-mails, Internet platforms, and, most recently, Internet image telephones. However, they do not seem to be very fond of writing letters or postcards.

The patriarchs of the most influential, well-to-do families enjoy certain supremacy within their family. On the other hand, they are obliged to take care for the well-being of all family members. Thus, in the strict sense of Confucianism, nepotism is not a flaw but rather a binding obligation. As a result, entire companies and even governing bodies are occupied by members of a single clan. Many big companies and also entire *chaebols* were destroyed because incapable children and relatives were employed instead of professional managers not related to the family owning the company.

3.12 The Development of the Status of Women

Professor Eun Ki-soo [9] of the Seoul National University wrote in an essay in 2008 that the discussion of sexual subjects has increased incredibly in Korean television programs. He argues that despite this development, opinions concerning marriage still remain very conservative while divorce is still seen as evil.

Furthermore, illegitimate children are not approved of as well. According to the essay, besides the Philippines, in East Asia, Korea is the country with the severest standards concerning gender relations before marriage. Because women increasingly start to attend universities and work in organizations, Eun thinks that they are likely to face a dilemma, as on the one hand they are still obliged to the ideal of "the perfect mother," while on the other hand, they wish to be successful and contribute to the living standard of their family. According to him, sociologists relate the decreasing birth rate of the nation to this dilemma.

Eun's female colleague Lee Jae-kyung elaborates on the same situation as follows [10]: "Traditional family values were thought to be the safeguard for preserving our identity from Western influences. However, sociodemographic statistics indicate otherwise." Lee remarks that the younger generation thinks different than the older generation when it comes to dates, sex, love, marriage, and motherhood. She believes, however, that some more time will pass before gender equality can be observed when it comes to the distribution of tasks such as professional engagement, housework, and bringing up children.

Male Koreans usually pay respect to women in general and to mothers in particular. Crude harassments are rare and women are usually able to walk the streets unmolested, even late in the evening. Nevertheless, in certain quarters of big cities one might by chance encounter a robber or gangster or sit in a taxi with a dubious driver.

An increasing number of men in Korea worry that women might start to dominate the country. A member of parliament committed suicide at his best age in a spectacular action in autumn 2013, by jumping from a bridge into the river Han. He left a message, warning that a period of suppression of men was about to start. According to my own observations, Korea is still far away from such a situation—even if men are indeed learning to push baby carriages.

In most public organizations, women in leading positions are still rare, although some made their way up to top positions in recent times. On average, Korean women who work full time still earn 39 % less than their male counterparts. This has not changed in the last 10 years.

Korean women among themselves are very sociable. They like to go on joint excursions and picnics and sing and dance together. Usually, they laugh a lot and are cheerful with each other. In particular, visiting public saunas and going to evening bathes is popular as this offers the opportunity to exchange rare news and gossip and to share rather intimate experiences.

3.13 Liberal Education and Formal Vocational Training

The current technological economic success of South Korea, as well as its desired position within the international community of nations strongly depends on a comprehensive system of general education and vocational training. Almost the entire nation is convinced of this and thus ready for substantial sacrifices. The parents spend a lot of time and financial means for the education of their children, who in turn focus on their studies and forgo leisure time as well as pretentious hobbies.

Learning always had a central position in Confucianism. Schools have existed in Korea since the fourth century A.D.—initially for the upper classes but since 950 for all citizens. For a high position in the government, a person had to go through severe public examinations. This was quite different from Europe, where over the span of hundreds of centuries, the service in high governmental or military positions was reserved for children of the nobility only. A compulsory education was introduced in modern times and the government attached great importance to the education of its population because their skills and diligence were regarded as the only "raw material" that South Korea had to offer. The enthusiasm in South Korea for education is probably much higher than in European or American countries. Kern [11] reports that 54 % of the South Korean population considers the costs of education their highest priority in their household budgets, even more important than costs for the rent, nutrition, car, traveling, etc.

Young women, wanting to get married by all means prefer a so-called SKY partner: S stands for Seoul National University (SNU), K stands for Korea University, and Y for Yonsei University. These three institutions have the reputation to be the best when it comes to learning and providing the biggest chances for a professional career.

Although 55 % of all high schools and 78 % of all universities and colleges are privately owned, the budget for education, research, and development is with 20.3 % the highest position within the national budget, exceeding expenses for social expenditures and defense [12]. In an international comparison, the so-called PISA test, for instance, this resulted in the first place in natural sciences and the second place in mathematics. This further partly explains why Korean smartphones and flat screens dominate the markets all over the world. On a government initiative, all schools in the country were connected to the Internet as early as in 2002. This was further made possible as the whole country was provided with a fiber optic network, which is superior to the copper cables that were used in other countries before.

Positions in all ministries and increasingly in the parliament are occupied by university graduates, mainly from the field of technology, natural sciences, economy, or law. Apart from government expenditures, the private spending on education is very high. Korean parents are prepared to make substantial sacrifices for the education of their children. 37.2 % of the funding for educational institutes come from the private sector, whereas in the OECD, the average is only 16.1 %. In this respect, it has to be kept in mind that a high percentage (over 90 %) of young Koreans between 15 and 18 get a high school degree.

According to *The Korean Herald* in November 6, 2014, "Korean children [are] least happy in OECD." An index of happiness identifies the Netherlands as the happiest nation, leading with 94 % ahead of Iceland, Finland, and Spain with 90 % and Korea trailing behind with 60 %—as the last of all OECD countries. The scope of this problem was elucidated by an article of the next day in the same newspaper, which claims that nearly 30 % of all South Korean children between 9 and 17 have seriously thought about suicide. To quote: "Rushing off to school in the morning without a proper breakfast, bullied by peers, their rights as children abused by those in authority, and spending hours at cram schools before coming home late at night to parents who seem to be only interested in the child's academic performance."

Half of all children going to kindergarten have to pay tuitions in various school subjects, which cost their parents approximately $130 dollars per month. Korean school children (starting at the age of 6) usually get up at 7.00 a.m., arrive at school around 9.00 a.m., and return home around 5 p.m. After some homework, they can enjoy some time watching TV or surfing in the Internet. The majority of children aged 10–12 and 16–18 attend a cram school (*hagwon*) from 8 p.m. until 10 p.m. These cram schools are quite expensive and require high financial contributions from the parents. They prepare the children for the tests for the admission exams for better high schools and later for better universities. Both institutions are urged by the government to keep a failure quota of around 30 %. The difficulty for Korean students is to qualify for higher institutions—not to pass final examinations. For a graduate of a famous university, his field of study is less important than being a life-time alumnus of his former alma mater and entering the dense network of his former fellows.

Within this context, the concept of an "open university" is interesting. It permits late developers as well as any blue-collar workers without a formal education to obtain a diploma from a university, if they pass a difficult examination.

The most favored fields of studies are medicine and law. Three quarters of all candidates declare to pursue a career in these fields. Both subjects offer above-average income opportunities and a rather safe position. The government, however, promotes above all majors in engineering and natural sciences.

Additionally, many museums, theaters, and concert halls facilitate education all over South Korea but are clustered particularly in Seoul. Citizens of all ages frequent them, but in accordance with the average age of the population, the majority of visitors are young people. The big Sejong Auditorium is located at the impressive Sejong-no Boulevard and offers stage plays, concert events, and opera performances. The seats are comfortable with a screen in front of every seat that indicates the time and provides useful information. It is financed by also showing advertisements. Four spacious spots are reserved for wheelchair users. Not only the conductor, chorus, singers, and orchestra belong to the performing team, but also an announcer, as the South Korean citizen, used to permanent service, wants to be always well informed. The program booklets sometimes make exaggerated announcements, by, for instance, stylizing a local tenor as a new "Pavarotti" or hailing a native composer as a "Mozart of East Asia."

3.14 Physical and Mental Recreation

Life in Korea in general is rough and hard. This judgement is related to former working situations and income conditions. Though these conditions have clearly improved, everyday life is still determined by haste, impatience, rivalry, and the will to succeed at any price. Despite—or maybe because of—these circumstances, Koreans long for harmony (*inwha*). Living in harmony with neighbors, coworkers, and the environment as well as tranquility and good health create an evenness of temper. The term "*gibun*" describes the mind-set of a human being. Ideally, not being stressed, self-respect, acknowledgment, and praise create a good *gibun*. To damage the *gibun* of another person may sever any relation and create a bitter enemy. The usual Korean greeting "*anyong haseyo*," which means "are you in peace," tries to spread a generally good feeling, thus contributing to a common positive *gibun*. Preferably, one tries to avoid bad news and also does not impart them on others. If delivering bad news cannot be avoided at all, the evening is the best time, because otherwise the whole day would be ruined. In the evening, all tensions of the day and eventually suffered frustrations can be flushed away with alcohol, preferably together with good companions. Loud singing further releases the exhausted spirits.

The great musicality of Koreans is striking. Recently, many excellent male as well as female vocalists alongside conductors and instrumentalists come from South Korea. They excel in classical music, especially Italian operas. The renowned German weekly newspaper *Die Zeit* noticed in its edition from February 17, 2011: "No German opera-house gets along without a vocalist from South Korea anymore." By the same token, common citizens love music and songs as well. In the middle class and upper classes, learning an instrument is a marker of a good background. It is also of great importance since musical training enhances functions of the human brain.

The degree to which Koreans enjoy music might explain the success of karaoke, which was imported from Japan. Alone or with a partner, one faces the karaoke machine and sings unaccompanied by real instruments into a microphone and follows the lyrics on a video screen. The machine does not only make the voice audible but enriches it and one might feel like Caruso. After his appearance, the singer often feels happy and confirms that his *gibun* is in a quite comfortable state. It is interesting that usually individualistic Europeans prefer to sing together with others, as in a chorus, for example, whereas usually socially minded East Asians favor solo-singing.

The enthusiasm for music is not only shown by actively participating but also by listening to music. In television shows, the audience frequently is swinging and clapping along the songs. Performances of popular music on television are frequently aired and can be enjoyed almost daily on one of the numerous television channels.

In the private sphere as well as in business relations, it is always of advantage when the communicating parties commonly have a good *gibun*. That is why Koreans do not feel very comfortable in Western countries. Manners, which are perceived as cool, as well as abstract logical argumentations, relatively wide physical distances, and the eloquence of business partners in their native language, do not lead to a good *gibun* as at one's own home ground.

Rather distantly placed seats and high tables do not create a jolly environment produced by a narrow seating arrangement on cozy couches and benches or on warm lacquered paper on the floor around low tables. In Western cultures, a certain distance is kept between people and perceived as comfortable. One or two meters are considered as pleasant without creating a social trench. On the contrary, Korean partners might prefer an intimate zone well below half a yard, sometimes leading to physical contact. Occasionally, business partners even exchange slaps on their arms or shoulders. The physical proximity, also called "skinship," cannot promote a mental propinquity. Therefore, body odor has to be avoided as it can irritate an Asian, who is not used to humans smelling and rather associates body odor with animals.

In Korea, spacious private rooms in offices are regarded as luxurious. Hence, open plan offices with a few flexible partitions are generally preferred to isolated single rooms. These rooms are reserved for reasons of prestige for the top managers, who, however, are usually moving from one place to another within the office building.

The habit of some Europeans to reserve a spot in a public environment, such as a lecture hall or at a swimming pool, by laying down an object is normally not tolerated. When boarding means of public transportation, there is no real code of conduct. Jostling, one squeezes into a subway compartment only to peacefully share the narrow seats in great physical proximity with an unknown neighbor. Any scuffling for public space is considered unnecessary, as theses spaces are being considered common property.

According to *The Korean Herald* from December 18, 2014, the average Korean enjoys a daily free time of 3.6 h and spends 51 % of this time watching television and 12 % with surfing the Internet and social networking.

3.15 Some Sociopsychological and Sociocultural Aspects

As mentioned before, one very important asset for a Korean is his name. The own reputation and integrity have to be defended at all times as well. Saccone writes that "If losing your life is your personal death, then losing your reputation is social death" [13]. Therefore, it is highly recommended to be very careful when judging another person, especially with respect to his reputation. Generally, a foreigner is well advised to refrain from criticizing Korea or a Korean person. Respect for the name of another person is also shown by always attaching a mark, for example, an academic title (professor), the trade (judge), rank in the company (department head), position in the military (general), an official position (minister), or universally *seonsaengnim*, which can be translated to master, director, or pundit. When talking to a person, whom one does not know, one would not approach him with "Mr. Kim" but "Kim *seonsaengnim*."

In a discussion, the personal title will be preferably avoided. As we have seen, even among close family members, terms for younger brother and older sister are used instead of using private names. The use of private names is strictly off limits among other family members as well.

Closely connected to one's name is the term "face." In East Asia, it is crucial to always "keep one's face." It is equally important to take care that another person does not lose face by an inconsiderate word or act. If one exposes or ridicules another person, one might have a lifelong spiteful enemy. A proverb says "if I lose face, I lose everything; though to lose everything does not necessarily mean I have lost also face." Western people usually cannot imagine how important "face" is to East Asians, who often prefer suicide to loss of face.

One of the many intricacies of the Korean language is its reflection of social statuses. One can speak "up" or speak "down" depending on the status of the speakers. A person of a supposedly socially higher rank might react vigorously when he feels that he is not addressed properly. A multitude of verb endings expresses various levels of politeness; for a foreigner, it is nearly impossible to distinguish all the appropriate gradations.

Smiling is a good way to keep face in unpleasant situations, especially when in a bad mood. Europeans or Americans usually have little problems to admit not knowing something. Koreans find it rather distasteful to confess that they lack knowledge about something they assume they should know about.

Similarly, comparisons are not popular because one side can lose face, when considered inferior in any respect. In particular, Anglo-Saxons are fond of all types of competition, which is why they like sports and contests. For Koreans, sport is not necessarily a game except among good friends or acquaintances. To compete with unknown persons is considered risky, as one side is likely to lose, thus creating an unnecessary loss of face. In regional and international matches, however, the other party is perceived as an enemy and Koreans fighting not for themselves but for the national colors. Winning makes a hero, losing is shameful. In Western countries "the winner takes it all" and gold, silver, and bronze medals are only awarded at international championships. In Korea, like in other East Asian countries, preferred outcomes of a competition are numerous winners. At school sport days, there exist different categories that consequently produce many winners. All participants are divided for instance in a "red team" and a "blue team" which compete with each other. Therefore, apart from individual winners, everybody wins with his red or blue team either a gold or silver medal. Nobody leaves the meeting with empty hands.

Whereas the younger generation is exempted from personal frustrations, at least at sport events during their schooldays, as adults, Koreans usually have to fight if they do not want to be outrun. A general haste, restlessness, and often also impatience can be noted in Korea. "*Ppalli*" (faster, faster) is a phrase that can be heard very often. Inactivity, let alone leisure time, is considered in the modern business bustle almost sinful. His work ethic distinguishes Koreans from most foreigners. In many Western countries, the person finishing his job first and leaving is considered the smartest guy. In Korea, sometimes those who are the last to leave their work place are admired. Though South Korea is certainly a very successful industrial nation, her productivity in labor is ranked last among the OECD members *The Korea Times*, March 26, 2014). In general, productivity is measured by the output per hour. Working too fast often results in insufficient results and repairing faulty products is time-consuming and expensive. Perhaps, too many hours in offices and workshops are also spent in discussions and meetings as well as with superfluous, lengthy speeches of the bosses. Diligence does not always equal efficiency.

Generally, Koreans work hard and assiduously; many of them as long as possible with many old people working until they pass away. Glancing at the watch is despised. Likewise, one should not mind to work on Sundays and public holidays with a few exceptions like *Suseok* (Thanksgiving Day). Many workers and white-collar clerks hardly take a day off. But even if a compulsory period of leave would be regulated by law, it can be suspected that most Koreans would use this time for some kind of money-making. In big companies, especially in the field of manufacturing and logistics, the working time is strictly regulated; but leaving the working place at an early hour does hardly lead to leisure time. Instead, the time is used to further educate oneself or to work on a second job.

In small family businesses, nearly endless working hours are prevail, which are not always caused by poverty but often rather by the desire to be able to afford a more luxurious life style or to become rich. Occasionally, owners of a small kiosk or a vegetable shop have surprisingly large assets on their bank accounts. Those are mainly used to finance the education of the children. It is not exceptional that the owner of a snack bar has a son or daughter studying in the USA and has to pay almost $100,000 per year for his or her tuition and housing. Occasionally, prestigious family festivities, a luxurious apartment, an expensive motorcar, or most exceptionally a fancy vacation will be financed as well. Academic efforts are only highly respected if they produce material wealth and an idealist hardly earns any admiration. The contemporary symbol of success is the rich man. Therefore, the everyday life revolves around the issue of earning money. Even a New Year's greeting card might read "Pu ja doi soi yoi" a phrase that translates into "We wish you to become rich" instead of wishing good health or a peaceful time. Even the numerous Christian sects in Korea try to rake in monetary wealth, although the bible claims that it is easier for a camel to pass the narrow eye of a needle, than for a rich man to enter heaven. People are so obsessed with becoming rich that they are often willing to break laws if they feel that these laws bar their way to wealth.

In contrast to this conspicuous consumption, Koreans are basically investors—in different respects: They believe to invest in their bodies by buying and consuming healthy and rich food. Many leisure activities are sacrificed in favor of purchasing real estate to secure the future of the family and presents and kindnesses are distributed in order to win the favor of a person who could be of use in the future.

The contemporary Korean looks much more into the future than back to the past; basically, he is optimistic and thoroughly convinced that he can achieve (almost) everything, an attitude of the "can do." This results now and then in an exaggerated opinion of oneself. The nation lost quite some credit in October 2010, when it believed that it would be easy to take part in the "Formula One Circus." At the opening day of the test races, however, one was confronted with a lot of embarrassing shortcomings, which received international press coverage. Mishaps, caused by overconfidence, are common in Korea and many accidents and disasters in Korea have their roots in this overconfidence. Apart from that, many Koreans have a tendency not to believe in laws and are inclined to circumvent them whenever feasible.

Because of the geography of South Korea peninsula, its population exhibits certain characteristics of inhabitants of island nations such as Great Britain or Japan. They are not used to share roads and rails; a foreigner is a rather strange subject and not considered a neighbor at all. Furthermore, the uniqueness of their nation and culture is emphasized and they find it often difficult to make conservations in foreign languages.

Usually, Koreans do not necessarily expect heavy blows and thus are skeptical toward insurances. Only Western insurance institutes like the German Allianz have initiated an insurance industry in South Korea in the last twenty years. Typically, it was initially based on insurances for education expenses. To reckon evil events makes a South Korean uneasy and disturbs his *gibun*.

Apart from the virtue of smiling, most Korean people like to sing or express their feelings by making music. Korean singers are worldwide member of famous music ensembles and love classical music. High-class orchestras exist across the country, most of them in Seoul. But they are also various excellent singers of popular music of all types, whose concerts are frequently sold out and who regularly appear in television shows. Outstanding, excellently performed big musical shows are very popular and can almost compete with American productions.

The mind-set of Korean is well expressed in Korean traditional popular music. In the aftermath of the tragic, more recent Korean history in general and the division of the nation in particular, many songs that mourned the current state were produced. These songs express the ardent desire of the country dwellers for unification with their families, partners, and friends. The characteristics of this kind of music are derived from an old folksong, named "Arirang," which in the course of time, has become a second national anthem. It has been played for at least 600 years from the Yalu River in the north to the southern shores of the peninsula. One contemporary CD was produced in North Korea as well and here, at least, we can see a common ground between these two nations. The word *arirang* cannot be translated into another language. Korean children grow up with its bemoaning tunes and Koreans all over the world sing this song fervently, thus expressing their feelings in a musical way. One Korean saying claims that this tune belongs to their life like the rice on the fields.

Originally "Arirang" was sung while working. It has a melancholic modulation, though it is meant to help overcome the pains, sorrows, toils, oppressions, and more in general, all difficulties of life. A famous part of the text reads "to get over rough mountains." During the Japanese colonialization, it became a symbolic song for all Koreans and was sung with an almost religious devotion, amplifying the homogeneity of the nation and its hopes for a better future.

This emotional vocal music is adapted to the respective time and different regions. It is connected to everything that stimulates the mind. Therefore, many *Arirang* festivals are celebrated and numerous restaurants are named after the song, while a television channel with this name transmits news to Koreans abroad.

With its deep, melancholic mood, the song encourages the listener to move on and to survive and characterized the nature of the whole nation. The typical Korean notion of "*han*" is related to the idea of the "Arirang" as *han* expresses feelings of injustice and being underprivileged. The counter term to *han* is the positive concept of *meot* that facilitates a feeling of lightness and elegance and procures an optimistic will to live.

Among many other traits, the vitality of Koreans is also reflected in their propensity for collective celebrations and parties are vividly enjoyed. Important events within a family such as weddings, obsequies, jubilees, or promotions are celebrated more sumptuously than in most Western countries. According to the national custom, guests are expected to contribute to the financing of a birth, a wedding, or funeral service by giving cash gifts. These donations are submitted near the entrance in a special envelope. The amount of money given is determined by the social status of the person who is giving the gift. Besides the relatives and friends of the family, the supervisor of the hosts is frequently invited as well. Consequently, companies need a special budget for such obligations.

A delicious and opulent banquet is mandatory for these parties. On occasions such as an official feast or a picnic of a small family, the center of the entire event is the meal. Food is also the main topic of conversation just like the weather in West European countries and there are numerous cooking shows on TV, while heartily eating scenes are central to family dramas.

When traveling in foreign countries, Koreans frequently miss their native food and thus take a lot of their favored dainties with them in their luggage. If Koreans have to live for a while in a foreign country, they quickly find a way to obtain Korean ingredients, sometimes even importing them from their home country to make sure that they do not have to abstain from *kimchi*, tofu, rice, noodles, or garlic. The Korean diet is neither fatty nor sweet but rich in proteins and based on seafood and vegetables. In general, the Korean cuisine is very healthy.

The life expectancy differs between the sexes. Women usually live six years longer than men. This might be entailed by the enormous stress of the business life and the formerly high consumption of alcohol and tobacco might have contributed to this situation. However, the number of smokers has decreased over the years.

In Western countries, the lifestyles of men and women are coming more similar. In South Korea, quite the contrary is the case as the difference in the respective lifestyles is emphasized. Western women are often considered less female as Korean women emphasize their femininity, while an increasing number of women are entering higher positions such as head of ministries, lawyers, or CEOs of banks. Within families, women have the saying as well, although often indirectly. In public, men are still widely respected and they are often the legal authority in their family.

Koreans are often perceived as very emotional. This may be an innate attribute and enhanced by the hot food, which is consumed on a daily basis and this influences the *gibun* of a person. As already noted, *gibun* has to do with the balance of the mind. This balance can be determined, among other things, by winning or losing face. The loss of face has a very negative effect on the *gibun*. The *gibun* can further be disturbed by a lack of respect of persons who are considered to have a lower social status. It seems that the disturbance of the *gibun* is related to lower-ranked people bothering higher-ranked ones. Also, having to listen to bad news can disorder one's *gibun,* and therefore, a lie is often preferred, which is hard to comprehend for many Westerners, as such a behavior violates the eighth commandment.

For Koreans, a harmonious relation among people is most desirable. Even in business matters, it might be more important than financial results. In any case, a harmonious relation counts more than an adherence to principles or so-called truths. In order to "keep face" feelings and desires are hided in good Confucian conduct. In the Korean society, many things remain unspoken only to sometimes suddenly lead to an outburst of a person. That is why "*nunchi*" is highly regarded. *Nunchi* is a recognized virtue to listen and to find out the true *gibun* of another person, in particular that of superiors or discussion partners. Literally translated *nunchi* means "eye measure" and is the art to read nonverbal clues of another person. People who are skilled in this art are referred to as "*nunchi ppareuda*" (quick to apprehend one's mind). On the contrary, someone who is bad in judging another person is "*nunchi eoppta*" (lacking *nunchi*). Quick and witted people are able to read another person's gestures, intonation of assertions or pitches of voice.

Korean scholarly works on the character of other Koreans are full of contradictions [14]. Most of them agree that the merits of Korean people are their tenacity, perseverance, valor, and the fact that they are hard workers. People are considered affectionate and emotional, upright and proud; they have a strong inclination to autonomy and independence, but respect foreigners. Furthermore, Koreans are described as creative, cheerful, benevolent, peaceful, forgiving, and to love jokes.

These scholars are very rigorous in also enumerating the weaknesses of Koreans. The most frequently mentioned flaw is the widespread factionalism, followed by an extreme formalism, the latter putting the state above the citizens. Furthermore, it is mentioned that Koreans are not accurate and love to erect faulty facades. Promises are easily broken and many depend too much on authorities. It is criticized that flunkeyism prevails and that education does not encourage any self-reflection. Rational thinking seems to lack as well and gives way to a deep involvement in spiritual matters such as religion and philosophy resulting in superstition. Last but not least, Koreans are said to have a short memory, lack tolerance, and despise compromises, while they have a weakness for vain titles and a propensity for exaggerations.

Of course, human traits are always complex and include many different features. In Korea, it is much influenced by Western values as well, which became dominant after 1945. Korean scholars further emphasize the influence of the climate and topography on the character of people. In the mild southern regions, Koreans are rather meek and have flexible attitudes whereas in the rugged mountainous regions of the north, they seem to be more stubborn and narrow-minded while exposing a strong will power.

One might find these character sketches in everyday life in Korea and they might be helpful for a general orientation. Nevertheless, human character traits are much more complex and are subject to scientific psychology and sociology for those who have a deeper interest in this matter.

Among all other races, Koreans are closest to the Chinese. As the population lacks basic democratic virtues and common discipline, from very early times on, they have developed formal rites, not only for important events, but for everyday life as well. A general politeness can be noticed and people speak courteously to each other in public. They exchange compliments and frequently bow lightly to any associates. This does not necessarily prove kindness but is rather a sign of good manners. A lack of this good behavior might be considered disrespectful and trigger negative feelings.

3.16 Religions in Korea

None of the world's major religions, including Hinduism, Buddhism, Judaism, Christianity, and the Islam has been developed in East Asia.

Due to the frequent rain in Korea, which results in high humidity, no artefacts were preserved as in the Near- and Middle East, except for those made of stone-like materials. Some stone relics from an unknown past have survived the millenniums, many of them resembling the dolmen found in many places in Europe. They possibly served as tombstones for special personalities. The way their remains were preserved does not only indicate that the person was to be remembered respectfully, but it further suggests that people believed in life after death. In many civilizations, such burial customs mark the beginning of religious conceptions. Some research scientists of earlier civilizations link these tombs to Shamanistic imaginations, related to the mind-set of prehistoric hunters as well as the belief to be able to hear whispering voices from the afterlife. Until today, many Koreans believe that the ghosts of deceased are still hovering in our world.

Since ancient times, as in most other known civilizations, women play an important spiritual role in Korea. Usually, women are the bearers of religious movements which, however, were devised, developed, systemized, and organized by outstanding male individuals. Confucius (551–479 B.C.), which literally translates into "Master Kong," did not found a new religion, but established a system for a prosperous and peaceful state. His ideal was to organize mankind in relation to nature. Accordingly, men should be in harmony with the entire cosmos and the way to a harmonious character was education. Education distinguishes human beings from animals and consequently, education must be accessible for everyone. According to the Confucian understanding, the main goal of education is to obtain four virtues: humanity, justice, filial piety, and rites. This, however, would mark an ideal that can ultimately not be achieved. Still, the nobleman will take upon this mission with ceaseless efforts. The greater his achievement the higher should be his worldly position. Such an approach establishes a natural order, which is necessary as any collective cooperation needs rules.

This Chinese framework of moral and political conduct was adopted by the Yi Dynasty (1392–1907) in the form of Neo-Confucianism. It was followed by the entire nation like doctrines of a religion and was by and large successful in keeping a social order. It is likeable that this religion has established a culture of the written word instead of the sword and a rule of scribes instead of warriors. A negative impact, however, was its neglect to strengthen the economy. Instead, it builds up a strong military force. Above all, the main principle of Confucius, which demanded equal chances for everybody, was neglected as well. Instead, the feudal and greedy class of the *yangban* was established, which prevented the deployment of the vital and creative vigor of the nation. In lieu, rites and formalism suffocated the energy of the population. The focus on the family, which was also an ideal of social order, led to group egoism instead of promoting a sense of nationhood. This might have further promoted a Korean preference for factionalism and their zeal to form small groups instead of larger units. In summary, Confucianism (*yugyo*) has shaped the consciousness of the Korean nation more than a strict religion could have done.

Another crucial factor that affected the mind-set of many Koreans is Shamanism (*musok*). Though it is rarely an organized religion, it has satisfied the spiritual needs of Koreans for a very long time. A considerable majority of the population adheres both secretly as well as openly to Shamanism. Women are much more active within this field. A female (*mudang*) or male (*baksu*) Shaman is called on the occasion of illnesses, weddings, births, and burials into the house of the concerned family. They are also asked for an interpretation of the future, to mediate controversies, as well as for general counseling. Sometimes, family member seek the advice of a Shamans in their small temples away from the turmoil of the cities.

Ancient practices that existed before contemporary dominant world religions emerged are still being practiced in great variety and intensity. On one hand, these practices are closely related to the worshiping of ancestors; on the other hand, they are nothing but pure superstition. During these cultic practices, the Shaman focuses on satisfying the countless goddesses and ghosts which are believed to live in any home and can become very unpleasant in their resentments. This applies particularly to those deceased whose eerie appearance at the night is most dreaded. If such appearances occur, Shamans are supposed to help with a form of exorcisms (*gut*) that is performed in a small circle and tend to turn into psychoanalytic group therapies at the best. Executed in larger groups, they are often accompanied by long ceremonial performances and resemble a folk festival. In a positive sense, these practices help to preserve the rich national folklore of Korea.

Shamanism is not a religion in the specific sense; it is a global phenomenon and displays different characteristics in different regions of the world. The Korean manifestation derives from the Tunguse language and was introduced into the intellectual world of Europe [15] via the Russian language. A large part of the male Korean population hesitates to talk about their attitude toward Shamanism. Women, especially older ladies, however, all the more are happy to share their ideas concerning old traditional beliefs. Thousands of fortune tellers make their living in this high-tech country by catering to the demand of citizens seeking predictions on their future. Thus, it is not very surprising that a delegation of Shamans, together with representatives of the prevalent religious communities, attended the state funeral of the former President Roh Moo-hyun. In daily life, we find numerous Shamanistic symbols in Korea. For instance, dried fishes are placed at essential places of buildings and even on machines in factories, serving as symbols that should prevent mischief. At formal openings of prominent buildings, Shamanistic ceremonies are not uncommon at all and sometimes, these ceremonies seem to be more important than insurance policies.

For the practically minded Korean *pungsu* plays a significant role in his daily life. The rules of *pungsu*, better known to Westerners as Feng Shui, are widely observed in Korea. In the Chinese language, it means "wind and water." Indeed, within the climate zone of China, Korea, and Japan instructions taught in Feng Shui or *pungsu* make sense, for example, when suggesting that doors should not be located at the northern side of buildings as icy winds blow from the north in winter. Consequently, living quarters should be located on the warmer southern side. (Due to different climatic suppositions, this system would not work in South India.)

It is generally accepted that green plants have a comforting effect on the room climate. However, whether they can also protect us from the negative effects of electro-smog is still unclear. The same might apply to the supposedly baleful influences of subterranean watercourses. No construction of any importance is planned without the verdict of *pungsu* experts. Many of their instructions are very impractical in everyday life and they are costly. In factories, they may even hamper rational operational processes. Nevertheless, it is sometimes advisable to permit respective ceremonies when the subordinates feel better and safer after their performances.

Buddhism was already introduced around 372 A.D. via China, following the Silk Road into Korea. For almost thousand years, a flexible form of Mahayana Buddhism determined the minds of Koreans. In the old kingdoms of Shilla and Baekje, it became the state doctrine and almost led to a theocracy. This religion attracted the Korean mind because of its non-dogmatic form and an easy adaptability to Shamanism. With its solicitude and clemency, it appealed especially to women. Also, artists were greatly inspired by it and many admirable works of art were produced under its influence. Yet, with the outset of the Yi Dynasty, Buddhism was suppressed and pushed into a passive role, while Confucianism started to shape the Korean mind-set for the next 500 years.

Buddhism regained some importance during the Japanese colonization, as the Japanese were keen to assure that there was only one religion within their empire. Today, almost eleven million people are professing Buddhists in South Korea. This fact makes the social life in the Republic much more colorful and vital. It is quite interesting to observe that modern Buddhism has adapted some rites from Christianity, whereas early Christians had originally adapted parts of the Buddhist Liturgy.

In contrast to Buddhism, Daoism (Taoism) cannot be defined as a religion. It is rather a form of conduct of everyday life, worldly wisdom, and practical philosophy. Daoism, developed in China, is the moral of the simple and natural things in life. It was represented by wise, educated, Chinese men. Its emotional and sensitive character is considered to be especially close to the female inner life. The ideas of Dao are traced back to the old master Lao Tzu (who lived approximately at the same time as Confucius around 500 B.C.), to whom the standard book of Daoism *Tao-te-Ching* is attributed, although this book might have been written two hundred years later. It emphasizes a life without bustle and greediness which leads to contentment and harmony. Metaphorically, as the flow of water shows, in the longer run, soft power defeats hard power.

Although Daoism officially does not play any role in Korea, its influence on the behavior, aestheticism, and, above all, on Korean arts can hardly be overestimated. Additionally, it influences the Korean way of thinking. Daoism emphasizes the intuition and encourages men to be spontaneous. This philosophical tradition considers naturalness, spontaneity, and being able to cope with changes as excellent virtues. Actions that do not necessitate a lot of energy are also considered ideal. Within Daoism, the belief in rites and magic are widely popular. Somehow Daoism closely resembles ideas expressed in Feng Shui.

Prior to the arrival of Christian missioners, Korean envoys had had contact to Catholic missionaries at the court in Beijing. Upon their return, these Korean envoys established and took care of numerous flourishing Christian communities. Because the new belief was quickly considered dangerous for the Confucian bureaucracy, Christians became subject to persecution. The beginnings of Christianity in Korea were marked by heroic confessors, who frequently ended as martyrs under the sword.

Currently, eleven million Protestants and five million Catholics form a Christian majority. These denominations, however, are deeply divided. In particular, Protestantism is steadily growing and supported increasingly by the upper classes. The former President Lee Myung-bak, for example, turned out to be a keen patron of this religion. The success of Protestantism is based on the fact that it does not question the values of Confucianism. On the contrary, it adapts much of its reasoning, for example, a nearly ascetic conduct of life. Protestant missioners came to Korea as teachers and medical doctors and thus were perceived as agents of modernization. They were welcomed by public authorities and did not experience the martyrdom of the Catholics who had arrived earlier.

Pope Francis visited South Korea in the summer of 2014. He has gained much popularity because of his modest and human behavior. This was in stark contrast to the behavior of various leaders of the numerous protestant sects in Korea. As a consequence, Catholicism became more popular and has recently won many new supporters.

Visually, many big cities in South Korea are dominated by usually peaked church towers, topped with huge crosses blinking in red or white at night. In contrast, round Buddhist temples are hidden modestly in the tranquility of parks, groves, or forests. Five of the ten biggest churches in the world are located in South Korea and send out the second largest number of Christian missioners into the world. Only the USA delegates more missionaries. The various protestant churches compete intensively for the most glorious cathedral, the best orchestra, the largest chorus, the most sumptuous gowns in the liturgical setting, and, above all, the best clergymen who are able to preach passionate sermons. Women are the majority of their followers. An important token of their power rests with the volume of donations, which are utilized to finance kindergartens and hospitals. The entire practice of financial management is hidden from the eyes of the public. Thus, the government recently canceled the immunity from tax exemption for churches.

These communities of reformed Christians are split into numerous sects with an eloquent charismatic leader. Their doctrines, more often than not, deviate from the traditional theology. The most esteemed and dominant sects are very affluent and their leaders are also politically influential. Some of these sects exhibit the character of economical corporate groups. A few of them are quite exclusive and might even refuse to grant other Christians access in public worship under a dubious pretext.

The Yeouido Full Gospel Church under its charismatic leader, reverend and owner Cho, counts more than 800,000 members, who are expected to bestow up to 10 % of their income to their section. On top of that, they are expected to make donations after the service. In order to collect as many donations as possible, not only a tray or basket is circulated during the service, but there are offices and garages under the nave with machines that allow making donations by using credit cards. Occasionally, newspapers report about distribution disputes. At the beginning of 2011, such disputes climaxed in fist fights between leaders of some sects in front of a church in Seoul. Reverend Cho wanted to retire from active service around 2012 and wanted to install his son as his successor. The Internet and other media reported that he argued about his pension scheme, requesting roughly 13 million dollar per year.

Among these sects, the Moon sect has a special position. Its founder Moon Sung-myung considered himself as the Messiah of a new religious organization. His community is partly organized by following the structure of the Vatican. It has also borrowed many elements from other faiths. Moon ultimately wanted to unite Christians, Buddhists, and member of other religions or creeds. Consequently, he placed himself above Jesus, Buddha, and other originators of religions. The name Unification Church = *Tongilgyo* (originally The Holy Spirit Association for the Unification of World Christianity) reflects his idea to establish a home for the spiritual needs of all people; it is maybe derived from the universalistic view of Daoism. This Unification Church is active all over the world and has many followers in the USA. Moon had purchased the Washington Times and thus some influence on the public opinion in the USA.

Born in North Korea, Moon was a strong anti-Communist. He amassed considerable economic wealth, which was supposed to be used to gain influence in politics in order to protect his movement against a variety of adversaries. He wanted to establish a "holy international elite" that one day, headed by himself, was supposed to rule the world. Though turning 93, Moon's Unification Church counted hardly more than two million followers and did not fulfill the established aims. Moon build a gorgeous white dome on a wooded mountain slope roughly 90 km east of Seoul in the vicinity of *Gapyong*. This place is the spiritual center of his community and is called "Palace of Peace." It used to be the residence of him and his family as well. The administration headquarters are located in Seoul. Within sight, he erected a modern hospital, the lobby of which reminds of a luxurious hotel. Not only is the facility regarded as exemplary, but the medical standard and the quality of the physicians and the equipment including the latest model of a magnetic resonance scanner are considered to be outstanding as well. The admission is open for all citizens and the charges are relatively moderate. The top two stories were reserved for the exclusive use of the patriarch and his family. Moon passed away in September 2012. One of his sons and his wife are now the leaders of the sect.

According to Maull [16], the *Tongilgyo* conglomeration owns trade and production enterprises in the following sectors: Tea, pharmaceuticals, textiles, and machineries. It has invested in a multitude of stock-marketed enterprises and shows the strength of a *chaebol*.

One of our acquaintance, an engineer and versed businessman, summarized his view on this sect with the following sarcastic and striking comment: "Reverend Cho and others simply make money with Jesus; Messiah Moon made even more money, however, without Jesus."

The number of Christians and Buddhists in Korea amounts to 27 million believers, which makes up about 54 % of the 50 million inhabitants of South Korea. A considerable number of people are Confucians, which cannot be considered a religion as mentioned above, but more as a guideline for the conduct of life for common people and as a philosophy for more sophisticated persons. Tiny minorities follow hardly countable sects and movements in this country, which is absolutely tolerant with regard to religious beliefs. Therefore, there are about 30,000 Muslims who live in the country. This number is slowly increasing. Arab traders came to Korea as early as in the Unified Shilla period (around 700 A.C.) and the late Goryeo period (around 1200 A.C.), bringing their faith with them.

Different from other oriental countries, South Korea does not have a state religion or even a dominating doctrinal theology. Instead, a wide spectrum of convictions, spiritual attitudes, and confession of faiths exist that often intersect and permit double and triple affiliations. Sometimes, it is claimed, for example, that Koreans turn to Shamanistic practices when encountering calamities while they turn to Confucian teachings in their everyday social life and that they regard Buddhism as their philosophical background. Finally, brides often prefer a Christian type of wedding. In this country with highly emotional people, almost every religion finds a very fertile soil to spread their beliefs.

Last but not least, a Korean Council of Religious Leaders exists. This organization is composed of senior heads of the country's major faiths, and they meet regularly in order to enhance a mutual understanding and promote common interests. This might be an exemplary model for religious tolerance rarely matched anywhere else in the world.

3.17 Philosophical Approaches

The director general of the National Museum of Korea writes [17]: "The Korean Culture of the old kingdoms culminated in the harmony and unity with nature on one side and in the belief of the religions of Shamanism, Buddhism and

Confucianism on the other side. Above all in this religious thought stands the immaterial existence and thereupon the culture of Korea is substantiated." This quote could evoke the idea that religion in Korea might have taken the place of philosophy.

To a certain degree, the Western world is familiar with the names of famous Chinese philosophers as well as with their thinking and teachings. Apart from Zen people know much less about Japanese philosophy and hardly anything is known about Korean philosophy. Only a few Western scholars work on this subject as this requires Chinese and Korean language skills to master the scripts in the respective language. Looking at the history of philosophy in the world, we find a list of approximately 950 outstanding personalities in the "Routledge Encyclopedia of Philosophy" [18]. Among these names, there are only 80 from East and South Asia: China (35), Japan (21), India (15), and Korea (9). The great majority of philosophers come from Europe with some contributions worth mentioning from Arab countries and North America.

The low figure of Asian philosophers can be explained by the fact that their works are not translated into common Western languages and thus are simply unknown. Additionally, it has to be acknowledged that the philosophical tradition begins with the old Greeks and is by and large of Occidental character, reflecting the mind-set and lives of monotheistic beliefs.

Metaphysics is a major topic of Western philosophy and stems from characteristics of the Indo-German languages, using, for example, copulas which do not exist in East Asian languages. The famous German philosopher Martin Heidegger, for instance, investigated in his most famous book "Being and Time" (*Sein und Zeit*) what it means for a human being to be. A whole range of ideas is built on copulas such as "time is the meaning of being." Such a chain of reasoning cannot be constructed in the Chinese or Korean language and are difficult to translate. Probably an East Asian framework of thought can therefore not be compared to the concept of Western philosophy. In a strict sense, however, philosophy has a universal character as it predominantly deals with logical reflections of fundamental issues such as ethics, art of government, or aesthetics. Because logic is everywhere the same, there cannot be only a "Korean logic" and thus a merely "Korean philosophy."

Europeans often approach the cultural region of East Asia with ideas of old Chinese ideals of harmony and heavenly balance. The formula "Heaven—Earth—Man" can mislead people to see this as the key to the East Asian mind-set. Eikemeier, a scientist who works in the field of Korean Studies [19] deconstructs such an idea of a triadic formula, pointing out that the formula rather reflects a principle of order which deals with reality and circulates around mediation and coordination. "The circumstances in question are indeed frequently facilitated and rather complex, but not refined and speculative. They are concerned with the Korean everyday life and conduct of life in relation to objects, behavior, and mentalities as experienced by the majority of the population." Eikemeier continues that "Felicitous harmony with the universe is out of question; instead, one has to speak much more of human self-reference and human self-certainty." The scholar concludes his essay with the sentence: "This means that a foreign observer as well has to bid farewell to the concept of an exhilarating cosmic unity as well as to the 'Land of the Morning Calm'" [20]. This quote clarifies that philosophy has to be clearly discerned from religions and myths, which require believing and do not longing for insight.

Western cultures are based on the thoughts of antique philosophers and myths of a Christian precept. Similarly, Eastern cultures are based on old Chinese fables and the spiritual character of Buddhism. The West, however, realized its progress on the one hand by turning to natural sciences and technologies and, on the other hand, by developing democratic societies. Yet, Confucianism ignored the natural sciences for a long time just as they rejected a spirit of objectivism, which permits debates and critique, which again are necessary for change and progress. It was only at the end of the Joseon period (1392–1910) that a movement of "Practical Learning" (*sirhak*) emerged, which challenged and doubted "the old ways." At that time, this was a radical mental revolution. However, unlike the Japanese, the followers of *sirhak* did not want to adapt Western political, economic, and military achievements.

Like in any other great cultural nation, Korea incorporates multiple dichotomies: Spirituality and rationality, great arts and simple manual work, kindliness, and cruelty. Thus, despite the fact that their fellow citizens generally strive for entirety and harmony, Korean philosophers indeed have to deal with dualisms.

Unquestionably, Korea belongs to the great global civilizations, although it was geographically remote, politically secluded, and maintained many cultural idiosyncrasies. One positive aspect of globalization in the sense of Adam Smith is certainly to increase the wealth of nations by the division of labor. Yet, the mingling of different cultures can indeed create a certain homogeneity in the world. Instead, the diversity of cultures should be globally amenable. Within this context, Koreans with their unique culture and spontaneous hospitality can contribute greatly to the international scene. Being aware of their potential, Korea currently makes many steps into this direction.

3.18 The Roots of a Sociocultural Behavior

Initially, Koreans regarded themselves as the members of a single family of origin and thus as a pure race. This idea led to a unique national identity. Presently, the South Korean society experiences a far reaching change which, above all, alters the mind-set which leads to great generational gaps. Most likely, this change will be mastered successfully and enter a consolidated democratic, society acting under commercial considerations within a free market system, which will gradually enhance and improve its social security system. The nation will be increasingly integrated into the modern Western community; nevertheless, some important cultural characteristics will be enforced rather than disappearing.

Korea shows a great homogeneity with respect to the people, customs, food, and language. Unlike in the Chinese language, there are no dialects in the Korean language. Despite of all this, we can observe quite different attitudes within the population. Traditionally, there always persisted an antagonism between the authorities and the population. The government and the court followed classical Chinese manners, whereas the general public had rather amorphous habits and lived in almost chaotic conditions. They apparently followed the strict rules of the authorities; however, these rules were not really accepted. The population of the peninsula defined themselves as genuine Koreans with a deeply embodied self-conception. However, they lacked a conception of the state. Koreans temporarily set their reclusiveness aside to defend the country when an enemy invaded the nation. Nevertheless, a complete identification with the country did not happen. Only the lately demonstration of the Tapgol Plaza (1919) against the Japanese occupational forces can be considered as the beginning of a common national self-confidence.

Henderson [21] refers to the fact that no castle towns, guilds, port authorities, or chambers of commerce existed in ancient Korea. Likewise, there were no organized casts of dyers, merchants, weapon producers, etc. He writes about "undefined organizations, fluid positions, resistance to rules and law, and transitional ownership." This situation did not foster the development of specializations, an overall discipline, hierarchies, or loyalties as in Europe or Japan. The historian further notes that even when leadership persisted, it was "rough, gang-like, and unruly." Therefore, something like a clear-cut outlines of professions or business hierarchies did not exist either in the past. It was not uncommon for an "entrepreneur" to be concerned with livestock farming on one day, only to turn to the production of cooking pots the next day as he produced, stored, transported, and sold everything on his own. Basically, an entrepreneur abhorred the relation of employer and employee as well as any other kind of dependency. This is the main reason why important branches of industry did not develop beyond the ordinary crafts as business people detested the organization in larger companies. A tough competitive pressure, the appetites of the government, relatives, and criminals were all seen as big disadvantages of such a system. Instead, it was felt that the small shop owners, who often remain hidden, lived much happier as he could manage his own time and proceed as he wishes.

Even though people did live in company of others in narrow quarters and market communities, which were considered to have some advantages, according to Henderson, people still considered this as a mixed blessing. He further elaborates that "there is an inability to cohere, take common stands and develop accepted leadership." Within such an atmosphere, it is evidently difficult to find rational solutions to problems and to compromise. Permanent jealousies and dissensions impede to find common solutions of political, economic, and social tasks. At all times, there were personalities in Korea, who together with their attendants held quite different views.

Confucian societies tend to be built on hierarchical orders. People are not considered to be equal and therefore try to find out whether one is superior or inferior to others. For this reason, title-laden name cards are of great importance. Equally, the social status of a person is defined by income and wealth. If all that does not help to determine a pecking order, the same is established by psychological or, on lower levels, even physical power struggles. Such rankings can be found in families, sports clubs, religious communities, or any other type of public communities. In general, "higher-ranked" persons are then reluctant to accept democratic elections and always desire a special treatment.

Another "cultural abnormity," described by Henderson, is the fact that in former times, nobody could stay long enough in his official position in Korea to successfully carry out projects. Discontinuation was the rule rather than the exception. In 518 years, the capital of Seoul was governed by no less than 1375 lord mayors, who often changed on a monthly basis. Reasons for this were the idea to prevent the ever looming danger of corruption and anxieties that one person could become too influential and thus powerful enough to usurp higher positions. Furthermore, Koreans are obsessed with the idea of punishment and are likely to chase somebody away from his position if he makes a mistake. The tendency to frequently recall ministers as well as high government officials could still be observed under Syngman Rhee. Pak Chung-hee then tried to stabilize the structures of the higher civil services.

As a result of the above-mentioned practices, Koreans tried by all means to avoid to be considered a specialist or stupid expert (*chaengi*). Instead, they frequently were interested in many different things and always looked out for new opportunities. Similarly, they were constantly ready to take on potential rivals or to move into new fields of operation. This behavior had rather egoistic reasons and was not based on the idea to contribute to a greater good.

This explains why Korea did not have a strong base for its economy. Kim Il-sung in North Korea tried to counter this situation by erecting huge government-owned enterprises. In South Korea, Pak Chung-hee counted on charismatic entrepreneurs, who founded big conglomerations (the *chaebol*), which were directed by well-versed experts with a great knowledge, who always remained flexible and pragmatic in their conduct of business. The ability to change thus became a valuable attribute to test new technologies, to transfer businesses to other regions, to dismiss outdated know-how, and to face ever-new challenges. The modernization of the Korean economy was initiated in the *chaebol* and only today effects small as well as mid-sized industries.

All this further clarifies why the country probably needed a taut almost military leadership during a certain period of time. Korea lacked—like her former mentor China—to some extent a specific, important cultural quality, namely discipline. It is necessary to ensure that, metaphorically, all wheels of a big machine mesh effectively. In order to avoid an inflexible system, however, limited room is necessary that allows unlocking the creativity and readiness to work of Korean people.

Although Koreans differ from the Chinese, the Korean mental attitude is closer to the Chinese mind-set than to the Japanese. They share with them notions of jealousy and resentment, from which a tendency to disagree with others. Bitter rivalries, which unnecessarily consume resources, can be observed among leaders in parties, unions, as well as all kinds of clubs.

3.19 Spirit of *Seonbi*

Maybe the essence of the previous three chapters can be summarized under the term "*seonbi*." Koreans possess unique cultural traits that are rooted in the geography of the country. The geography determines the climate, which in turn determines the vegetation, fauna, and the living environment of human beings, including their food, tools, clothing, as well as their common social behavior. The fertile soil and the abundant maritime resources made Korea self-sufficient. The cultivation of rice promoted teamwork and the formation of intimate groups. These were later further enhanced by Confucianism, which demanded modesty and working in a harmonious society. Professor Han, an emeritus from the Seoul National University, claims that Koreans "love to group together" and that "is the cultural DNA that we have inherited from history." [22]

Koreans take pride in the saying of Confucius that the people east of China seem to be particularly honest and righteous. They are also proud of the fact that Confucius had stated that he would like to live among these people. Various Korean scholars have therefore repeatedly claimed that at least in this respect, Korea could hardly learn anything from their Chinese neighbors.

The *seonbi* culture originated from Shamanism. The mythical ruler Dangun was not only described as a wise and righteous king but also as the head of shamanistic rites, which are closely connected to the natural environment. In this respect, the cult of Shintoism and their Tenno rulers in Japan, a country with similar scenic landscapes, are quite similar to Korean Shamanism. The Chinese characters of *seonbi* refer to superhuman beings living in wooded mountains.

The early rulers of Gojoseon claimed to be descendants from heaven, who were supposed to take care of humanity and provide their subjects with all necessities, including military protection. During the Gogureyo period, festivals were held, during which people competed in dancing and various forms of martial arts such as archery and wrestling. Those who obtained high scores were called *seonbis* and were invited to assist the rulers, who govern the state. They taught common people how to write and read the difficult Chinese characters and introduced them to religious practices. Furthermore, they also spread the knowledge of how to construct bridges, roads, fortresses, and monuments. In times of war, they formed battalions of brave soldiers.

This tradition was further perfected in the kingdom of Shilla by the *Hwarang* (or S*eonnang*). This was a group of young men, who were spirited patriots, and often decorated like women with flowers and precious stones. (Probably they stood in the tradition of ancient Amazon fighters.) The most outstanding personalities were entrusted with high positions in the civil administration. When Confucianism and Buddhism were introduced in Shilla, their teachings blended with the *seonbi* culture, which also comprised of elements of Daoism. Around 600 A.D., the five commandments of the *Hwarang* were stipulated: To be loyal to the king; to show filial piety to the parents; to honor friendships; to never retreat in battle, and to not kill without a just cause.

In the later Goreyo Dynasty, the matching cultures of the *seonbi* and *Hwarang* were amalgamated and special emphasis was placed on a culture to suit the natural environment of the country. This was in line with the idea to take care of local citizens and the old concern of Dangun and Gija to benefit all mankind.

With the growing influence of Confucianism, officials were subdivided into civil and military officials. This meant that the military lost its former all-encompassing power.

The Yi Dynasty embraced Confucianism and its strict version, Neo-Confucianism, was gradually adapted to the Korean environment. The early kings and leading scholars kept some elements from Buddhism but basically studied the Chinese classics of Confucianism, interpreting them and developing their own teachings. In the absence of a better alternative for the word, "*seonbi*" was spelled with the same Chinese characters used for "scholar." Indeed, governmental examinations for higher civil positions required the knowledge of classic Chinese literature and its local interpretations. In the course of time, people started to equate *seonbi* with the *yangban*, who had a supposedly lazy scholarly lifestyle. But ultimately, honest *seonbi* were considered to be virtuous and modest scholars, whereas *yangban* were regarded as plainly greedy and corrupt.

Nevertheless, the working class, especially in rural villages preserved the spirit, manners, and customs of the *Hwarang* of the Shilla period. They gathered to celebrate festivals and to take care of the costly funerals of family members. Communities were built to jointly dig irrigation systems, erect public facilities, and something like an insurance system was established to help unfortunate members of the community in times of misfortune. To some degree, these communities exercised a kind of democratic self-government among themselves. In times of hostile foreign raids, so-called righteous armies were formed, which fought against invading Japanese, Mongol, or Manchu troops. It was this spirit that nourished the independence movement during the Japanese colonial rule that plagued the intruders with countless ambushes.

The younger generation in the south of the peninsula perceives the *seonbi* as rather useless literati who are in sharp contrast to hard-working laborers and managers. They feel as real, authentic Koreans; however, and at the same time, they are very open for global ideas and exchanges. Their self-confidence nourishes their longing for participation and democracy.

Unlike in South Korea, the population of the north is educated to expect that their government, in the manner of the old kings, takes loving care for its subjects. The regime insists on its pure Koreanness and their people being the "cleanest race" in the world. North Korea rejects all foreign influences and is preoccupied with its ideology of autonomy and self-reliance. North Korea has never been a member of the Comecon (The Council for Mutual Economic Assistance), a socialist economic community and has never strived to be integrated into more or less capitalistic associations like the ASEAN (Association of Southeast Asian Nations), or an international organization like the GATT (General Agreement on Tariffs and Trade). The nation claims to be unique and wants to preserve this status without any compromises.

In the face of a widening gap between few people who are rich and an increasing huge majority of poorer citizens, some old-fashioned Korean patriots lament the vanishing of old virtues. They are concerned that the recent cult of money in the south is going to destruct the country's valuable cultural heritage and: "Many of them feel a nagging sense of moral inferiority to their more orthodox brethren" [23] in the north. The feeling of a moral superiority leads to the fact that more than 50 % of all North Koreans are loyal to their regime, despite all the hardships they have to suffer. The future will show whether the isolation from the rest of the world and the highly intelligent propaganda of the regime within in the country will hold out against globally rapidly progressing IT technologies.

3.20 Government and Administration

After centuries of internally competing states, monarchies, the arbitrary rule of the *yangban*, especially in provinces, as well as times of foreign rule, and military dictatorships, today, South Korea is an independent and democratic state. This new, modern state functions—to the surprise of some Western nations—worked very well. Korea still has a central administration, but it is progressing toward establishing more reasonable regional and local autonomies.

As a result of numerous reforms, today South Korea has a constitution which is at eye level with the constitutions of other developed democracies. Besides the generally acknowledged human rights, it obliges the state to take all efforts for the well-being of its citizens. This includes the rights to pursue one's own happiness, to find a job, being paid fair wages, a minimum wage, to have access to education, clean surroundings, help in case of disablement, protection of the private sphere, and the right to found unions. The constitution further determines the separation of powers into three branches, namely legislative, executive, and judicial.

The legislative branch consists of the National Assembly (*gukhoe*), which is compiled of 246 deputies directly elected by the people and another 54 sent by the parties, in proportion to their election results. All 300 deputies are elected for a period of 4 years. For the parties, there exists a minority stake of 3 %. Presently, there are only four parties in the parliament. The main function of the *gukhoe* is to pass new bills with a simple majority (therefore, the deputies are commonly called "lawmakers"). The government or ten deputies, respectively, can submit a bill to the parliament. It also decides on contracts regarding financial commitments as well as on the national security, military affairs, and international treaties. Any veto of the president can be overruled by the National Assembly with a majority of two third of votes. The *gukhoe* is a one-chamber parliament.

The executive branch is headed by the president, who is directly elected by the people for one five-year term. As head of the state, he represents the nation both internally and externally. He presides over the state council, which should have at least 15 and not more than 30 members, which he picks himself. He also appoints his deputy and the prime minister. For both appointments, he needs the approval of the parliament. The president is also the commander in chief of the South Korean armed forces, and it is his duty to work toward a peaceful reunification of the country. The president has the right to suggest new laws to the parliament. He cannot dissolve the National Assembly, but the National Assembly can impeach him in case of a serious misconduct.

The president can declare martial law but needs the subsequent approval of the National Assembly. A number of agencies are at his disposal: The National Intelligence Service, other security services, a commission against corruption, an advisory council for science/technology, and a committee for small- and middle-sized businesses. Finally, there is an office for control and investigation, which supervises the financial behavior of the central as well as the regional and local authorities. This council further scrutinizes the abuse of power and faulty behavior of public office bearers.

The prime minister remains in the shadow of the president. Nevertheless, he pursues a couple of important functions as he proposes members for the state council or recalls them. He directs the antitrust authorities, the office of intelligence service, and the emergency plan service. Presently, there exist 17 ministries. Besides the more common ministries, there is also the Ministry for Unification; the Ministry of Culture, Sports and Tourism; the Ministry of Science, ICT and Future Planning; the Ministry of Maritime Affairs and Fisheries; and The Ministry of Gender Equality and Family. Besides the ministries, there are 16 offices for specific fields such as taxation and custom duties, statistics, the police, agricultural development, supervision of food and medication, safeguarding of copyrights, and the promotion of small- and middle-sized industries. These offices are directed by vice-ministers, who originate from a related ministry and thus have expert knowledge within their field.

During the military dictatorship of the country, the head of the National Intelligence Service was considered by many politicians to be the second most powerful man after the president. It was founded in 1961 under its former name, "Korean Central Intelligence Agency" (KCIA) and has been severely criticized by the public because of past abuses. It was renamed into "National Intelligence Service" (NIS) and reorganized in 1999. Behind the scenes, it is still quite active, but its name has lost the dread of its colloquial name "Angibu," which was formerly attached to the KCIA.

The entire governing body rests on the service of 850,000 government officers. They are divided into three categories: Career officers, special administrative employees, and civil specialists employed on a contractual base. The latter are particularly well paid as they are hired for highly qualified jobs. The wage of the majority of the other two categories is divided into nine categories, and bonus payments are granted for exceptional performances.

Of the 850,000 civil servants, 550,000 work for the central government and only 300,000 are employed for the provinces and municipalities. This shows that the local autonomy is not much developed yet. There are 16 regional district administrations, including seven for the cities of Seoul, Busan, Daegu, Incheon, Gwangju, Daejon, and Ulsan and another nine for the provinces of Gyeonggi,

Gangwon, North Chungcheon, South Chungcheon, North Jeolla, South Jeolla, North Gyeongsang, South Gyeongsang, and Jeju. These nine district administrations comprise of 235 lower administration units: 72 cities (*si*), 94 rural districts (*gun*), and 69 autonomous districts (*gu*).

3.21 Legislation

Confucianism strived to educate and influence people to become virtuous, thus making a legislation superfluous. It emanated from the concept of *ye* (in Chinese language *li*), which was regarded as a manifestation of the heavenly. From the period of the early Joseon Dynasty (1392) and the beginning of Neo-Confucianism, *ye* and law were mentioned in the same breath [24]. If the citizens would follow the moral principles, worldly laws would be unnecessary. Due to the ambivalent nature of human beings, including Koreans, this idea remained an ideal. In reality, many crimes were committed which were punished draconically and capital punishments were enforced with cruelty.

The first laws in Korea had Chinese roots and were mainly monitored by the nobility. With the start of the Yi Dynasty, an increasing number of common rules and customs of the Korean society were codified. These laws were supposed to be oriented toward the social reality of the nation and protect Korea from being overwhelmed by the Chinese culture. This was less important for the penal legislation than for the family law. For instance, for centuries it has been a custom for grooms to move, at least temporarily, into the house of his in-laws and the children were brought up in their household as well. In the line of succession, martial children had equal rights—regardless of their gender. This was fundamentally different in China and Japan. The situation started to change gradually with a growing influence of Confucianism. After the Japanese colonial rule, Japanese laws became valid. The Japanese introduced the first complete legal system in Korea. It was, however, partially replaced after 1945 by Anglo-Saxon laws. Indeed, both legal systems did not meet the needs of the traditional Korean society.

But the Koreans use to say that there exists a considerable gap between the laws and the reality of life as complex situations can hardly be grasped by legal paragraphs. Professor Choi [25] elucidates five scopes within which a clash of formal Western laws and traditional Korean social structure cannot be avoided:

- Universalism versus individual endeavors,
- Impersonal versus personal relations,
- Competition versus cooperation,
- Individual versus collective responsibility,
- Readiness for conflict versus the pursuit of harmony.

First of all, the idea that the introduction Western rules alone would result in the creation of a modern society seems rather unrealistic. Secondly, the contradictions described above could, under changing circumstances, create a complex combination of variables that would lead to significant behavioral insecurities among citizens.

Nevertheless, it is clear that the Korean economic miracle could not have happened without a narrow interrelationship with the global economy. The acquisition of capital and capital investments, technological license agreements, and studies and vocational trainings abroad have been necessary for further development. Nowadays, the integration into international institutions and the broad global exchange of commodities and know-how between devolved industrial nations are the driving forces that foster an economic expansion. Cooperation with highly developed partners in the USA, Europe, and lately also Asia would have been impossible without a modern international legislation. Every successful international deal results in a contract, which will not be realized without generally accepted rules.

This also applies to interactions within the country. South Korean economic laws match the international level for more than 20 years. This applies to company foundations, accounting, insolvencies, internal and external trade, local and international investments, finances, securities trading, all the necessary regulations in everyday management, labor laws, proprietary rights, and sophisticated tax laws. The legislation for economic laws is very close to international standards. When it comes to the implementation of existing laws, Korea is still (although this trend is decreasing) rather inflexible. A willingness to arbitration seems much bigger than in Western countries. This applies, above all, to business partners in the small and middle-sized businesses, which prefer to settle their disputes without the judiciary.

3.22 Judiciary

The Korean Constitutional Court of South Korea was established in 1988. Its president is appointed by the President of the Republic from a range of constitutional judges. The appointment has to be approved by the parliament. Out of the nine constitutional judges, respectively, three are appointed by the president, three by the parliament, and another three by the chairman of the Supreme Court. They have to be at least 40 years old and have to have worked for a period of no less than 15 years as a judge, prosecutor, or lawyer. They are all appointed for a six-year term and can be reelected until they turn 65. One exception is the chairman, who can be reelected until he turns 70.

The Supreme Court has 13 members besides the chairman. It is considered an independent branch of the government. The chairman is appointed by the President of the Republic with the approval of the parliament. He serves a six-term office or until he turns 70 years old. The other 13 judges are also appointed by the President on the proposal of the chairman of the Supreme Court. Again, the approval of the parliament has to be attained. All judges serve for a term of 6 years and can be reelected until they turn 65. Prior to their appointment, they have to have worked for no less than 15 years as a judge, prosecutor, or lawyer.

This professional training is followed by a mandatory educational period of two years, concluded by a rigid final examination. Besides the Supreme Court, there exist a Family Court, an Administrative Court, and a Patent Court. The Supreme Court decides on the appeal of the five appealing courts and also confirms the validity of elections.

The jurisdiction in South Korea is threefold. Besides the Supreme Court, there exist high courts and district courts in 13 larger cities of the country. They include 44 branch courts and 102 urban courts. A judge decides in the district courts on all common cases. However, in cases of suits filed over $ 100,000, or in major crime cases, which might result in a life sentence or even the death penalty, a panel of three judges is required. Complaints on legal decisions can be filed to the five appealing courts in the cities of Seoul, Daegu, Busan, Gwangju, and Daejon. The judiciary system ensures—like its US-American model—a high degree of "checks and balances."

3.23 Parties and Elections

According to the constitution, the parties—which can be founded freely and are established in large numbers—are assigned with the task, to articulate the political convictions of the citizens and to organize their will. All actions have to be based on a democratic proceeding. The parties support candidates, who run for elected offices in common elections in order to work for the well-being of all citizens and to serve the public interest.

After the Pacific War, many small political parties emerged. These parties were rendered insignificant or were even temporarily forbidden by the military dictatorships which followed. It was only from 1987 on that free and direct elections of the President of the Republic became possible again. Currently (March 2014), there are four political parties presented in the parliament.

So far, there are no very influential popular parties, which have dominated the politics of the country over several decades. Instead, a constant coming and going of bigger and smaller parties as well as parties merging or splitting can be registered. There are both conservative and socialistic tendencies, but party members gather first and foremost around eloquent or demagogical personalities with charisma and pathos and their networks, which often have a regional character.

An independent National Election Commission manages free and fair elections for all citizens on all levels of administration: locally, district-wise, and nationally. In general, all citizens have the right to actively vote, starting with the age of 18 and they have the right to be elected for a public office with the age of 25. The parliament is elected by all citizens of the country for four years. It passes the bills, deals with the national financial budget, with the foreign policy, and various other controlling fields of public life. In case of grave misconduct, it has the right to push dignitaries out of their official positions (right for impeachment).

3.24 Criminality

All types of crime—except economic crimes—have decreased in South Korea with an increasing affluence of the people. Serious criminality is on a similar level as in Western European countries and in Seoul, it is lower than in most urban centers of the Western world. The operating ratio of the police successfully persecuting criminal offenders is higher than in most Western countries. The death sentence continues to exist, yet it is rarely enforced.

Petty crimes, however, are rather common in South Korea. Pickpockets are frequent, embezzlements in companies are almost a constant nuisance, and especially when it comes to cheating, the delinquents prove to be very creative. Many people mistrust each other when no particular loyalty prevails. When losing an item, there is almost no chance that somebody will turn up and hand it back to the righteous owner. Moving is an especially risky undertaking. Another particular threat is posed by the practice of using stamps instead of signatures to sign contracts. These stamps can easily be copied or stolen and if one's *ingam* (a special stamp for the real estate business) goes missing, one might even lose one's house or land.

The high number of civil servants charged for offenses in South Korea is remarkable. *The Korean Herald* reported in its November 3, 2014, issue that 1202 police officers, 264 prosecutors, and other officers of justice, 136 officials of the tax authorities, and in total 11,458 civil servants were recorded in 2013 for having committed various offenses. The charges were predominantly concerned with bribery. In its issue from January 12, 2015, the same paper grumbles that "Korea has a long way to go when it comes to tackling corruption." According to the international Corruption Perceptions Index (CPI) from 2014, Korea is ranked 43rd of 175 countries surveyed, and only ranks 97th in terms of public trust. The big business conglomerations are so powerful that the government has little jurisdiction over them, even when bribery, tax evasion, and price fixing are concerned. If their owners are prosecuted and convicted by courts, they are frequently bailed out by top-ranking politicians as these owners are needed for investment decisions and the national economy would be badly hampered without them. Consequently, if they are convicted, their terms are cut short or suspended. The existing anticorruption laws are rather severe, but they are hardly enforced—at least when it comes to influential bosses. For ordinary citizens, the rules more often than not, apply. *The Korean Herald* believes that overseas investors will be discouraged by this code of conduct, which thus stalls the economic growth of the country.

One central problem is the widening gap between well-to-do people and the impoverished part of society, which provides for the rich families that live in expensive high rising buildings with sophisticated security systems.

Another delicate problem in South Korea is organized crime, which affects the whole society. It derives its basic income from "protection money" from smaller shops and the so-called pleasure industry. It further controls gambling and prostitution. This kind of mafia (in Korean *kkangpae*) has expanded to Japan and controls large parts of the Japanese *yakuza*. Their members are predominantly naturalized Koreans either from North or South Korea.

In Japan, the *yakuza* is an open problem which is discussed in the general public and described in detail in literature, and there are daily reports about them in the newspapers. However, in Korea there is a peculiar silence when it comes to the relevant criminal alliances. In contrast to the *yakuza*, the *kkangpae* in Korea does not appear in public and are only feared in respective circles. Occasionally, their services are used unlawfully. It was reported that some companies used them to collect money or to evict real estates. In former times, even the government is said to have used them to disperse violent demonstrations. The *kkangpae* rather have the quality of groups of thugs, whereas Japanese *yakuza* groups are involved in major crimes and are accused of numerous homicides.

Almost 50 % of foreign offenders are Chinese. In fact, many Chinese prefer to stay on *Jeju* Island. Unsurprisingly, the province has the highest number of crimes in South Korea. The tense relations with North Korea trigger a lot of espionage activities from both sides—a popular topic for many TV shows in which more often than not the Communist side is accused of numerous murders, also on South Korean territory.

3.25 The Real Estate Business

The population density on spare soil, suitable for urban expansion, is high. The real estate prices in the countryside and in small towns are still affordable, but they have skyrocketed in urban centers. Additionally, people are attracted by the idea to live in large cities and thus move toward metropolises such as Seoul. Not only are the job opportunities and comfortable way of life including shopping facilities, medical care, educational facilities, the proximity to important official places, and public authorities attractive, but there prevails a certain snobbism and feeling "having made it" that prompts city dwellers to look down at the country pumpkins.

Building high-rise buildings is the answer to tackle the problem of the scarce building plots. When driving from the airports of Gimpo or Incheon toward Seoul, one will be impressed by endless rows of buildings with 15–25 floors, built using a simple, monotonous architectural style. These buildings cover hills and valleys, shimmering in gray, white, and beige colors. Among them are some towering skyscrapers which often exhibit unique architectural characteristics. In recent years, more and more bold avant-garde constructions have been erected and famous architects from of all over the world participate in the planning, designing, and construction of new skyscrapers. The shoddy buildings of the 1970s are gradually torn down and replaced, using some of the reclaimed land is used to green the area.

The great majority of the population lives in common high-rise buildings, which are usually rather narrow, whereas more affluent citizens reside in smart-living towers with much more comfort and security. However, most skyscrapers are occupied by big *chaebo*l offices and international hotels.

Many of the very wealthy people in Seoul live in so-called villas. These are buildings with four to six floors and designed for only 30 families. They offer a modern living ambiance, while they copy different building styles from different times and places around the world. Villas are often entered via luxurious lounges with elegant ladies at the reception desk or, more frequently, one drives through marble subterranean halls to one's own parking lot. These parking lots contain up to seven automobiles for all conveniences of the family. Besides the full service that is offered in villas, the latest developments of in-house-electronics are available. Additionally, well equipped fitness centers, golf-training lots, beauty parlors, as well as baths with a sauna and pools can be used by the residents. There are lounges for parties, music or movies, cafés, and playgrounds for children. Such luxuries, however, come at a price and a build-in kitchen alone in such an apartment can cost 350,00 dollars.

Single-family houses are rather scarce in the big cities and often belong to old families or extremely rich people. In Seoul, such houses can be found in the urban district of Seongbuk-dong, where the "Blue House," which is the Korean counterpart to the White House in Washington, D.C., is located as well. This is where diplomats, ministers, and *chaebol* families reside. Sometimes, artists and professors, who do not like to settle in high-rise buildings with their community vibe, live here as well. In the suburbs, there are modest houses of families who have lived there for many decades. In the Southwest of Seoul, in the direction of Incheon, there are still some slums that are inhabited by impoverished people, waiting for the area to be gentrified. In the countryside, we find many people living in their own houses. Some of these houses are modest, most are quite orderly, and a few can be called impressive.

In recent years, many residential areas for the middle class have developed, for instance in Seongnam, Daejon, Daegu, or Masan. These areas are built for 40–400 families and include generous common facilities such as small parks, playgrounds, fitness-studios, cafés, and underground parking lots. Many of them do not find a buyer, because the income situation in the provinces is much more modest than in crowded urban areas. Due to a shrinking population, the demand for such apartments will further decrease in the future.

These apartment buildings are in general better equipped than those for the majority of the population in Western countries—although Europeans might miss fireplaces, tiled stoves, a small garden, or swimming pools. The majority of Korean homes is rather standardized. This uniformity makes it unnecessary to invest into a new home and, on the other hand, makes it easy to find new tenants. Because of these circumstances, many Koreans change their lodgings with ease and workers can easily move to places where they can find employment. Similarly, enterprises can smoothly move to another, better location since most of their employees will follow. The nomadic lifestyle of the old Tunguse and Mongols who always followed their livestock to better grazing grounds may be still engrained in the modern Koreans. Mobility and flexibility are important factors of a modern industrial society, which permanently requires new patterns of thinking, learning, replacing everything outmoded, and even moving to other countries.

Koreans like to abandon whatever they despise and in this sense, flexibility serves as a mode of self-fulfillment. Thus, the field of real estate properties is especially mobile and less static in South Korea.

For two decades, the shortage of living spaces triggered permanent price increases. This led to the attitude to look at apartments not as a home, but as a means to increase one's wealth. In particular, clever housewives took part in this thoroughly capitalist system. They uncovered localities which were promising with respect to becoming more valuable and made an advance payment—sometimes many years prior to the completion of a building. These buildings then often had doubled their value when they were ready for new tenants. At first, this only created wealth on paper since a new flat had to be purchased after selling and moving out of the old home. The new flat was often just as expensive as the former one, due to increasing prices. Yet, if a second apartment could be acquired in due course of time, the liquidity could be used for further speculations with almost no risks. This set into motion a merry-go-round which enabled, for example, a famous female minister and professor to purchase a total of 52 apartments which permitted her a luxurious lifestyle.

Professional residential estate speculators borrowed enormous sums from banks. The money was easily granted, as only first-class furnished apartments were bought, which served as excellent guaranties. This made it possible for investors to construct huge housing complexes. During this period, some foreign expatriates had to leave their flats, because the owner had sold them. When moving into a new apartment, very often no rent was required. Instead, the proprietor asked for a high "key money" of up to 75 % of the value of the estate, which in turn was used by the proprietor to acquire new apartments. When these apartments were subsequently sold, the key money could be easily repaid by the value increase of the sold buildings. This so-called *Jeonse* system, which could be regarded as a win–win situation for both sides, is probably globally unique in its form and intensity. Nevertheless, it is recently coming to an end as there are no longer huge gains as real estate prices are no longer increasing but rather decreasing.

An attenuated form of this rental system is the *Wolse* system. Here, one has to pay the owner the rent for one to three month. These payments are entirely paid back at the end of the contract. Additionally, a lower monthly rent is charged as well. It remains to be seen how these systems will work in times of higher inflation and very low interest payments by financial institutions. Some people feel that, despite high taxes on owning multiple houses, their money is better invested in real estate than saving it on bank accounts.

These codes of conduct led to a construction boom, which supplied the nation with much needed housing facilities, created many jobs, and pushed the GNP. Many citizens became rich without real net output. These times are now coming to an end. Today, some 100,000 apartments stay empty and the real estate market is facing hard times. In general, the prices for real estate are falling, except for a few very exclusive locations. The construction industry, which has significantly strengthened the economy, is anxiously looking into the future. Therefore, the government has initiated various infrastructural facilities.

The reasons for this development can be found in the saturation of the housing needs and continued construction activities off the actual needs: Simple living units of the past cannot be sold because of the increased expectations of people whereas expensive apartments are hard to sell because of a lack of affluent customers due to difficult economic circumstances. Only very prestigious locations remain rather untouched by these developments. However, the drastic decrease of the birth rate in South Korea will further enforce a shrinking of the real estate market.

In big cities, small rental rooms of only 3.5–5 m^2, called *gosiwons,* have existed ever since. They serve as temporary retreats for those who are preparing for exams for famous universities or the civil service. Poorer families start to cram into these places as these facilities do not require any deposits.

3.26 Internet Platform (*Taekgeul*)

The Internet can promote the exchange of ideas and experiences, thus generally contributing positively to communication processes. Yet, the Internet can also be misused. Therefore, a critical approach to this medium is absolutely necessary.

The recent President of the USA, Barak Obama, was not the first candidate, who used the Internet in general and social networks in particular, for his electoral campaigns in 2008. Indeed, it was the South Korean presidential candidate, Roo Moo-hyun, who in 2002 employed this modern medium and appealed to his young supporters. To the very surprise of older politicians, he won the election with a landslide. His success marked the beginning of a new age of democracy.

The many positive actions that contribute to a fruitful exchange of opinions and ideas are countered by the misuse of thousands of other Internet users. For instance, it is difficult to verify the information that in some places, the prices for real estate are dramatically dropping. The same is true for the immediately released counterinformation, which claims that the prices of these properties are indeed increasing. Both opinions appear as news, but they are released without any references. Here, the Internet still remains a no man's land.

In October 2010, 782 anonymous entries could be found on the Korean *Yahoo* platform that attacked the politics of President Lee Myung-bak rather incompetently and randomly insulted him in a filthy habit. These "authors" merely voiced their personal desire to relocate to North Korea as soon as possible. Yet, subsequently, only one case of such a relocation became known. It will certainly remain unknown whether the authors were writing from the North or the South as, despite its general backwardness (except in the production of weapons), North Korea employs IT specialists with a great reputation.

In another instance, a famous and successful actress in South Korea committed suicide, because she could not endure the slandering offences that were continuously spread on the Internet. The general public kept wondering if primitive dirty fellows, rivals, or even other agencies were at work to discredit her.

It can be observed in modern industrial societies that technical achievements continue a positive development, while morals and education increasingly decrease. This probably makes a basic education for Koreans in ethics, morale, and philosophy—which might substitute the diminishing virtues of Confucianism—just as mandatory as subjects such as mathematics, physics, biology, and chemistry. The openness toward different religions causes a much desired tolerance and pragmatism in South Korea. However, it also leads to arbitrary attitudes since many sects patchwork the contents of the world religions to use them as it pleases. Traditional values are weakened, morals become hazy, and superstition replaces common sense.

Not only young people waste a considerable amount of time with unproductive games, obtaining unnecessary information, and engaging in shallow dialogues. Besides, a lot of precious time is lost by frequent commercial calls. Hence, a reasonable control of the Internet will become a great task for the future in Korea as well as elsewhere.

3.27 Cultural Aspects

In the global public, the image of Korea is determined by its countless, oftentimes cruel wars against internal as well as external enemies. Of course, one has to keep in mind that Korea has never started a war in its long history. In recent times, Korea is instead recognized as a nation which is extremely successful in technological and economic matters.

Studying the very long history of the country, however, proves that it is above all a nation of culture. From the early production of ceramics to the mythical stories of the country, which was deeply influenced by the aesthetics of Daoism in the arts and crafts, it shows a rich production of cultural assets. At the peak of its expansion (about the middle of the eighth century A.D.), the former southern metropolis of Gyeongju (*Kyongju*) was considered one of the most magnificent cultural centers of the world. It has long since disappeared, and today, we only find a little town on the historical site. Only a few selected remains like the *Bulguksa* temple or the *Sokkuram* grove at the borders of the old city survived. Both sites were restored and belong today to the Unesco World Cultural Heritage. Together with the National Museum of Gyeongju with its famous art collection of sculptures and gold works, they represent the splendid historical past of the town. This city with the oldest observatory in Asia is also called "A Museum without Walls."

Within the walls of the wonderful National Museum in Seoul, we find unique pieces of art. Many displayed objects—and many more, which are preserved in the spacious storehouses—are donations of distinguished Korean personalities. Not only in Seoul, but almost everywhere in the country do we find a great variety of museums and exhibitions of all kinds of arts and genres. This great variety is stunning if we take into considerations that these are just the remaining pieces that were preserved throughout centuries of unrest. Many objects have been destroyed in wars or were stolen by invaders. Between 1592 and 1597, the Japanese alone systematically pillaged the whole country. Until recent times, Western foreigners tried to steal cultural assets from the country. On his latest official visit to Seoul, President Obama returned some precious historical seals, which had been stolen by soldiers during the Korean War. Furthermore, many paintings and scripts fell victim to unfavorable atmospheric conditions. When walking through Korean museums, it is noteworthy that we see almost only local displays, whereas in London, Paris, Berlin, New York, or Tokyo, many objects are exhibited that arrived there through theft, force, or deceit. Korea still has to claim a variety of incalculable cultural assets from institutions around the world.

As in many other great cultural nations, national heroes emerge from the fields of economy, natural sciences, sports, or entertainment while only very few are known from the fine arts. Admirers of the old Korea lament the vanishing of the poetic and artistic abilities of the nation. Nevertheless, great efforts are taken to support and strengthen the performing arts. Seoul has become a global center for concerts, exhibitions, and symposia of all kinds. Lately, some Koreans have gained international fame in the field of literature and the movie business. All leading newspapers of the country—including their English editions—cover daily important cultural events such within the movies, all sorts of music, exhibitions, literary publications, or any other artistic outputs both nationally and internationally.

3.28 Sports

As in many other nations, original Korean sport disciplines are derived from martial arts. Archery is one of the categories in which Korea excels in international competitions. Koreans have already won numerous medals at world championships and Olympic Games.

Korean combat sports such as *taekgyeon*, *hapkido*, and *taekwondo* are quite well known; the latter is very popular and the national *taekwondo* association counts approximately 3.8 million members. It has also become an Olympic discipline. *Ssireum*, a form of wrestling similar to the Japanese *sumo*, is popular as well. In the past, hard-working Koreans did not have much leisure time and thus could not spend many hours to practice sports. Consequently, people concentrated on professional sports that would allow them to earn money such as baseball, golf, boxing, soccer, ice skating, and recently cycling as well as tennis.

In the USA and Europe, sports-minded people can find countless private sport clubs. As idealists, they can practice many marginalized types of sports such as rowing, canoeing, diving, sailing, and different kinds of track and field, as well as swimming, fencing, or certain winter sports. In South Korea, the *chaebol* and their owners generously sponsor some kinds of sports. As a result, Korea won an Olympic gold medal in baseball (Beijing), a long-standing domain of the USA. South Korea also produces many fine golfers, especially outstanding women. For a long time, Kim Yu-na was the queen of ice skating while both men and women won a lot of medals in short track events. Even an Olympic bronze medal was won by the South Korean soccer team (London). In the realm of amateur-like sports, not many noteworthy outcomes can be notified. Exceptions are perhaps found in marathon races, occasionally shooting competitions, boxing, table tennis, fencing, weight lifting and swimming, where one Korean swimmer won an Olympic gold medal in Sydney (400 m freestyle, Pak Tae-hwan).

Instead of private sport clubs, the athletes practice in schools or universities and, above all, in company facilities. This is why there are many active basketball, volleyball, and handball teams. The big *chaebol* leaders usually head a particular sports association such as soccer, boxing, archery, etc. They are of course expected to support this association with all organizational and material means. The Samsung chairman Lee Kun-hee even serves as member of the International Olympic Committee.

Many business tycoons are die-hard baseball fans. Thus, eight out of the nine clubs of the Korean top baseball league are dominated by the *chaebol*. Most of these top managers have studied in the USA or Japan and have played this game themselves. Baseball ranks among the most popular sports in both countries, the USA, and Japan. Enormous funds are invested into the clubs and their players earn fabulous salaries and bonuses. Just as the *chaebol* dominate the whole nation, baseball dominates the South Korean TV channels. Only golf enjoys a similar coverage of the airtime. Though soccer becomes increasingly popular among young sporty people, it has great difficulties to survive against the concentrated power of the *chaebol*-sponsored baseball clubs. But the situation is gradually changing because some *chaebol* have started to sponsor their own soccer teams.

Hiking and trekking are very popular sports among members of all age groups. People pay much attention to dress and equip properly—something that can be observed for all other physical forms of training as well. If one wants to play a little bit of baseball, this first requires to buy an almost professional outfit. This behavior is a bonanza for companies selling sportswear or equipment for indoor and outdoor activities.

Literature

1. Ministry of Culture and Information (1982) A handbook of Korea, 4th edn. Seoul, p 82
2. Ministry of Culture and Information; cit. pp 435–536
3. Ministry of Culture and Information (2004) Handbook of Korea, 11th edn. Seoul, pp 275–276
4. Lueras L, Chung N (eds) Korea; Honolulu 1981; p 316
5. Compare Lovell J, Lovell A (1984) Korean impact on Japanese culture. Elizabeth (NJ), Seoul
6. Wittvogel K (1981) Oriental despotism. New York/Yale, p 6
7. Ministry of Culture and Information; Handbook of Korea, 11th edn; cit. p 183
8. Compare S, James C (2009) The art of not being governed. New Haven
9. Eun K-S (2008) Family values changing—but still conservative. In: Kim KD (ed) Social change in Korea, Seoul, pp 146–147
10. Lee, J-K The South Korean Family. In: Kim KD (ed) Social change in Korea; cit. p 158

11. Kern, T (2005) Suedkoreas Bildungs- und Forschungssystem; in Th. Kern/ P. Koellner (Eds); Suedkorea und Nordkorea; Frankfurt/ New York, p 166
12. Kern T; cit. p. 161
13. Saccone R (2001) Negotiating your way through Korea; Elizabeth (NJ)/ Seoul, p 128
14. Kim J (1991) The Koreans; their mind and behavior, Seoul, pp 31–44
15. EikemeierD, Schamanismus; in Ch. Auffahrt/ J. Bernard/H. Mohr; Metzler Lexikon Religion; vol. 3. Paginismus - Zombie; Stuttgart/Weimar 2000; p 241
16. Maull H, Maull I (1987) KOREA; Muenchen, p 109
17. Chung Y (1999) Die alten Koenigreiche; Muenchen 1999; p 8
18. Routledge Encyclopedia of Philosophy; London/New York 2000
19. Eikemeier D (1989) Himmel - Erde - Mensch; in K. Kitamura; KOREA; Zuerich 1989; p. 122
20. Eikemeier D; Himmel - Erde - Mensch; cit. p 190
21. Henderson G (1978) Korea—The politics of the vortex. Cambridge (Mass.), pp 225–226
22. Han Y (2014) An intellectual history of Seonbi in Korea; Paju, p 13
23. Myers BR (2011) The cleanest race. Brooklin, NY, p 58
24. Deuchler M (2004) Neo-confucianism in the early Joseon Dynasty: some reflections on the role of Ye. In: National Commission for the UNESCO; Korean Philosophy: Its Tradition and Modern Transformation; Elizabeth (NJ)/ Seoul, p 51
25. Choi D (1982) Western law and traditional society in Korea. In: Ch. Kim J (ed) Business laws in Korea; Seoul, pp 34–64

Chapter 4
State and Economy—Essential Development Principles

4.1 Falling Victim to Rapacious Neighbors

Korea could have been a prosperous and happy country in world history. It has a wonderful landscape, fertile plains crossed by rivers, a nice climate with distinct seasons, and tough, strenuous people. In the northern regions, it has rich mineral resources and is only scarcely confronted with natural catastrophes such as floods, sometimes leading to landslides in the mountainous regions. These circumstances lay the foundations for a successful economic development. Furthermore, the access to China, which is itself a great civilization, provided the nation with useful know-how and helpful input. However, Korea was attractive to its bordering countries in the north, east, and west, which ultimately prevented an uninterrupted development of the nation, and it repeatedly fell victim to its greedy neighbors.

In particular, Siberian and Mongolian nomadic tribes left their bloody footsteps all over the peninsula. They sacked the riches, devastated cultural assets, robbed gold and silver, kidnapped women, and killed and enslaved a substantial part of the population. The first devastating invasions of recent history took place between 1215 and 1381 and climaxed with Kubilai Khan in 1274 and 1281. The outrageous conqueror wanted to invade Japan and twice assembled mighty forces in Korea, which had to provide the costs for the equipment, ships, food, and auxiliary troops [1].

The bellicose Khan started both attempts from the southeastern corner of Korea. The local population, experienced in shipbuilding, had to construct a huge fleet, which they had to furnish as well. Both attacks failed because of the vigorous resistance of the Japanese samurai and due to seasonal typhoons, the so-called divine winds (*kamikaze*). They dispersed the fleet, sank numerous ships, or caused heavy damage. The main burden of these failed operations was carried by the Koreans. Only one-fifth of the second armada of Kubilai Khan, including 4400 ships and 140,000 men, escaped the military and natural catastrophes. The Mongols had completely overextended the range of their domain from the

D.K. Schneidewind, *Economic Miracle Market South Korea*,
DOI 10.1007/978-981-10-0615-9_4

Near East to the Far East and were not able to manage the numerous insurrections against them with their limited own human resources. They were frequently entangled into Chinese and Korean revolts, especially at their southern borders. Only around 1380 did the Mongolian reign over Korea finally end and left the country completely worn-out with the crafts, agriculture, and trade paralyzed.

With the beginning of the Yi Dynasty (from 1392), the state regenerated and Joseon under its outstanding king Sejong recovered and was led to new intellectual, cultural, scientific, and economic heights. The enlightened monarch implemented a series of successful reforms and initiated many military and civil structures. The crafts, trade, and agriculture blossomed. Because a formal patronage (*sadae*) of China was acknowledged, Korea enjoyed a long period of peace at her Western front.

Yet, on its eastern front was stricken with many disturbances. Over many decades, Japanese pirates had plagued the coasts and their towns. Also, a considerable number of Japanese had settled in the south of the country from the mid-fifteenth century. These settlers engaged in revolts and started combats with the inhabitants of their guest country. These difficulties were finally overcome; however, they had a long-lasting weakening effect on Korea.

Roughly a century later, another blow came from Japan when Shogun Toyotomi Hideyoshi had the insane idea to conquer China. Korea denied Hideyoshi's troop to pass through the country. As a result, in 1592, 150,000 Japanese warriors invaded the country, reached Seoul in only 20 days, and continued their way to the river Yalu, the border to China. The Korean troops were no match as they were neither well organized nor did they have modern weapons like the Japanese, who had firearms. While crossing the country, the Japanese destroyed dams, irrigation systems, bridges, palaces, temples, and all different kinds of buildings and houses. The Japanese fortunes of war ended when the Chinese entered the battlefields and pushed the samurai back, who were not prepared for the cold Korean winter and did not have any provisions. Meanwhile, the ingenious Korean admiral Yi Sun-shin had cut off the Japanese support at the southern harbors.

The Japanese attackers had to hastily retreat. Yet, they took time to take along with them all valuable art and old scripts that they could get hold of. Additionally, thousands of artisans, craftsmen, and scholars were departed. After this withdrawal, the Japanese reappeared in 1597 and rushed across the country up to Pyeongyang. Again, the Chinese rushed to help and the Japanese fleet was again fatally damaged at the southern shores. But afterward, Joseon was economically paralyzed. More than two-thirds of the farmland was devastated. The nation was thrown back for 100 years. These traumatic events are unforgotten in Korea until today.

The slow recovery was ruined with the next invasion, this time from the Manchu of the north in 1627. They came with a giant army and overran northwestern Korea, because the Yi government was loyal to the Ming Dynasty and the Manchu intended to conquer China. Joseon did not keep the strict neutrality it had promised in 1636, and therefore, the Manchu ventured upon a second invasion. "Subsequently, a tremendous amount of gold, silver, grain and other products of Korea, as well as a large number of skilled workers, were sent to the Manchu court. Needless to say that the war with the Manchus and the tribute goods sent to them caused a tremendous economic strain and hardship for the Korean people" [2]. But in 1644, the Manchu overpowered the Ming, established the Ching Dynasty, and took over the rule of China as a whole. They considered Korea as a loyal vassal state and allowed the nation to take care of its internal affairs. Afterward, Korea cut itself off from the rest of the world and inflicted the death penalty on those who dared to enter the country. This radical, and to a certain extent almost fatal, decision disconnected the nation from all international know-how.

At the beginning of the nineteenth century, Korea was ruled by weak child-kings, respectively, their guardians. Due to its seclusion from the outside world as well as permanent internal discordances, Korea lost touch with ongoing global developments. This led to the nation falling behind when it came to technological know-how and was responsible for its economic weakness, which ultimately resulted in military vulnerability. This development did not remain unnoticed by some foreign powers.

Beginning in 1895, Japan had established its presence in Korea and successively taken over the administration of the state. Many small riots failed to change the situation. On the contrary, they rather disturbed a persistent economic recovery of the country.

Japan's aim was the extension of its territory in order to widen its economic basis. It had recognized that its main rival on the other side of the Pacific, the United States of America, had a much bigger economic platform that was necessary for a modern great power to stand its ground. (A platform that Russia does not possess anymore and that China is working for very hard at the moment). Therefore, Japan modernized its neighboring country and its socioeconomic structures. The educational system was substantially reformed, Western measurements and weights were introduced, and the public finance was put under Japanese control.

Korea was used as a deployment zone and source of supplies for the Japanese in the Japanese wars with China (1985) and Russia (1905). Within the country, the Japanese military suppressed any resistance and finally perfected the annexation of Korea. Thenceforward, Korea delivered mineral resources, food, and blue-collar workers for the Japanese industry and, at the same time, served as a sales market for its colonial ruler. Japanese conglomerations, traders, and farmers poured into Korea. In 1911, the number of Japanese immigrants had already passed 200,000. The best farmland was expropriated and issued to Japanese settlers. In particular, the fields of the Jeolla Province, which were renowned for the excellent rice that was produced there, were in the focus of the colonizers.

The colonizers made sure to have control of all educational institutions and adjusted them according to their needs. They wanted to make sure that Koreans were educated to become solid and loyal workers were and not bright students. Consequently, they lowered the quality of the teaching contents. In this context, it is also worth mentioning that the Korean society nevertheless profited a lot from the administrational systems, the agrarian know-how, the industrial management, the communication system, and the traffic infrastructure, which were left by the colonial powers after the Second World War. Japan had indeed invested huge amounts in these fields that had been rather underdeveloped prior to the Japanese reign.

The end of the war in 1945 brought no salvation to the country, which had been maltreated for centuries. A few days after the dropping of the atomic bombs on Hiroshima and Nagasaki, the Soviet Union hurried to enter the war in the Far East and marched into Korea on August 10, 1945. The Soviet Union was connected to Korea via a small border strip. The Soviet troops stopped at the 38th parallel, which they had agreed upon with the Americans to serve as a demarcation line. Again, the fate of the peninsula was at the hands of foreign powers. The Allied Forces agreed on an American, Soviet, and Chinese trusteeship of Korea for five years. However, this did not happen, because both Koreas proclaimed their own government, thereby sealing the division of the country. The industry remained in the north, whereas the south continued to focus on farming—a bad deal for both sides.

4.2 Internal Discordances

Besides invasions by rapacious neighbors, the country also suffered severe setbacks due to internal rivalries and discordances. A striking example for this is the history of the three Kingdoms of Shilla, Baekje, and Goguryeo. These kingdoms fought each other between the fourth and the ninth century A.D. During their fights, they called upon foreign auxiliary troops for support. For instance, Shilla asked China for help, while Baekche called for Japan. Later, Shilla united the three kingdoms, yet a part of Goguryeo, under the lead of General Tae Chopong, did not join the union but set up another state in Manchuria, called Parhae (also Balhae or Bohai), which comprised of a large part of northeastern Korea. Although many inhabitants belonged to local ethic groups like the Mohe (later called Jurchens), Parhae was actually a Korean state. Nevertheless, it tried to conspire with the Japanese in order to attack Shilla from the east.

Likewise, at the end of the nineteenth century, various Korean factions alternately courted the Chinese, Russians, and Japanese to gain their support instead of acting in the best interest for their country.

For South Korea, the civil war turned out to be as devastating as earlier fights against the Mongols, Japanese, and Chinese, when their ruler Kim Il-sung plotted a nasty war. The military campaigns devastated the country beyond comprehension. In the course of the military actions, Seoul was conquered four times by the north and was entirely destroyed. North Korea suffered from the bombardments of the US Air Force, which neither spared housing compounds nor dikes or irrigation systems. Bewildered, the world witnessed the brutality between North and South

Korea. The atrocities continued in the South even after the armistice, when all fellow citizens who were suspected of Communist convictions were murdered and Socialist activities were relentlessly suppressed on the island of Jeju and in the province of Jeolla.

Hostilities between different groups have a long and fateful history in the country. "The word 'Korean' became synonymous with factionalism even in international communist circles" [3]. Wherever an organization or community is established, there is also an opposition. Both sides hardly compromise and are not too keen to live peacefully together, but prefer intense quarrels. This quarrelsome character of Koreans can be found in all organizations, on administrational levels, and even in sport clubs or in property managements. Maybe the *chaebol*, as huge business conglomerations, are an exception as they are ruled by patriarchal owners.

Since democracy is mainly defined by the art of compromising, many people wonder about the stability of democracy in South Korea today. It is generally agreed that it is indeed rather strong. The politicians as well as the voters appear well educated concerning the modern democratic systems. The negative images of dictatorship in the neighboring north, alongside negative past experience with military dictatorships in the country, are deterrent examples for South Korean electors. The challenge of dealing with conflicting opinions is, after all, good for competitions, and competitions are one of the keys of market success.

4.3 Resistance to Changes for Conservative and Structural Reasons

Modern Korea is well known for its ability to swiftly and dynamically follow changes in many fields. However, the effectiveness of the society can be slowed down by the division of a rich minority that makes all decisions and citizens who are only cogs in a machine and become increasingly poorer. This could easily divide the South Korean society in the medium and long term. Traditionally, there has always been a social rift in Korea. During the 500 years of the Joseon period, there was an upper class of civilians and military officials of about 10 %. Their status derived from scholarly examinations about the doctrines of Neo-Confucianism. Serving in government was the only desired form of employment, and their authority was unchallenged by the other 90 % of the population. Their orders were simply followed. Commoners had to contribute with their manual services and tax payments in kind and money. Though openly commoners paid respect to the upper class, they silently despised them. In many popular songs or plays, they ridiculed them for doing nothing meaningful and for only adhering to scholarly disputes.

The general opinion was that the king should first and foremost take care of the well-being of his subjects. However, only very few exemplary rulers followed this idea, as for example King Sejong the Great (1418–1450). Other rulers did only hardly respect this dictum or even dismissed it completely. During the time of the Goryeo Dynasty (918–1392), a selection procedure for higher public offices as well as for military organization was established. It was based on official public examinations with very high requirements. The studies for the examination necessitated the knowledge of traditional Chinese writings and its classical commentaries. In Korea, these writings were mainly the lessons of Confucianism, whereas the rich works on Daoism were generally neglected. The Confucian writings focused extensively on the statesmanship and the question of how to shape a harmonious society within a hierarchy, thus defining the role and positions of rulers and servants, fathers and sons, and husbands and wives. After having successfully passed the examinations, no more than 10 % of the citizens—excluding slaves, who made about 60 % of the population—could climb the social latter and work in offices of the *yangban* level. This class was freed from any type of manual labor and taxes.

The *yangban* status was actually not hereditary. But the sons of *yangban* had the best chances to succeed in the public examinations. Marriages between members of the *yangban* class and people from other classes were strictly forbidden. Consequently, the *yangban* remained among itself. In the close proximity of the royal palace, the rulers usually made sure that the *yangban* took care of the well-being of their subjects. The great majority of the *yangban*, however, lived far away in provinces and it took days of travel until they reached the court. Away from the control of the royalty, they only cared about their own prosperity and that of their families. Their behavior was sometimes despotic, and they were even empowered to decree death penalties. The well-being of the citizens was of no real interest to most of them until more modern times (about 1850).

These circumstances were described in a legendary romance, the Chungyang Tale. It is still very present until today in numerous stage productions, plays, narratives, and movies.

Once upon a time a young man of letters of high standing lived in the city of Namwon in the far away province of Jeolla. He fell in love with a commoner beauty. They promised each other their eternal love as he left for the capital. After a few years, the young lover successfully passed the difficult examination for public services and was appointed to a high position at a distant court of the capital. Meanwhile, in Namwon, a new *yangban* was appointed, who was attracted to the young lonely beautiful woman. When she refused to marry him—keeping her former promise in mind—he sentenced her to death because of disobedience.

Her secret fiancé meanwhile held the honorable position of an *am haeng eosa*, which meant that he was a secret inspector of the king and travelled incognito through the provinces in order to uncover wrong doings. He arrived in due time at Namwon, dismissed the despotic *yangban* from his offices, and received a special permission from the king to marry his beloved fiancé and to live together with her in the capital.

The substance of this legend is considered until today by high government circles as ideal. A memorial of the heroine Chunhyang was erected in 1920 in the lovely Gwanghallu park of Namwon. Until today, it is a very popular tourist destination.

Besides the *yangban* and the commoners, there also existed people of low standing, who either worked in fields that were despised by the majority such as butchers, tanners, or executioners or served as slaves for the government and higher-ranking persons. This group of people made up 50–60 % of the entire population. These people could not be promoted to important offices, no matter how intelligent they were. Thus, the development of a broad middle class was slowed down and consequently no healthy medium- or small-sized businesses were established. This in turn led to the fact that there was hardly any demand for goods and services on a big scale. The national economy was, on a long term, doomed to stagnation.

Even in the democratized population of South Korea of today, similar structures are still visible. The class barriers, however, can be in general bypassed by everybody with a proper education. The upper class of perhaps 5 % includes the *chaebol* owners, high-ranking officials, and many *nouveau riche* families. 75 % belongs to properly installed administrative officers, normal managers, skilled workers, and farmers. The last 20 % is comprised of relatively uneducated people who live and are work for low wages, for example, as taxi drivers, delivery drivers, messengers, housekeepers, small retailers, and unskilled laborers.

Many people are dissatisfied with their social circumstances. Some are going on strikes and even more gather for protest marches. So far, the situation has improved through the general economic progress for the majority of the population. The government is thus anxious to ensure a continuation of the economic growth in order to avoid tensions and problems.

There have always been socialistic and Communist tendencies in South Korea. Most of leaders of such formations have been exposed and eliminated. The majority of South Koreans perceive The Northern Regime as horrifying and discouraging. The race for the better social system is convincingly won by the Southern democracy. In South Korea, people know that at least 90 % of the inhabitants of North Korea live in extreme poverty and are hungry. Thus, Communism has become synonymous with poor living standards, except for the dictators in charge and those close to them. Kindermann [4] once said that pluralism should never be allowed in a Socialist society. This of course does not apply to the 10 % of his leading cadres and their privileged helpers.

In addition, we have to take into account that in the Far East—China, Taiwan, Korea, and Vietnam, and to a certain extent in Japan—material wealth is considered as the most desired objective in life. There is little understanding for the Christian parable of a wealthy man, who will rather pass the eye of a needle than enter paradise; instead, a wealthy man is rather idolized in East Asia. The capitalistic greed for material wealth in modern China led to an enormous growth of its GNP and is admired by South Korea.

South Koreans marvel at those who have become immeasurably rich by creative business ideas, but most people do not mind how one accumulates wealth. Economically meaningless financial manipulations, speculative stock trade, erratic real estate businesses, gambling, and even criminal practices are likewise admired, and successful people are not met with envy as in Europe. Instead, one tries to learn their methods or secrets. Many Koreans are not immune to gambling, but in general, they study and work very hard. One hardly finds luxurious cars in Seoul that were scratched with a key, although their owners tend to brag with them, even if they cannot really afford such a car. Like in China, there is no such thing as a car that is too big for a man or a handbag that is too expensive for a woman.

4.4 Insecurities in the Postwar Years (1945–1960)

It is generally known that good luck and even more good timing are fine perquisites for economic success, but there are not such things as miracles in the realistic sense. Still, South Koreas' spectacular growth in the last 40 years comes very close to a miracle. As pointed out in earlier chapters, the initial situation was conceivably unfavorable. Losses through neighboring nations and by internal devastations prevented the accumulation of noteworthy state properties and private properties.

The *yangban* class suppressed the vitality and creativity of the people. There was no age of Renaissance concerning ideas and attitudes as neither the industriousness of Calvinism nor the Protestant work ethic prevailed. The permanent state of defense since the division of the country in 1945 devoured enormous financial means, which had amounted to 20 % of the national budget for a certain time. The compulsory military service was set at 18 months, after it had been 30 months for several decades. This withheld valuable working forces from the economic system as well as investment resources.

Like many economically successful nations (Switzerland, The Netherlands, Denmark, Japan, Germany, Singapore etc.), South Korea does not have significant mineral resources. In all these countries, the right economic mind-set was the driving force behind their economic achievements and led to welfare of the population. Unfortunately, in many of these countries, this attitude seems to decrease. Initially, Germany served as a model for Korean. But from the seventies of the last century, the USA has taken this role, as this nation is considered more dynamic. However, since the hard and productive labor in the USA is partly replaced by financial strategies, which are plotted behind comfortable desks in offices and which normally do not contribute anything useful for the economy, China has become a new and admired role model. Presently, South Korea seems to turn to this new economic colossus.

After World War II, compared to North Korea, South Korea found itself in an unfavorable situation. In the first instance, it was not supported by the USA, whereas The Northern Regime was established and provided for by the USSR and China. The Communist country quickly had a modern army, a great number of modern weapons, and even state-of-the-art jet fighters. When the occupational forces left the country in 1948, as it was mutually agreed on by the USSR and the USA, South Korea was left behind almost defenseless.

North Korea had almost all mineral resources of the peninsula. In particular, coal was important as a primary source of energy. On this basis, the Japanese had already erected a noteworthy heavy industry as well as a chemical industry there. Both industries were further expanded with the assistance of the Soviet Union. South Korea, on the contrary, was a purely agrarian country and of no economic interest for the USA. Nevertheless, the South Korean government made a very important decision, which became one of the most important bases for the later development of the country: a wide-ranging agrarian reform. Significantly, such a reform also marked the beginning of the rise of Japan. In the Philippines, however, it caused a permanent paralysis of the economic engagement of its population.

In former times, the inhabitants of North Korea were considered to be serious-minded and energetic, whereas their southern compatriots had the image of being rather easygoing. In the past, the kings in Pyeongyang even forbade marriages of the nobility with southern women. The fact that the *yangbang* system was less widespread in the northern and northeastern parts of Korea than in the west and south is as well noteworthy.

Another distinction between the two countries was that Kim Sung-il in the North patronized the industry, as it was supposed to provide the basis for his military strength, while Li Sung-man in the South was an ambitious ideologist, who did not show any particular interest in the economic field or concerning technological ideas and did not engage in these fields. He further lacked any competence in these decisive sectors. Both politicians were fervent patriots and wanted to unite the nation—and of course both wanted this to happen under their leadership. The rather tall Kim Sung-il was initially considered as a tough man, who had already fought against the Japanese in China as well as in Manchuria. His adversary in the South, with an average stature, had instead acted predominantly—without any success—in the international diplomatic arena and had lived for many years during the war in the USA, where he had studied and got a doctoral degree. He liked to be called Dr. Syngman Rhee and was married to an Austrian woman, a fact that did not support his low popularity.

Kim Sung-il clearly controlled—backend by Stalin—the North, whereas Rhee had many political rivals in the South. The majority of able and farsighted personalities from the Northern provinces had fled to South Korea, mainly to Seoul. Rhee's many appeals to the Americans were met with lukewarm or no responses at all. After the initially disastrous military defeat following the armistice, he engaged in political maneuvering. Rhee was a descendant from a *yangban* family and had no vocational or practical experiences. Consequently, he had no specific plans to develop the society. Additionally, his government lacked administrative knowledge after the retreat of the Japanese. Rhee, a die-hard hater of Japan, did not even consider for a moment to make any use of the former administrative officers. Another big problem he had to face was the infiltration of South Korea by northern squads that organized numerous acts of sabotages.

The USA had rather naively expected that South Korea would automatically develop on its own, despite its lack of experience and tradition in democratic rules, into a typical democratic country. But under the reign of Syngman Rhee, who increasingly behaved like an autocrat, a number of insurrections, which were often triggered out by students, occurred in the south. He bloodily suppressed these insurrections, although it was known that some North Koreans were involved in the actions and Rhee became increasingly unpopular.

Facing a hopeless candidacy in the 1960s elections, Rhee announced his retirement and went into exile in Hawaii, where he passed away in 1965 after a sixty-year-long fight for his country. Nahm [5] notes: "The bureaucratic political heritage and the feudalistic social order of the past, the legacies of Japanese colonial rule, and the division of the country constituted insurmountable obstacles to the promotion of democratic institutions and a new way of life." It seemed that most of the leading Koreans of that time still lived with the mental heritage of the Yi Dynasty and simply omitted the importance of a prospering national economy.

Until the retirement of Rhee and the end of the First Republic, there was very little economic progress in South Korea. This was, among other things, caused by the lack of scientists, technicians, economists, and managers, caused by the fact that the education of these specialists had been rigorously suppressed by the Japanese occupants. A further reason for the lack of an economic progress was the enormous expansion of the population after the 1953 armistice that plunged South Korea into poverty and caused a drastic inflation. There was a fundamental lack of capital to establish an export-intensive industry and to import the necessary sources of energy, food, and raw materials.

4.5 The Era of Pak Chung-hee and the Military

In the late 1950s, the Americans started to supply South Korea with food, fertilizer, and capital. But the successors of Syngman Rhee could not really handle the demands of the market economy, which was insistently claimed by the USA. As soon as in spring 1961, a bloodless coup *d'état* terminated the Second Republic (the first armed uprising since 1392). 250 military officers under the lead of a second rank military major general Pak Chung-hee took control of the country and restored order.

The nation remained under the major general politically underdeveloped. Yet, it soared to the status of a mighty industrial nation. Park became the father of a Korean "Economic Miracle." The nation was lucky enough to have the right man at the right time at the right place. At later times, this general with his understanding of democracy would not have had any legitimacy to rule the country.

The major general, born in 1917 in the small town of Gumi in the northern Gyeongsang province, was of humble origin and is suspected to have been attracted by Communist ideas when he was younger. After a brief period as a schoolteacher, he joined the Japanese army under the name of Takagi, Masao. In Manchuria, he enrolled in an officer's school, served successfully as an officer, and entered the Japanese military academy in Tokyo where he climbed to the rank of a lieutenant. Living in Manchuria, he observed how the agrarian country reached a high industrial status under the command of the Japanese army within only one decade. After the Second World War, he graduated from the Choson

Defense Guard School, a kind of police academy, which became the core of the later South Korean army.

Leftist elements of this unit staged the Yeosu Rebellion and were subsequently crushed. Park, being a member of the South Korea Workers Party, was sentenced to death as he was suspected to have actively taken part in the unrest. Later, he was pardoned and his death sentence was turned into 20 years in prison. After he submitted secret structures of the party and names of their leaders, he was released and got an assignment at the intelligence of the army. Park was appreciated by some higher militaries, which saved him from some critical situations when he, for example, predicted an invasion from North Korea seven months before it happened. During and after the Korean War, Park was repeatedly promoted. Maybe because of his Communist experiences, he became an implacable opponent of all Socialist systems.

It is said Park hated and admired Japan at the same time and used it as a role model. He became almost synonymous with military discipline and technocratic leadership. According to him, democratic forms of government were to be installed only at a later point in time. Very ambitious five-year plans were established under his leadership—and surpassed. The free enterprise system was continued, but it was put at the service of a long-term sustainable development of the state. Following the Japanese example, this was planned by a competent ministerial bureaucracy (administrative guidance = *haengjeong chido*).

The slogan of the Park era was "*kyeong chae chaeiljuui*," which translates into "economy first." The admirable economic growth required sacrifices and came with a high price: Manpower was rigorously exploited, the freedom of citizens was confined within limits as, for instance, the freedom to travel was annulled, and the gap between cities and the countryside temporarily widened. The focus on Seoul became overwhelming, the level of foreign debts inflated, and a few conglomerates, the famous/infamous *chaebol*, grew as almost all capital reserves were concentrated on them. This paralyzed small- and medium-sized companies, and the retail trade was shoved aside to cheap markets and small street outlets. Quality goods had to be sold directly at front doors, a trade route that later became almost obsolete. Its function has meanwhile been taken over by increasingly big department store chains and supermarkets, in which the *chaebol* invested heavily.

Economic pioneers such as Chung Ju-yung, who founded Hyundai in 1950, or Kim Woo-choong who build up Daewoo in 1964, as well as Lee Byung-chull, who initially founded Samsung in 1938 as a trading company and reinvented the company in 1969, turning it into the most powerful conglomerate in Korea today, were all authoritarian figures with a "can do" (*hamyeon teonda*) character. They were hungry for success, self-assured, hardworking, and much disciplined. Besides these positive qualities, the typical Korean evils of nepotism and corruption could be observed that later became the Achilles heel of the *chaebol*. Any period in the development of an enterprise (or that of a nation) requires a specific type of action. The development of South Korea from an underdeveloped agrarian state to a leading industrial power initially demanded robust pioneers, who trusted their socio-economic instincts and will to power.

Workers, who had to acquire their skills and competences on the job, were numerous and therefore cheap. Production know-how was obtained to a large extent by license-taking from Japan. Product development was replaced by swarming out into industrialized nations in order to either obtain licenses or by spying them out. Foreign rivals within the country were stopped by takeovers or by the government assigning monopolies. The necessary basis of raw materials and energy sources were obtained by export promotions, whereas at the same time, non-desired imports were rigorously dismissed.

The first necessity was the provision of finance. Capital was provided by joint ventures, preferably with US-American participation as well as government guarantees for overseas capital acquisitions. The various subsidiaries of the *chaebol* also created capital with numerous internal financial transactions, which were neglected by the authorities. The price for this was paid by accepting governmental guidance, which could be loosed by corrupt deals with omnipotent bureaucrats and, ultimately, in the time after Park, with leading heads of state. There was hardly any room for real democratic rules. In particular, regional and local authorities were deprived of their autonomy in favor of central bureaucratic powers in the companies' headquarter.

In a second step, the workers were to be further trained to develop their ability to evolve their own sophisticated production know-how. In order to decrease license payments, research capacities had to be expanded and deepened. Complex management structures needed to replace the high-handed decisions of authoritarian patriarchs and, above all, a modern financial system had to be introduced. Last but not least, slowly but steadily, democratic institutions had to be further developed.

In a third phase, universities had to be modernized and improved to an international standard. Internationally accepted accounting standards enable corporate governance and a system of fair taxation. All layers of society should cooperate freely and autonomously run institutions. These new networks should then be integrated into the global economy and other organizations. In Korea, a former "hermit kingdom," the drastic changes were surprisingly successful and the very self-confident nation takes this for granted.

Initially, the Japan example was followed, and the Korean government defined the main objectives. Instead of widely dispersed entrepreneurial visions, this enterprise was controlled by governmental planning authorities that mainly controlled the scarce financial means of the state. Nevertheless, the economic planning did not result in rigid five-year plans as in many Communist countries at that time. Instead, plans were discussed and drawn up together with the big conglomerates and continuously observed and permanently flexibly adjusted.

I took several decades until the South Korean economy developed itself from own initiatives and strength and established itself on an international basis. Similar evolutions can be observed with numerous developing countries today. South Korea was followed as a model, especially by China in a couple of instances.

The globally admired ascend of Korea from the rubble of war to a leading technological and economic power has to be ascribed to the diligence and hardships that South Koreans endured. President Park, however, has to be given credit that he overcame the traditional resistance to change and personal sacrifices of the population. He took action against old social tensions and pragmatically worked without pretensions. He had to fight the aspirations of the Confucian-infused officialdom. The elite of the *yangban* was basically contempt for commercial and technical issues. The five-year plans of his government served as a meaningful and expedient framework for the industry and the general public to achieve his goals.

Park had to overcome animosities of his compatriots against the Japanese when he pursued realpolitik in establishing diplomatic relations with Korea's old foe Japan. "The needs of the time compelled Park to lean on Japan, inextricably tying South Korea's economic future to that of its neighbor" [6]. In Japan, there was also a strong opposition to reconcile with the neighbor. After Park had signed a treaty with Japan that normalized the relationship between Korea and Japan on June 22, 1965, in Tokyo, the economic relations between the two countries increased dramatically. Huge amounts of capital were invested by Japanese companies; Japan gave heavy loans to Korea and allowed to obtain many licenses from the advanced Japanese industry. Furthermore, half a million Japanese tourists annually brought hard currency to their Western neighbor. Many Korean businessmen used the New Year festivities and other holidays to attend managerial educational programs in Japan.

If the country wanted to achieve within a quarter of a century what other developed nations had achieved in a full century, the state had to set clear aims and to distribute the limited financial resources among the desired projects. The president and his able advisors had always a keen eye on the skillful planning abilities of Japan. The neighbor had to fight a lack of natural resources and capital as well. The Korean government further tried to avoid mistakes that Japan had made. The long-term plans of South Korea stretched roughly over 25 years and from 1962 to 1986. The plan involved two parts: (1) it put the relevant industrial fields in a sequential order and (2) at the same time, aimed at improving the quality of the output by completing five phases: (1) direct protection stage, (2) targeted support stage, (3) independent development stage, (4) full-scale international competition stage, and (5) world-class stage.

The First Five Year Plan involved the strengthening of the infrastructure and promoting the educational sector. At the same time, modern power plants were built. The government directed its special attention to stimulating the export industries, initially including the textile industry. Eventually, the agrarian base was invigorated to save foreign exchange reserves by replacing the import of food supplies and to secure the livelihood of the rural population.

The second five-year plan extended of the industrial sector. Labor-intensive industries within the fields of electrical appliances, precision mechanics, plastics, and food were promoted. The construction of roads, highways, railway lines, harbors, telephone circuits, and high tension cables was pursued with great enthusiasm.

The third and fourth five-year plans focused particularly on the heavy industry, the steel industry, and the chemical industry. This fostered the construction of ships, heavy machinery, and later automobiles. The chemical industry initially concentrated on petrochemicals and fertilizers before it started to include synthetic fibers and resins. At the same time, the rubber and light metal industries became more active as well. Gradually, sophisticated engineering projects were mastered with the construction of plants and whole industrial complexes.

Even the fifth plan (1982–1986) still bore the hallmarks of the meanwhile assassinated president. The liberalization of the financial markets and the privatization of banks were envisaged as well as establishing a free market and ending the monopolies of the *chaebol*. The new generation of politicians wanted to increase the efficiency of the enterprises by giving leeway to new forces. Particularly, small- and medium-sized enterprises were supposed to produce for the domestic market. The agrarian sector had to face a decreasing demand for rice as a staple food, cultivate products like special fruits and dairy products, like yoghurt or cheese, and raise livestock such as sheep and cows.

All these measures led to technical and economic results that amazed the world. Obstacles to such a clear and focus-oriented planning would have been competition, demand, and suddenly changing circumstances. Park closed the domestic markets over two decades for foreign competitors. This enabled local Korean companies to gain strength, and their products could meet the demand of the national market as well as the US market, which was generously opened to Korean products as well. This of course demanded an increasingly high quality of the offered products.

One example of the newly required flexibility was the question of how to handle the oil crisis. When the oil-producing countries suddenly quadrupled their prices, Korean planners believed that the Middle Eastern countries would become rich overnight and were likely to invest this newly acquired wealth. These countries were in need of modern infrastructure such as roads, harbors, and power plants. The staff of Western companies was unlikely to work in dry deserts where only unfamiliar food and beverages were available at a place that lacked entertainment. However, the disciplined and undemanding Korean workers could be dispatched in great numbers. Thus, Korea could create cash and ensure the oil supply at the same token.

The distinguished expert on East Asia, Vogel [7], ranked Park among three other national leaders, "who inherited countries in great turmoil modernized their nations by building new systems and initiated very rapid growth, causing transformations that continued after them." The other three leaders he mentions are Mustafa Kemal Ataturk (Turkey), Lee Kuan Yew (Singapore), and Deng Xiaoping (China).

The pioneers, who controlled the *chaebol,* were men trusted by Park. Thus, they jointly pursued a policy that caused a lot of undesired effects for the nation. After the untimely death of the president, nobody was able to keep these men and the powerful bureaucracy in check. Personally, the almighty president lived a modest life. He resided in a relatively unpretentious mansion in a park in a far eastern district of Seoul. His wife Yook Young-soo was—in contrast to her husband—very popular among the entire population. She was assassinated by a North Korean agent in an earlier attempt to murder the president. Park himself was killed on October 1979 by the chief of his own intelligence service because of his individual ambitions [8].

Park had indeed faced a strong opposition. The leader of the opposition, Kim Dae-jung, had gained so many votes in the 1971 election that Park's governing party had slipped below 50 %. In the summer of the same year, Korea‘s economy suffered from the drastic increase of the oil prices, a high inflation, and the decline of the economic growth, followed by the downfall of many important companies, including some powerful *chaebol*.

Whereas monstrous agglomerations in the industry were the result of the planning bureaucracy, the government took care to organize millions of small agrarian operations. Initially, the rapid upswing of the country did not only pass the farming industry, but it even weakened it when many workers left for the cities to find well-paid jobs in factories. In 1970, on the initiative of President Park, the S*aemaul Undong* (New Village Movement) initiative was launched. Within this movement, the state did not operate with economic plans but mainly offered guidance for self-help, collaboration, and diligence.

The governmental Saemaul Undong Central Consultative council built 78 training centers on central as well as regional bases, which spread the movement to districts and villages. In these centers, more than 150,000 male as well as female management personnel were educated. Above all, they learned to be enthusiastic about the movement alongside teamwork, group dynamics, and social interactions, which were taught by using case studies. Purely theoretical performances were taboo, and all emphasis was put on practical work. This management staff inspired people in villages across the nation. The communities then elected democratic committees and its leaders. Some of the objectives were scientifically proven methods of cultivation, buying jointly used machines, efforts to keep the community healthy, family planning, efficient housekeeping, and implanting the ideas of *Saemaul Undong* in elementary schools.

The government helped by constructing roads, paths, wells, sewage disposal plants, storage facilities, and plants for agricultural processing. They further provided financial means to start these projects. Outstanding personalities and communities with special ideas that showed great initiatives were awarded medals and ribbons, for example, for the beautification and greening of public sites, places, and streets. *Saemaul Undong* was a huge success. Today, the quality of life in the formerly notoriously poor villages is sometimes higher than in some towns. The income of the rural households has tenfolded only within a few decades. The government emphasizes the non-material gains of an increased willingness to cooperate and a general optimistic and progressive spirit of the rural population. The traditional great disparity between cities and rural areas was significantly reduced, and there was never again a serious shortage of food in South Korea.

This successful movement that has by now a dynamic of its own was also strongly supported by Park's successor Chun Doo-hwan. Delegations from Thailand, Malaysia, Singapore, and the Philippines traveled to Korea to study the movement and tried to introduce it in their countries as well. The Korean model, however, cannot be easily adapted to other nations as it is based on a specific philosophy of the local mentality and a particular national conscience.

Under Choe Kyu-ha, the temporary successor of Park, tendencies of the first cautious steps of a democratization of the country were observed. Nevertheless, the political forces were entangled in factional disputes, and again, the military entered the stage. Under the leadership of major general Chun Doo-hwan, martial law was declared. A new constitution was ratified, which was a mixture between a presidential and parliamentary system. Chun was elected as the new president for seven years. He saw himself as the successor of Park in economic matters and developed a realistic attitude toward the necessity of an efficient national economy.

This seemingly restored the conditions similar to the circumstances under Park. However, Chun's reign was slightly more conciliatory than Park's. The economy was no longer planned only technocratic. Instead, the ideas and demands of businessmen and economic associations were taken much more into account. It was believed that the economic crisis could be overcome. Chun's rather strict leadership caused unrest among students, who demanded basic human rights, an independent administration of justice, freedom of press, and a direct election of the president by the people. Unfortunately, such idealistic demands neglected the economic requirements or considered them secondary. In general, however, it was recognized that the prioritized export should be reduced in favor of the development of the domestic market. The tradition of the five-year plans was continued, and the economy continued to grow. The bureaucracy and *chaebol* continued their intrigues, and this time, the president was personally involved in these machinations.

Whereas China participated in the 1988 Summer Olympics in Seoul, North Korea did not. However, China had warned North Korea to not intervene at all and thus had helped to ensure peaceful games. The People's Republic of China observed with an increasing benevolence and most interested the economic development of South Korea.

Chun Doo-hwan was succeeded by Roh Dae-woo, another former general. Roh came into office, because the leaders of the opposition Kim Young-sam and Kim Dae-jung run against each other. Thereby, Roh won the majority of votes against the combined numerical superiority of his rivals. Roh acted carefully and pursued policy that oscillated between former relations and ideas of his political opponents. A sixth five-year plan was established and consistently followed. This provided for a further improvement concerning the field of mechanical engineering as well as a solid entry of South Korea into the electronic industry. Farsightedly, the complete country was supplied with a broadband cabling system using fiber optics. This measure turned South Korea into the leading country concerning Internet access. At the same time, South Korea entered the automotive industry. This move was smiled at by all international experts and was considered little promising. The promotion of the middle class and a general liberalization was continued.

Similar to Japan, South Korea held on to the stately guided industrial policy, which was built on mighty conglomerations, evaluated by highly intelligent bureaucrats, and partly subsidized by governmental funds. Nevertheless, the officers of the administration gradually lost their capability to assess the increasingly complex and ramified economy. At the same time, the demands of consumers became more complex. The entire economy needed a liberal democracy to meet the requirements of the markets.

Roh Dae-woo's term of office ended unglamorously. Yet his foreign policy was quite successful as he established diplomatic relations with the so-called countries of the Eastern Bloc. Simultaneously, both Korean states joined the UN. He is also credited with the tacit approval of a democratization of South Korea.

4.6 Economy Under the Auspices of Democracy

Kim Young-sam won the elections of 1993, and his election marked the end of the time of the military. During Pak Chung-hee's term, they had energetically helped to strengthen their homeland. They had not cared much for their personal well-being and did not, as many politicians within democratic systems, focus on personal ambitions. While politicians want to be reelected and therefore try to avoid unpopular decisions, even if such decisions are reasonable, the military does not care too much about the wishes of the people, if these desires do not seem to help or even obstruct the economic growth of the nation.

The economic strengthening formed a growing middle class that became increasingly important. Its offspring developed a strong political conscience and formed the base for a sound democratic behavior of this new class. They actively engaged in politics and made a transition from a military dictatorship to a democratic system possible without the force of arms. The subsequent presidents shared with the former generals the passion to further develop their country. However, they could rely on an already strong national economy which allowed them to make democratic compromises and gave them more leeway for social developments as well as tougher line toward the *chaebol*. The military leaders had known that they needed the managerial talents of the *chaebol* leaders and thus had given them great freedoms. This led to an increase of corrupt practices, which ultimately also infected Park's successors.

Kim Young-sam vigorously fought corruption. His endeavors culminated when Chun Doo-hwan and Roh Dae-woo were accused of taking briberies. Chun was sentenced to death and Roh to 22.5 years in prison. Both had accumulated private wealth worth over half a billion dollar each. Their sentences were later mitigated and finally both enjoyed a full pardon. Roh duly paid all penalties imposed on him, whereas Chun paid a little bit more than half of the penalty, retaining the position that he had no money left. He insists to be a poor man by now, living only from what his sons provide him with.

In the future, all civil servants in higher positions as well as members of the parliament had to disclose their entire financial circumstances. During Kim's term of office, it became evident that the state bureaucracy was no longer a senior partner of the economy, but had turned to its actual determination: to provide the legal and social framework for a well-functioning economy. Kim Young-sam also granted some local authority autonomies that they had lost before.

The economy continued to grow. Yet, at the end of his term, the financial crisis of 1997/1998 struck Asia and it especially hit South Korea, which was still a financially unstable country. Rescue came from the International Monetary Fund (IMF). Until today, great parts of the population in Korea do not like to acknowledge this help, as the financial aid was tied to strict conditions that were imposed on the country. Nevertheless, most of these restrictions turned out to be very beneficial for the modernization of the nation. Following Kim Young-sam, the younger Kim Dae-jung became president in 1998. After the brief interruption by the Asian monetary crisis, the country continued to grow. The national administration became subject to a reform, and the country was aligned to the principles of a free market economy. With his so-called Sunshine Policy, Kim was initially successful in his efforts of a rapprochement with North Korea. The two nations agreed to set up a special economic zone close to the DMZ at Gaesong. Yet, it was then discovered that North Korea continued to develop nuclear weapons. This discredited Kim Dae-jung and his authority declined rapidly while the conservative forces increasingly gained power.

To the general surprise, Socialist Roh Moon-hyun won in the next election and served as president from 1993 on. He started with a so-called clean policy and did not tolerate any type of corruption (both presidents before could not be accounted for any personal enrichment; however, they had made sure to receive considerable donations from the *chaebol* for their parties).

In particular, young people supported Roh as a liberal new hope with a strong democratic mind. He became an advocate of social justice and pleaded for a "fair distribution of the national wealth." For instance, his administration levied taxes on those who owned more than one house or apartment. This measure also had the purpose to stop real estate speculations in the country, especially in Seoul. As most wealthy citizens of Seoul are owners of a number of houses, apartments, and offices that provide for their income, Roh, from the very beginning, faced fierce opposition. In the field of foreign policy, Roh tried to continue the policy of his predecessor to dissolve tensions with the North, but he soon had to recognize that North Korea did only take benefits from the south without giving anything equivalent in return. Roh's party lost the next election to the conservative politician Lee Myung-bak, a former lord mayor of Seoul. Taking responsibility for corruption cases, in his family, Roh committed suicide, although he himself was most likely innocent. This Socialist politician was popular but had no or only very little influence on the Korean economy.

4.7 Dynamics Under Lee Myung-bak

Whereas the three predecessors of Lee were occupied with ideas of civil rights, democracy, and social security but had no practical economic experiences, Lee, a former top manager, showed a very friendly attitude toward economical and entrepreneurial questions and had a lot of experience within the field of civil administration. Like no other president before him, he approached the USA, put North Korea in its place, further expanded the good relations with China, and developed a friendly relation with the new Japanese prime minister, Hatoyama, Yukio. Lee had the vision of developing an economic union of China, Japan, and Korea.

In 2008, the political opposition gathered huge crowds in the streets to protest against the import of American beef. At the same time, the USA was the second largest export country for Korea and South Korea exhibited a considerably negative external trade balance with the USA. This shows how easily emotions can take over rational thinking in Korea. Yet, the whole event rather had the feel of a public festival, as only a few participants listened to the address of the oppositional leader in front of the city hall.

Lee Myung-bak faced strong adversaries. Reconciliation with Japan is still a difficult subject in Korea, as many Koreans find the compensations that have been paid for the lootings and abuses during the Japanese colonial reign, insufficient. Furthermore, they are irritated by historical interpretations in Japanese textbooks. Many Koreans also fiercely object territorial claims of the Japanese concerning the small rocky islands of Dokdo, which are located in the center of rich fishing grounds and supposedly have some mineral resources. It seems to them that Japan does not acknowledge that it has lost the war and thus has lost all its former Korean territories.

Lee sympathized with the construction industry and, immediately after having taken office, annulled the taxation of second real estate properties. As mentioned before, ministers have to report their sources of income as well as their properties. Thus, it was revealed that all members of the cabinet indeed owned dozens of apartments.

Lee Myung-bak was known to promote projects that secured employment and profits for the related industries. As a mayor of Seoul, he had already restored the Cheonggyecheon, a small river that had flowed underground for decades in Seoul. This project necessitated the expensive demolition of an elevated highway and hundreds of houses, and many shops lost their attractive location. These shop owners became bitter enemies of the ambitious mayor (Fig. 4.1).

Fig. 4.1 A green aisle through downton Seoul—the renaturalized Cheonggyecheon stream

Today, the small river is a popular tourist attraction and has developed an interesting flora and attracted some amphibians. The riverbed is situated approximately seven meters below the city streets and has walkways on both sides. This allows people to stroll for several miles through the center of the city and still feel a bit like being in nature. The citizens of Seoul make frequent use of this opportunity; however, hardly anyone knows that it is quite costly to maintain the necessary pumping system around this artificial piece of nature.

Another project which is of questionable usefulness is the Pan Korea Grand Waterway, a canal that connects the harbor of Incheon with the Han River. The construction was very expensive, because a stony watershed had to be divided. Numerous bridges of the Han River are built so low that they do not allow larger vessels to pass and the river is known for dangerous floods. Lee had envisioned that big cruising ships would dock at Incheon from where passengers would embark on small ships to arrive between northern and southern Seoul. From this point, a splendid boulevard was to lead to the Sejong-no avenue, which leads directly to the royal palace at the northern edge of the city.

The final part of the plan has already been completed: Fountains, flower beds, and a new golden statue of King Sejong the Great have been installed. This, again, led to many complaints as the statue of King Sejong is clearly smaller than the statue of the great Admiral Yi Sun-shin, which is located approximately 150 yards away. Many Koreans feel that this is inappropriate. Further complaints are voiced as the former wide avenue had to be narrowed for this installation and frequently causes traffic jams.

Lee liked to support water conservation schemes. His "Four Major Rivers Project" became particularly controversial. The whole drainage area of the four most important rivers of the country, the Han, Nakdong, Geum, and Yeongsan, was restored and caused enormous financial expenses and will continue to require high maintenance costs. The basic ideas of the project to control the rivers, improve the water quality, beautify the landscape, and create sites for sports and leisure are certainly commendable and the future will show whether the benefits justify the costs.

South Korea is not only a country of tunnels, but also a land of dams. More than ten quite large dams have been constructed and 1200 dams of medium size regulate rivers and torrents in the mountains. All in all it is reported that 18,000 dams exist in South Korea. The bigger ones create water reservoirs to produce hydroelectrical power, which contributes 2.2 % of energy to the total generation of electrical energy. Newly planned projects meet the stern resistance of the adjacent residents and are hard to put through.

The project of an artificial city 70 miles south of Seoul is carried on. Some government offices have already moved to this new location. Sejong City is first and foremost built for scientific and research activities. It is supposed to relieve the overcrowded capital where there is almost no free space left as Seoul is surrounded by the borders of the province of Gyeonggi.

Another idea of Lee seems not to be actualized. He thought about digging a canal from Seoul to Busan, thus crossing the entire country from the northwest to the southeast. The mountainous landscape of South Korea would require hundreds of locks that would increase the costs of the project to a degree that the complete financial capacity of the nation could be endangered. The economic advantage of the canal, however, would have be only very limited.

The dynamics of the era of Lee Myung-bak do still persist, though he more or less only pursued ideas of his predecessors Pak Chung-hee and Chun Doo-hwan.

4.8 Liberalization and Increasing Standards of Life

In the previous chapters, the history of the economy of South Korea seems to be almost completely intertwined with its political developments. Weggel [9] elaborates on this by stating that: "In traditional Asia, the economy as such has never played a self-reliant role. This means that there was no formally independent economical bureaucracy, a specific economic science, or a history of economy on its own accord."

Nowadays, the course of the economy in Korea is no longer determined by bureaucrats alone. The entire environment has become more liberal and many forces are working together. The trade association, the Federation of Korean Industries (FKI), has become quite influential and confident. Indeed, the mighty *chaebol* such as Samsung, Hyundai, SK, and LG (called "Big Four") still play a dominant role. Nevertheless, medium-sized enterprises that hardly existed before start to play an increasingly important role. Because none of the "Big Four" begrudges the position of the chairman of the federation to another *chaebol*, they agreed in recent years to appoint a representative of a medium-sized company. The term of chairmen has meanwhile been reduced to periods of 1.5 years as it was feared that this person could become too powerful.

Lee Myung-bak followed the tradition of conservative presidents to prioritize the economic development of the country. His successor Pak Geun-hee has so far refrained from actively fixing her aims and rather relied on moral or idealistic roll calls. In conclusion, one can say that in its long and eventful history, Korea was never in the position to establish and stabilize a flourishing national economy over a longer period of time. The north of the country abides in its wretched tradition, whereas the South—mainly due to President Pak Chung-hee—initiated a new, dynamic phase which ultimately position South Korea among other industrial nations.

An international ranking list regarding the per capita income in relation to the GNP (Gross National Income) of the top 35 nations shows the following figures as in 2013 in US dollar (Table 4.1).

Arithmetically, Liechtenstein has the highest GNP rate per capita, but its data are irrelevant as this small country has an enormous number of daily and weekly commuters.

All these countries (except the special cases of Qatar, Saudi Arabia, and Kuwait) are predominated by a free market economy, and the government does not—or only hardly—play a role in managing economic objectives or structures. Among these 35 nations, ministates such as San Marino, Andorra, Liechtenstein, or Nauru are not taken into consideration.

Table 4.1 International ranking list of per capita incomes

Rank	Country	GNP (per capita)	Total GNP (in $ billion)	Population (in million)	Birthrate (children per woman)
1	Luxembourg	110	511	0.5	1.6
2	Norway	100	60	4.6	1.9
3	Qatar	100	203	0.9	2.2
4	Switzerland	81	650	8	1.5
5	Australia	65	1.505	20	1.9
6	Denmark	59	331	5.6	1.9
7	Sweden	58	560	9	1.9
8	Singapore	55	300	4.6	1.3[a]
9	USA	53	16.800	306	2.1
10	Canada	52	1.825	33	1.6
11	Austria	49	450	8	1.4
12	Kuwait	48	185	2.5	2.7
13	The Netherlands	46	800	17	1.8
14	Finland	47	260	5.2	1.8
15	Ireland	46	262	4.1	2
16	Iceland	46	15	0.3	2.1
17	Belgium	45	507	10	1.8
18	Germany	45	3.640	82	1.4
19	VAR (Emirates)	44	396	4.4	2
20	France	43	2.740	64	2
21	Great Britain	40	2.540	61	1.9
22	Brunei	40	16	0.4	2.1
23	New Zealand	40	181	4.1	2.1
24	Japan	38	4.900	127	1.3
25	Hong Kong	38	274	7	1
26	Israel	37	292	6.4	2.9
27	Italy	35	2.070	58	1.4
28	Spain	29	1:360	40	1.4
29	Bahrain	27	32	0.7	2.2
30	Oman	25	81	3.2	2.9
31	Saudi Arabia	25	745	28	3
32	Cyprus	25	22	0.8	1.5
33	South Korea	24	1.222	49.5	1.2
34	Bahamas	24	8	0.3	1.9
35	Malta	23	10	0.4	1.4

Status 2013 for GNP and population; birthrate about 2010
[a]In the case of Singapore, a very high immigration rate has to be additionally taken into account
Source IWF; Birth Rate UN Data

Table 4.2 Identification data of further important countries

Country	GNP (per capita)	Total GNP (in $ billion)	Population (in million)	Birthrate (children per woman)
Russia	14.8	2.120	141	1.4
Poland	13.4	516	39	1.3
Argentina	11.8	488	39	2.3
Brazil	11.3	2.245	190	1.9
Turkey	10.8	830	71	2.1
Mexico	10.6	1.260	109	2.4
China	6.7	9.200	1.329	1.6
South Africa	6.6	277	44	2.6
Indonesia	3.5	870	235	2.5
India	1.5	1.870	1.130	2.7

Source IWF; Birth Rate UN Data

Furthermore, for reasons of comparison, the following important countries are listed as well (Table 4.2).

Concerning this list, one has to take into account that the varying exchange rates and purchasing power parities do not always facilitate an objective image.

South Korea is only ranked 34th as far as the GNP per capita is concerned. With respect to the absolute GNP, however, it is ranked 15th and justifies its membership in the G-20 (Group of Twenty), an international community of the politically and economically most important states of the world. Concerning its population, South Korea is ranked 17th, but its low birthrate together with China, Japan, Poland, and Italy ranks it last in this category, which seems to be something that needs to be thought about in the future. In the immediate future, however, this point might not be too problematic due to the baby boomer generation of the 1980s and high life expectancy, which is on a comparable level with Great Britain and China.

With regard to global trade, South Korea occupies the 13th rank with imports and ranks even 11th with exports as the nation exports more than 45 % of its entire GNP. The main imports are energy supplies, chemical products, and special machines, mostly from China, Japan, the USA, and Saudi Arabia. The main exports of South Korea are electronic products, road vehicles, as well as ships to China, the USA, and Japan.

The overall volume of imports in 1960 was only US$330 million and increased to US$435 billion until 2008. It is interesting that the share of food items decreased from 10 to 1.5 %. The overall volume of exports in 1960 was merely US$22 million and increased to impressive US$422 billion until 2008.

The structure of the exports changed dramatically within these 46 years (Table 4.3).

Market requirements and bureaucratic planning went hand in hand with this development. Government officers systematically promoted industries that generated high added values and thus achieved high profits, while being able to compete on global markets concerning the quality and price of their products. Relevant

Table 4.3 Changes in the export of important Korean products

1962	Silk, tungsten, fish, animal fats, timber, textiles, machines, clothing, and simple chemical products
1988	Textiles, electronic components, steel products, footwear, ships, road vehicles, marine products, machines, and electrical devices
2008	Communication equipment, engineering products, road vehicles, ships, chemical products, machines, electronic components, measurement and control technology applications, steel, and electrical devices

industries did not exist and needed to be established, and specialists had to be educated. Korea, as a former agrarian nation, is justly proud of having learned to produce industrial "world-class products" in such a short period of time.

In his retrospective account of the 2002 FIFA World Cup, which was jointly organized by South Korea and Japan, Song [10] determined that Koreans had become very confident with respect to the future of South Korea's economic success as well as concerning individual prospects. South Korea, essentially an agrarian nation, ultimately entered the circles of the modern industrialized nations.

Meanwhile, the living standard of the population increased enormously, yet remained quite unequally distributed. South Korea shares this situation with many other industrialized nations, as the increasing complexity in the fields of technology, economy, and society requires more and more education and training and does hardly tolerate an introspective lifestyle. The standard of the South Korean middle class has considerably improved compared to countries with a similar level of growth. However, concerning the statistical average income—including the incomes of the numerous millionaires—the country has not yet reached a position among the top twenty nations with respect to the per capita GNP. The governmental planning offices knew about the problem to balance investments into the future with an increasing private wealth. However, the global external influences and the growing private demands of the population restrict their scope.

Over a period of more than 500 years, Koreans had hardly developed any significant economic initiatives. The course of the national economy depended on the instructions of a stubborn government that was not in favor of changes. Therefore, until the late nineteenth century, stagnation prevailed until Korea was forced open by the Japanese. This, however, happened only in favor of Japan's own egoistic interests. Individual initiatives were in general not supported.

The foregoing figures show that South Korea ranks among the upper middle class of nations. Though it is still far away from dominant powers such as the USA or China, it can no longer be considered an undeveloped, underdeveloped country, needing help from other nations or denying aid to less developed nations. Professor Kim Seong-kon from Seoul National University reminds his compatriots that numerous people in the world admire the superb achievements of South Korea within many different fields (*The Korea Herald*, October 15, 2014).

After the war, hardworking entrepreneurs had participated in modeling the economy, but the development rigorously remained in high dependency on the state. Only later, with a real democratization, did a free market economy grow. In particular, the development of medium-sized and small-sized enterprises thrived, as they were no longer neglected by the administration but actively supported.

Currently, the government increasingly withdraws from the actual economic affairs. Yet, it still formulates objectives and supplies promising developments with credits, guarantees, and tax incentives. Internally, it lets the liberal market economy take its course and loosened those rules that controlled and limited the international exchange of commodities and services. This is why entrepreneurship and creativity are vigorously unfolding within the possible framework.

The state pursues the primacy of protecting the independence of the country and, at the same time, the primacy of improving the common good. In this respect, it does not hesitate to intervene in the markets to ensure an optimal supply for the people. Indeed, this task should be the ultimate goal of the national economy. The pharmaceutical industry is a good example for this principle. The state sets "reasonable prices," which prevents excessive pricing and thus unduly profits for shareholders and bonuses for executives by overcharging sick people. The national health system in South Korea seems to be relatively reasonably priced, and the control of the pharmaceutical market is one reason for this. Korea knows that a "completely free market" would be utopic and that an efficient, functioning market economy needs reasonable rules. Similarly, a soccer or ice hockey match without rules would also not make much sense.

4.9 Determinants of the Economic Development and Planning

Until the Japanese occupation, which started around 1900, the country was economically in a sort of "long sleep." The colonizers woke South Korea from its slumber, however, only to satisfy their own necessities. The south of the peninsula seemed to be a pure agrarian state. In the chaos of the war between the two Koreas (1950–1953), cultivation areas were badly damaged. The same was true of northern cultivation areas. After 1951, Korea almost starved. The industry and trade were completely paralyzed, and there was almost no available capital and there was a total lack of foreign exchange in order to import food, primary energy, and technical know-how. Indeed, South Korea was on one level with Mali or Mozambique.

The causes that enabled such an economic growth out of a hopeless situation need to be evaluated. South Korea's recovery has been unprecedented in modern economic history. With respect to absolute numbers, China has achieved something similar by now. Nevertheless, the South Korean GNP per capita in 2013 was almost US$24,000, whereas in China, it was less than 7000 dollar in the same year. Of course, it has to be taken into consideration that the upswing of China started only around 1979 and the purchasing power parity of the two currencies can hardly be compared.

The timing of the Korean turn for the better, however, happened under very unfavorable circumstances. In contrast, China was neither divided—with the exception of Taiwan, which makes only 1.7 % of the total population—nor did it (proportionally) have to bear enormous cost of defense. Furthermore, China has rich mineral resources and a global prosperity could be enjoyed by the country. This provided for powerful distribution markets and, at the same time, drew international investors, who were willing to invest in the promising Chinese market. Among these international investors were a large number of Chinese businessmen, who had formerly emigrated and who did not hesitate to invest capital in their home country. Likewise, great investments were made from Hong Kong and Taiwan.

In the following, some of the determining factors will be introduced that enabled South Korea's growth. Experts from Korea as well as from foreign countries agree that one so-called soft factor had a great share in Korea's success story—and it is still in effect. This "soft factor" is the unique vitality and dynamism of the Korean people, which is accompanied by assertiveness as well as national pride, and the traditional willingness to learn.

4.10 The Vitality of Koreans

While material prerequisites (hard factors) were missing in South Korea, most people in the country had still kept an enormous vitality throughout the troublesome years. After living in South Korea for only a few months, one observes a clear difference to people in Japan. In both countries, the pace of life is quick and sometimes hectic. Although the Koreans are generally friendly and helpful, they are more impatient and always accelerate their speed. If anything is offered for free, they usually plunge—without being ashamed—for the desired objects and even give a thumbs-up in triumph. Often, we recognize in subway stations that people stand less orderly in line to wait and many passengers wriggle forward once the train arrives, sometimes even elbowing other passengers. In this situation, everybody only acts in his own interest, yet takes care of his friends or relatives that might accompany him. Generally, there exists a rule to drive on the right side. Nevertheless, cars will overtake other cars from all sides on the highway and tracks are crossed. It can be frequently observed that drivers of large cars are more reckless—including drivers of trucks and public busses. Thus, the congested traffic in cities is almost a blessing as despite this reckless driving behavior, only few accidents occur and damages are mostly limited to car body damages. The speed limit on highways is 68 mph (110 km/h) to prevent major catastrophes.

For a Westerner, watching Korean television is very revealing. More than 35 % of the program deals with historical or family-centered dramas, 25 % focuses on eating and agricultural production, and 10 % each are concerned with concerts and sport events. Family dramas are often very emotional and the audience tends to respond very emotional to the story. On the contrary, sensitive conversations as well as political or even philosophical discussions only occasionally take place.

Some Westerners are surprised of Korean eating habits and the central role that food plays in the Korean culture. In rarely any drama series or film, dinner scenes are missing. The news also use some air time to discuss issues of nutrition, agricultural production, and food logistics, giving special attention to seasonal specialties. In lively scenes, delicious foods are consumed and the thumbs-up is given to underline the delicious taste of the food, all accompanied by enthusiastic sounds. People from all backgrounds and of all ages can relate to this form of food consumption. One can consider this as a token of the vitality and joy of life in South Korea.

According to their convictions, Koreans eat mainly extremely healthy food such as such as mussels, crustaceans, fish, eggs, and fresh vegetables, which are all generously mixed with ginseng and garlic and seasoned with pepper and chili. Sometimes, the hands are used to eat, in order to speed up the process of swallowing the food. The eating procedure is frequently accompanied by smacking the lips and quaffing. Everybody seems to like soups and those are hastily ladled out or sipped directly without hesitation from the bowl. In popular eateries, everything will be gulped down with plenty of Korean *shucho*, a local liquor, containing 22 % alcohol. The Korean obsession with food stems from the fact that they regard a strong and healthy body as the most important capital, which enables a vital work performance. However, the rich and spicy food can occasionally lead to sanguineous outbreaks with some people.

It is not very surprising that fans get very emotional and exclusively support their team when important sport events are shown on TV. But when it comes to international competitions, there hardly exists any idea of fairness. If Korean competitors are obviously unfairly dealt with, as in the 2006 Winter Olympics in Turin, this causes extreme anger and those acts are classified as hostile acts of foreign countries. It does not matter that this concerns only a sporting event without any vital importance for the state.

The Korean man has to create a self-image of being a tough daredevil. He is inclined to face opponents and sometimes does not know his limits. An enormous willpower, which often might be considered stubborn, can be attributed to many Koreans. Often, they even stick to impossible aims—and occasionally achieve them. From time to time, these character traits lead to an overestimation of one's abilities that end in risky ventures. The mandatory military service for young men does not spare them of a very sturdy physical and mental education. Certainly, these men are better trained for survival in critical circumstances than the often pampered Central Europeans.

As soon as possible on the peninsula, people threw themselves into available work and took any chance offered or task required. Generally, the people prefer self-supporting jobs and worked up to seven days a week, from six in the morning (if necessary) until midnight. Those who work in major enterprises where their workday ends at 6 p.m. frequently work a second shift at another place and occasionally even engage in a third job on weekends and public holidays. For example, taxi-driving at night is a possible additional job for some people. Many citizens are indeed forced to work more than one job to improve their modest regular income. However, people who already have a high income are always ready to work for additional earnings, to fulfill their almost unlimited desire for a higher standard of life. Leisure time is considered to have a limited value.

4.11 Educational Will and Aspirations

The combination of a good standing in society and a high income appeals to almost all Koreans. The most preferred vocational activity of the middle and higher classes is therefore found in the big *chaebols* and the public service sector, in the latter preferably in a ministry. The road to these positions is full of hardships. Most gifted pupils and students work toward this goal from early in the morning until late at night. Only excellent grades permit access to the top universities, which are necessary if applying for a position in the ministries. 75 % of all female and 69 % of all male Koreans get access to college. If one browses through the relevant "Who is Who" volumes of the high society, usually the universities from which the person graduated are mentioned.

In the fields of economy, technology, and science, many noteworthy personalities got their Ph.D. in the USA and a few graduated from Germany, Japan, Great Britain, and France in scientific fields. It can be generally stated that an academic education in rather pragmatic disciplines such as engineering, economy, medicine, or law is mandatory for a successful career. This is likewise necessary in the upper level civil service, in particular in the pertinent ministries. Ministers who have not qualified for economical or organizational assignments are rather the exception than the rule. The times in which high militaries have ruled the country and self-made men controlled the *chaebol* have definitely passed.

Besides the academic qualifications, having a good network of important people is important for personal success. Here, the focus is on family relations, which lead to numerous marriages among the upper class. Alumni relations are likewise important, especially if one has graduated from a prestigious university. In Korea, local affiliations are also important. People from one's own region or county enjoy a preference when choosing a person for a qualified position. This is quite unique to Korea. It could happen that a voter elects a person from his own province, disregarding a candidate from his own party or his long-standing political convictions.

In his strong determination to become part of the upper class, the aspiring Korean will seek the assistance of people who might be of use and avoid the companionship of less promising fellows. This results in a general suspicion toward people he does not know and everyday life encounters, while people one knows are generally trusted. When meeting a person for the first time, many Koreans subconsciously wonder how to make the best use of him or her and whether this person could be useful (or harmful) at all.

4.12 Dedication to Prestige—The Importance of Face

In South Korea, material wealth seems hardly to be used for personal convenience but is rather a sign of prestige and is thus openly displayed. Rich people like to flaunt with the size and extravagance of their home. Assertions of 500 m^2 (5380 square feet) are not rare. But when moving into the flat, the size usually shrinks to an actual size, which is about 60 % of the total size as ails, floors, elevators, verandas, terraces, garages, all types of common spaces, storage rooms, etc., have to be deducted. Furthermore, the thickness of the mortar and sometimes even of the walls are included in the total size of the apartment. Nevertheless, differently from other East Asian regions, the overall size of residences in South Korea is rather big.

In previous times, stylish furniture was produced as well as wonderful pieces of art. However, contemporary Koreans seem to have a different taste. Instead of focusing on the quality or design, it will frequently be emphasized that a famous architect or designer, possibly from overseas, was employed to design the flat. Generally, the location of the home gives much more prestige than furnishing it with tasteful paintings and sculptures, selected antiquities, or flower arrangements. Carpets are usually not used at all. Of course, houses or apartments of the upper class are often furnished with precious furniture and pieces of art. The most important aspect about them, however, is that these artefacts are more expensive than what other people own. Modern kitchens and manifold electronic devises including robots also help to give "big face" to their owners. In some instances, a large part of the living rooms is dominated by a giant television set, which in some instances is not even switched off when entertaining guests.

European visitors to South Korea are surprised to see relatively few small cars, which constitute a majority in European cities. This is due to the fact that a bigger car supposedly leads to a higher reputation. Foreign cars are especially popular. A well to do family in one of the top apartments in Seoul possesses often an off-roader for golf activities, a big sedan for representative purposes, a smart car for the wife, and some sport cars like Ferrari, Maserati, or Porsche for certain outdoor activities and for the children. All cars are always polished. Upper-class families also employ a driver for their convenience and prestige. It turns out that the absence of small cars can be explained by the huge bodywork of many cars that still only have a small engine.

When it comes to presents and dinner invitations, usually only an expensive choice is a good choice as an average entertainment would signify a loss of face on both sides. This attitude culminates at important celebrations such as weddings, anniversaries, and similar occasions. Numerous guests are invited and usually pampered in prestigious hotels. These occasions need to be planned with great cares since the image (face) of the whole family is concerned. Thus, compromises cannot be tolerated.

Even the Korean middle class can hardly afford not to play golf at the weekend or to obtain a membership in a prestigious hotel or club of an exclusive department store. Naturally, one has to frequently go shopping or attend an extravagant event in Singapore, Tokyo, or Shanghai and spend holidays on Hawaii, in Switzerland, or at Californian coast. Similarly, the selection of the kindergarten, schools, or higher educational institutions for the young family members is crucial. It is important that these institutions need to offer an excellent education as well as benefit the prestige for the whole family. When negotiating a wedding, these choices matter a lot and sometimes ambitious mothers of the bride bend the truth a bit by claiming for example that her daughter graduated from a prestigious university, when indeed she only attended a college for a few semesters.

The road to social success inevitably leads through hard learning and successfully passed final examination of a prestigious university into a ministry position or a recognized *chaebol*. Such a career can sometimes be replaced by a lucky marriage or assets inherited from the parents. In some cases, wealth accumulated by real estate investments might be helpful as well. In all of these cases, a rich person is generally admired by Koreans as this person can gain prestige by their financial means. Craving for recognition can be seen as one of the most powerful motivator and strongest driving force behind the action of many Koreans.

The influence of nationalism seems to be less obvious. Most Koreans consider themselves to be good patriots. In external relationships, meaning Korea's standing in the world, they are proud of any national achievements and closely identify with them. They read in the newspapers and are delighted when Samsung surpasses the Japanese *keiretsu* Sony in one or more industrial sectors. During the 2010 Winter Olympics in Vancouver, the chairman of Samsung paid a suite in the Hyatt Hotel for the South Korean ice-skating star Kim Yu-na to spare her the frugal accommodation in the Olympic village. Even unskilled workers of a minor enterprise, who often are skeptic about multinational groups, applauded this deed, because they believed that it contributed to the victory of the national star, which they personally took pride in.

Concerning internal relationships, the primary focus of Koreans is their own family and not the nation. As already mentioned before, most Koreans traditionally do not trust high-ranking officials of their country. Not only entrepreneurs and top politicians shovel the wealth of their clans frequently onto bank accounts outside the country, even owners of small kiosks try to withdraw themselves from the duty to pay taxes. Avoidance of taxes seems to be a national sport, though this becomes increasingly difficult because the competences of the tax administration are growing. In terms of mass psychology, Korea is hardly different from other states. This also matches the mind of affluent parents who withheld their sons from the due military service by letting them study in the USA. It is also remarkable that many Koreans prefer foreign products to local goods. Here, egoism prevails over patriotism.

In many instances, the approach to corruption in South Korea is interesting. Officially, corruption is vigorously fought. Nevertheless, many "realists" point toward the fact that obstacles can be overcome and the course of a matter can be accelerated in many cases. Corruption is therefore often considered as stimulating for the national economy and is maybe comparable to animating drugs, which however have very negative consequences in the long run.

It is also a fact that rhetorically gifted politicians are able to mobilize national enthusiasm if the well-being of the home country really seems to be in jeopardy. When in 1999, Koreans felt that their country might be overrun by foreign countries (represented by the International Monetary Fund), hundreds of thousands of patriots followed a general trend (not following a public roll call) to make their precious metals available for the disposition of the state.

In summary, it can be stated that the enormous motivation to obtain material wealth among Koreans stems from the desire of a favorable self-presentation. This is true for individuals, for one's own family as well as for larger groups. Finally, this observation is valid within South Korea as well as on the international floor.

4.13 Primacy of Implementation Versus Planning and Decision

South Koreans are united concerning many common goals. Nevertheless, they compete furiously with each other on a personal level and show an utmost particularism. An outstanding personality was necessary to focus the motivation of Koreans on the general national development. At the right time, the country found such a leader: Pak Chung-hee. For a long period of time, his name could hardly be mentioned since he had the image of an abominable dictator. Indeed, today, there would hardly be an appropriate position for him. However, the general public slowly starts to recognize that Park was indeed godsend—without posthumously approving his undemocratic procedures. In any case, he can be called the father of the industrialization of South Korea.

Park, as a former high military person, acted self-confidently, disciplined, and autocratic. As an ardent patriot, he made every effort to organize his country independently and make it a better place, meaning to get it out of its economic miseries. Park's approach was described as pragmatic, considerate, and resolute. His unpretentious behavior and modest demeanor were admired and no secret bank accounts were found with him. As a rationalist, he prohibited *gut*, an obscure shamanistic practice. He did neither display beaming charisma nor personal charm and remained rather unpopular with the population. This was in contrast to his wife Yuk Young-soo, who enjoyed a nationwide admiration and popularity because of her warm, sympathetic character.

Park hated democratic decisions which required the consent of all people involved. He liked to make his own decisions, yet as a good listener, he was fond of getting systematic and all-encompassing information. All questions were discussed with one or the majority of his seven economic advisors. These advisors had the right and even the duty to voice objections. The final decision was however passed by the president.

While most enterprises as well as political operations usually involve an extensive and qualified planning, in most cases, the implementation remains unsatisfactory. Likewise, there does hardly exist any noteworthy literature on business administration or implementation. As a practical man, Park knew that even brilliant decisions are of no use if they are not or only badly implemented. Thus, he prepended a four-step decision implementation:

1. Stipulating a fundamental principle,
2. Establishing a basic policy,

3. Developing the outlines of the proceedings,
4. Carrying out the political intentions.

The responsibility for carrying out a project was assigned to a responsible minister, who was in charge of the project and its success or failure. Therefore, the respective minister made the final decision concerning the practical procedure on-site. President Park than practiced his "management by walking around," thoroughly inspecting all relevant facilities in the various phases of their progress. Park set priorities with a drastic development of the export industry and substituting the import of consumer goods. These measures had already been considered important by his predecessors; however, because of a lack of abilities and competences, they had never gotten off the ground. The president liked plans that meticulously pointed out a complete cluster of projects and the precise time sequence in which they were to be accomplished.

The most important step was the creation of a modern chemical industry and the erection of a giant petrochemical complex at the southern cost of the peninsula. Fuel was very important for logistics, chemical fibers enabled to establish a modern textile industry, and the production of fertilizers improved the results in the agricultural sector and allowed to significantly reduce the import of food. Furthermore, the production of explosives helped to set up a large-scale armament industry. First, the basic materials had to be produced, before producing semi-finished products and ultimately completed products. Schematized in the sense of a cascade from top to the bottom, these included basic petrochemical items, followed by synthetic yarns, textile materials in the supplementary processing, and finally fine garments. In all stages, the products had to be fit for export, which means they had to meet high-quality standards.

The second priorities were the iron and steel industries. They enabled the production of various types of semi-finished products for the manufacturing of machines, vehicles, and industrial installations. However, initially crude steel and particular types of semi-finished products were exported, because it takes quite a long time until specialized machines can be constructed that meet the high demands of the global markets.

When building up a heavy industry, one has to reflect on the fact that South Korea did not have any experience in this field, whereas after World War II, Germany and Japan could draw on their rich, almost 100 years of experiences. The Koreans replaced experiences by disregarding risks and an unshakable self-confidence. Weapons had never been produced before in Korea, and successfully manufacturing them for the own demand, South Korea did not need to import them anymore. Another prominent substitution of imports was the production of vessels for the fishing industry, which could also be successfully sold to foreign countries.

Right from the beginning, the Park administration pursued the objective to build up a light industry as soon as possible and to cope with the lower part of the above-mentioned cascades. The next target would be the electric and later the electronical industry. Ultimately, the vision was to establish a car manufacturing industry and the construction of huge vessels for deep water operations. They were supposed to serve the needs of the average customers and, at the same time, permit global sales campaigns. It was entirely clear that world-class products would be necessary to reach these ambitious goals and to conquer the global markets. All these targets were developed out of the blue. There were no companies with experiences in the various fields to be handled. Here, Park relied on the power of the *chaebol*, an enterprise type that will be explained later. All targets were faced with five-year plans, which simultaneously demanded quickly increasing exportation quotas.

Export increases of annually 40 % were envisaged. These increases were always obtained or slightly exceeded. In 1964, everything started with US$120 million and the target had been set at 10 billion dollars for 1977. This goal was finally achieved. By 2012, 548 billion dollars were obtained.

The ever-increasing industrial volume required many laborers, yet, on the one side, the gradually progressing rationalization in the countryside created a need for new jobs. The government took care of those who were willing to work and who were willing to earn their living abroad. A great number of laborers were used to rebuild the infrastructure of Vietnam and even more worked on the Arabian Peninsula, especially in the Gulf States. They were initially employed by Western construction—and engineering companies. Afterward, they were quickly employed by Korean enterprises that took advantage of the skills that these workers had obtained and used them in the realm of structural engineering, civil engineering, and plant construction in Korea as well as overseas.

4.14 The Change of Awareness Among Citizens

It is the merit of Pak Chung-hee that great parts of the South Korean nation were pulled out of its traditional, fatalistic conscience and that its inherent vitality was adapted to the requirements of a modern technological progress, basically driven by scientific research and technological developments.

As it is generally known from old Korea (*Joseon*), the social classes consisted of scholars, farmers, craftsmen, and merchants as well as the classless people with the status of slaves, who comprised more than 50 % of the population. The scholars developed the unique class of the *yangban* that controlled Korea for some time. They believed that all resources of the nation were at their disposal, though they did nothing to produce anything and did not take care of the resources. Traces of this attitude supposedly can be found among some high-level bureaucrats of today. As "scholars," the *yangban* perceived themselves as literati, who occupied themselves with old Chinese scripts in order to discuss them in a dogmatic way without any respect to practical purposes. They refused to work on any practical matter. Always clad in meticulously white garments, they liked it to be carried around in comfortable sedan chairs so that they did not have to walk in public at all. They did not care about the fact that the common people were enthralled in an eternal cycle of poverty (*borigogae*) and lacked chances to develop.

Park opposed the old "*yangban* mentality" with a technologically oriented view of life, in which technologists decide about and supervise the guidelines of the national economic development. On a wide scale, engineering processes were set in motion, which had to be economically utilized in order to improve the entire economy of the nation. This then permitted in turn to distribute blessings to all people. O Won-chol [11], one of the seven economical consultants of Park, writes: "At any rate, the most advantageous situation results from the situation, in which the head of the state is himself a previous technologist." Park being a former responsible artillery officer, well acquainted with arms, machines and logistical systems, entrusted only technologists with the necessary strategical planning and processes. First, the right fields of application had to be identified before the required related competences and skills had to be defined. Afterward, the essential capabilities had to be developed in the form of necessary human capital. Finally, after the implementation of the planned targets, some million jobs were created for sufficiently trained laborers.

The president was aware that the spirit of the troops was important in combat. Thus, he knew that it was not enough to inspire the leaders, but the whole masses needed to be aroused. During the Japanese occupation, many patriots had fervently fought the colonists, but the masses had remained rather indifferent. In June 2014, the then prime minister nominee Moon Chang-keuk said that: "… the symbol of the people of Joseon (1392–1910) was laziness. They were lazy, lacking a sense of independence and were inclined to rely on others …" (*The Korean Herald*, June 13, 2014). Most likely, these people were not motivated—or even demotivated—to engage in useful work as they did not get anything for their efforts.

Now, the president provided a sense of awakening. He challenged the whole social system and demanded that everybody went above and beyond his limits. Without extraordinary efforts and substantial privations, an economical breakup cannot be achieved. In this respect, South Korea is an exemplary prototype for an economic and social development. Park went as far as to instruct the population to dress orderly and to always look presentable, taking care of their outward appearance.

The president succeeded not only to inspire the common people. Among those who strived to contribute to the new purpose were many descendants of the former *yangban* class. They took on the social competition with intelligence and diligence. Furthermore, the president changed the public awareness of the nation as a whole. This was necessary because Korea permanently had to learn to catch up with the leading nations and had to cope with contemporary challenges.

In the period after Park, the results of the big leap forward had to be consolidated and the whole management instruments had to be refined. This required new proceedings. In these fields, unity cannot be forced, but consent has to happen on a broad base. In a mature nation, the technology as well as the whole social structure of society turns increasingly complex. This development in turn requires a thorough commitment and an extensive identification of all participants involved. But any developed national economy necessitates from time to time a vigorous change and the pushing of new developments. These developments can hardly succeed in a democracy against the will of the majority as they require temporarily extraordinary efforts, the preparedness for change, and renunciation of habitual customs. Only sensible, wise, and courageous leaders can bring this forward.

The development of human resources was therefore preeminent for the Korean nation. First with emotional addresses and then increasingly with the material support of the government, an intensive educational system was established for the entire society. Up to 90 % of an age group acquires the matriculation standard and more than 65 % achieved an extended education at universities and colleges of advanced technology. This is the only way in which a nation can maintain a high technological standard and cope with a society which has to deal with an increasing advance of communication means and high technology. The state takes care of the education of the researchers and teachers; it provides universities and a qualified infrastructure and patronizes special talents. It further provides an insight to the parents and their offspring that it is worth the trouble to make sacrifices for education in order to later reap the fruits of all the efforts. The rather large campuses of elite universities, even in the heart of the densely populated Seoul, create a prolific climate to study. That meets the will of the majority of the population that is interested in education.

Therefore, a discussion whether a government administration should decide about the right way or if the forces of a "free market" should rule is obsolete as both have to cooperate to avoid wasting funds and risking losses by frictions. Initially, Korea looked at Japan as a role model, as the country initiated a fabulous commercial development with a clever administration. The leadership of Korea now has to take care of private initiatives and make sure that as many creative ideas as possible will push through. Pioneers have to be supported, and it has to ascertain that the *chaebol* will not restrict them.

The country was indeed very lucky that together with its ascent into the circle of advanced industrialized nations, a peaceful breakthrough of democracy happened from 1987 to 1988. This development evoked a lot of international appreciation. It further enabled the state to increase social contributions, to reduce the bureaucracy to a certain extent, and to start an offensive to cut back the omnipotence of the *chaebol*.

There were neither examples nor traditions for the democratization of Korea within the country as it had been the case in the USA or some European countries. At all times, there had been insurrections against authorities by exploited people who were deprived of their rights. In recent times, such upheavals were initiated and led by student groups and leftist labor movements. Kim [12] notes that this has changed since 1987, when a broad middle-class elite started to play an important role within the state. Most likely they contributed a lot to the process of democratization, because they provided political ideas, strategic thinking and behavior, and a civilized culture of discussion to the whole movement.

Moral concepts play a decisive role in the development of a society. Contemporary Korea has diverted in the last decades from a conservative ethos of Confucianism with its respect for experience, authorities, and hierarchies and embraces liberal values of individual freedom and the pursuit of happiness as well as the right for equal chances for all.

According to Kim [13], cosmopolitan ideas from innate democratic countries such as Great Britain and the USA contributed to this change as well as the Christianization mainly to Protestantism, of a substantial part of the Korean population. Calvinistic frugality and acquisitiveness fell on fertile ground. Furthermore, the idea that the fate of local groups should be managed in their own institutions according to local conditions was considered attractive. It was not favorable for the Catholic Church that it tried to direct Korean affairs from far away Rome. When dealing with East Asian people, one always has to keep their traditional values in mind that sometimes differ considerably from Western concepts.

4.15 Dispatching Coal Miners and Nurses to Germany

Unquestionably, governments should assert the headlines of the economic policy of their country. However, once it comes to details, bureaucratic planners without practical experience are at a loss, even when having a good basic theoretical education.

To prove this thesis, the program of dispatching Korean coal miners and nurses to Western Germany at the end of the 1950s will be briefly given as an example. At this time, there was a shortage of qualified and skilled workers in Germany, while the Korean government was interested in earning additional foreign currencies [14].

The foreign ministers of the two countries agreed to set forth experts, using the euphemistic title "Technical Cooperation" [15]. In reality, jobless academics and other people with high qualifications in Korea applied for jobs in Germany, attracted by the high wages that were offered. In fact, most applicants had never seen a mine from the inside before. Nevertheless, the Germans succeeded in quickly training these intelligent people in both vocational as well as language skills. Soon the Koreans felt superior to their German colleagues, who despised them for wearing fine suits and neckties during their leisure time. When recognizing that they would never make it to management positions, most Koreans left the coal mines and took on other jobs or founded small companies. Many left the host country either for the USA or their home country, which had meanwhile made substantial progress.

Many Korean nurses had a qualified medical training and were actually needed in their home country. Thus, the local authorities wanted to dispatch only visiting nurses without a lot of medical education. Yet, German hospitals were looking for well-trained and educated nurses. The majority of nurses were disappointed because they mainly served as helpers and had less access to qualified services, although they became very popular with German patients because of their abilities and devoted services. Meanwhile, the German embassy in Seoul informed the foreign office in Bonn, Germany, that a shortage of qualified nurses was expected in the rural areas of Korea [16].

Like their Korean male colleagues in the coal mines, the nurses they watched in disbelief at their monthly wage accountings, which showed only half of the amounts promised in their contracts because of the excessive German deductions for taxes and social security contributions. Most of the women originally intended to return to South Korea, yet meanwhile, they had reached an age, which was formerly considered as unseemly for younger women. Thus, they often married in Germany either one of the "coal miners" or a German. Because their children and grandchildren normally did not speak sufficient Korean, they usually did not consider to return to Korea. Some did take this option into consideration when they turned older; however, the enormously increased costs of living in Seoul made such a decision almost impossible. As a result, more than 30,000 Koreans live in Germany today. The Korean government arranged a big party in Frankfurt in 2013 and expressed its appreciation for their contribution to the national financial situation in former times.

Despite the best of their intentions, the official bureaucrats of both governments ultimately did not achieve the planned results.

Literature

1. Ladstaedter O, Linhart S (1983) China und Japan, Wien/Heidelberg, pp 315–316
2. Nahm AC (1988) Korea—tradition and transformation. Elizabeth (NJ), p 125
3. Breen M (2004) The Koreans, New York, p 117
4. Kindermann G-K (2005) Der Aufstieg Koreas in der Weltpolitik; Muenchen, p 336
5. Nahm A cit. above p 474
6. Lee M-Y (2011) The Vietnam war—South Korea's search for national security. In: Kim B-K, Vogel EF (eds) The transformation of South Korea, Cambridge, p 434
7. Vogel EF Nation Rebuilders: Mustafa Kemal Atatuerk, Lee Kuan-Yew, Deng Xiao-Ping and Pak Chung-hee. In: Kim B-K, Vogel EF (eds) p 513
8. Maull HW, Maull IM (1987) KOREA, Muenchen, pp 56–57
9. Weggel O (1991) Kultur und Wertvortstellungen im asiatisch-pazifischen Raum. In: Schneidewind D, Toepfer A (Hrsg) Der asiatisch-pazifische Raum; Landsberg, p 43
10. Song B-N (2003) The rise of the Korean economy. Oxford, p 311
11. Won-Chol O cit. above, p 499
12. Kim S-S (2008) The role of the middle class in Korea democratization, Seoul
13. Kim S-S cit. above, pp 109–110
14. Choi S-J, Lee Y-J (2004) Umgekehrte Entwicklungshilfe - Die Koreanische Arbeitsemigration in Deutschland, Goethe Institut, Seoul without date
15. Auswaertiges Amt; Deutsch-Koreanisches Protokoll ueber ein Programm zur voruebergehenden Beschaeftigung von koreanischen Bergarbeitern in westdeutschen Kohlezechen: Archiv Nr. 6; Bonn, 16 Dec 1963
16. Deutsche Botschaft (German Embassy in the Republic of Korea); Entsendung koreanischer Krankenschwestern und Krankenpflegehelferinnen; V 6 - 8-/155/71; Seoul, 17 Mar 1971

Chapter 5
Powerful Conglomerations—The Chaebol

5.1 Development of the *Chaebol*

Already before World War II, when Korea was still part of the Japanese Empire (though a rather underprivileged one), following the Japanese example, there existed groups of enterprises in Korea (named *chaebol*) which had established themselves in various fields of business such as production, trade, and financing. These enterprises resembled the Japanese *zaibatsu* (which were called *keiretsu* after the war) but were much smaller than their powerful role models. The Japanese administration in Korea mobilized these enterprises for the needs of the Japanese wartime economy. According to the Chinese characters, the word *chaebol* can be translated as "glorious rightful family" or simply as "business family." Metaphorically, it can be also understood as a "monopoly."

Usually, the phenomenon of the family-ruled companies is considered typical for Korea. But there are also numerous huge conglomerations in the West that are under the influence of major clans (Walmart, Volkswagen, Glencore, Philips, and Exor for example), and even in the People's Republic of China, 40 % of all major companies are reported to be owned by families. Yet, most of their top managers are normally hired from outside the family.

As repeatedly mentioned, in Korea the family is considered as a safe haven and the father is traditionally the one constant factor in social relations and can rule with great authority. For this reason, the owners of a *chaebol* tried to employ as many relatives as possible in their companies, starting with their own children. This has to do with the tendency of Koreans in leading positions to found and continue dynasties. Furthermore, the children have to obey the father as a person of absolute respect, something which cannot be necessarily expected to the same degree from distant relatives or people from the outside.

D.K. Schneidewind, *Economic Miracle Market South Korea*,
DOI 10.1007/978-981-10-0615-9_5

The word "*chaebol*" has still a magical sound for many Koreans, although only a few conglomerates can be considered *chaebol* in the traditional sense. In the first place, the term describes an enormous massing of affiliated enterprises, working in many different fields. The *chaebol* like to call themselves a "group" or "group of companies." But the conception of "group" is not really valid as these conglomerations do usually not draw up consolidated balance sheets in the sense of a modern international rendering of accounts.

Kim [1] believes that without the propagation of the "classical *chaebol*" in Korea, neither capitalistic-minded entrepreneurs could have become active nor would stable economic structures have developed. These conglomerations facilitated the introduction of an industrial policy to the early presidents of the Republic after the war: Syngman Rhee and Pak Chung-hee. This further established bureaucrats who directed the whole economy with their "administrative guidance."

Rhee was democratically elected in 1948, but behaved increasingly like a power politician with dictatorial traits. He nationalized the formerly Japanese enterprises of public areas such as finances, transportation, communication, and energy. Managers who had already worked before the war as well as managers of newly established companies after the war were members of Rhee's Liberal Democratic Party. Particularly, managers of the construction business helped to finance the party and in return obtained licenses and foreign exchanges. An economy of favoritism developed in which making profits had much more to do with personal relations than with progressing productivity.

Initially, leading entrepreneurs wrangled with government bureaucrats for power. Under the influence of the Korean War, ultimately a centrally run system that emphasized a strict anticommunist system prevailed. This led to an enforcement of the state agencies and a weakening of the civil society. During this time, in cooperation with the bureaucrats, the leading capitalistic figures accumulated an enormous wealth within their family enterprises. Not all of them succeeded in saving this wealth into the present time.

The military coup of 1961 aimed to remove the prevailing corrupt system. It further wanted to make the country independent from imports and consequently from foreign powers. In order to achieve these goals, an own strong export industry needed to be build up. For this purpose, Pak Chung-hee and his regime depended on the financially strong and powerfully managed *chaebol*. Of the 30 biggest *chaebol* existing as of today, only three were founded during the Park period or thereafter.

At the beginning of his term, Park was inclined to a central state economy, an obvious decision for a former traditional military leader. It was reported that Lee Byung-chul, the legendary founder of the Samsung group, convinced the president that only a relatively liberal market economy would extricate the necessary managerial initiatives and creativeness, which would be essential to achieve an international competitiveness and to ensure the supply of modern commodities for the population. Fortunately, General Park was a good listener and was extremely open for new ideas. His confidence in Lee Byung-chul was rooted in the fact that this entrepreneur was one of the few Koreans, who had studied abroad, namely at Waseda University, a top university in Japan.

The former major general regarded the *chaebol* in the same way he had looked at his old military units that he had trusted and leaned on as a commander. On the one hand, he depended on the *chaebol* leaders but on the other hand had to convince them of his superior leadership and command them in a convincing style. A controlled relation developed, which resulted in advantages for both sides. A powerful modern industry was build up from zero, and up-to-date technologies were developed within a short period of time. The management of a big army of laborers and the conquest of foreign markets were only possible with an intelligent leadership, military discipline, will, and know-how of industrial management, all of them focused on ambitious targets with a concentrated input by all means. Less than half of all *chaebol* leaders of that time had a higher education. This had been hardly possible to obtain during the time of Japanese occupation. But these personalities excelled with their natural intelligence and an acquired assertiveness. Until today, *chaebol* leaders, without exception, have of a solid academic education which is partly surmounted by postgraduate studies abroad. In contrast to this, their fathers could be considered preponderantly "self-made men." Yet, although they had less theoretical management know-how or even expert knowledge, they made up for this with an iron will to succeed, to always learn new things, and by not being afraid of new challenges.

Besides hospitals and other medicinal establishments, colleges, universities, and research institutes belong to the orbit of many *chaebol*. The old founders of the *chaebol* wanted to express with them their affection and proximity to the public well-being as well as demonstrate their apprehension of science. Certainly, they also wanted to erect memorials for themselves. This reminds of the generous foundations and grants of many patrons in the USA.

In the following, the development of some important *chaebol* like Samsung, Hyundai, SK, and LG will be traced briefly, followed by another eleven groups.

5.2 Leading Chaebol

5.2.1 Samsung

"As Samsung goes, so goes Korea" is a variation of a saying in respect of General Motors for the USA. At present, Samsung's CEO, Mr. Lee Kun-hee, lies in hospital after a heavy stroke, while the whole nation is reading his medical records in alarm whether he will fully recover or, if not, his son and possible heir, Lee Jay-yong, can shoulder the heavy burden of leading the mighty *chaebol*.

The tough entrepreneur Lee Byung-chul founded a small commercial company that traded with food items and textiles in the city of Daegu in 1938. After the war, the company also entered the production of these products. The founder was heavily influenced by the Japanese society and economy, because he had spent some educational years in Japan. He admired the powerful *zaibatsu* such as Yasuda (today Fuyo Group), Sumitomo, Mitsubishi, and Mitsui. Following the example of Mitsui (literally meaning "three wells") and Mitsubishi (literally meaning "three stones"), he named his company Samsung (literally meaning "three stars"). Concerning the organization of the company, the Mitsui Group became later his model. However, his enterprise remained ridiculously small for quite a long time when compared to the Japanese colossus. In 2013, Samsung reported sales of about US$225 billion and a profit of US$30 billion. The members of the Mitsui Group are only loosely connected, and there does not exist anything like a consolidated balance sheet. Nevertheless, Samsung has very likely caught up with the former model of its founder.

The old Lee Byung-chul lacked charisma but had a talent for strategy. Kim [2] reported that Lee changed President Park's mind, who originally intended to integrate some important *chaebol* into an Economic Reconstruction Association (*gyeongje jegon chokjinhoe*) [3]. He convinced Park that it would be better to give free hand to the entrepreneurs of the *chaebol* than letting bureaucrats make decisions concerning the national economy. Thus, the powerful president was ultimately content with his role of passing the objectives of the economic development forward and to leave the matter of economic progress to private management instead of trusting the governmental management with this task. This decision unleashed countless entrepreneurial initiatives. The *chaebol* were integrated into the general framework of the Korean industrial revolution, but they were quickly released to the tough competition with their huge global rivals.

In 1961, the *chaebol* founded their own exclusive association of enterprises, the Federation of Korean Industries (FKI). Lee Byung-chul became its first chairman and developed it into a powerful organization. The FKI has about 450 member companies as of today and is open only for the big industry. There is another association that represents the middle and small industries.

Besides his entrepreneurial expertise, Lee also developed considerable financial skills. He wanted his *chaebol* to rest on many pillars and thus successively entered all relevant industrial segments with Samsung, such as petrochemicals, shipbuilding, electrical appliances, construction and engineering, and aviation. Due to government regulations, an entrance into the banking business was not possible. The letter rule still applies today. This is why Samsung extended into the insurance industry in the last decade. Its focus within this field is the insurance of water and fire damage. The investment business has become similarly important and resulted in the foundation of Samsung Securities.

Meanwhile, the electronic sector of the *chaebol* became the most famous and successful business branch of the conglomeration. Originally, it started with the production of inexpensive household items like washing machines, television sets, microwaves, and private computers of average quality. Yet, Samsung Electronics quickly turned to the top quality level of its overseas rivals and evolved into a market leader with "DRAMS and SCAMS" (dynamic and static random access memories) as well as with semiconductors. Subsequently, Samsung invested in the research and development of electronics and became a global leader in the field of liquid crystals together in sharp competition with the Japanese electronics giant Sony. Measured at its sales volume, Samsung is presently regarded as the biggest technology enterprise in the world.

Though Korean enterprises are highly profit-oriented, they like it to accentuate their endeavors for the general well-being of the population. Accordingly, Mr. Rim, a Samsung manager [4], explains the corporate colors of the *chaebol* as follows: The most important color is blue, which stands for top technology, green symbolizes the commitment to health and the environment, and white hints to the company's direct engagement concerning social responsibilities such as medical care or scholarships for gifted students. The founder Lee, Byung-chul claimed to not only contributing to the quality of life of the Korean people, but also contributing to the well-being of people all over the world.

Career account of B.C. Lee:

1910	Born in Gyeongnam into a well-to-do family
1929	Finished grammar school (SAT exam)
1934	Studied political sciences at Waseda University Tokyo
1938	Founded a rice mill at Masan
1939–1942	Invested into real estate and forwarding businesses (all failed)
1948	Founded a trading house (Samsung)
1953	Founded the sugar plant Cheil
1954	Founded Cheil Textiles Co.
1961	Elected as the chairman of the Federation of Korean Industries
1964–1987	Chairman Samsung Corporation
1964–1966	Founded various charitable foundations
1968	Chairman of the daily newspaper JoongAng Ilbo
1968	Director of the Sungkyunkwan University
1969	Founded Samsung Electronics
1973	Founded Cheil Communication
1975–1985	Founded and operated various cultural establishments
1977	Founded Samsung Construction & Engineering
1977	Founded Samsung Shipyard
1982	Bestowal of an honorary doctoral degree by the Boston University
1997	Deceased in Seoul.

The chairman was well aware of his extraordinary life story and already in 1955 liked to be addressed as *Hoam* Lee Byung-chul. (*Hoam* roughly translates into: "to fill a space with clear water like a lake and, at the same time, stay unshakably in it like a rock.") In his later years, Lee took endeavors to be academically recognized like many other Korean personalities. These people like to emphasize that their nobility is based on the traditional ideal of scholarship and cultural values (in contrast to Japan, where the sword is recognized as the sanctuary of the samurai). Arthur Schopenhauer's aphorism that "common sense can replace almost any degree of formal education, but no education can replace common sense" applies to Lee Byung-chul as well as for some other founders of classical *chaebols*. Lee further incorporated a great fighting spirit and a strong tenacity which both enabled him to attack time and again after every defeat.

In February 2010, the huge family of the owner celebrated posthumously the 100th birthday of its legendary founder. The *Korean Times* in its online paper:

"Samsung Group, Korea's largest conglomerate, celebrated the 100th birthday of the late *Hoam* Lee Byung-chul's at the Hoam Art Hall in Seoul from February 4th to February 19th. On this particular occasion, Lee's family, both former and incumbent Samsung executives, other entrepreneurial leaders, politicians, and bureaucrats attended and commemorated Lee's 100th birthday. All attendees honored and paid respects to a man, whose epic career had spanned the formation of Korean conglomerates from times of harsh authoritarian rule to its transformation into a capitalist economy." Lee was celebrated as the "Father of Business" and even as the "Father of the Korean Industry." Yet, trade unions did not manage to establish themselves in his company.

Unquestionably, this visionary enterpriser kept a particular interest in the research and development of products and new businesses and was a master in their organizational planning. He fully grasped the chances that opened up during the industrialization of South Korea in the era of Pak Chung-hee.

Like most of the Korean *chaebol*, Samsung is not focused on only one business branch unlike most Western enterprises, but it is active in various areas. Besides the well-known electric and electronic business, Samsung is active in the fields of petrochemicals, shipbuilding (it is indeed the world's second biggest ship constructor) and construction and engineering (Samsung Construction and Technologies). The latter was involved in three building projects concerning the highest buildings worldwide, namely the Petronas Towers in Malaysia, the Taipei 101 in Taiwan, and the Burj Khalifa in Dubai. The *chaebol* is further active in the insurance industry and operates a huge retail business. Countless other business branches, such as the fashion business, are likewise entered by Samsung. The Samsung Group is the biggest producer of food in Korea and operates a theme park, the Everland Resort located south of Seoul.

In 1987, Lee transferred the leadership of the *chaebol* solely to his son Lee Kun-hee (born 1942), who was not the first born of his sons. He led Samsung to the absolute peak of the Korean industry and made sure that it became one of the leading companies within the group of international enterprises. Lee seemed to be one of the very rare cases, in which a son inherits the abilities of his father and even replenishes them in certain fields. This globally minded man graduated in economics from the Waseda University in Japan and completed a MBA from the George Washington University in the USA.

Presently, Samsung has sales of approximately US$370 billion, employs roughly 280,000 people worldwide, pays US$18 billion taxes to the Korean government, and combines 22 % of all Korean exports. The president of the company Lee Kun-hee invests heavily into research and development and advances the further globalization of this conglomerate. An investment of about US$9 billion in Austin, Texas, is especially noteworthy. The net sales of Samsung Electronics in China surpassed those in South Korea for the first time in 2013 (18 % of sales versus 10 % at the home market). By region, Asia/Africa accounted for 47 % of all sales, the Americas for 30 %, and Europe for 23 %.

Between April 2008 and March 2010, Lee Kun-hee and his conglomerate endured a crisis when the son of the founder was accused of corruption and tax evasion. He received a two-year suspended sentence. Although corruption and tax evasion are common offenses in Korea and almost considered petty offenses, in this case, however, the amount in question exceeded US$120 million. For two years, Lee resigned from his chairmanship without appointing a temporary replacement or successor. As not unusual in East Asia, he openly and humbly apologized on television before he reentered his position. Though the public opinion condemned the machinations of Samsung, the majority of the people could understand that Lee Kun-hee did everything to ensure the stability of his *chaebol* and to secure the jobs of his employees without taking any direct personal financial advantages.

Lee tightened the group by merging some companies and by selling others. The focus on the core businesses had very positive outcomes for the company. Only the request of the government to sell its automotive business to Renault was regretted. Nevertheless, Renault could not succeed alone and presently Samsung and Renault are building up a joint business. Yet, it becomes difficult to gain market shares in a domestic market, where Hyundai/Kia account for 70 % of all automobile sales. According to its own statements, Samsung is the world market leader with memory chips (40 %), flat screens (23 %), and smartphones (20 %). In the domestic market, the Samsung family dominates the retail business with numerous department stores and supermarkets.

However, some entrepreneurial extravagances survived like the ownership of the Shilla Hotel in Seoul which is considered as one of the top hotels in the world. The company also owns the fifth largest theme park in the world (Everland) and Cheil, a communication agency (marketing, advertising, public relations, event management), which is globally active and has already advanced to number 19 among big agencies. The Samsung Medical Center (SMC), which includes a number of hospitals and medical research centers working on a charitable in principle, is highly esteemed in Korea. They get over $100 million annual support from the group. Additionally, there are financial contributions to the oldest university of Korea, the Sungkyunkwan University which was founded in 1398.

Compared to most Korean enterprises, Samsung survived the financial crisis of 1997 relatively well, despite its ongoing dynamic developments. In most Korean firms, the change from one generation to the other was not always as successful as with Samsung. Most Korean university graduates dream of working for this *chaebol*. Among the major customers of Samsung are most famous enterprises such as Apple, Dell, Hewlett Packard, or Sony. Significant contracts that were concluded in the last years were projects such as a building for renewable energies of 2500 MW in Canada, providing Shell with storage capacities for liquid gas (total value of the order US$47 billion) and—within a Korean consortium—the erection of nuclear power plants in the United Arab Emirates.

Important managers of the group can expect above-average incomes but generally only get a contract for one year. The working atmosphere of the *chaebol* is described as extremely stressful. This is illustrated by the death of Samsung Electronics' vice president in 2010, when the 55-year-old top manager jumped from his luxury apartment in South Seoul. He left a farewell letter in which he pointed out that an extreme workload and responsibility had resulted in depression and ultimately caused his dramatic suicide. Just one year before, he was awarded the title of "Best Engineer of Korea." Particularly, small mechanical engineering companies, to which Samsung outsources technical services, suffer from the continuous pressure of their commissioner and many of them went bankrupt.

For some years, the firstborn son of Lee Byung-chul, Lee Maeng-hee, plagued his younger brother with legal claims with respect to the company's assets. Ultimately, the court ruled that the transfer of the group from the father to his younger son was entirely legal. Now, Lee Kun-hee has to take care of a smooth transfer of the business to his only son, while at the same time somehow satisfying his two daughters. The oldest daughter, Lee Boo-jin, is already the president of the Shilla Hotel and manages Samsung's duty-free business. The younger daughter, Lee Seo-hyun, became the president of Everland and manages a couple of fashion brands.

5.2.2 Hyundai

Chung Ju-yung was a man with strong leadership abilities. He lived from 1915 to 2001 and only had an elementary education but excelled in work ethics, personal courage, and a particular instinct for business opportunities. His father expected him to take over his small farm in the village of Ansan, which is today part of the province of Gangwon in North Korea. But the son escaped to the port city of Incheon and took a position as a dock hand. He later moved to Seoul and worked as a delivery boy before he succeeded to conduct some clerical work in a rice mill and advanced into the bookkeeping department. In his later career, he profited a lot from his accounting knowledge. When he was 25, Chung started a small repair shop for automobiles. However, he lost it to a fire. Unflinching, he rebuilt the shop, and after the war, his Hyundai Auto Repair Company was regarded as fairly successful. But he was more attracted by the building trade since the beginning of a construction boom promised higher profits. Syngman Rhee already entitled him to erect major projects including the construction of bridges—a task which he executed with great self-confidence and success.

The later President Park became fond of this entrepreneur and entrusted him to build dams, roads, and power plants. Chung and his company became famous when they build the first motorway from Seoul to Busan. This led to new contracts with the Gulf States, which he also completed successfully against all odds. His interest in shipping was sparked by these projects, and he entered the field of shipbuilding. From this field, he moved into the production of cars and continued to advance in the electronics business.

Before Chung retired in 1987, he divided his *chaebol* into five units, which were all managed by sons or other close relatives:

1. Hyundai Motors Company
2. Hyundai Construction Company

3. Hyundai Heavy Industries
4. Hyundai Precision Industries
5. Halla Group (satellite *chaebol* with the business branches cement, automotive parts, construction, and mechanical engineering, which was founded by a brother of Chung Ju-yungs).

"Chung Ju-yungs incredible ascent from rags-to-riches was closely interwoven with South Korea developing into a nation with a key position in the global industry" [5]. Together with the founders of Samsung, LG, and Daewoo, Chung is one of the most prominent personalities of postwar Korean history. Chung Ju-yung ran in his later years as a presidential candidate. As a Korean patriot, he was very much concerned with the relationship of the two Koreas and he maintained connections with North Korean leaders.

In 2005, the conglomeration adopted a new format with five holdings:

(1) Hyundai Marine
(2) Hyundai Automobile
(3) Hyundai Department Store
(4) Hyundai Development
(5) Hyundai Heavy Industries.

As of today, Hyundai Motors, together with its acquired affiliated companies like Kia, commands a market share of 70 % in South Korea, though 3/4 of the produced sedans are sold overseas. The group already belongs to the five biggest automobile producers in the world (together with Toyota, General Motors, Volkswagen, Hyundai, and Ford). It is by far the biggest group within the conglomeration. The oldest son of the founder, Chung Mong-koo, serves as its chairman since 2000. He is a graduated engineer and served in various functions in many member companies of the five holdings. Between 1998 and 2000, he was a chairman of the whole conglomeration before he concentrated on the automotive business, which he brought to a top world level by applying rigid quality requirements.

Like Samsung's chairman, he was accused of financial irregularities and convicted to three years in prison. The sentence was later converted into a "donation" of 1 billion dollar for charity and he was ultimately pardoned in 2008 by the administration of the Lee Myung-bak government (whose president formerly served as an executive within the same *chaebol*).

Hyundai Motors does not only produce sedans but manufactures trucks and busses a well. An interesting establishment is Hyundai Rotem. This enterprise produces railway vehicles and tanks. The Korean newspaper JoongAng Daily (September 20, 2009) proudly announced that "Korean tanks roll into the global markets." These combat tanks belong to a "luxury segment," and Rotem consequently charges high prices. In 2009, Rotem sold military equipment for more than US$400 million. Recently, the company got its first order to deliver 38 trams to Turkey as it has developed an efficient, ecofriendly low-floor tram.

Presently, Hyundai is not considered any more as a complete *chaebol*, though the group is still ranked second in Korea. This *chaebol* has overexpanded at the end of the last century and has diverted from its core businesses. Therefore, the weaknesses of Hyundai became evident during the financial crisis of 1997/98. It split up into many individual units. Among them, Hyundai Motors survived comfortably with a lot of foreign capital. Currently, the company makes good profits and it has accrued a considerable solvency.

Another huge section of Hyundai, the Heavy Industries Group is headed by Chung Mong-koo's sister in law, Mrs. Hyun Jeong-eun. This group is engaged, among other things, in the production of elevators, the shipping industry, and tourism. Therefore, as typical for a *chaebol*, it meddles in different branches and seems to be deeply indebted. Another group of the company is Hyundai Heavy Industry, which focuses on shipbuilding. According to the legend of the company, it was founded by the late Chung Ju-yung after he persuaded Greek shipping companies to contract the purchase of several ships. With these contracts, he convinced banks in London to give him a credit that he used to found the company. This business branch later absorbed parts of the former Samho *chaebol* and thus entered the steel production business. Chung Mong-koo, chairman of Hyundai Motors, has already expressed his interest in this business, probably as a source of supply for his automotive assembly factories.

Another famous part of Hyundai companies is Hyundai Engineering & Construction. This part was the pride of the founder and stands for the glorious success of the entire group. Chairman Chung Mong-koo and Chairwoman Hyu Jeong-eun competed to acquire the majority of shares when the Korean Exchange Bank offered them on the market. Of course, the widow of Chung Ju-yung's older brother had no chance against her brother-in-law, who has much more financial means.

Actually, these two people did not like each other at all. The *Financial Times* [6] described their relationship as follows: "But within South Korea the Shakespearean family frictions between Mr. Chung and Mrs. Hyu overshadow all financial calculations and potential effects of synergy." Chung Mong-ku has the advantage of being the oldest living son of the founder. On the other hand, the husband of Hyu Jeong-eun was the favorite son of the founder, who acquired the status of a martyr, when he saved his father's face, who illegally paid some hundred million dollars to North Korea in order to enable a meeting between President Kim Dae-jung and President Kim Jong-il. Hyu Jeong-eun's husband, the younger son of Chung Mong-woo, committed suicide by jumping from the company's headquarters in Seoul.

For a long time, the Korean government has pursued a policy of dissolving of massive company conglomerations like the *chaebol*. Instead, the government prefers enterprises that focus on a core business and do not waste their energies for diversifications and family feuds. As long as the patriarch Chung Ju-yung was alive, these problems did not occur in the company as he was a benevolent but severe dictator. Until his death, he lived close to the place of his first employment as a bookkeeper of a rice mill business in the district Insa-dong in Seoul. He lived a modest life and led an exemplary family life with his wife and eight children (all boys). He acquired full recognition of the industrial society when he was repeatedly elected as a chairman of the Federation of Korean Industries. Obviously, he could not arrange his succession in a way which guaranteed a smooth development for his enormous lifework. Like most *chaebol* leaders, he was not capable to understand the perspective of laborers.

His son Chung Mong-koo is likely to become the successor of his legendary father. He was already decorated with two international honorary doctorates, one from the National University of Ulan Bator and another from the Connecticut State University. He is preparing his son Chung Eui-sun for the role of "heir apparent."

5.2.3 SK

The SK group recently became the third largest business conglomeration in Korea. It was founded in 1953 by Chey Jong-hyun when the textile enterprise Sunkyung was purchased. In 1976, it obtained a government license to establish an international trade company, which opened the way for the company to become a classical *chaebol*. With the acquisition of the Korea National Oil Company and the Korea Mobile Communication Service Company, two entirely different lines of business were added to the conglomeration. This *chaebol* has developed enormously under the leadership of the son of the founder Chey Tae-won (Choi Tae-won), who was married to the daughter of the former president of South Korea, Roh Tae-woo. Like his colleagues in the other two top *chaebols*, he was sentenced to three years in prison because of financial irregularities and pardoned without serving a day of his conviction. In 2012, the chairmanship was handed over to the former President Cho Dae-sik.

Today, everybody in Korea knows SK because it is famous for its wireless services in mobile communications and the Internet and it is a pioneer within the field of mobile phones. The *chaebol* is the second largest manufacturer of semiconductors (magnetic and optical memories) worldwide; this section of the company is known under the name of Hynix.

The role of SK in the energy industry is even more important. The company ran the first oil refineries in Korea and it is as of today globally engaged in exploring fossil energies. It, for example, hit the headlines with the development of gas fields in Eastern Siberia (Kamchatka) and—in alliance with Chevron—new and sensationally productive oil wells off the coast of Brazil.

Starting with the oil business, the step toward the petrochemical industry was not too far. Propylene oxide was produced, which is the base for the production of polyurethane. This branch of the company also produces biodegradable materials. It is further an important manufacturer of polyester fibers. The chemical branch expanded into the life sciences. Drugs such as anticancer agents and medications against schizophrenia were developed. Later, SK engaged in the manufacturing of lithium batteries and developing electrically driven vehicles, which is a highly future-oriented industry.

In 2007, the group was split into the investment branch (SK Holding) and seven operating units: SK Energy, SK Telekom, SK Chemical, SK Construction, SK Networks, SK Gas, and SK Insurances—all of them listed at the stock market.

Like other *chaebol*, SK could not resist to acquire a well-known hotel, the popular Walker Hill in the eastern part of Seoul. In hunt for profit, the very popular Korean folk shows in the hotel were canceled since and a Casino, which is much frequented by Chinese tourists, was established instead.

5.2.4 LG

Koo In-hwoi and his son Koo Ja-gyeong built in 1947 [7] a production facility for cosmetic creams at Busan. Because it was difficult to find plastic fastenings for tubes in Korea, they decided to enter the production of plastic products. Besides the tube fastenings, they soon further produced soap dishes, combs, and toothbrushes. Being in touch with their clients, they moved forward to engage in the production of toothpastes (the most famous brand being Perioe) and soaps. The requirement for primary materials prompted them to invest in oil refineries. This in turn introduced them to the tanker business, which in turn introduced them later into the insurance business for maritime shipping. Because all these businesses turned out to be very successful, they accumulated a considerable financial wealth. The founders looked for branches where they could invest their fortune and believed that electrical appliances would be a good choice. Soon, they started to produce radios and quickly entered the electronic business. This *chaebol* later became a pioneer for the production of glass fiber cables. LG is a perfect example for a *chaebol* that incorporates horizontal as well as vertical diversifications.

Presently, LG (which is an abbreviation of its former name Lucky Goldstar) is one of the globally leading enterprises in the field of semiconductors and telecommunication business. The current chairman, the third one in the succession line, Koo Bo-moo, hires and educates excellent managers. He formulates his own, philanthropic philosophy of management and devotes his free time to ornithology (according to Gongto [8]).

Whereas the founder families of Hyundai and Samsung have direct control over their groups by holding great capital shares of their central enterprises of the group, the Koo family confines to a more indirect control. Within their *chaebol*, the numerous members make only minor mutual investments. The two main enterprises of the group, Lucky Ltd. and Goldstar Company Ltd., have only less than 30 % of the shares of the group at their disposal. This is also called a pyramidal form of control.

LG is considered a conservative *chaebol*. Already its founder Koo In-hwoi supported the Confucian virtue of harmony. Initially, the majority of all top managers came from families related to the Koo family, as well as from the family of the husband's wife. Presently, mainly professional board members are selected for top positions, based on their abilities and not on their family ties or age. Decisions within the group are made independently and are basically decentralized.

Besides the basic businesses such as telecommunications, electronics, displays, and chemicals, there are many other joint enterprises in a broader wickerwork of interests. There are for instance also firms which produce and sell wine or soda and take challenges of the solar business. Special expectations are placed with the newly founded company LG Life Sciences. This company is the reason why the logo of LG has recently been translated into "Life's Good."

After a hesitant start, LG initiated in the 1980s a global expansion of its business. Currently, there exist more than 150 branches and 50 joint ventures. LG is the fourth biggest *chaebol* in Korea. It has no records of financial problems, no scandals are reported, and there were no major collisions with the trade unions. The group shrank because the families of Koo and Hu decided to control their interests by themselves, and thus, the GS group separated from LG and LG sold its department stores (GS Square) to the Lotte group.

5.2.5 GS Group

This *chaebol* seceded from the LG Group in 2005. Thus, the owner families of Koo and Huh (Heo) started to operate solely within their prevailing business interests. The name "GS" hints to the origin of this company, Lucky Goldstar (LG), by interchanging the initials.

The joint venture between GS Holdings and Chevron operates with Caltex, Korea, the nation's second largest refinery. Other prominent companies of the group are Haeyang City Gas. With Seorabol Gas, GS Nanotech, and GS Fuel Cell, the group is involved in future-oriented technologies. Besides its interests in the field of energy, the group operates within the retail business, especially in mail order selling. It is active in operating convenience stores (CVS) and supermarkets (GS 25), and in the long run, its aim is to extend into all global markets. The group also produces prepared meals and operates the Mr. Donut chain. It further runs an advertising agency and leases out real estate. Like all other main *chaebol*, GS maintains an engineering and construction unit as well.

The *chaebol* sells sports equipment and articles and is well known for its activities in professional sports. For instance, it owns the soccer club FC Seoul.

The current chairman and CEO, Mr. Huh Jin-soo is known as an open-minded and friendly person. He was just reelected as the chairman of the FKI.

5.2.6 The Amazing Lotte Group

This group is a very atypical *chaebol* and only climbed to its recent position within the last few years. Its founder Shin Kyuk-ho was born in Ulsan and lived after the Second World War as a businessman under the name Shigemitsu, Takeo, in Japan. There, he studied at the Waseda University, married a Japanese woman, and assumed Japanese citizenship. He still has the habit to alternately live one month in Korea and one month in Japan. Thus, half of his business empire is ruled from Tokyo. He started by selling food products in Japan and was very successful with chewing gum—an item that he had encountered on a trip to the USA. This product, until then unknown in Japan, became popular in the postwar years in the country. After some time, he became quite prosperous and decided to make significant investments in his home country, initially mainly in real estate, which was very cheap at that time.

He invested into new fields of retail and always kept a watchful eye on the real estate business. He derived the name "Lotte" of his conglomeration from the heroine of a German novel by Goethe. Concerning his business, he always remained close to the consumers (retail business, housing units, hotels) and avoided highly risky businesses in the heavy industries and investment goods until later.

Lotte commands a wide network of retail outlets. Many of them operate shops that work around the clock. In recent years, the takeover of an American chain of convenience store of Unitas Capital caused some sensation. With more than 3500 outlets, Lotte owns about a quarter of all Korean CVS in the country and is number two behind FamilyMart (a chain of the Japanese trading house Itochu with 4800 outlets).

Regionally, Lotte expands especially into China. Here, a Chinese–Dutch joint venture and likewise the supermarket chain Times with 65 outlets were absorbed. Lotte is also expanding in other Southeast Asian markets.

Apart from supermarkets, Lotte also owns more expensive department stores (36 in South Korea, 9 in Seoul alone, and more are planned). This business will further go overseas, mainly to Vietnam and Indonesia. There exists already one deluxe department store in Moscow.

Additionally, Lotte is famous for its hotel business; the most distinguished one is located in the center of old Seoul. It also serves as the head office for all global activities. Presently, 15 units are known, among them those located in Japan, Guam, Vietnam, China, and Moscow.

The company further owns apartment blocks and an amusement center in the southeast of Seoul. Of the approximately 60 business units of Lotte, an engineering and construction company was also established, which mainly takes care of the *chaebol*'s own projects. A petrochemical branch and a financing branch, which focuses much on the credit card business, insurances, and asset developments, have been established as well.

Still active at an age around 93 years, the old Shin Kyuk-ho wants to see two of his last dreams come true: the creation of an own beer brand and the completion of the Lotte World Tower. This building with its elegant design will be the highest building east of the Arabian/Persian Gulf. The brand Cloud Beer was introduced in the first half of 2014, and the tower will be completed in 2016.

The Lotte group achieved all this despite the fact that (officially) in Korea everything is unpopular which is of Japanese origin. The last sales figures reportedly are approximately US$80 billion. The *chaebol* mainly employs family members as top executives. The older son was entrusted with the Japanese business, while the second son supervises the Korean operation. Only recently did the patriarch, who looks rather young, relieve his older son from his duties in Japan. This move might signify that the second son will become his successor. Presently, a succession feud rages between the two sons.

Of course Kepco and Posco are bigger than GS and Lotte; but they lack the characteristics of a classical *chaebol* such as a single-owner family, a patriarchal founder, and the diversification into numerous business branches. Instead, both companies were originally owned by the government. Kepco was privatized in 2002 and Posco in 1997. Kepco (Korea Electric Power) supplies Korea with electricity, and it takes pride in operating modern nuclear power plants. The company is listed on the stock exchange. Posco (Pohang Iron and Steel) is the second largest steel producer in the world and operates with 30000 employees at the southern coast of South Korea. Posco is a public limited company, and up to half of the shares are owned by foreign capital.

5.2.7 Daewoo—An Example of a Drastic Failure

Kim Woo-choong, another extremely successful entrepreneur of the postwar period, for a long time, was considered the most successful businessman of the nation and also its hardest worker [9]. He founded the *chaebol* Daewoo, which was well-known overseas and considered a flagship of South Korean industry. The company ranked as second behind Hyundai. Kim came from the textile industry and entered one after another the fields of heavy industry, automotive production, and electronics. Although the founder only owned relatively few shares of the companies of his group, people spoke of a "one-man empire." He ruled his companies with an iron fist. Similarly, he was always in conflict with the trade unions. However, it has to be mentioned that at this time, these organizations had only little understanding when it came to economical necessities.

In the wake of the Korean financial crisis in 1997, the Daewoo *chaebol* collapsed because it was laden with excessive foreign debts. The new administration did not provide any support as it had been customary in former times. This triggered the most spectacular bankruptcy in the history of Korea and an inconceivable loss of US$80 billion was reported and Daewoo broke into pieces. Many parts of the group still operate successfully as of today under different names.

Kim Woo-choong who is 79 by now still lives outside the country and is convinced that the breakup of his conglomeration was unnecessary and happened due to the pressure of the IMF (International Monetary Fund). He was in conflict with the bureaucrats' economic policy making team, which opposed the idea of him solving the debts crisis by raising funds instead of cutting debts.

At the same time, other *chaebol* with famous names collapsed like Daewoo [10]:

Kia
Halla

Hanbo
Jinro
Haitai
New Core
Sammi
Cheonggu
Daenong
Ssangbangwool
Hanshin Construction
Soosan Heavy Industries
Taeil

Some of these companies were saved by other *chaebol*, and some of them were totally restructured and continued to operate under new names, sponsored by other investors, and lead by other managers. This earth-shattering event was considered necessary by the government as well as by the majority of the local business society.

5.3 Actual Ranking of the *Chaebol*

Within the last decades, various *chaebol* ascended, while others descended. Some even disappeared, while others were newly established. There have been fusions and split offs, and sometimes the names of companies changed as well. During the time of the late military dictatorship, some *chaebol* were nationalized, some were regrouped, and a few were newly founded. During the term of President Kim Young-sam, a new phase of successful privatization of various national enterprises started.

Under the guidance of some dozen owner families, roughly three dozen powerful conglomerations established over time. The biggest daughter companies with their affiliated firms could be also called *chaebols* or, to use a more modern term, *keyul*. All in all, about a hundred agglomerated groups of companies are nowadays considered to be *chaebols*.

In the following, 20 of the most prominent conglomerations are listed (Table 5.1).

Most of the affiliated companies of the *chaebol* are listed on the stock market. The assets and number of employees vary considerably. Nearly all *chaebol* only sparsely publish their business figures. This has to do with the secretiveness, which is still preferred by Korean enterprises. Yet, it is also related to the many corporate interconnections and the various joint ventures, which make it very hard or even impossible to obtain figures.

The statements do not comprise figures of the hundreds of subsidiaries both within the country and overseas. It further has to be mentioned that many relations do change significantly in the course of time.

Samsung has occupied the top of the list for a couple of years. In former times, it sometimes swapped positions with Hyundai, which clearly is second behind Samsung. Hyundai's position has become even more stable after the company has

Table 5.1 Ranking of the 20 largest *Chaebol* in Korea (2013)

	Chaebol	Sales in US$ billion	Total balance in US$ billion	Number of affiliated companies	Number of employees (in 1000)	Main fields of business
1	Samsung	317	304	74	265	Electronics, E&C
2	Hyundai A.	146	167	57	155	Cars, automotive, E&C
3	SK	144	133	80	79	Telecom., energy
4	LG	108	94	61	143	Electronics, telecom.
5	Kepco	84	172	24	53	Electricity supply
6	Posco	65	77	46	39	Steel
7	GS	63	53	80	33	Retail, Energy, E&C
8	Lotte	60	85	74	91	Retail, real estate
9	Hyundai H.	56	53	26	42	Heavy industry, shipbuilding
10	Hanwha	36	34	51	35	Chemicals, insurance
11	S-Oil	29	11	2	3	Refineries
12	KT	26	32	57	67	Telecom.
13	LS	25	18	51	14	Cable, electronic equipment
14	Hanjin	23	37	48	31	Air and sea transport
15	Dongbu	22	17	64	17	Chemicals, electronics
16	CJ	16	22	73	54	Food, entertainment
17	Kumho	16	17	26	22	Tires, air transport, petrol.
18	Shinsegae	16	23	29	47	Retail
19	Doosan	16	28	22	24	Machines, E&C
20	DSME	15	17	19	17	Sea technology

This list of conglomerates does not include organizations like Korea Gas (which is government-owned), Korea Land & Housing (which is a public institution), or Nonghyup (which is an association of Korean agricultural enterprises)
Source Bank Korea; FTC (Fair Trade Commission) of Korea

integrated Hyundai Engineering & Construction (not yet included in the foregoing ranking list). The so-called Hyundai group (Heavy Industries) is not yet visible on this list. Currently, the third position is occupied by SK. LG is on the fourth place as it shrank by the secession of the GS group.

5.3.1 Posco (Pohang Iron & Steel Co.)

Placed as number five among the big business groups, the company does not have the characteristics of a classical *chaebol* as it is a public company that is not owned by a family. It further concentrates only on one specific business section. Posco belongs to the biggest steel producers in the world. It is basically a sound business with good profits; however, according to *The Korea Times* from March 17, 2015, it is endangered by powerful politicians who want to install confidants as chairmen, from which they expect favors in turn.

5.3.2 Kepco (Korea Electric Power)

Like Posco, Kepco is also not owned by a family. This *keyul* ranks sixth among the big Korean business groups. It concentrates on supplying the nation with electricity. The company was founded in 1882 and was government-owned. Meanwhile, it is listed on the Korea Stock Exchange. Besides the national power supply, it specializes in the export of nuclear fuel power plants, in particular to the Arabian hemisphere.

5.3.3 Hyundai Heavy Industries

As pointed out above, the Ulsan-based Hyundai Heavy Industries was formerly part of the Hyundai group. It is mainly engaged in the shipbuilding business, where it has a leading role in the world. However, it is currently struggling due to China's powerful entrance into the shipbuilding industry. Besides container ships and chemical tankers, Hyundai engages in the production of machines and off-shore engineering. The group is also active in the field of green energy by producing wind rotors and solar cells.

5.3.4 Hanwha

Hanwha (number ten in the ranking) was founded in 1952 and has supplied in its earlier days the military with explosives. To many business people, it is still known by its old name Hankook. With about 30,000 employees in over 50 subsidiaries, the group works predominantly in the chemical industry. Recently, it took over defense-related business operations from the Samsung group. Hanwha has also constructed many high-rising buildings and it operates shipbuilding wharfs. It further takes interest in the insurance business. In order to become a global leader in alternative energies, it acquired in 2012 the German solar company of Q-Cells. The current CEO is Mr. Kim Seung-yeon.

5.3.5 S Oil

This atypical *chaebol* was established in 1976 as Ssangyong Refinery. Its products are petroleum, petrochemicals, lubricants, polysilicones, para-xylene, and propylene. The conglomerate is considered as one of the most successful "downstream operations." The Saudi Aramco Co. owns 34 % of its shares, and the CEO is a Saudi. The group is regarded as very profitable.

5.3.6 KT

This group is not a classical *chaebol* either. It was established in 1981 as a public corporation and privatized in 1985. The shares are widely spread, and with approximately 7 %, the National Pension Fund (NPF) is the biggest shareholder.

KT originally served as Korea's first telecommunication company. Its affiliation KTF developed and manufactures mobile phones and terminals as well as android smartphones. Both units have merged in 2009. The group engages in wired as well as wireless telecommunication and high-speed Internet, operating its own satellites. Though the business is generally focused on South Korea, it has also developed interests in China, Taiwan, the USA, and Canada.

The management is independent from any major shareholder, and the group is rather a modern *keyul* than a traditional *chaebol.*

5.3.7 LS

LS Corporation is actually a holding company with mainly four units: LS Cable Systems (power and communication cables), LS Industrial Systems (electrical and automation systems), LS-Nikko Copper (copper smelting and refining), and LS Mtron (machinery and technical components). This group resembles more a real *chaebol* as it is controlled entirely by the Koo family, which also owns the huge LS group.

5.3.8 Hanjin

Hanjin was established in 1945 as a transport company to serve the US Forces. Later, it made a fortune during the Vietnam War. As of today, its containers can be found on all seven seas. Hanjin owns and operates over 150 own containerships, and the conglomerate can be called a full-service logistic provider. It also acquired Hanjin Heavy Industries, which was founded in 1937 and became famous for its creative engineering, for instance the process of underwater welding. It also specialized in building special ships such as tankers, cable layers, and icebreakers. The engineering and construction branch of the *chaebol* excels in building bridges, shipyards, and airports. In 1969, the national airline KAL was privatized and Hanjin took over the airline. The budget carrier Jin Air also belongs to the group, and in 2013, 44 % of Czech Airlines were taken over as well.

The vice president of Korean Airlines, Mrs. Cho Hyun-ah, daughter of the group's owner Mr. Cho Yang-ho, showed a rather ignominious behavior in December 2014, when she ordered an airliner, which was already on the runway to return to the gate as she insisted to expel a cabin manager, who protected a stewardess, who had served nuts in an "improper way" to the vice president of the airline. Cho Hyun-ah then had forced both the cabin manager and the stewardess to kneel down while verbally and physically abusing them. *The Korean Herald* from December 16, 2014, considered this incident a "beastly event" and voiced its opinion that leadership positions in companies should not be distributed by birthrights and instead should be filled by the most qualified persons. The paper reflected the public opinion that the second and third generations of the *chaebol* families attribute with their arrogance to the prevailing "antibusiness sentiments" in contemporary Korea.

5.3.9 Dongbu

The Dongbu group was established rather late in 1969 by the active enterpriser Kim Jun-ki as a small construction company named Miryung Construction. It quickly grew with the development of South Korea and important segments of the economy. Its 42 affiliations employ 35,000 people in the fields of steel, electronics, fertilizers, shipping, as well as engineering and construction. It also expanded aggressively into financial services such as insurances and securities. The managers of the conglomerate are considered to be particularly energetic and creative. Like in many other *chaebol*, the ownership is somehow shrouded in mystery. It looks as if 45 % are portfolio investments and 55 % belong to major shareholders, the latter most likely being member companies of the group. The founder Kim Jun-ki owns approximately 10 %, and another family member Kim Nam-ho owns 3 % of the shares. Though this firm looks like a typical family-ruled *chaebol*, Mr. Lee Soon-byung is its CEO.

5.3.10 CJ

CJ, which stands for "Cheil Jedang," is perhaps a good example of how the rise of the *chaebol* fostered Korea's modern economy by using the power of family clans and operating in an economical vacuum. It seized almost all business opportunities in Korea and left very little for entrepreneurial talents that followed later, except for entirely new technologies like the IT industries. The increasing unbalanced spread of the country's wealth might become in the medium to long run a major obstacle for the nation.

The ingenious founder of the Samsung group, Lee Byung-chul, established around 1953 the Cheil Jedang, company which went into the production of sugar and flour and later conquered the cooking oil and nuclear acids market. From this base, he moved into the business of processed food and frozen food. The next step was to found a pharmaceutical company, which produced hepatitis vaccines and alpha interferon, an anticancer medicine.

From 1992 on, the management started to distance itself from the Samsung group, and in 1997, it ultimately spun off from it. The CEO was Lee Maeng-hee, the oldest son of Lee Byung-chul, who decided that his second son Lee Kun-hee would become the heir of the Samsung Empire. This decision was contested by the older son, who then lost all following legal cases.

The new group branched out into media enterprises, a family restaurant chain, and a music cable channel and established the first multiplex theater in Korea. CJ Entertainment became highly influential in the rising Korean pop culture business. In the bitter family feud, Lee Jay-hyun followed as president and CEO and his sister became vice president of CJ.

In quick succession, the group established the bakery chain "Tous Le Jour" and the coffee shop chain "A Twosome Place" as well as the steak house chain "VIPS." The group started to operate more globally. Further diversifications led the company to the field of home shopping, logistics, and financing (investment and securities). The group has meanwhile occupied rank number 16 among the *chaebol*.

5.3.11 Kumho/Asiana

Pak In-chon established this group with a single taxi in 1946. It is by now successfully engaged in the petrochemical industry. Overseas, it is known above all for its tire production. Furthermore, Asiana Airlines, the second largest Korean airline, belongs to the group as well. It frequently was considered the airline with the best service worldwide. Furthermore, some Korean budget airlines belong to the conglomerate as well.

In total, 30,000 people are employed at the group and work in 30 affiliated companies. It operates bus lines and is engaged in shipping, logistics, leisure and entertainment, information technology, engineering and construction, as well as financial industries. The tire production of Kumho belongs to the biggest companies of this kind in the world, which maintains production facilities in Korea, China, and Vietnam.

This *chaebol* also suffers from family feuds. For many years, Pak Sam-ku and Pak Chan-ku, the two sons of the founder, who both are chairman of the company, have their offices on different floors in the company's headquarter in Seoul's Sinmun-no. Yet, there are no joint discussions, and the secretaries ensure that the two men do not accidentally run into each other at the main entrance.

When Daewoo went bankrupt in 1999, Kumho acquired too many of its subsidiaries. Nevertheless, despite this decision and the international financial crisis, the group managed to get through perils and hard times.

5.3.12 Shinsegae

In 1930, when Korea was ruled by the Japanese, the Japanese Mitsukoshi group established a department store in Korea. The department store was purchased immediately after the end of WW II in 1945 by Lee Byung-chul, the founder of Samsung, who renamed it into Dongwha. In 1963, the name was again changed into Shinsegae ("new world"). This department store became the first modern retailer in Korea and introduced the first credit card system to the country. Shinsegae erected seven department stores in all major Korean cities and operated the largest department store in the world in Busan.

In 1991, Shinsegae separated from the Samsung group. It developed a new brand, e-mart, which became the largest retailer of Korea with nearly 100 discount markets. In 2006, the group acquired all 16 Walmart stores in Korea. It makes great efforts to extend into the Chinese market, where Korean consumer brands are happily accepted.

Shinsegae is managed by the members of the Lee family. However, they maintain a friendly relationship with the Samsung group. This branch of the family controls 51 % of the shares of which Lee Myung-hee alone owns 17 %.

The Korean media consider Shinsegae and Lotte to be "archenemies" fighting for supremacy in the local retail market. This rivalry sometimes even becomes rather personal. For instance, when the heir of the Shinsegae group, Chung Yong-jin, recently assumed that his counterpart at the Lotte group, Shin Dong-bin, might be interested to take over the country's second most successful airline, Asiana Airlines, he immediately wanted to take part in a bidding to acquire this company. However, once he was informed that Lotte was not seriously interested to buy the airline, he quickly dropped this plan.

5.3.13 Doosan

This *chaebol* belongs to the oldest businesses in Korea and was established as a department store in 1896. Later, it expanded into the business sectors of trade and services. After WW II, it started to engage in different fields of the heavy industries including engineering and construction. It published the Doosan Encyclopedia, which is a major encyclopedia in Korea, and it has acquired the Chung An university. It further owns a professional baseball team (OB Bears). But as of today, the group consists of two major sections:

1. The field of technical facilities and machinery. This includes the construction of power generation plants and nuclear stations, desalination plants, and plants for the chemical industry. Doosan also takes a leading role in the production of equipment and machines for the construction industry. For instance, in 2007, the conglomerate acquired the Bobcat Company, an American subsidiary of Ingersoll Rand. It further produces large diesel engines and is a leading company in Korea concerning hydraulic techniques. It is engaged in a joint venture with the German Babcock Company concerning construction and maintenance of energy production and boiler engineering. Within the technical fields, many parts of the bankrupt Daewoo group were taken over.
2. The section of consumer goods and services. A variety of activities belong to this section, as Glonet biochemical products (such as emulsifiers, skin care products, phosphatides, and ingredients for organic farming), packaging materials, fashion articles, pet food, restaurant chains like Kentucky Fried Chicken and Burger King, sales of magazines, as well as information and communication services among others.

Presently, Pak Yong-man (Park Yong maan), the son of the founder Pak Seong-jik, is leading the *chaebol* together with cochairman Pak Jeong-won. The son of the latter, Pak Seo-won, seems already to be designated to become the heir of this group. The most important affiliate company is Doosan Heavy Industries & Construction Co. Ltd, which is run by Pak Gi-won (Park Geewon) as CEO and chairman. It is remarkable that this company has a foreign name on the list of managers: J. Bemowski, a former Mc. Kinsey executive.

As typical for many family-run *chaebol*, the group is to some extent "shrouded in mystery." Doosan Corporation (a former beer brewery) serves as the official parent company, listed at the Korean stock exchange. This made the group more transparent and helped to establish a professional auditing and secured healthy profits for the shareholders. But the vast majority of the shares (including preferential and non-voting shares) are held by funds, and individual ownerships can hardly be traced. "The Group" is always named as the highest authority. Therefore, one has to look at the top management in order to conclude who is, after all, in charge of the decision making and who is benefitting from the corporate efforts. This hide-and-seek game is most likely set up to confuse potential rivals and foes.

5.3.14 DSME

This group is called Daewoo Shipbuilding & Marine Engineering. Because it is not a family-owned company, this company is also not a classical *chaebol* and has more features of a modern *keyul*. The group claims 1973 to be its founding year as this is the date on which Okpo Shipyard of Korea was founded. In 1978, the Daewoo Shipbuilding & Heavy Machinery (the very mixed conglomerate of the famous entrepreneur Kim Woo-choon) acquired the Okpo Shipyard. The first profit was made only in 1991. After the sensational bankruptcy of the Daewoo group in 1999/2000, the Daewoo Shipbuilding was spun off in a debt for equity swap.

This enterprise concentrated successfully on ocean technology and became a leading company in the four fields of shipbuilding (tankers, container ships, ice-breakers as well as submarines and other military ships), offshore installations, plant building, and energy production (wind rotors).

31.5 % of the shares are owned by the KDB (Korea Development Bank) a government institution, and the NPF owns 8 % of the share. Additionally, other Korean capital and funds from Chinese, Arabian, Russian, and Singaporean investors seem to be involved. Ko Jae-ho serves as CEO, and currently, his reelection is hotly debated as there is a strong opposition against the government choosing a bureaucrat for this important and demanding position.

In addition to this top fifteen, there are further internationally acknowledged *chaebol* such as Aju, Amore, Byucksan, Hansol, Alla, Hyosung, Isu, KCC, Kiswel, Kolon, Kyobo, LS group, Nongshim, Orion, Poongsan, Ssangyong, Taekwang, Taeyong, Woongjin, and the YTN group.

On some Korean lists, NH Nonghyup is grouped on the fifth position with a turnover exceeding US$70 billion; but this organization is actually the cooperative umbrella organization of the Korean National Agricultural Cooperative Federation and not at all a classical economical enterprise or conglomeration.

5.4 Financial Institutes/Banks

With regard to the balance sheet total and the total number of employees, banks and insurance as well as investment companies belong to the most important enterprises of the country. Of course all these insurance and investment enterprises, which belong to a *chaebol*, are not included in this ranking.

In Korea, banks have to follow the legal obligation to engage only in financial businesses and not to engage in industrial undertakings. Since the financial crisis, all financial institutes are subject to the strict requirements of the IMF. It is noticeable that many Korean finance institutes, especially banks, are owned by foreign shareholders. This should probably help to increase the security of these institutes and to anchor them in the world of global finances. Some of the insurance and investment companies are headed by rich owners, whereas the banks are more or less under governmental control (Table 5.2).

Within the relatively young insurance and investment business, Samsung Life Insurance, Samsung Fire & Marine Insurance, and SK Holdings need to be mentioned as well.

Table 5.2 Ranking list of the 8 largest Korean financial institutes (2013)

Name of the institute	Total balance in US$ billion
Woori Financial Holdings	341
Shinhan Financial Group	311
Hana Financial Group	295
KB Financial Group	292
Industrial Bank of Korea	213
Korea Development Bank	168
Korea Exchange Bank	105
BS Financial Group	47

Source Bank of Korea

The financial branch of the cooperative umbrella organization of the Korean agrarian industry, NH Nonghyup Head Union, shows a balance sheet of around US$220 billion and could be ranked among the institutes named above. However, it is unclear to which extent non-financial positions are also included in this number.

5.5 Founding Characteristics of the *Chaebol*

For a few years, the *chaebol* have now been in a phase of transformation. Originally, almost all of them were founded by one entrepreneur and has been ruled in a patriarchal manner by him and members of his family. These *chaebol* initially operated in a kind of vacuum when competition was concerned. They did not have to fear any established rivals since there were no real competitors within the country and rivals from abroad were generally not admitted to conduct large-scale business in Korea. The local companies enjoyed many privileges by the government as long as they obeyed the "guidance" of the planning bureaucrats, which meant to enforce the economic power of the country, to export as much as possible, and to strive for a global top position with regard to all relevant technologies of modern development. Thereby, they created jobs and procured the necessary foreign exchange for South Korea.

Because the *chaebol* had not been members of financial institutions or powerful industrial groups—different from other Western or Japanese systems—they first did not have to be concerned with observing commercial or financial criteria. Instead, they were fully focused on creating sales and conquering market shares. Thus, financial gains were initially secondary. Only the owner families were able to treat themselves with different kinds of luxuries. The conglomerations financed their growth predominantly with loans, which were usually obtained from overseas instead of being generated at least partially by a capital accumulation within their own enterprises.

The owners of the *chaebol* competed among themselves to become the most powerful company, thus adding to a good reputation of the owner families. These families strived for power, wealth, and prestige in order to enable an affluent lifestyle. The disadvantage of this approach was that no professional management class could develop that would have occupied positions of control and execution on the boards of big companies. Thus, the complete management system often lacked rational decisions. The top managers further could not organize themselves in national or international organizations. National associations and committees generated rules in favor of a few powerful families, instead of taking care of the well-being of the whole nation.

Within the FKI, the *chaebol* families build a national circle of power of owners and manager families that joined the system either by marriage or through a network of militaries, academics from universities, religious circles, and political parties. In upper-class golf clubs, wellness centers, or private kindergartens and schools, these people wish to remain among each other.

The well-to-do owner families oriented themselves by comparing their *chaebol* with the companies of their rivals in terms of high domestic market shares and the number of employees. The desire to triumph over other *chaebol* families often significantly influenced many decisions of the corporate politics. In recent times, the management of the *chaebol* has become more rational and caught up with global standards. Nevertheless, many children and other relatives started to own thousands of related companies. In its July 7, 2012 edition, the *Korean Times* lamented that the numerous companies connected to the *chaebol* make most of their business with their affiliates. This would lead to manipulations such as creating excessive profits—often overseas—and minimizing tax burdens.

For the majority of the average Korean citizens, the word "*chaebol*" has a magic sound and they seem to be a symbol for wealth, influence, and power—attributes formerly associated only with the high nobility or political potentates. Marrying into a *chaebol* family was always a dream for handsome sons or beautiful daughters and this has not changed significantly. For over half of a century, competent board members would hardly criticize the action of *chaebol* family members. Sometimes, deviating opinions were even met with sanctions. During the time of the military dictatorship, high-ranking militaries and bureaucrats were recruited when they retired at the age of 55 [11].

The early patriarchs of the *chaebol* have aged. They tried to involve their children, their own relatives, and the families of their wives into the business—no matter whether they are commercially talented or not. Trust and loyalty were the more important criterion. By all means, they tried to have their own son become successor of their own commercial empire. However, modern science of genetics have proven that a child inherits only in less than one percent of all cases the ingenious genes of his or her parents. The mathematical probability that a grandchild inherits special abilities of his predecessors is consequently rather small.

Unlike an innate entrepreneurship, of course management techniques can be learned. Thus, the children of *chaebol* families are sent to the best schools and universities in Korea and overseas. But as every experienced manager knows, an academic title does not at all guarantee an entrepreneurial dynamism. We think that in the medium run, the *chaebol* will be in a healthy process transforming into regular public corporations, although their owners might enjoy the property of their shares for a long time.

5.6 Transformation of the *Chaebol*

The alliance of patriotic bureaucrats and vivacious owner entrepreneurs working with energetic chairmen was well suited for the start-up of the South Korean economy. This system has become outdated by now.

Apart from some exceptions, the family character of the *chaebol* is about to vanish. This process is partly related to the inappropriate behavior of some company patriarchs and their children. Some of them ended up in prison, whereas others floundered on their incompetence or feuds within their family.

Thousands of qualified positions in the giant *chaebol* had to be filled with qualified people not affiliated with the owner family. These employees were not necessarily loyal. Almost all *chaebol* started internal training programs—an expensive as well as time-consuming procedure. Samsung partly chose a different path. Besides providing an internal training program, the company also hired excellent employees from other companies and even from foreign countries. This saved time, which is one of the most crucial aspects in the fast-paced electronics business. Another advantage of their approach was to acquire external know-how and to learn about different management practices, bringing them to the corporate group. In this sense, Samsung was a pioneer of using qualified overseas labor and managers within Korea.

During its quick development, the Korean industry was initially based on foreign know-how, which could not exclusively be obtained by taking licenses. Consequently, local as well as global joint ventures were established and shares in foreign enterprises were bought. The use of specialized foreign labor, however, was limited to some departments and, if possible, in subsidiaries. Usually, these foreign workers were easy to control as they could hardly speak or read Korean. Yet, accounting, auditing, and concerning tax provisions require a sound knowledge both orally and in writing in *hangeul*. Consequently, almost no foreigner could ever enter the inner circle of the corporate power of Daehan Minguk.

Since the reign of the Two-Kim-Governments (Kim Young-sam and Kim Dae-jung), the non-military rulers were determined to break the power of the *chaebol*. Initially, their endeavors were based on proofing that they were corrupt and evaded taxes. The success of this approach was rather limited, as the counterparts of the *chaebol* were more often than not to be found among the bureaucrats. After the financial crisis of 1997, substantial evidences were found when several *chaebol* had been considerably weakened or even broken down. This was interpreted as a proof for their inefficient management. Until 2003, besides Daewoo, 13 well-known groups became insolvent, among them famous names such as Kia, Hanbo, Jinro, and Halla. During the era of the military government, the market forces could not freely operate as the *chaebol* were considered dependent parts of the national economy, and thus, the government would have saved them by all means.

As early as in 1991, Deputy Prime Minister Choi Gak-gyu supposedly publicly demanded to separate the ownership and management of the *chaebol*. Throughout the years, this led to many conflicts between the top government and the giant conglomerations. The latter defended their position by massive corruption as well as by their own political efforts. Nowadays, the government tries to control the *chaebols* but knows how important they are for the well-being of the nation and thus refrain from too drastic measures and even pardon executive culprits.

It is quite disconcerting that *chaebol* leaders and their offspring consider their giant enterprises as "their own," because they usually do not own more than forty, thirty, or even only twenty percent of the shares, while the majority lies with public shareholding.

After the financial disaster of 1997, the IMF (International Monetary Fund) made regulations concerning the Korean economy. They did not only demand Korea to rigorously cut down expenses but also requested that Korea would follow internationally accepted accounting rules for businesses, which would further lead to a greater transparency of the firms. These were the conditions of the IMF for granting the nation the much needed credits. Until these rules, most *chaebol* had regarded bookkeeping as a suitable means to hide the real financial as well as economic situation of their enterprises. Consolidated balance sheets of major groups were particularly useful to shed light on the covering-up tactics of the various affiliated companies among themselves. It was almost customary that some group members had among themselves and in cooperation with the headquarters pushed their claims and debts around as they needed in order to cover losses or to avoid taxes. Even intragroup bills of exchange could be discounted, and the banks took part in that game.

After new modern accounting and auditing systems were introduced, the treasury had quick access to the relevant tax requirements, which improved the financial situation of the government budget significantly. High taxation is unpopular everywhere in the world. Yet, in East Asian countries, the dislike of government charges carries an idiosyncratic character. People want by all means to keep what they have earned. East Asian people do not believe that others (bureaucrats) can make the best use of their money. As much the administration becomes more rational, this view is changing as a related society bears advantages for all members of society.

The mutually supportive group of government bureaucrats is usually suspected to transform into a parasitic termite colony. This has frequently happened in the past, especially in non-democratic systems, and led to waste, uneconomic behavior, and excessive debts. In former times, bureaucrats had been called "robbers" in Korea and this stigma still seems to stick to them. But as a token of a good development, the measurable figures of honesty to tax expenses and justice of revenues have improved considerably. In comparison with many European nations, the Korean government is careful not to overstretch the tax burden as this could damage the most important commitment of all participants of the national economy. The Korean civil servants of today are encouraged to display economic efficiency and good public service.

Whereas foreign capital could buy shares of Korean financial institutions, the average share that can be bought from a big industrial conglomeration is limited to 15 % until today. However, meanwhile, there exist some hundred joint ventures in South Korea and even a lot of 100 % foreign companies. Similarly, the *chaebol* and some other progressive companies invest in all important foreign markets. As a result, their business practices and management behavior become increasingly international as well.

The *chaebol* invest roughly 40 % each in Asia and North America, respectively, the biggest world markets. Predominantly, they pursue the objectives of securing their own export volumes, gaining access to interesting international finance markets, and avoiding rapidly increasing wages in the local labor market, and the opportunities of strategic alliances, predominantly in sales but also in research and development.

While routine tasks abroad were usually accomplished by foreign staff and technical experts, the bulk majority of managerial personnel consisted of Koreans. Many of these qualified Korean expatriates were promoted to managerial ranks after returning from their time abroad. They help to create a new global conscience in their parent companies; therefore, the multinational Korean conglomerates will slowly but inexorably develop into transnational conglomerations.

5.7 The Future of the *Chaebol*

The ranking order of the *chaebol* is constantly and sometimes very quickly changing. Everything in Korea has the tendency to advance fast, and managers are not shy of drastic changes at any time. The nearly almighty power of many business tycoons permits even significant decisions within a short period of time.

Out of a dozen of powerful conglomerations of the period of military rule, which were considered almighty and slightly mysterious, more than a hundred business models have developed, which are subject to constant ups and downs. Many have to retire from the rough Korean competition, and others come into being with new innovative business concepts. The legendary founders of the traditional *chaebol* were looked at with a mixture of admiration and fright. The present leaders of the *chaebol* are likewise not popular, but they are respected and serve as examples for many followers. This is an advantage for the national economy, which enjoys many business start-ups.

Korea has learned that the production of commodities and service features set up the strong backbone of a national economy, which enables a competition with other countries. This economy is driven by determining the needs and satisfying them with a world-class range of goods and services. It further seems important not to be financially dependent.

The financial industry is the great transmission belt which keeps everything in motion. The rise of the Korean economy is related to the fact that for a long time, the government controlled all financial means. The *chaebol* could therefore concentrate on production and logistic issues. Only in recent years did they accumulate their own financial resources and built up financial institutions such as insurance companies. Some of them have accrued huge financial funds, which caused the government to impose a special tax of 10 % on "excessive financial reserves." The *chaebol*, which owe much of their outstanding position to former privileges granted by the state to further propel the country's economy, should indeed refrain from non-productive financial games.

An efficient and competent system of finance is essential for the development of a national economy. However, dealing with and creating of huge profits with mathematical models rather than performance-based tangible results might lead to misallocation of resources. In all East Asian countries, including South Korea, the majority of the population reveals besides diligence and intelligence a distinct preference to take risks. Thus, the speculation with financial papers is as popular as gambling. The TV channel Arirang (January 3, 2011) asked, during a New Year special, a young girl about her career wish. Her rather sly answer was "I would like to do investment banking." Hopefully, for the well-being of Korea, she enunciated just a rare attitude of the future working class.

Economically, President Pak Chung-hee was the right man at the right time, at the right place. He released his country from a miserable economic situation and turned it into a global competitor. Nevertheless, he would not at all fit into a modern democratic society. Under his rule, the *chaebol* rose to international strength and turned Korea into a global powerhouse. But their outdated attitudes do generally no longer fit into the modern industrial world. It is highly questionable whether leadership positions should be awarded by birthright. Some of the *chaebol* are already transforming into modern enterprises. These companies should no longer be called *chaebol* but *keyul*.

Currently, many *chaebol* are first and foremost busy arranging their heirs. On the one hand, they try to put their offspring in leading top positions, and on the other hand, they try to avoid inheritance taxes wherever possible. To some degree, this paralyzes their efforts in the daily business. Some of the heirs are well educated and seem to be able entrepreneurial successors of their predecessors, while some others are quite well trained but probably lack top management qualifications, and many others are nothing but children of their fathers.

Recently, the government started to support small and medium-sized enterprises as they build the base for any healthy industrial society and employ most of its members. For the better or not, most of them see the *chaebol* as their role models because they promise a wealthy and comfortable life to their owner families. According to the *Financial Times* from July 7, 2012, more than 90 % of all companies listed on the stock exchange in Korea are under family control.

Song [12], a professor of economical sciences of the Seoul National University (SNU) and likewise a prominent personality of the Korean business bureaucracy, is convinced that the formation of business groups in Korea that are in keen competition with each other is an important factor contributing to the quick growth of his country. This spirit of rivalry and competition must be kept up for Korea as long as possible.

The Korea Times [13] reported in April 27, 2011, that an advisor from the staff of President Lee Myung-bak had proposed to use funds from the huge NPF to invest them into the most important *chaebols* in order to gain a certain control of these giant conglomerates that are so vitally important for the national well-being. The author of course has severe doubts that direct interventions of the bureaucracy would be an appropriate way to promote the national economy in a progressive and competent way.

The reputation of the *chaebol* in the general public is, however, decreasing. Every day, the newspapers report about scandals involving bribery, embezzlements, drafts, and the imprisonment of *chaebol* leaders and inappropriate behavior of third- and fourth-generation members of *chaebol* families, who believe that the law does not apply to them due to their inherited wealth.

Literature

1. Kim Y-T (2008) Bureaucrats and entrepreneurs, Seoul, p 43
2. Kim Y-T cit. above, p 14
3. Kim Y-T cit. above, p 46
4. Rim K (2007) Paradigm shift and challenges for Korean industry: case study of Samsung. In: Malich J, Pascha W (eds) Innovation and technology in Korea, Heidelberg, pp 65–67
5. Steers RM (1999) Made in Korea—Chung Ju-chung and the rise of Hyundai, New York, London, p 5
6. Oliver C (2010) The Financial Times, edn from 24 Sept 2010
7. Kim Y-T cit. above, p 81
8. Gongto (2005) (a kind of Who is Who of prominent Korean personalities), Korea 1 %, Seoul, p 143
9. Saccone R (2005) Koreans to remember, Seoul, p 136
10. Kim Y-T cit. above, p 222
11. Pohlmann MC (2005) Suedkoreas Unternehmen. In: Kern TH, Koellner P (eds) Suedkorea und Nordkorea, Frankfurt, New York, p 132
12. Song B-N (2003) The rise of the Korean economy, Oxford, p 76
13. The Korea Times (2011) Pension fund urged to reign in Chaebol, edn from 27 Apr 2011

Chapter 6
Challenges of the Business Leadership

6.1 International Approximations of Leadership Processes

Globally, business leadership in the industry and within the administration is becoming increasingly alike. This is due to practical constraints as well as the activities of globally operating consulting firms and because of globally operating famous management-gurus. In particular, the requests of a fair rendering of accounts of the serious, transnational financial community paved the way to an international standardization in South Korea as well. This is of course much appreciated by the tax authorities.

Not only are the structures of the enterprises becoming more similar worldwide, but also the processes of internal proceedings are assimilated, though to a lesser degree. For example, there exists only one, universal science of physics and a Brazilian physics or Chinese physics cannot exist. This leads to the same nature of technical processes. However, economic science is not a natural science with its strict laws and nature constants. This discipline is closely related to the social sciences and is based on psychology, social psychology, and on experiences—even though it also makes use of technology and mathematics.

6.2 Different Styles of Personnel Management

At first glance, a firm is all about calculating and major management data such as planning and operating results are reflected in figures. But in principle, men act by making individual decisions and operate in markets with millions of individuals. Either side pretends to make basically rational decisions but in fact, all decisions are to large degree subjected to emotions. Actions and reactions of individuals are therefore often difficult to predict as we all have a different history, grew up or live

D.K. Schneidewind, *Economic Miracle Market South Korea*,
DOI 10.1007/978-981-10-0615-9_6

in different climates, are used to different food, have deviant social customs, and are subject to other rules and laws. As a result, East Asian countries—including Korea—differ considerably from Western nations regarding the management of personnel.

Frequently, parallels are drawn between the management style of Japan and that of Korea. This includes the strict inventory controlling system, deliveries "just in time," severe quality controls, and the circles of staff engaged with the improvement of almost any operational matter. Furthermore, the formal hierarchies are identical. Yet with regard to these structures, the regular staff in Japan has a far greater freedom in their operational jobs than in their Korean colleagues.

Korean shareholders are at pains to pursue their matters as in the Anglo-Saxon world, whereas the Japanese take relatively little interests in their companies. Within the *chaebol,* the control of the owner families is almost a hundred percent. Still, some important principles of "Asian Style Management" can be observed in Korea: the consideration of long-term business objectives, the intensive engagement with the employees and their education, and keeping a mental flexibility which permits the enterprises to quickly respond to any challenge. Additionally, the great attention for customers and the willingness to provide any kind of service have to be mentioned.

On the occasion of a marketing presentation in the fall of 1981 in Tokyo, the strategy consultant Edward de Bono from the UK put a gray cat on the floor into a square built by tables. He then asked the assembled managers: "What do you think in which direction will the cat move when it wants to leave the square?" Nobody was prepared for an immediate answer. De Bono explained that the gray cat represented the general consumer, whose decision making can hardly be predicted as he might act spontaneously. All participants agreed that the decision of the cat could be influenced by a titbit or by making loud noises. However, the behavior of this rather stubborn animal could in general not be determined.

Of course, it would be very helpful to first thoroughly study the nature and temperaments of cats as well as the surroundings and the situation of the animal in order to be able to influence its behavior. This knowledge could be applied to the behavior of customers as well. All human beings are similar with respect to their basic needs at birth; however, later they are decisively shaped by various, specific local environmental influences and climatic conditions as well as moral concepts of their society. All managers who interact with human beings should thoroughly study their basic needs and their sociocultural imprinting. This is especially true for the particularly original Korean markets.

Internationally educated and experienced enterprisers and managers always remain with one leg in the global world or in the culture of their host-country and with the other leg in their own. Even a very centralized enterprise such as Coca Cola does no longer globally use the imperative slogan "Drink Coca Cola" but pays attention to Asian mentalities and rephrase their slogan into "Let's drink Coca Cola." Of course, all enterprises are subject to the prevailing laws of the country of residence and have to observe quite different local laws concerning personnel management.

When German companies cross the national border, they quickly meet with different habits in Denmark, Poland, or France. Despite some common ground, the differences are sometimes even greater with North Atlantic cultures in North America, Latin America, South America, or with Slavic social systems in Eastern Europe or Russia. More deviant are the mentalities in Africa, although African countries are frequently influenced by British, French, or Portuguese colonial education. When approaching Islamic–Arabic cultures or cultures influenced by Hinduism or Confucianism, the socio-psychological differences become much more obvious. Within the latter, Korea takes a peculiar position.

Naturally, there is nothing like *the* Korean enterprise. Almost every company has its own spirit and develops its own corporate culture, even up to a point where they create their own corporate language. Furthermore, Korean enterprises summon strength from the history of their country, experience, and many specific characteristics from a country that is perceived as absolutely unique.

All moral concepts and structures of Korea are strongly imprinted by Confucianism. One of the most prominent characteristics of it is thinking in hierarchies. The scholars were at the top of society. Civil servants were selected from their rank by severe examinations, which initially tested the knowledge of the old literature as a subject. With the advance of the Neo-Confucianism, this changed; the well-being of the state became dependent on practical virtues and competences such as the construction of waterways and streets and, most importantly, agrarian skills. Therefore, master builders, artisans, and farmers enjoyed special privileges. The trade was also recognized as being vital, yet within the hierarchy merchants ranked at the last position, only followed by people without an affiliation to one of the esteemed categories of the upper society.

Whereas in Europe and Japan important and famous enterprises, which do partly exist until today, had already developed since the late Middle Ages, such a traditional entrepreneurial system did not exist at all in Korea. On the contrary, the economy of the country was not structured for continuity and showed a rather amorphous and partly even chaotic character. The main structuring element of the nation was always the military with its hierarchies and enforced discipline. Likewise, at the beginning of the modern national economy of the Republic of Korea, hierarchies of the *chaebol* dominated the economy as well as the experiences of a long military service of their managers and staff.

Different from many Arabian countries, which have an intensive Islamic background, Korea has been for more than a hundred years a secular country. Most Koreans try to find their fortune during their earthly existence through hardwork and industrial striving. There never did exist a clear idea of a possible afterlife as within East Asian religions and spiritual beliefs.

Self-confident nations such as China, Japan, and Korea as well as their southeast Asian neighbors such as Vietnam, Thailand, Cambodia, or Laos wisely adapt everything that seems technically, economically, and organizationally beneficiary. However, they are increasingly keen to take care for their own cultures and by no means want to become dependent from other nations. The US American Professor Patterson [1] argues that one reason for the rapid development of East and South

Asia is the rivalry between the different countries from this region as they all show the nationalistic endeavor to catch up with other developed states, or even to surpass them.

The Japanese management is still—though to a lesser degree—following its own patterns, which are sometimes regarded in Western countries as "exotic"—despite the fact that they are often copied from the West. Unlike Japan, Korea is likely to follow US American principles. It is therefore difficult to realize certain insights into the business administration in Korea, because there does not exist a generally accepted corporate culture but rather specific systems of the various *chaebol*. As family enterprises used to think in terms of generations, a long-term goal has prevailed over a short-term maximization of profits. Such an approach met with the expectations of the military dictatorship, which looked for a long-term future of the nation, its security, and keeping it independent.

As repeatedly mentioned, the *chaebol*, however, are subject to a far-reaching change. This has already happened in the employer–employee relationships. The exuberance of labor after 1953 was replaced in the latter decades by a shortage of skilled workers. The oppression of the workforce under military dictatorships with low wages and few rights that seemed necessary to quickly overcome the prevailing poverty in Korea was replaced in the following decades by democracy and strong trade unions, which achieved remarkable improvements concerning the income of workers. Because of the earning power of the enterprises, this was not only possible but also fair and raised the purchasing power of the population considerably.

However, the employees did not always take the individual situations of the companies into considerations and neglected the worldly wisdom that life cannot always move upwards. This is especially true for economic developments that include both booms and crisis. A Chinese wisdom has it that in front of a mountain, there always lays a valley or at least a plain. Similarly, a car cannot always be steered straightforward through the traffic. Concerning the development of incomes, there are times when the pedal needs to be used to accelerate the speed or needs to be stepped on, always depending on the actual traffic.

In the case of South Korea, one always has to take into account its rivalry with the Communist, self-proclaimed "state of workers and farmers" in the North. This situation triggered a special motivation to show the superiority of its own societal system.

6.3 The Employees

In Anglo-Saxon countries, there is a tendency to look at the capitalized value of an enterprise, to take care of a healthy ratio between the input of financial resources and its profitability. The working force is considered predominantly a cost factor and only secondarily as consumer potential.

In large parts of Europe, the generally accepted political objective is to achieve a well-being of the population on a broad scale; for this purpose, the working people have to be educated and trained. Well-meaning industrial patriarchs directed their companies in this direction and remained popular.

In Japan, an ideal of the equality of all citizens was propagated for a long time. One basic slogan was "*kaisha wa hito nari*" (the company is its people). Like all other stakeholders of an enterprise, the employees obtained shares of the achieved profits. In turn, the employees were expected to sacrifice their personal life for the companies they worked for.

How to classify South Korea within these models? The country's tough, hard, able, and willing to learn workers have a great share in the economic success of the country. They worked for the bare survival of their families and to overcome the threat from the North, which was economically (and militarily) much more advanced in these years. Working was considered a quasi-sacred act: Without working, there was no food for the family. Within the *chaebol* however, they would be just small cogs in the wheel. In big traditional companies, the old Japanese concept of total devotion was common. Called *myeolsabonggong*, it was usually rewarded by a lifetime employment.

Until today, the average work time is up to 50 % higher than in Middle Europe. But a lot of this time is consumed by lengthy meetings and after hour dining, the notorious *hoesik* (literally meals with coworkers). They usually end in drinking parties and often last until after midnight. Recently, they are much detested by young wives and their husbands. Formerly unheard of, they now demand payment for these extra hours. This sounds like a social revolution to the bosses. The *chaebol* are setting up factories overseas in Vietnam or Bangladesh due to increasing labor problems at home. Many workers have lost their confidence that they will have a chance to advance by working hard. Instead, slogans such as "We pretend to work reasonably well, because they pretend to treat us reasonably well" are being heard. This sounds as if Korea is becoming more "normal" and that the time of "wonders" has passed.

President Park intended to develop a collective prosperity and modern weapons with the industrial power of the *chaebol*. Nevertheless, the founder families of the *chaebol* with their entourage of relatives and favorites, together with the official bureaucracy, determined the fate of the enterprises. Rights to have a say for employees remained unknown. Thus, the companies' gains were not fairly distributed.

With the progress of democracy after the period of the military dictatorship, the distribution of the profit become increasingly just. The term "just" applies to a distribution according to achievement, effort, ability, and (with a decreasing tendency) age. Victims of this system were the disabled, uneducated elderly people, and those who are incapable or reluctant to obtain an education. Political endeavors are made to support those who are poor without fault on their part. Regrettably, democracy has been initially misunderstood as a system of self-service and the masses did not understand that the enterprises need a certain accumulation of financial means for further investments.

Of course the employees do identify with successful and famous companies, because they provide a little bit of prestige and the subsistence of life. But an unconditional loyalty to one's own enterprise, such as in Japan, did not develop. Secretly, most individuals dream of establishing their own private firm. For decades, there was almost no chance for an entrepreneur to grow in the shadows of the *chaebol*. But with the opportunities of the new electronic age, the number of people setting up their own, new businesses is considerably increasing. The government supports this development and especially promotes the service industry as new jobs can be generated in this field quite easily.

Formerly, an employment with a big firm was considered as a lifetime affair. But in recent years, so-called flexible working relations became usual. As a result of this hire and fire system, employees became notorious job hoppers. But in general, almost everybody is looking for stable jobs in the government or government-related public organizations.

6.4 The Management Level

Every larger working team needs organization and directing of the workload—regardless whether men in blue overalls or with white collars are involved. The generally quick development of the companies in Korea offered most competent people the chance to grow into respectable middle management positions. These people are traditionally seeking the proximity of their direct superiors.

The Japanese claim a peculiar relation between an employee and his superior, the so-called *amae* (leniency, sweetness, or clemency). This exists with a similar intensity in Korea as well. Personal solicitude is gratefully accepted from the superior and as far as possible returned, above all, with loyalty. This means that the younger, and consequently weaker, member of the workforce recognizes his departmental head as a kind of mother-substitute. He longs for much love and care and a very close relationship with his boss, which resembles the sweetness of the relation between infant and mother. The superior protects the younger person entrusted to him even when the young man makes mistakes. In return, the younger person shows almost blind dedication to his boss. Unavoidably, this leads to petty jealousies among the employees since the head of department has to do favors to many if not all members in order to be successful with his group. It has to be mentioned that this behavior is about to change with the younger generation.

Following the Confucian idea, all companies—such as the society as a whole—are hierarchically aligned. Like the government bureaucrats and the military, Korean enterprises show a lot of differences in status as well. Unlike in North America or Germany, all members of a company will be addressed—except the lower-ranked *jigwon*—by their title in the enterprise as well as in general public and sometimes even within the family. For example, one would say "Kim Jeonmu" or "Lee Gwajang" instead of "Mr. Kim" or "Mr. Lee" (Table 6.1).

Table 6.1 Ranking list of titles within Korean companies

Korean	Japanese	Anglo-Saxon	German
Hoejang	Kaicho	Chairman	AR-Vorsitzender
Sajang	Shacho	President	Vorstandsvorsitzender
Jeonmu	Senmu	Senior board member	Vorstandsmitglied
Sangmu	Jomu	Board member	–
Isa Daeu	Torishimariyaku-Bucho	–	Stellvertretender Vorstand
Bujang	Bucho	Head of department	Hauptabteilungsleiter
Chajang	Jicho	–	–
Gwajang	Kacho	Manager	Abteilungsleiter
Gyejang	Kakaricho	Group-leader/team leader	Gruppenleiter
Jigwon	Shain	Qualified employee	Fachkraft

In different enterprises, a variety of more titles such as deputy chairman, deputy department head, and deputy section chief exist. In Korea, three different classes are distinguished among the *jigwon*. This reminds very much of military ranking orders.

For all these organization systems, democratic structures are hardly suitable. This is evident in the case of military orders. In this respect, the Korean professor Yi [2] asks: "Is the bureaucracy of all modern states not organized by Confucian hierarchical principles though under different names?" Like an army, for the general public, an enterprise seems like a monolithic entity headed by managers, who exercise a strong leadership, directing the company with firm hands and leading it with high spirits into the right direction.

In Korea, there exists only one board of directors, whereas in some countries there exists a "supervising board," which is responsible for the general policy, control, and to appoint and remunerate the executive board members, and an "executive board" which is responsible for actually running the company. In recent times, usually the chairman is the person who controls and runs his enterprise. In Korea, he can make decisions without the consent of the other board members, who are not his colleagues as in some other countries. In the case of Korea, the chairman is usually the head of the founder family of the enterprise and owns more shares of it than anybody else.

The company is theoretically controlled by some "outside directors" sitting on the board. However, they are usually not familiar with the details of the enterprise and more often than not have only little knowledge of business management. At the best, they give good advices, sometimes because of their life experience and a mature personality, but usually they only sit on a sinecure and are in some way related to the owner families.

In former times, every board member of the bigger companies used to be a member of the founder family. Because many *chaebols* have become extremely diversified, hundreds of qualified outside managers had to be employed over the years. Nevertheless, whereas family members in many cases had been sitting in their executive chairs for decades, the employed managers remain rather shortly in their positions. *The Korean Herald* reported as of February 2015 that the executives of Hyundai Heavy Industries retire in average when they are 57.1 years and executives of LG retire already with 51.4 years. The retirement age of executives of other important *chaebol* is located between these numbers. The tenure of top managers was revealed to be between merely 3.4 and 8.1 years. One can only wonder why these organizations treat the know-how and experience of their key staff so wastefully.

There are special regulations for banks because these institutes are traditionally quite fragile in Korea. In particular, their "outside directors" are subject to rigorous restrictions since 2010. These new rules have been worked out by the Korea Federation of Banks. The persons must be appointed for at least two years but can serve a maximum of five years, whereas 20 % of them have to be replaced every year. The elected people have to come from fields closely related to business life. They cannot get stock options or other incomes calculated on the base of the profit targets of the bank. Their income has to be published just as donations to organizations close to them. These "outside directors" have to take part in further training courses in order to increase their competence and to prevent an unnecessary outflow of financial means from the banks. Similar regulations would be highly beneficial for most other enterprises as well.

6.5 The Korean Trade Unions

In Europe, the associations of trade unions introduce democratic procedures from the outside into the companies. In Germany, this results within the coal, iron, and steel industry in an equal representation of the workforce on the supervisory board.

With the process of democratization in South Korea, the central organizations of the trade unions are indirectly present in the companies as they take care of labor laws or political concerns. However, the wages and salaries of the employees are negotiated by the individual company unions. Within these unions, the ranks of *gwajang* and above are not represented, though exceptions with respect to the membership in the prevailing union are negotiable. There is no codetermination concerning general issues of the companies whatsoever.

The powerful central organizations of the unions exercise considerable pressure on the firms in Korea and have improved the conditions of the working class to a great degree. They have achieved a tremendous general rise of wages and salaries for skilled employees. In some cases, the wages were probably increased too quickly. Consequently, South Korea has developed to anything else but a low-wage country. The incomes of unqualified labor fall behind the general development. This is insignificant for the production of high-quality goods by skilled labor craft; and even more so in the fields of research and development.

Employees conducting sophisticated tasks in the sales and marketing departments as well as in the general administration demand high financial compensations. The increasing income gap between the incomes of skilled and unskilled workers is a global phenomenon. This is especially significant in Korea, because unskilled workers are usually loan workers, who are not organized in trade unions. They pay a high price for the flexibility of the enterprises.

In Korea, nearly 60 % of all employed people work in flexible contractual relationships. The Cambridge professor Chang [3] observes that Korea has one of the most flexible labor markets in the world. This situation was caused by rationalization measures in the aftermath of the so-called Asian crisis 1998.

In many countries, this situation leads to people asking the government to take care of this gap by providing social financial reliefs. Yet, in Korea, the common public still believes that disadvantaged people should work harder and put more effort in their work and, above all, their education. Omissions in this respect at the younger age have fatal consequences in the future.

Apart from the sad fate of the unskilled workers, the system of the company trade unions is very advantageous in the sense that the regulation of wages is linked to the productivity of the firms. This avoids the paradox which can be frequently observed in European enterprises when the general trade unions force an increase of wages on companies in the red, thus jeopardizing the very existence of these enterprises and their employees.

6.6 Treatment and Position of Employees

As increasingly the necessary or desired qualifications for a job in a modern industrial society are momentarily not available on the domestic labor market, the companies educate their employees in their own training courses or send them to partner companies or subsidiaries in the USA, Japan, and—to a smaller degree—to Europe. When employing highly educated candidates, especially small- and medium-sized companies prefer graduates from technical colleges or universities of applied sciences to those from top universities, as the latter ones are often career-minded and soon want to become top managers, thus causing unrest among colleagues. The situation is quite different when scouting specialists for chemical and pharmaceutical tasks in laboratories or in sophisticated areas of engineering such as nano-technologies for instance.

A further problem is to keep the qualified employees in the company, since the labor market offers a wide range of opportunities to them. For skilled workers and at lower management levels, financial means are the most attractive arguments. The total income of an employee comprises two-third of a fixed monthly income, which is calculated by established rules such as educational qualifications, age, which stands for experience, and of course the hierarchical ranking. The other third of the income are bonuses. The latter ones are awarded according to the individual achievement, which is judged by the personal superior. The size of the bonus is generally determined by the performance of the company as it is computed in the annual profit and loss statement.

The bonuses are usually paid annually (in some cases twice a year) and their amount can vary drastically, for instance, between three- and six-month salaries. Because these bonuses are also subject to the personal appraisal of the superior, there can be a considerable spread between the individual total incomes. The system provides the superior also with an effective means to control his subordinates. In more recent times, the payment of bonuses is increasingly replaced by a system of individual premiums.

Additionally, there are allowances for social reasons such as contributions to housing costs, commuting expenses, family leaves, and educational costs for children, or even the annual preparation of *kimchi*. These allowances depend on the general company regulations as well as the assessment of the superiors. There are a lot of special subsidies such as those for personal education, the maintenance of cars, separation allowance, down payments for rental apartments, loans or guarantees for an own apartment or house, special family parties, and funerals. The superior is thus able to influence the commitment and loyalty of the staff to the company.

A good-working atmosphere is considered crucial and especially the middle management takes care of this. They will continuously show a social, humane understanding to the workforce. In this respect, common evening events play an important role. On such occasions, a lot of fun is involved: Everybody dines well, sings loudly, and drinks too much. The expenses are dealt with differently: Often the company pays for the evening, sometimes the employees settle the bill, and in rare cases the superior pays the bill from his own pocket. In the same sense, the company supports the establishment of any types of circles such as tennis, baseball, chess circles. Sometimes the employees go hiking or mountain-biking together.

The upper management is naturally susceptible for financial incentives as well, which are especially substantiated by high bonuses. However, for them chances for further education, prospects of promotions, and a higher prestige with the company title (*bujang* for instance), which reflects a prestigious car and a "trust money," are more important. The delicate privilege of the "trust money" was to be used to finance invitations—especially of business partners—presents for customers and employees, and personal representational expenses. In former times, it could be as much as half a monthly salary. Recently, the tax authority has limited the amount and strictly makes sure that the money is not misused by asking for correct vouchers [4]. The "trust money" was a way of the company to show its absolute trust to its managers and it further enforced their self-confidence.

However, most important are the chances for promotion. The secret goal of almost every executive is the position of *sajang* (president). Achieving this goal comes close to a divine mission. Occasionally, some departments of an enterprise are legally split, only to promote somebody to the rank of a *sajang*. To become chairman or *hoejang* of a company is almost exclusively reserved for a company owner or his close relatives.

For all above-cited reasons, employers and employees anticipate long-term employment relations. In former times, changing to another enterprise usually meant to climb up the career ladder starting from scratch. Yet, meanwhile, because of the increasing shortage of able managers, headhunter offices have come into being and find jobs for specialists or outstanding executives, which naturally do not like to start with minor challenges but desire to directly enter leading positions.

The enterprises do not only publicly laude their employees and promote them but they also publicly disapprove of them, delay promotions, and even degrade their employees (the latter ones are absolutely unthinkable in Japan, where in comparable situations mangers are put in the backwater). It can be generally stated that the loyalty with the company increases with the hierarchical rank. If this loyalty is not returned by the company, frustrations can hardly be avoided. The concerned manager will usually look for another position outside this enterprise and, nowadays, usually employ a headhunter for this purpose. In a few instances, strong personalities chose to become entirely independent and founded their own enterprise in order to show their outstanding abilities.

6.7 Notes to Management

In the "land of the morning calm" stubbornness, a spirit of contradiction, and the willingness to conflict is remarkable. Because the willingness to compromise is quite limited in Korea, managers with social skills and the ability to mediate between conflicting parties are most appreciated.

Superiors usually set very demanding goals and appeal to the ambitions of their subordinates to achieve goals that are almost out of reach. The employees are usually proud to be challenged and appreciate that their abilities are not underestimated.

Disciplinary misdemeanors are dealt with at a council of elders which imposes sanctions. A customary proverb has it "that one Korean is always stronger than three Koreans;" accordingly executive officers often have to mediate between seemingly incompatible opinions.

A Korean staff is composed of acknowledged individualists, whose characteristics might lead to great creativity. However, the superiors have to direct the independent activities into orderly and reasonable directions. The often extroverted pride of one's own abilities frequently leads to self-confident requests and always more fastidious tasks, which sometimes leads to an inflated self-esteem. A lot of accidents happen in Korea due to an exaggerated opinion of oneself.

The companies usually recruit their employees directly from qualified colleges and universities. Afterward, they are generally drilled and specifically trained within the firm. These processes lead to a characteristic corporate culture. The period of training is generally accompanied by a certain time, during which information is gathered and during which the new employee assists in special areas of different departments. The system of job rotation is experienced in later periods of the career and always requires a high degree of flexibility and is almost never reduced to only one workplace and one particular working group. The deployment for different working places supports the understanding of the connections within the enterprise and enables the members to superior positions in later times.

Regular transfers, especially within the areas of construction and supply, also prevent the notorious "Korean illness," which is the corruption in all enterprises and other organizations. This phenomenon causes time and again great problems for companies and the government. Corruption does not always happen due to greed or a lack of conscience for the negative consequences but because one has obligations toward family members, former mentors, or close friends, which have to be honored at some time.

Traditionally, women cooked tea for male superiors and other staff members. They also ran errands and performed minor office work. Today, women are often very precise and reliable and are therefore used predominantly in bookkeeping, accounting, and data processing. In the course of the last fifteen years, they worked to be promoted in different fields of administration. The term "career women" already exists in Korea as well. The advance to executive positions carries dignified titles and is sometimes supervisors of male employees. This is still rare, but happens from time to time. This development reflects a fundamental break with Confucian traditions and means a real social revolution for older staff members.

6.8 In Pursuit of the Ideal of Harmony

An enterprise consists of many—in some cases tens of thousands—individuals, who all have different temperaments. An ideal of business management in Korea therefore is the establishment of harmony (*inwha*) among the members of the company. Harmony generally requires reciprocal loyalty, which means that the management is loyal toward its employees and vice versa. They tend to see the enterprise as a family and the employees as confined to them as members of an entire household. That is why they strive for a patriarchal management style. They are strict when it comes to duties but they show understanding and joviality in all interpersonal relations. The managers strive for an open atmosphere and a maximum of information between the partners. This is not an easy task in a country in which the inhabitants like to shroud their life in secrecies and become only talkative for the evening drink. An ideal chief should be a friendly example for all employees, making it psychologically difficult to deceive him. The negative attitude of the former *chaebol* toward trade unions stems also from the fact that they tried to alienate employees and managers and endeavored to win them over to external socialistic organizations not compatible with the objectives of their own company.

Joint activities, a humorous atmosphere and in certain difficult situations generous financial allowances, are very helpful to create and maintain of a healthy working atmosphere. In many instances, this is achieved through a small social fund, which is made available by the head office to various departments. Real joy for working and great loyalty derives from a healthy working atmosphere. The executives have to prove with their personal behavior that the relations are not one-sided and from the top to the bottom, as it is the case in most Western enterprises. "The management demonstrates this by personal attention to the individual needs of the employees and their families" [5].

Thinking idealistically, this establishes a chain of men working hard for their companies, their families, and, in the end, also for the whole nation. This builds a bridge between the traditional Confucian virtues and the requirements of modern management. In all instances, the feelings of people have to be respected and the dignity of the superiors has not to be questioned under any circumstances.

The frequent lack of discipline among male Koreans is met by the mandatory period of military service for every young man. This experience promotes comradeship and the common pursuit of challenges. The "comrades" will be formed within group cohesion; their strengths are channeled to a common achievement and directed against the "enemy," who in this case is the competitor or rival. The superiors should have learned to take responsibilities and to achieve the best possible education for their confidantes, who should in turn express their gratitude with their willingness to perform their duties.

Nevertheless, Korea is not a land of milk and honey; on the contrary, hardwork prevails. The very best workers are commended, materially awarded, and honorably promoted. Those who fail can expect punishment, pity, or contempt. This system of "carrot and the stick" (*sin sang pil bol* in Korean) creates a strong tension and immense pressure inside enterprises. Therefore, harmonious relations are very important in order to ventilate excess pressure that could reduce labor achievements.

If these harmonious relations are destroyed, chaotic circumstances within the enterprise might be the result. Clumsiness and abuse of authority of superiors will quickly outrage employees. This can be expressed in emotional actions that will cause great damages to the companies, both material-wise and image-wise. The Korean industrial world has already experienced several persistent strikes, which are more often than not caused by outside trade unions but were provoked from the inside by employees. When the British Standard Chartered Bank wanted to abolish the system of payment by seniority and replace it by remunerations according to merits, 2600 employees entered a strike of two-and-half months in the summer of 2011, retiring the whole time to a hotel more than a hundred kilometers east of Seoul. Ultimately, they achieved their goals.

Such events are becoming increasingly frequent in companies that follow too eagerly modern Western management methods and neglect the Korean culture and mentality. When introducing unusual methods and processes, it is recommendable to take time and to be ready to communicate a lot. It is sociologically proven that changes are always better handled within groups.

It is a good and successful practice to express corporate principles and to integrate them in a written "corporate philosophy," but this assumes that the management truly believes in and lives according to these principles. Many companies in contemporary Korea seem to accept a reasonable mix of national and international principles, which shows the strengths of both models. Useful procedures are accepted while not useful ones are dismissed. The giant Korean *chaebol* and *keyul* with their modern administration systems which are very successful in global markets prove that such a pragmatic conduct can be quite effective.

6.9 Finance and Accounting

As already mentioned above, around the turn of the millennium, the International Monetary Fund managed to implement important criteria with respect to the profit and loss account, as well as for the general accounting system for larger companies in Korea. This is an important precondition for the firms knowing realistically about their situation with regard to their liquidity, profitability, and their defined financial goals and objectives. The disclosure of these important data naturally leads to a greater acceptance at the stock markets and contributed to the fact that large portions of the capital of the *chaebol* are now in the possession of other market participants rather than the owner families of the founders. The protection of the institutional and professional investors as well as for portfolio management was considerably improved as well.

These measures also created pressure for the firms to disclose profits and pay dividends, which ended the efforts to only achieve sales and market shares at nearly any costs. Of course, price wars are still selectively fought for strategical reasons, in order to strengthen market positions, or to take over rivals.

During the military dictatorship, only a few selected *chaebol* received a lot of capital. Under such circumstances, a healthy small- and medium-sized industry could hardly develop or flourish as a severe lack of capital was always notorious for the Korean economy. In principle, certain ministry officials are still steering the development of some projects by tax incentives, preferential credits, or guaranties. But in general, today the *chaebols* have to accumulate their own capital or to procure it from the free capital markets.

The recent Commercial Code of the RoK orders that 10 % of the annual cash dividends have to be withhold as legal reserves until the total reserves equal 50 % of the issued share capital. This procures a certain financial stability of the companies.

The Japanese *keiretsu* only have a low depth of production and therefore established an enormous network of dependent suppliers as well as distributors. Their Korean counterparts, however, found a middle way producing important parts themselves while working also with an extended net of suppliers. Whereas the Japanese *keiretsu* allow their junior partners some financial leeway—at least in better times—the Korean subcontractors always had to live with the hard pressures of their principals, which made it nearly impossible to accrue even small financial reserves for them.

The general situation has meanwhile clearly improved and vivid small- and medium-sized industries have flourished, which only depend on the giant conglomerates on a limited scale. The government considers the existence of the *chaebol* still as necessary for big projects. Yet, it has learned from the Western societies that a sound industrial society has to lean on healthy small- and medium-sized enterprises to a great extent as well.

Medium-sized companies quickly establish an orderly financial management and a transparent accounting system, following North American examples. Many Korean parents let their offspring to study at US American universities. After their return, they work in Korean enterprises—more often than not in the company of their parents, where they apply what they have learned abroad.

Nevertheless, instead of transparency, chaos prevails in numerous rampantly growing small and diminutive firms. This reflects the predominating mentality of particularly older and middle-aged Korean business people to veil profits, to continuously lament about the "bad course of one's own business," to manage in an authoritarian style, to practice nepotism in the best understanding of Confucianism, and to engage in corrupt practices. Nevertheless, slowly but steadily the tax authority succeeds to shed light on this chaos and force people, who did not pay taxes for decades, to make a fair contribution to the public interest. Groups of the small enterprises sometimes make a lot of money, have considerable credit balances at banks, and are looking for high loans, when they see a chance to conclude yet another speculative real estate business. (Another part of this book provides some information on the almost bizarre Korean real estate market) [6].

6.10 Taxation

As late as in 1948, a Korean Tax Law Committee worked out an orderly and fair taxation system as it has been in use in most developed states in the world for a long time. The economically important direct taxes such as income taxes and corporate taxes are settled in corresponding tax acts. Indirect taxes are the value-added tax (VAT) and the special excise tax, a kind of luxury tax for products of refined consumption.

Other taxes that are important for the entrepreneur are the estate duty, a tax on the reassessment of assets, and a tax on excessive profits, as well as a duty on securities.

There exists the principle of "no tax without a relating law." Other than the laws, there is a "Presidential Decree" that can be issued in very special cases. However, it is subordinated to the formal laws. Regrettably all tax laws are subject to rather frequent changes and therefore deprive the enterprises of reliable planning.

A National Tax Tribunal takes care of the legal protection of tax delinquents; it is independent from the tax authorities. The taxpayers can object decisions of the tax authorities at the National Tax Tribunal. The National Tax Service (NTS) is also independent from the tax authorities and cares for the collection of taxes. It has six regional and 99 local tax offices at its disposal.

Basically there exist national and local taxes. The national taxes are subdivided into the common national taxes, the custom duties, and taxes which are bound to special expenses, for instance to the educational system.

The local taxes are subdivided into taxes for the provinces, for the districts, and for the cities. With respect of the latter ones, there are discerned common taxes and taxes fixed for special expenses.

The common taxes of the districts and cities comprised of inhabitant taxes, landowner duties, and duties on utilizable agricultural land, duties on tobacco, vehicle taxes, and taxes on fuel consumption.

For foreign expatriate managers, income taxes, corporate taxes, and the VAT are personally important. Additionally, taxes on registrations, an inhabitant tax, and taxes on licenses and custom regulations have to be paid. With respect to the custom regulations, there exist treaties with many foreign governments such as the USA, Canada, the EU, and others. In fact, however, numerous, narrow-minded special provisions were invented and are applied. These extra-provisions are really not worthy of a significant industrial nation. Between all developed states, it is agreed that private property during a move can be imported without restrictions (with the exception of one vehicle per household). However, in Korea, there are numerous nit-picking exemptions: Only two carpets are permitted, liquor is not permitted at all, antiquities are strictly examined and in doubt arbitrarily heavy duties have to be paid, and last but not least, one can expect steep taxation in the case of electrical appliances. In practice, nevertheless, it appears that the private property of foreigners moving to Korea is handled with leniency.

After listing so many taxes, it is good news to report that there do not exist direct taxes on properties and no trade taxes, which is very reasonable because, after all, every country lives from a thriving economy.

The Republic of Korea together with many other countries has signed double taxation treaties. These treaties are supposed to avoid a double taxation as well as to prohibit tax evasions. Consequently, in some cases, the tax burden of foreign corporations, companies, or individuals can deviate from the national treatment.

Foreign citizens residing in Korea have to submit their entire global income to Korean tax liability. The disposal of real estate or capital participation in Korean companies is considered an income, even if they are listed on the local stock exchange. People with a permanent residency or who have lived twelve months or longer in Korea are considered residents. Persons who do not permanently live in Korea have to pay taxes only on their local income. People who live less than 183 days per year in the country are free of any taxation.

Income from interest or dividends is subject to withholding tax; the percentage ranges from 14 to 30 %, depending on the case.

The income tax rate is progressive. It starts with 8 % and ends with 35 % for national taxes. There are a lot of tax allowances for instance for married couples and families, for elderly people, physical handicaps, health costs, certain insurances, the education of children, or acknowledged donations.

A person who lives in Korea has to hand the declaration of the liable income tax for the previous year to the NTS until May. The principle of self-assessment applies to the submission of the tax declaration. An offence of the basis of proration, the form of the declaration, or the stipulated deadline for submission is fined. Taxes have to be paid immediately with the submission of the declaration; a prolongation can be granted on request. An offence of the regulation can be fined with an additional 20 % of the tax liability.

For foreign residents, there exists the attractive possibility to file the tax declaration with the US American Chamber of Commerce in Seoul. In this case, a tax deduction of 30 % will be granted, because it is internationally well known that in the USA the tax liability is calculated on the basis of one's entire income worldwide and that offences are severely punished.

As additional taxes to the income tax, an inhabitant tax and a capitation tax are raised, which are due for natural and juridical persons. The inhabitant tax amounts uniformly to 10 % on the income tax. The capitation tax is regionally determined by different criteria. A natural person has to pay between US$10 and US$50, if he/she is in business.

In recent years, the taxes and social charges mounted to 23.7 % for a single person and to 21.4 % for a couple with two children (in Germany for instance it was 55.5 % for a single person and 46 % for a family in average). In an international listing of "the more net from the gross," Korea ranked first ahead of Great Britain, Switzerland, Luxembourg, and Japan [7].

Because the national debt was proportionally the lowest of the OECD members, it looks as if the Korean state is governed quite efficiently.

The taxation of the enterprises is adjusted to the taxation of profits. The corporate tax is raised for all enterprises which aim at profits as their business target. That means that it is required from all firms as well as from companies limited. Any juridical company construction in order to save taxes is generally void.

Like natural persons, all corporations are subject to tax liabilities with their entire worldwide income. The formal seat of a company or its management is decisive. The period of the business year is generally freely eligible; it has, however, to comprise 12 months. Practically, almost all companies have decided to use the calendar-year as their business year.

Globally, the taxable income is calculated as the difference between the operating income and the operating expenses. The corporate tax law provides precise definitions for both. Liquidation gains and gains from fusions or split ups of corporations are not counted as earnings. Furthermore, the rise and fall from previous years are tax-free, just as alterations of the capital stock. Incomes from the common operating business as well as from leasing, asset redeployment, asset transfer, and new assessments of properties are considered as normal income and are therefore taxable.

The Korean enterprises have to follow the accounting principles of double-entry bookkeeping. The principles of an orderly accounting are laid down in the Korean Accounting Standards.

If a company shows a participation of foreign capital or has substantial international business relations, the income determination is subject to a separate examination of the financial authorities. This proceeding should prevent to put off profits in foreign countries through unfair transfer prices; in this respect, the "arm's length price principle" is applied, which means that prices with foreign partners can be agreed upon only if they would have also been charged to third independent business partners. During the last century, corresponding practices were proven to some international companies, in particular to those in the chemical business, which got major punishments. The law provides even prison sentences for the responsible managers in these cases.

On the corporate tax, an inhabitant tax and capitation tax is also levied as in the case of income taxes.

It was already mentioned that many Koreans like to juggle with real estate. This can have a lot of consequences with respect to the taxation as for instance, selling real estate, the multiple ownership of accommodations, the classification as a luxury residence, or the type of location. Taxation can be lowered for instance, when a municipality wants to encourage citizens to settle. Yet, it might be increased by five times, if densely populated areas are concerned (sometimes in Seoul or Busan) and a further settlement is undesirable. The taxation of accommodation units can vary from 0.3 to 7 % depending on its location and design. Real estate for commercial use is taxed between 0.3 and 0.6 %; however, it may be suspended, if the municipality wants to encourage industry to settle. The taxation rates are subject to frequent changes of laws and often depend on the currently ruling parties and their social determination.

Taxes are also due on water vehicles and flying objects. Motorcars are taxed according to their cubic capacity and the difference between privately and commercially used vehicles is drastic. For private cars, 200 Won are charged per cubic centimeter, whereas for commercial cars only 13 Won per cubic centimeter are charged.

Taxes on registered offices will not be charged if the total space is smaller than 330 m^2 or has less than 50 employees. The basis for proration depends on the entire space of the office and the total amount of the wages and salaries of the employees. Per square meter, 250 Won have to be paid and 0.5 % of a monthly salary of an employed person.

At the beginning of 2011, South Korea has introduced the International Financial Reporting Standards (IFRS), which were elaborated by the International Accounting Standards Board (IASB) in London; the latter one is a powerful organization of the associations of certified public accountants in 120 countries. This organization should replace the US American GAAP as a worldwide standard for accounting.

6.11 Decision Making

Any communicative relation will be accompanied by small and major decisions. This is most obvious in course of the daily business. The times, in which the higher superiors in the government and the *chaebol* always made their will to a decision, are over. This has unleashed an enormous creative power of the Korean people. They decide in which company they would like to work and can start a company of their own at any time. Nevertheless, it is quite normal in the vertically organized Korean society that important decisions will be made by persons who are hierarchically higher placed.

In bigger Korean firms, decisions are made in the form of cascades from the top. On each level of the cascade, the actual leader has his own scope of decisions. This increases from the bottom to the top. The superiors instruct the employees what to do and tell them the time limit, but they may carry out their proceeding in their way. The boss is trusting his specialized workers, who are usually well-trained and he knows that they are more familiar with the machines and all the circumstances than he himself. He lets them do their job self-confidently and proud of their personal abilities.

That is why the companies have also established an extensive system to put forward proposals, which are directed to the ambitions and the creativity of the employees. Useful proposals are awarded with high extra pays. This system is generally regarded as very successful and has saved millions of dollars for many enterprises and made resourceful employees extremely happy.

As long as the founders of the *chaebol* lived and lead them, they decided on all important matters. They gave their enterprises a particular mark and those developed their own corporate culture that reflected to a high degree, the personality that established them. Managers on all levels believed that they knew how the founder would want things to be done. But most of the old patriarchs do not live anymore and the related matters have become extremely complex. Most of the decisions that have to be made nowadays are discussed by highly qualified people meeting in competent panel discussions. This reflects the tendency of a modern participatory style of management.

Generalizations about the management style of the *chaebol* are a delicate matter, especially, because many things are in a constant flux. Almost all procedures of a *chaebol* are subject to continuous changes. One might carefully say that the hard factors (structural conditions) of management are already quite international, whereas the soft factors (social conditions) keep a strong Korean component.

Some of the big *chaebol* are real transnational enterprises and hold a high percentage of their assets overseas; thus having removed themselves partially from domestic circumstances. However, the planning bureaucracy is still influential on decisions, which are highly important for the national economy. It has the sole overview of the national resources and acts in the interest of the state. The bureaucracy can assist very important projects with the allocation of funds, guarantees, or tax reliefs and thereby can pave the way, for instance, for research and development. The ministerial bureaucracy controls to a large extent banks and independent financial institutes. This secures a primacy of the "real economy" over a "virtual financial community." This is why Korea did not fall victim to untrustworthy property funds from the USA in 2008 and was only indirectly hit by the global financial crisis. One had indeed learned from the preceding financial Asian crisis ten years before.

6.12 Common Business Behaviors

The Korean business consultant Yang [8] proposed in 1988 the following "ten commandments" to conduct business in his country:

1. One should always have a formal introduction at his disposal
2. One should never be without business cards
3. One should never assume that matters uttered in English are completely understood by the participants of a conversation
4. One should not push too hard to get ones point through and force a partner aside
5. One always has to invest in human relations
6. One should never put a partner in an embarrassing situation, instead one should constantly try to praise his achievements
7. One should always be a good host and reversely enjoy an extended hospitality
8. One should go to the greatest lengths to understand the matter of the counterpart
9. One should avoid applying abstract Western logic to ones arguments
10. One should always be alert and be well-informed about what is happening

Elaborations of the ten points:

(1) One should better not approach someone directly, but try to be introduced by a respected person or institution (prominent banker, head of an association, respected politician, famous professor, top manager, university, financial institute, and ministry).

(2) Business cards play a crucial role when introductions are made. Both sides can obtain information from them about their position in a country obsessed with hierarchies (company, rank, membership of organizations, academic qualification, address of the company, and private residence).

(3) Even if a Korean manager fluently speaks common English, he usually is not able to describe complicated matters. This applies to a normal interpreter as well, unless he is a technical expert and was trained in foreign countries. Therefore, it is highly recommended to obtain written minutes right after a meeting.

(4) In a meeting, one has to be very well prepared, polite and patient, stand always firm, and above all show in any situation a calm dignity. Contrary positions may be left aside, put back, or cleared by an intermediary. The opposite side likes to hide behind a collective team and is fond of frequently taking time to think disputed matters over.

(5) Documents (even laws) do only set up a basis for negotiations and are most disliked when referred to in discussions. It is also not popular to formulate them too much in detail, because tomorrow, the circumstances might already change and thus, one has to meet them with a flexible attitude. Good human relations are most helpful under such circumstances and they might—together with trust and respect—enable compromises and even concessions.

(6) Koreans are generally quite emotional and also very sensitive; this has to be kept in mind particularly in all cases where the "face" is concerned. If the partners pay respect to each other, a relaxed and positive atmosphere might prevail which leads to good feelings (*gibun*) permitting now and then to surprising concessions.

(7) Whereas in Anglo-Saxon countries invitations for entertainment—particularly in case of customer relations—are frowned on, they have to be gladly accepted in Korea. To be able to become partners, drinking leads to friendship and to good feelings trust. A comradely atmosphere can also be created by playing golf together, which is an extremely popular sport among East Asian managers. The relations might be further improved by small tokens and presents. In order to protect oneself against obligations, it is highly recommendable to give presents in turn and also to take turns inviting each other.

(8) Sincere personal relations lead to mutual trust. When trust is established, a word can procure more safety than a well-phrased contract. Therefore, it is important to assess the partner with empathy (*nunchi*). It is helpful to have knowledge about his family, education, mind-set, and hobbies as well as his personal data such as his birthday and anniversaries.

(9) Only when conversation partners have lived for a very long time in Western countries, one can try to use Western logic. But it is rather recommended to sound out the empathy (*nunchi*) and feeling (gibun) of another person. Finding out the most common emotional denominator is usually the safest way for successful negotiations.

(10) Change is omnipresent in contemporary Korea. Like the fleeting modes, changes in the fashion and preference in the structures of manufacturing and organization happen within the enterprises and with them, the mind-set of the people. Our Western society has become rather hesitant and slow concerning changes and they sometimes seem too rapid for us—even if we try to follow them. If operating in South Korea, one always has to keep up with the latest developments. For the marketing departments, market research is crucial. Only regular test sales assure a realistic evaluation of actual market trends; surprising developments are rather the rule than exception. Much attention has to be devoted to market trends that might point to the future.

These "ten commandments" have partly relativized but are generally still valid.

6.13 Negotiations

Negotiating and haggling seems to be in the Koreans blood. This happens between civil persons in daily life as well as between citizens and public authorities, associations, firms, and formations of the retail industry. It happens also inside enterprises, between the enterprises, in the dealings of the enterprises with public authorities, and finally also between the authorities and the political forces.

In almost all cases, Koreans negotiate with each other and all parties know the socio-psychological rules very well. Sooner or later they obtain results, which are usually connected to mutual concessions; those are commonly declared as improvements in order to keep face. Even in the case of lawfully fixed facts, they normally find skillful forms of interpretation.

A fundamental difference exists within the institutions of the military. Here, the rule is led by a hierarchical understanding—as in most places in the world—and commands need to be just obeyed.

International political or commercial negotiations are sometimes quite difficult, depending on the cultural environment of the negotiators. A special case of its own are negotiations between North and South Koreans as both know their mentalities and positions very well, but have meanwhile developed very different mind-sets which turn out to become irreconcilable. In the course of the last decades, South Koreans have gained much global input which decisively broadened their international horizon. This does not apply to North Koreans.

Generally speaking, the objective of negotiations is to bring together two conflicting points of views; the outcome should be that both sides can live with it. In many Western countries, the scope is restricted by rules and laws and steadfast power positions. This is basically the same in Korea; but extremely tough negotiation partners try even in a clearly inferior position to get somewhere with concessions. They proceed following the idea of Taoism that constant dropping wears in the long run the hardest stone. Koreans believe that after all, anything can be negotiated—though within limits. Time flows and thus circumstances change and open up new opportunities; no process is forever completed.

People who are influenced by monotheistic religions such as Christianity, Islam, or Judaism are inclined to establish articles of faith with unalterable convictions that are not negotiable at all. This is different in the more flexible and tolerant East Asian religions. One can see nowadays in modern China how doctrines can be watered down, circumvented, or even washed away. Nevertheless, even among Christians, Muslims, or Jews there are people, who, despite their religious beliefs, look out for themselves and try to hypocritically circumvent their principles with sophist's methods. Men are unfathomable and in many instances not immune to persuasion.

According to Saccone [9], there exist three prejudices concerning negotiating:

1. One negotiates only in determined situations and under determined premises. In North America or Western Europe, one can negotiate prices at a flea market but not in a restaurant.

Wrong: Even in a restaurant one can get additional quantities or little presents.

2. One negotiates at a fixed time, at a fixed place, on a fixed agenda.

Wrong: One can negotiate at anytime, anywhere, and on anything.

3. One should have a genuine talent for negotiating or needs at least a long and thorough training.

Wrong: Any bright man can become a good negotiator with audacity, fantasy, and patience.

When negotiating, one can and one should have fun. Interesting people are frequently met, with the weapons of spirit and knowledge as one tries his strength against the negotiation partner like in a sporting competition—and very often, the pleasures of kind hospitality can be enjoyed.

For Koreans, the point in time is very important. Decisive chapters in one's life (birth, marriage, funeral, etc.) and to a slightly lesser degree business matters depend on the right timing. Such an event should by all means not be scheduled on a so-called unlucky day but should occur on a "promising lucky day." To fix these days, the traditional moon-calendar is consulted as all appropriate dates for respective situations are listed in this calendar. Particularly, older negotiation partners attach a high importance to this procedure.

An appropriate location for a negotiation is a cozy place, which provides a good atmosphere. This rules out a huge table in a dignified conference room. The latter is reserved for the final announcement of the results of the negotiation and for the proper toast. A Korean partner appreciates when he can decide in his country on the seating plan, where the picking order is of extreme importance. At any rate, his team is then strictly ranked in the seating order and everyone gets a place that underlines his dignity. For this purpose, round tables are less suitable. Instead, oval tables are much more appropriate. For the foreign partner, it is disadvantageous when sitting in direction of the windows, because this might divert his own attention. For the same reason, a room equipped with beautiful pieces of art is rather distracting and should be avoided. Similarly, one would like the service personnel to act as discretely as possible.

The usually male negotiation partners greet each other by shaking hands. On this occasion, the right forearm will be stretched and supported by the left hand as a token of special respect. The negotiation room will be entered with a positive attitude; it anticipates an advantageous result for the future of all participants, who are presently considered partners and not adversaries. All participants are elegantly dressed, smile continuously, and endeavor to speak distinguished and politely. At the beginning, the partners might talk about the weather, families, university times, sport preferences, hobbies, common acquaintances, traveling to distant countries, or even philosophical opinions. Political judgements or religious discussions should be avoided. Ideally, the participants discover as much common ground as possible. This greatly contributes to a pleasant atmosphere and helps to establish good relations as well as continues them. Polite bowing is always mandatory in Korea.

In a friendly atmosphere, the willingness to accept the partner is seemingly greater than in an impersonal, big conference room and also possibly leads to concessions. At any means, the own dignity and importance have to be demonstrated. One's own important position in the head office has to be underlined and a discrete hint to one's own personal relation to the top management and the owners of one's own company should be dropped. Koreans themselves like to mention their good relations to prominent people (name dropping) as well.

The foreign negotiator should be flexible but never show a sign of weakness. It is always advantageous to pay great attention to the partners of the discussion and to walk in the partner's shoes. Any controversial argument should be lined with politeness. All these suggestions will produce a good *gibun* of the negotiation partners and promote positive results.

The selection of a capable interpreter is a delicate matter. Basically, it is recommendable to bring an own interpreter. However, it is unlikely that an interpreter is a non-Korean, who is absolutely fluent in the Korean language (though the number of Westerners who learn Korean is increasing). A Korean interpreter should preferably live permanently overseas as this prevents the Korean partner from trying to get him on his side. It is most useful when he is familiar with the line of business or has at least successfully completed specialized studies.

It is always of advantage to learn some Korean words and phrases. This might not enable you to have a conversation in Korea, but the other side will appreciate the fact that a foreigner shows that he makes an effort to understand his country and uses a few words that sound familiar to the Korean.

When getting to the heart of discussions, issues should generally be discussed in Korea as the partners feel much more comfortable and open in their home country. It is further much easier for him to consult the head office in the last instance. Yet, it makes sense to invite the discussion partners to one's own home country during the course of the negotiations. This allows them to become familiar with the other company and to better understand aspects of complicated negotiations. Furthermore, many questions can be answered already beforehand. Last but not least, Koreans like to travel as this satisfies their curiosity and gives "face" to their fellow countrymen.

The discussion partner in Korea might unexpectedly suggest visiting an exhibition or an opera or arrange to visit his factory premises. Such suggestions are in no direct connection to the general negotiations; nonetheless, one should gladly follow such an invitation. It will enhance the reputation of the organizers, especially when the event is connected to some pomp and glitter. Finally, sealing the negotiated agreements in an almost ritual framework should by no means be turned down. However, it is possible to forestall this with an own invitation for a ceremonial event. In East Asia, substantial sacrifices of time have to be always made.

The foreigner is usually focused on quick decisions, but in East Asian territories, he has to be ready to invest a lot of time and patience. Likewise, one should be ready to approach a subject of discussion from a different side, or to look at it from a different perspective, discussing alternatives. Finally, one should always look for a common denominator. The result of the negotiations might look different from the original bargaining position, but it may have the same benefit.

Negotiating with bureaucrats is especially delicate. In such a situation, there is no equality of the partners. One has to get through such negotiations even if it seems impossible to achieve one's own targets completely. Anywhere in the world bureaucrats can be arrogant, cold, and very self-confident. However, in Confucian systems, these qualities are especially virulent, because the civil servants (public authorities) hold an old tradition and have acquired their position by visiting the best universities, having passed very difficult public examinations. The foreigner is not taken seriously as a discussion partner, because he can hardly be integrated into the complicated system of granting favors to.

In the past, the foreign negotiator was always in the awkward position of a petitioner. This has changed in recent times and the bureaucracy has learned to act predominantly as a service institution. Usually, it gives a hand in supporting projects, particularly in the case of welcome investments.

Even if there exists a difference in official matters, nevertheless, a foreign applicant might bring about a common interest such as similar experiences of academic careers, intellectual interests, or shared hobbies. Good relations to prominent people are also helpful to draw the attention of the public official. In such cases, it is absolutely appropriate to extent a correct invitation. If this invitation is accepted, a certain familiarity might develop. In case the bureaucrat might not be directly concerned with the presented problem, he still can help in pointing to loopholes in regulations or introduce a colleague, who can help to overcome certain difficulties. A Korean proverb holds it that even considering the given distance in public, private favors are sometimes granted.

Generally, it is helpful to know personalities from political circles either in Korea or in one's own home country. Such relations can open doors. Negotiating in Korea it is prudent to engage a person versed in legal matters; before signing contracts, the legal situation needs to be thoroughly assessed. Meticulous preparations are extremely helpful before entering negotiation.

6.14 The Service Sector

The service sector accounts for 60 % of Korea's gross domestic product and 70 % of all jobs. Yet, the government will further support this sector by deregulations and policy programs. Six fields seem worth to be further investigated: tourism, logistics, software, health care, education, and finance.

A willingness to extend service is generally not a strong point of Western societies while particularly in the business world it plays a crucial role in Korea. It is so natural that hardly anybody talks about it when he experiences a good service. However, one complains extensively and emotionally, if he is exposed to a less than perfect service. The service is not as refined as in Thailand or Japan, but it is nonetheless intensive and excellent from the Western point of view.

Before going into more detail about the manifold types of services in Korea, the most amazing type of service in South Korea will be explained: the delivery service, called *baedal*. This service is unique in the world and superior to countries with good delivery systems such as the USA and Japan. The delivery industry has rapidly grown in the last fifteen years. It employs almost 200,000 people and has become an essential economic factor.

Bae Hyu-jung wrote as of January 11, 2014, in *The Korean Herald*: "There are few things that cannot be delivered in this short-tempered, fast moving and tightly networked country." Meanwhile, the Koreans take the exceptionally customer-friendly *baedal* for granted. 1.5 billion boxes are recently delivered annually with a value of nearly US$4 billion.

The system is made possible due to the country's "*ppalli-ppalli* culture" (hurry-up mentality), by the excellent traffic infrastructure and communication systems, and an army of low paid, mostly young people.

The roads are full of hazardous motorcyclists, who are a nightmare for other users of the road. They squeeze through moving and stopping vehicles of all sizes, boldly ignoring any traffic sign. They make at least a dozen delivery-stops per day in order to ensure a sufficient income. Their neck-breaking maneuvers lead to numerous accidents every day. Special delivery companies concentrate on the door-to-door transportation of light parcels, documents, and groceries. They charge rates which are calculated on the basis of distance and weight. A parcel delivered to a distance of up to three miles costs 7$ and 15$ up to 6.6 miles. Even though these are not cheap rates, the service is very popular. The regular postal service would need five days to deliver parcels and letters.

Home shopping is very popular for almost all types of merchandise. It is widely advertised on television and numbers products, ranging from household goods, products for outdoor activities, textiles, beverages, and food items. The housewife sits in front of the TV screen at 9.00 p.m. and orders fresh mussels from a southern town, which she will receive already at 11.00 a.m. the next morning in an ice box at her 35th floor apartment in Seoul.

The most popular form of delivery is the food delivery service. A lot of people such as researchers and students prefer this service because they can save a lot of time. Another merit is the possibility to check smartphone apps that offer a variety of food choices and to make use of special offers. More than 70 apps compete within the food delivery category as of the beginning of 2014. Restaurants which deliver by either using special delivery companies or using an own small fleet of bikes save on service personnel and on restaurant space.

The delivery system is widely used by women (85 % by one count). Women who do not work watch TV almost all day and working women are afraid to go out after dark. Because a lot of women are afraid of male delivery persons in the evening, more and more female bikers are employed. The Seoul Metropolitan Government has installed small lockers close to apartment blocks. The delivery men put the parcel or letter in the locker and set a password. This password is sent to the recipient via text message and the order can be retrieved at any time.

Recently, the home shopping industry has been subject to strong criticism. *The Korean Herald* laments in its April 2, 2015, edition "Sadly, a filthy side to the business environment in the industry has also grown. There are so many entrenched foul business practices in the industry that the nation's antitrust watchdog called them 'a comprehensive assortment of irregularities.'"

Because the industry is considering the use of delivery drones, the installation of pick-up spots would become necessary. However, it seems unlikely that drones can be used in densely populated areas.

The smaller shops can compete with departmental stores and supermarket chains mainly because of their willingness to deliver bigger purchases to the customer's home. This service is most welcome to a housewife, who has just bought 20 beer cans, 10 big bottles of water, and 2 big water melons. The items are then often delivered by older, male members of the household of the supermarket. Huge discount stores like e-mart recently obtained their operating permissions only under the condition that they refrain from home deliveries and thus ensuring that small stores remain somewhat competitive.

In general, the different types of service in Korea can hardly be counted. Usually, they are added to purchased goods and performances. Service is such a natural course of action that Korean literature on economy hardly ever mentions it. It is also telling that the same word "ko-gaek" is used for both "guest" and "customer."

It is really a pleasure to go shopping in one of the great departmental stores in Korea. People are generally well dressed and their hair is well kept. There are often musical events and small art or other exhibitions. The service personnel is overwhelmingly friendly, extremely patient, and every time ready to accept complaints, even taking back items purchased half an hour earlier. The purchased items will be carefully wrapped, decorated with a ribbon, and frequently a little token of special service (*seobisu*), such as miniature samples or other small items, will be attached. As presents need to be packed perfectly, they are wrapped artistically and decorations for special occasions are added. Most departmental stores offer a service where presents are professionally wrapped for a little extra charge.

Department stores are open from 9.30 a.m. to 8.30 p.m., including on Sundays. This makes sense because only on Sundays do working people with their families have sufficient time for bigger purchases such as furniture, which require time for inspection and a careful selection. Stores are closed on one day during the week; yet, every store is closed on another day, so that customers can always find an open outlet. Because departmental stores usually house branches of banks, flower shops, shoe repair shops, and dry cleaning outlets—operating by the shop-in-shop system—the customer will save much time during his shopping tour in the city.

The personnel in hotels, restaurants, beauty salons, fitness studios, and the like is usually well-trained and ensure that customers feel special and important. It is no accident that Inchon International Airport was labeled recently for the ninth time the most convenient airport in the world; for 2009 and 2010, a Korean airline was recognized as the carrier with the best service internationally.

In small retail outlets, service efforts are naturally smaller and less time and money is invested in this sector. However, they still go into the same direction and even highly rationalized supermarkets and convenience stores do usually have someone to help put the purchased items into paperbacks and carries them on request to the car of a customer or a taxi. Taxis are quite popular because they solve the parking problem.

We have never seen anybody in Korea who has filled his own car at a gas station only to hurry through the rain into the station to pay his bill with his hands smelling of gasoline. At Korean gas stations (called *oilbank*), a small group of employees extends a loud welcome and somebody takes care to fill the tank, whereas another person cleans the windows and sometimes even the car interior. Afterward, another person takes the client's credit card to the cashier. Meanwhile, the driver does nothing except perhaps reading his newspaper. After leaving the gas station, the driver usually finds a wiping cloth, a key ring, a bottle of water, or a voucher for a car wash on his backseat. When paying cash, the change never has to be controlled as it will always be correct.

If a Hyundai breaks down anywhere in the country, one can phone the next branch of this company to get help free of charge within a few minutes (if close to a bigger town) and after some time in the countryside. When picking up a car from a vehicle repair shop, the customer will inevitably find a small gift and the car is meticulously cleaned inside and outside. Regular customers (*tangol-son-nim*) do not even have to move the car to and from the shop by themselves: It will be picked up and at the end of the year, the customer might get a present such as a repair kit or a bottle of liquor.

The organization of substitute drivers in Korea is quite interesting. They offer a 24-h driving service. Spontaneously meeting a friend and having a snack and some drinks on such an occasion does not pose a problem at all, because a substitute driver can ensure a safe drive home. Either the restaurant provides a telephone number or the guest has some respective phone numbers himself. Recently, coordination centers have been established, which direct drivers with own cars to the desired location. On request of the customer, the coordination center can also provide special cars such as a red Ferrari with a driver in livery with white gloves.

There are also substitute drivers available for customers, who drive their own car but are suddenly tired or have taken too many dry Martinis. The drivers arrive by foot, usually living close to the pick-up spot, driving the guest in his own car to his home and returning by means of public transportation. This service is available in many cities also after midnight and to far-away suburbs. In many instances, a coordination center contacts numerous drivers via radio. The drivers have then to react very fast in order to get the job before one of his many rivals gets it. It is generally assumed that the substitute driver is not insured against accidents.

This service exists in addition to an already-existing extensive taxi service net. Countless taxis patrol the roads around the clock. Because they are relatively cheap, almost everyone makes regular use of them. When it suddenly starts to rain, pedestrians might look in vain for an empty taxi. Returning from a supermarket or from the airport, loaded with heavy luggage most taxi-drivers are willing to carry the luggage to the fourth floor in turn of a tip. This is particularly appreciated by senior citizens.

A single traveler as well as participants of a meeting can ask (even around midnight) an agency to send a Russian interpreter or a Chinese translator. Likewise, one can get a car wash, or have things repaired in the household, or have a piece of heavy furniture moved. The term "service" is not negatively connoted at all as it is often the case in Western or Northern Europe countries. Koreans who live in foreign countries—especially those who are older or live with a handicap—usually frequently compare the service available to the service in their home country and often complain about the situation and prices for service in their host-country.

Resourcefulness and diligence make such a variety of services possible, which extends to any thinkable type of assistance for both companies and private persons. Within this field of industry, specialized enterprises, as well as loosely organized networks and individuals, have to be really fast to satisfy the customer.

When it comes to service, not only a flawless quality and competent handling are important but well-trained people play an important role as they take care of a pleasant and relaxed atmosphere. Immediately after the guest has taken a seat in a restaurant, a smiling waitress appears and offers a cup of tea and some peanuts and other appetizers in order to shorten the time of waiting until orders are taken and dishes are served.

The unusually high service standard is made economically affordable because time is only of little concern with regard to the productivity factor. Western industrial societies measure the productivity in time units. Therefore, the highly efficient industrial nations of Korea and Japan do badly in international comparisons as they do not pay much attention to the time used, but are primarily interested in the productivity per person (or head or arm). Traditionally, one has to work until the job is done, regardless of the time required, though the trade unions have by and large achieved to establish regular working hours, especially the manufacturing industry. However, many meetings and educational events are still held outside the working hours. For office workers and of course the management class, overtime is rather the rule than the exception. Furthermore, the strong identification with the own company requires to satisfy the customers. This is reflected in the pride of being a member of the enterprise and the truism that all income is, after all, derived from the customers.

Character-wise, Koreans are rather impatient and pugnacious. The high willingness to serve can only be generated by intensive training, the awareness of an immense competitive pressure, the good example of superiors, the increasing influence of consumer protection associations, and, last not least, the fact that the government does not grant comfortable transfer incomes to people who are able to work for a living.

People who do not work are stigmatized in Korea, but many people have to work even at an old age to make a living because they cannot enjoy a sufficient pension. Not a few older people roam the streets of Seoul and collect old boxes and other cardboard items, pushing them forward on small carts or on bicycles in all weathers. Additionally, many Koreans are generally hungry for money, regardless of the circumstances.

Although the Korean service culture is already highly developed from a Western perspective, a headline of the newspaper *The Korea Times* demanded in its edition from January 7, 2010, that "Korean firms need an improvement of their customer service" and that further efforts were needed to make their customers more satisfied and happy. This request does not only include industrial enterprises, but also hotels, educational institutes, and in general any kind of organization where clients have to pay money. Because the subject is principally considered as a very important issue, a national index for customer satisfaction, the so-called NCSI (National Satisfaction Consumer Index), was established. A ranking by achieved points is annually published. The ranking is almost every year subject to changes (Table 6.2).

Table 6.2 Ranking of service organizations in Korea

	Ranking 2014	Score		Ranking 2009	Score
1	Hotel Shilla	84	1	Yeungjin College	84
2	Lotte hotel	83	2	Hotel intercontinental	82
3	JW Marriott hotel	82	3	Chung Cheong university	81
4	The Westin Chosun hotel	81	4	Samsung Construction and trade corp.	81
5	Severance hospital	80	5	Daelim Construction	81
6	Samsung medical center	80	6	TaeKyung college	80
7	Intercontinental hotel	80	7	Sunkyunkwan university	79
8	Seoul St. Mary's hospital	80	8	Seoul Plaza hotel	78
9	Sunkyunkwan university	80	9	Lotte hotel	78
10	Asan medical center	79	10	Daegu transportation corp.	77

The theoretical maximum would be 100 points. It is of course no coincidence that the rewarded firms come from the service sector or are closely related to it. But even in the construction sector, no company can afford that its employees enter a house with dirty shoes or leave a construction site disorderly. Because the high schools, colleges, and universities are in severe competition with each other, they are consequently also a subject of the ranking. The national average of the NCSI in 2009 was 71 points, which shows an unusually high standard of service performances in the entire country.

But there is one very unpleasant type of service, especially for foreign managers and merchants in Korea (as well as in Japan): the problem of returned products. For instance, when the Han River floods the warehouse of a pharmaceutical wholesaler, he will sent the spoiled products immediately back to the producer, as he normally does not have an insurance policy. He would argue that the deal was sealed under regular business circumstances; a flooding or even a financial calamity, however, is not a normal circumstance and thus, he has the right to return the products. The latter case could also show that the manufacturer failed to produce attractive, well-selling products; it is a further common conviction that the bigger business partner has in general to shoulder unforeseen risks.

The manufacturer has no chance but to smile and to accept the returned goods. Of course, he is well advised to have a reserve in his calculations that means to add a certain percentage for such unforeseen events. In many cases, one has to investigate the given circumstances thoroughly in order to prevent a possible abuse.

6.15 Logistic Structures and Logistic Systems

To develop an economy, the distribution of goods and the transfer of services efficient traffic connections and communication systems are most important. This requires a good infrastructure. The government is aware of this need and invests sufficiently in such facilities. President Park constructed a highway from Seoul to Busan already in the 1970s.

Today, a dense net of highways covers the complete country, except the eastern side, which is only sparsely populated and also quite mountainous. The general speed limit in Korea is 68 mph, and thus, new highways are built with slightly narrower roads and shoulders while curves are slightly tighter than in most other Western countries. The extension of the net continues and numerous tunnels and bridges, which are quite expensive, have to be constructed. For all types of vehicles, the highways are subject to tolls. The mileage charge is electronically registered and directly debited to the account of the car holder.

The highways ensure smooth north–south connections, which were rather neglected in former times. Whereas the motorways have already reached the limits of their capacity on the northwest route of the country, they are still not too crowded in the center and in the southwest. Trucks are numerous on the freeways, though cargos such as sand, cement, or coal are usually transported by means of coastal shipping. Despite a good railway system, many people travel in buses and mini-busses due to their cheap fares. An ever-increasing vehicle on the freeway, however, is the automobile.

Besides the highways, the entire country is covered by a good road system and almost every village has a road connection which grants quick access to the general traffic network. Even most of the bigger offshore islands are integrated into this traffic network; this development is quite costly because of the many bridges and dams which have to be erected. Traffic jams are quite common in urban areas, as Koreans are extremely well motorized. This is especially true for the capital and its suburbs—the many elevated highways, tunnels, and nearly 30 bridges erected over the Han River can only slightly reduce the traffic.

Congestions are quite frequent on weekdays and holidays, especially close to touristic attractions such as the Seoraksan national park, which attracts many people for hikes. The same is true for the skiing attractions of Pyeongchang and Yongpyeong in the northeast of the country. Another popular target is the green island of Gangwha or the spectacular island-bridge of Incheon, both roughly 50 km west of Seoul. Streets are further crowded around the interesting maritime park of Suncheon in the southwest as well as in the vicinity of the old capital of the Shilla Imperium Gyeongju.

Seoul and its suburbs have an excellent subway network. Its platforms are separated from the rails and the incoming trains by tall safety partitions and the entire ticketing is handled electronically. All other parts of the country up to the mountainous regions are connected with the capital by railway. The trains are inexpensive, rather comfortable, punctual, and offer a good restaurant service.

A showpiece of the national railway system is the high-speed train of the KTX Bullet Train. In the rest of the world, only Japan with its *Shinkansen*, France with its TGV, Germany with its ICE, Spain with its *Alta Velocidad Espaniola*, and Russia with a high-speed train between Moscow and St. Petersburg offer a similar transportation service. The KTX was originally built with French technology, but due to a lot of complaints about technical defects, today, only Korean engineers are working on its further development.

These modern train units run between Seoul-Busan and Seoul-Mokpo with a maximum speed of almost 124 mph (200 km/h). The tickets, however, are expensive.

Korea is still dissatisfied with the general punctuality of the trains with respect to transporting passengers. In 2010, an average delay of 38 s was registered—a result that European train travelers can only dream of. However, Japan as a role model only had an average delay of only 18 s and the Koreans use this number as their yardstick.

High-speed trains which are quick, punctual, and comfortable are sweeping all day from north to south and back, but still a big portion of the domestic traffic takes place in buses, which are cheaper than the railway with its excellent service. But the bus stops at the service areas of the highways are equally or even more attractive.

South Korea is surrounded by the sea on three sides. Thus, it is not surprising that there are numerous harbors, which are however not very much used in the domestic traffic because road and rail offer much faster connections. Overnight ferryboat trips to a major island were quite popular until April 15, 2014, when the Sewol, a ship of almost 7000 gross-registered tons, capsized and more than 300 people drowned.

Yet, container and mass-transportation cargo are transported on ships, for instance between Busan and Incheon. Also hundreds of small islands still lacking bridges or dams are serviced by smaller boats and ferries.

The two major harbors (Busan and Incheon) have a vivid exchange of freights with all important global ports. But the international cruising business has not yet caught up with Korea except for Busan. There are future plans to engage in a large scale into the cruising business.

There are numerous domestic airports for local traffic. Some of them only see little aircraft movements and are obviously planned for the future. Only services to Seoul/Incheon, Busan, and Jeju are almost near their capacity. Some new low-budget carriers have considerably increased the starts and landings, for instance at Busan, where the construction of a large airport is already being considered. All international flights are directed from Incheon, Kimpo (Seoul city), and Busan. Jeju is an exception, as it serves many flights to and from China, which are rapidly increasing in their frequency.

Most of the traffic systems are in sharp competition with each other like all other business branches within Korea.

With respect to logistical services, companies as well as private persons like to hire specialized service companies. Enterprises have neither to take care of transportation services themselves nor do they have to keep stock capacities in times of minor demand. According to their needs, smaller or bigger vehicles are at their disposal. Likewise, means of transport with pallets, containers, and special units such as cold-storage vehicles are always available. The highly developed flexibility and the Korean art of improvisation permit the industry to extend a tailor-cut service system. The services for individuals have also to keep pace with industrial services; the requirements are on an equally high level.

Because the industry has introduced a rigorous "just in time system," there are only few storage houses in the country. Direct deliveries from the main factories take place in an exact 30-min interval.

Like in all industrialized countries, mainly standardized pallets and containers are used as they permit a quick and comfortable transshipment between ships, railways, trucks, and planes. To a large extent, the "ppalli, ppalli" (quick, quick) principle prevails.

The well-organized *taekbae* system enables a transfer of goods and messages from A to B to C and back to A. This system is also used by private persons. One can send luggage from one hotel to another hotel in advance and arrange at the same time that one of two pieces is sent back to one's home. People do not need special preparations and only a few formalities are required. The price for this service is also quite reasonable.

This agile behavior of the entire business life gives the impression that the country works like a well-lubricated machine, where all cogs reach into each other and the whole national logistic system operates smoothly like a clockwork. Apart from the professional logistic services, small family companies often use their own family members for transportation, especially in the *baedal*-system. The significant disadvantage of the whole system is that the roads are always crowded with vehicles and all drivers are pretty stressed.

Basically, Koreans are restless spirits, who rarely enjoy free time. The entire country has more characteristics of a "service park" than of a "leisure time park." Apart from the small upper-class minority, it is understood that everyone serves other people or other organizations. It is unthinkable that somebody takes time off or escapes into holidays when an urgent business or even medical assistance is required. The whole machine has always to run without any interruptions.

6.16 Organization of Labor

The successful development of industrialized nations is based on technical innovations, outstanding entrepreneurs, the establishment of capital markets, the foundation of a realistic accounting systems, and especially the sacrifices of employees who, for many years, have to work hard for rather poor payments. Additionally, in Japan, Korea, and China, a governmental industrial policy with an elaborated framework of planning helped to foster this development.

In Korea, initially foreign technology from the USA, Japan, and Europe was employed, and only in later years own noteworthy innovations were made. The capital markets were—and partially still are—supplied by overseas capital investors. A reasonable accounting system was only established starting in 1997. Like in Japan, a bureaucratic guidance was enforced. Yet, in Korea it was much more dominant than in Japan. Finally, like in other industrialized nations, the development rested on the shoulders of an impoverished workforce.

A utopian social justice is hardly considered by anyone in Korea as it is obvious that there are gifted and untalented, diligent and lazy, responsible as well as irresponsible citizens, which consequently lead to successful and unsuccessful human beings. That means the sense of justice is reduced to equal opportunities, which is difficult to ensure by the government since some people have inherited incredible fortunes, some got small properties, and the great majority has received nothing at all.

The workforce in South Korea partly opposes the government and big enterprises rather hostile and skeptically. It hears sirens in the North wailing and propagating the impossible idea of all citizens being treated equally. For some reason, the North refuses to acknowledge the flagrant inequality between the hungry citizens, which make about 90 % of the nation and the well-off rest that belongs to the military and functionary class. The daily reports in South Korean newspapers on the incomprehensible riches of *chaebol*-families arouse the rage of emotional fellow citizens.

Backed by the government, for a long time, almost all companies ignored the matters of their employees. The 1948 constitution provided minimum social standards, and trade unions were generally intended; however, they were later severely regulated and ultimately, during the regime of Pak Chung-hee, completely lost their power. This led to fierce strikes, dramatic riots, and anarchic socioeconomic conditions. Because Pak's priority was always to build an economically sound state, he took action and staged a military *coup d'état*. South Korea had to outrun the North, which was at that time economically considerably ahead of the South.

Because this in turn was not in the interest of Kim Sung-il, his system made sure that the southern labor movements were undermined by Communists, who caused considerable unrest. Under similar circumstances, Chun Doo-hwan seized power after 1980 and continued a military dictatorship.

During the term of his successor Roh Tae-woo, a democratic motion spread quickly, which was further expanded under his successor Kim Young-sam. Whereas the leadership wanted a slow democratization process, the worker's party considered democracy as a self-service shop. Rather naïve, many people immediately asked to double their incomes. This would have led to a collapse of the economy.

Fortunately, the income of the average employee was increased significantly, however, in reasonable steps. Similarly, the working time was reduced in several steps. Besides, Saturdays became work-free days and the Korean workforce today enjoys 15 public holidays—a number that is surpassed in the Asia-Pacific area only by the Japanese with 16 days off. In comparison, Australians enjoy only eight days off per year. Indeed, in 1969, Koreans still worked on Sundays and work-free Saturdays were only gradually introduced some years later.

This was a quite difficult period of time for the management. First, the managers had to show sympathy for the demands of workers, in order to show solidarity. Yet, secondly, they also had to keep the labor force in good spirits at their workplaces, and thirdly, the exaggerated requests had to be subdued and prolonged for a reasonable time. Otherwise, the firms would have been immediately ruined.

This strategy was not always successful and the consequences were vehement strikes and the foundation of more trade unions. The right to strike is firmly anchored in the Korean constitution. In those critical days, the number of strike days went up from two in 1984 to thirty-three in 1990. Between 1987 and 1994, the wages and salaries annually increased significantly ten percent per year, whereas the productivity increased only by eight percent. This period of catching-up stabilized the situation and in retrospect, resulted in a higher consumption by society. This in turn led to a higher demand for enterprises.

With the 1997 financial crisis, the number of strikes increased again. The reason was an increase of wages, which were leveled off to three percent in face of a higher inflation. Numerous companies downsized and many blue- and white-collar workers lost their workplace or were insufficiently paid while working in insecure working relations. The former practice of a quasi-lifelong-employment was abandoned.

Meanwhile, the main concern of the trade unions was less an increase of wages but more to secure the number of good-working places. The number of strikes decreased to only five days. The goal of the strikes in 1987 was to increase the income by 70 % and in 2004, the goal was at 84 % to achieve a favorable content of the labor contracts. There was also a remarkable turn in the economic sector: In 1990, 70 % of all strikes happened in the manufacturing sector, whereas in 2004, more than 60 % of all strikes were held in the service sectors. In particular in the 1980s, a huge number of strikes were carried out in favor of political issues. The most dominant desire was the demand to withdraw the 28,000 US forces deployed in South Korea (a claim obviously initiated by Northern sympathizers). These political strikes are not registered in official strike statistics.

In the country, central organizations exist alongside company unions. According to the reports of the Ministry for Labor, there were 6100 single unions with 1.54 million members as of the end of 2004. This results in only 10.5 % of all laborers being organized in unions. Whereas in most countries the conflict of interests between employees and employers is dealt with in meetings between the unions and employer associations, President Kim Dae-jung had founded in 1998 a so-called Tripartite Commission, in which the government is represented as a third party. This commission concluded a "social pact," which was recorded in 90 articles that aimed at the preservation of the national competitiveness.

The central organizations are mainly subdivided into two central organizations: The FKTU (Federation of Korean Trade Unions), which has been under government control from 1961 until 1987 and subsequently played a moderate role. In 1995, another organization was founded: The KCTU (Korean Confederation of Trade Unions), which represented much more radical points of view than the FKTU. Hence, it was only legalized starting in 1999.

Structure of the organization of the trade unions as of the end of 2004 [10] (Table 6.3).

These figures show that approximately 223 people were connected to the FKTU, whereas 425 were connected to the KCTU. It can be concluded that the

Table 6.3 List of important Korean trade unions

Organization	Number of individual unions[a]	Number of members
FKTU	3.714 (61.7 %)	780.200 (50.8 %)
KCTU	1.256 (20.9 %)	668.100 (43.5 %)
Independent unions	1.047 (18.4 %)	88.500 (5.7 %)
Total	6.017 (100 %)	1.536.800 (100 %)

[a]Predominantly corporate unions

KCTU is mainly active in larger companies. During the last years, the figures of memberships stagnated in general. Moreover, the FKTU had to register small losses while the KCTU registered a small growth.

The corporate unions (company unions) are mainly independent from the central unions; they are autonomous with respect to their structure, administration, and negotiating capacity. However, on the central level, there is a strong tendency of coordination within the KCTU, which significantly increases its effectiveness.

In the 1990s, a lot of fierce strikes were organized; meanwhile, their number has considerably decreased. Employees who are not organized in unions legally do not have any right to strike.

A strike can only take place, if the majority of all employees advocate it by a secret and direct vote. During a strike, the management is not permitted to reshuffle the working force or replace it by other workers. As soon as a strike takes place, the management is permitted to threaten the workforce with a lockout. For any losses that are caused by strikes, the management cannot ask for compensation. Nevertheless, it can ask for compensations in the case of wild (illegal) strikes.

The right to strike for civil servants and for employees in the armaments industry is subject to strong restrictions. In emergency cases, the administration can prohibit strikes or at least severely restrict them for medical care, public utility companies, the finance sector, very large companies, or the radio- and communication field. Such restrictions have time and again provoked illegal strikes and led to severe custodial sentences at court.

Recently, the main conflicts in labor relations occur in peripheral areas of the labor market as for instance irregularly employed workers in the field of construction or in the transportation business. This also concerns the situation of temporary workers in small industries, who would like to found their own corporate unions and are fighting for minimum wages that would grant them a reasonable income. If the opinions differ significantly, usually a conciliation procedure will be initiated to prevent a trial in court.

Presently, the minimum wage per hour is set at less than five US dollar. Whereas the income for unskilled labor is extremely low in Korea, it is in total not at all a low-wage country. In a "global ranking list," Germany is by far at the front with respect to the total labor cost per hour; nevertheless, Korea is already ranked tenth, ahead of, for instance, Sweden, Japan, the USA, Australia, and Canada [11].

The trade unions have an increasing tendency to demonize the ongoing globalization in general and transnational business relations in particular. Whereas all formerly Communist states (even Cuba) have recognized the fatal error of reclusion with no established social, political, economic, scientific, and intellectual bounds, North Korea tries to continue its struggle on its own. This impervious longing for self-sufficiency might preoccupy some last obstinate leftists. Because trade unions have meanwhile intermeshed themselves with all leading international union organizations, they will probably sooner or later come to the right understanding of the international division of labor. The big business on the other hand has to distribute in future the jointly produced GNP more reasonably among all participants.

Literature

1. Patterson, DP (2002) Asian management styles? The evidence from Korea. In: Rhee ZS, Chang EM (eds) Korean business and management. Elizabeth (NJ), Seoul, pp 238–246
2. Yi S-U (1983) On the criticisms of confucianism in Korea. In: Korean national commission for UNESCO, main currents in Korean thought. Seoul, p 127
3. Chang H-J (2010) 23 lies which they tell us on capitalism (23 Luegen, die sie uns ueber den Kapitalsimus erzaehlen), engl. London 2010 and Munich, p 297
4. Deutsch -Koreanische Industrie- und Handelskammer (AHK or DHIHK) (2005) Steuern in Korea (Taxes in Korea); 4 edn. Seoul, p 32
5. Jang S-H (1988) The key to successful business in Korea. Seoul, p 57
6. Compare Deutsch-Koreanische Handelskammer (AHK or DKIHK); cit. above
7. Focus (2010) Spitzenwerte bei den Abgaben (peak values at public charges), edition from 14/2010
8. Jang S-H, cit above, pp 73–75
9. Saccone R (2001) Negotiating your way through Korea. Elizabeth (NJ). Seoul, pp 17–18
10. Lee B-H (2007) Militant unionism in Korea. In: van der Velden S, Dribbusch H, Lyddon D, van Daele K (eds) Strikes around the world 1968–2005—case studies of 15 countries. Amsterdam, p 155–172
11. Focus, cit above

Chapter 7
Markets and Marketing in Korea

A great majority of the Korean population suffered from a shortage of consumer goods (non-durable goods) throughout their history. Basic commodities (appliances and durables) have been even more out of reach for the average consumer. A market for investment goods in the real sense did not exist at all, as all noteworthy investments were in the hands of public authorities, for instance, military complexes, palaces of the high nobility, or the construction of roads and bridges, respectively. Private enterprises of a certain size, like in Europe, America, or Japan, were virtually nonexistent.

7.1 Cultural and Societal Change

Dennis Hart [1] starts his book on changes in Korea, entitled "From Tradition to Consumption," in which he describes the changes from frugality to total consumerism, including the consumption of extreme luxury goods, with the following sentence: "This is a study of cultural change as a companion of capitalist industrialization." A few pages later he defines culture as a set of traditional convictions and imaginations used by people living and working closely together. The transformation from agricultural work to industrial production already forced a significant conversion of daily habits, but not of the consumer behavior. This can be explained by the fact that goods were predominantly manufactured for exports. Additionally, to a lesser degree, arms were produced and a national infrastructure was established.

Since mass production leads to decreasing costs, the Korean industry produced more goods than necessary and thus surpassed the demands of exportation and consequently had to find another market. In a second phase of industrialization, the necessary demand had to be created by means of modern marketing in the domestic market. This led to the first mass consumption in Korean history.

D.K. Schneidewind, *Economic Miracle Market South Korea*,
DOI 10.1007/978-981-10-0615-9_7

The Korean population had long cut consumption, partly for traditional reasons and partly because this seemed necessary as long as the industry had not financed its development. In fact, from a conservative point of view, this process is still not entirely completed, though a few *chaebol* have already amassed an excessive wealth.

The spread of mass communication, as well as being increasingly exposed to Western lifestyles and developments in Japan, and the sudden flourishing of democracy that strengthened social movements, sparked the Korean demand for high-quality products. Desires need to be inherent in man, otherwise advertisement cannot trigger them, and in general, the desires of human beings are endless. The thrill of new opportunities created a longing for new products, which surpassed any realistic extend and Korea lived beyond its means during these times. During the past decade, a relatively dynamic balance developed and the consumer spending started to almost follow the productivity obtained by the industry.

Nevertheless, a majority of the contemporary population is rather dissatisfied with its situation. They realize that the economy has stopped to make great leaps and environmental requirements lead to restrictions. However, people are provoked by the luxury consumption of a small "group of others," meaning a small number of people who became extremely rich within a short period of time and without working in a classical job. Instead, these people have often either inherited money or made a fortune by gambling, trickiness, bribery, or fraud.

Thus, in a country in which "face," indicating prestige and need for admiration, has such an important meaning, tensions arise. There is also an almost fetishistic ambition to keep up with people of the upper class. Koreans tend to always compare themselves to others, and they do not accept that others are better off for whatever reason.

Korea has a modest past, which was spiritually influenced by Shamanism and Confucianism. Today, it has quickly turned into a global materialistic society and there is hardly any resistance to this development. This Korean mind-set is already firmly established with citizens, who are younger than 45 and has caused a dramatic loss of the national identity. Though individual competition and aspiring personal success are rather new phenomena in the Korean society, hallmarks of Confucianism such as responsibility and reciprocity have not vanished [2].

Only 25 year after the end of the military rule, a well-paid, secure job that further assures a good reputation is considered the most desirable personal aim. The prevailing hedonism nourishes the expectation that all personal desires should be fulfilled in the shortest possible time. All male Koreans thus believe that they have to own the most stylish car, and their female counterparts believe that they always have to be dressed up according to the most recent fashion. The new urban generation sees itself in the center of a glamorous and varied life style.

Korean consumers are constantly exposed to television programs that suggest that this is indeed the lifestyle they should strive for. In fact, housewives walking from the kitchen via the hall to the living room can continuously follow the television program on different steadily running television sets. Similarly, dealers in their small shops are also exposed to a constant stream of commercials. At many public places, people are exposed to larger-than-life glamour girls on huge screens and golfers with arrogant faces and *blasé* attitudes across the green with their electronically well-equipped golf carts. Whereas the younger generation in Europe looks rather realistically into their future and, in general, does not have any exaggerated expectations, many young people in Korea still believe that they will eventually live in the dreamworld that the media landscape creates.

The Korean advertising industry disposes of several billion dollars (in Korean Won that would be trillions), and it continues to undermine traditional values of the society. Additionally, it ruins more often than not the good taste of people. The portrayed dreamworlds propagate nearly unlimited freedom, suggest fantastic professional promotions for almost everybody, and lift technology to a divine status. At the same time, environmental damages, traffic jams, and the numerous miserably paid service personnel are left aside. The pages of magazines are filled with stories and photographs of designers, astronauts, and mannequins, all of them living in dream-like apartments. However, the working day for most people is controlled by triviality, frustrations, boredom, and insecurity.

The wisdom and dignity of old Koreans had a high status in traditional Korean society. In recent times, even women aged sixty and older often dress and behave like young women. This is made possible by aesthetic surgery, cosmetic lotions, and above all hair dies. Sophisticated women avoid sunshine and always carry an umbrella with them. They pay a lot of money for questionable preparations which promise to change their often naturally brownish skin color into a ghostly white tone.

In public, people with an attractive, yet often superficial body, are very much admired, are called *ulzzangs* (*eoljang*), and are hysterically cheered at when appearing in a public place. Even on television, less attractive people are sometimes mocked, while exceptionally beautiful women are called *yeosin* (idols). Instead of significantly contributing to society, many people are more concerned to take care of their artificial white teeth and colored hair. Particular attention is paid to workout in order to meet the weight and sizes of professional models. For these purposes, an ideal Western persona is created as an idol for the perfect makeup, dressing, behavior, and even language; actually, over 70 % of all advertisements incorporate English phrases. A considerable part of the Korean society believes to be on a way to an unlimited, global, borderless consumer world. It is hardly recognized that historically most civilizations leveled out after a fast initial progress.

Professor Kim Ran-do, who is the director of the consumer Trends Research Institute of the Seoul National University, believes [3] that modesty is no longer a virtue of his fellow Koreans. The younger generation does no longer foster any inhibitions and is ready to show its self-confidence at any time, though this self-confidence is often not based on particular abilities or deep knowledge. According to him, the ridiculously high expectations of some young people have to be understood as a consequence of the fact that many of them are growing up as an only child and are showered with care and gifts. Different from their parents, these children do not define themselves anymore through their work place, their university, college, or organization and instead focus only on their own identity when they grow up. He describes this as a drastic change which is very different from the past, when people preferred a humble instead of a boastful conduct. In general, the older generations were considered to be workaholics, contrasting the more recent "self-holics." Today, young people are more inclined to spend money only on them, thus further fostering industries that produce unnecessary luxury goods. Together with the younger people, the entire population is to become increasingly trendy and their purchase decisions are predominantly based on outside perceptions.

If we denote Korea to be an "Economic Wonderland," this proves only true for a remarkably short time in which the nation grew from medieval structures to a modern market economy with overflowing shelves, similar to all other developed countries. In some market segments (flat screens, basic electronic commodities), Korea even is the global market leader. In November 11, 2010, the representative of an African country lamented in the "*Zweites Deutsches Fernsehen*" (the second German TV broadcaster) that South Korea had been called a developing country only a few years ago and now is producing world-class television sets, "whereas we cannot even produce nails."

A development that had taken almost 200 years in other countries was accomplished within only 50 years in Korea. Out of former frugal attitudes developed a vivid—and sometimes even wild—consumer frenzy. The accompanying social upheavals were relatively well mastered. The consumer behavior, the structures of physical distribution, and a modern range of marketing measures developed in rapid succession.

As already mentioned, the target of the conglomerates and bigger companies had first and foremost been market shares. Nowadays, one can say that market shares and profits are found equally important. Formerly, however, a diversification in all market directions was strived for, while presently, the market-policies are mostly focused on the most profitable segments.

7.2 Ancient Markets

Koreans associate a close sense of nostalgia with their traditional markets. Although there are only a few of them left in remote areas, they provide good picture of the authentic life of the traditional Korean society with its roots in agriculture and craftsmanship.

According to old Chinese annals, markets had already existed in the region of Jinhan around the time of Jesus Christ. According to a majority of historians, this would have been around the geographical area of the later Gyeongju (approx. 50 miles north of Busan). Around 500 A.D., the establishment of a market with many booths is reported at the eastern part of Gyeongju (Kyongju), the capital of the

Shilla kingdom. But it was only during the Goryeo Dynasty (918–1392) that they developed into orderly events with rules that were controlled by public authorities.

During this period, Buddhism flourished and Buddhist temples owned a lot of land and many slaves. This wealth allowed the monks to produce and trade rice, other sorts of grains, salt, alcohol, and various other handicraft products. The goods were often sold in close vicinity of the temple buildings.

Whereas agricultural markets were solely privately owned in the entire country, manufactories were divided in those of public owned and those privately owned. The public workshops were considerably larger than the private ones, and they were situated in towns with administrative precincts. Both types of manufactories had to pay the same amount of taxes. Sales were commenced by merchants as middlemen as well as directly at markets.

The biggest problem of the markets was delivery because means of transportation were not yet much developed. Waterways were dominantly used to transport mass products. The transportation of fruits was problematic, especially for fish and other seafood; by adding salt and hot spices, a certain degree of conservation was obtained.

In the northern parts of the country, ice was collected in winter and was securely packed in straw and stored in dark rooms. This enabled to keep even perishable food rather fresh until early summer. This storing technique is well known from the quarters of Seobinggo-dong in Seoul, which had a riverside harbor that permitted the delivery of marine products from the southern shores, hence offering a variety of seafood.

In the southern parts of the nation, ice was not available, and thus, food had to be treated with salt and spices in order to make preserve it. The tradition of preparing extraordinarily hot food has lasted in Korea until today.

Nationally important markets existed in the cities of Pyeongyang, Wonsan, Tosan, Hwangju, Songwu, and Gaesong (all of them belong to North Korea today) as well as Anseong, Chuncheon, Jeonju, Daegu, Namwon, Gurye, and Jinju, all located in the south.

The most famous place for trade in former centuries was Gaeseong (Kaesong). This city accommodated already rather early numerous manufactories, for instance, for brassware, crockery, and furniture. Instead of a five-day rhythm of market days, many booths were operated every day. The powerful merchants of the city appeared in all important trade centers of the country and maintained branches (*songbang*) in all corners of Korea.

Until the end of the Joseon period, specialized markets such as Damyang (bamboo products), Seoul (firewood), Daegu and Jeonju (medical products), Myeonchon, Suwon, and Hampyeong (cattle), Gurye (silk), or Gwangcheon (fermented fish and crustaceans) had developed as well.

Already in early times, markets were strictly regulated and illegal activities were severely punished in the entire nation. All markets had a public tax official. The opening hours were stipulated, and the market days—usually every fifth day, in accordance with neighboring markets—were precisely determined. Quite often, five markets grouped together so that one could offer or buy merchandise every day at another market. The locations of the markets were usually seven to nine miles apart from each other; this was the average time needed to go and return from a market at one day. The merchants used roads that had been built for public servants on horseback throughout the entire kingdom. Every seven to nine miles, there were small rest areas or lodging facilities. Their total number in Korea is estimated to have surpassed 2.000.

Measurement and weights were clearly determined and a catalog of punishments existed as well. This catalog indicated, for example, that twenty blows with a stick would be the punishment for drunkenness, 30 for swindlers and people using impolite words, and 40 blows were due if someone quarreled with a person of respect.

Starting in the seventeenth century, traveling merchants had organized themselves in guilds. From 1851 onward, market regulations were introduced on national, regional, and local levels and brokers needed a government license for their activities. They organized transportation and stock-keeping capacities, financed business transactions, took deposits against interests, and also issued bills of exchange. Unlike the manufacturing, trade and payment transactions were traditionally on a high level, which was furthered by a widely spread literacy and the ability to master figures.

The traders partially had their own market stalls, which were either open or roofed. Sometimes, they used publicly available stalls in the shadow of streets line with tents. Many of them recorded their transactions, and some already were capable of correct bookkeeping. Several of these traders promoted their products on huge boards, on which they placed product descriptions and price comparisons. Additionally, they tried to lure customers with free gifts or volume discounts. All these actions were indicators of an early marketing strategy. However, the favorite pastime of dealers definitely was personally haggling with suppliers and customers.

The more affluent merchants contributed to the entertainment of the visitors by supporting musicians, jugglers, or tightrope walkers, and financing religious ceremonies. Many farmers and citizens visited the markets not only with the aim to purchase something, but also for their amusement as these markets often were the only welcome change in their monotonous daily life. News was exchanged, old friends met, and new friends were made. Above all, weddings were arranged as there were hardly any other chances for men and women to meet outside their homes. Such traditional market places were extremely loud because of market criers, lively conservations, and heated arguments.

The times of such busy places of exchange are over. Modern markets are well organized, yet, occasionally, a trace of the former vital atmosphere has remained in some colorful stalls, even in Seoul. Around 1914, about 1.500 markets were counted in Korea. The last figure for South Korea was 569 markets in 1998 for a much bigger population [4].

7.3 Structures of Distribution

During the seventies of the twentieth century, many manufacturers used the system of direct marketing both in the countryside as well as in cities. Direct marketing means door-to-door sales, sales on open market places, and also sales by various types of street traders. Some companies employed real armies of sales people in the entire country.

These structures have meanwhile changed and are still subject to further changes. Today, the system of door-to-door sales can mainly be found in rural areas. Reasons for this are the fact that many housewives work today and cannot be approached at home. The women are also more sophisticated and want to go to different shops in order to be able to compare products and to have a greater selection.

Direct sales are still common when it comes to the distribution of pharmaceutical or cosmetic products, for instance, for the specialist trade. Hospitals and doctor's offices are preferably served directly by the pharmaceutical industry.

Another type of direct sales has spread within offices. Employees have not only used their close connection to co-workers in order to sell cooking pots or cosmetic items so them. Sometimes insurance policies or traveling packages were sold as well. Some of these employees are trained by specialized companies to organize a kind of snowball system to involve their acquaintances in a dense sales network. Crafty specialists train these people usually after work.

Open markets, both outside and those with roofed stalls, have held their ground. They are reserved for low-prized goods of daily use as well as durable commodities and simple appliances.

In recent times, extensive supermarket chains have developed, many of them being convenience stores. Most of these stores offer consumers' long opening hours and some open 24 h since working hours take similarly place around the clock. Therefore, a metropolis like Seoul does not grant itself any rest. A strong extension of this retail trade is forecasted for the years to come. The Lotte group, a forerunner when it comes to modern distribution, has recently bought the US-American chain "Buy the Way" and announced to considerably expand its sales, thus somehow acting as pioneers of modern distribution systems.

All these types of outlets are directly supplied by the industry, sometimes from their factories or from central distribution centers of chain organizations. Middlemen or wholesalers do hardly play a role today.

Like in all other industrial societies, the small private retail outlets suffer increasingly under the pressure of giant organizations expanding since the mid-nineteen nineties. The *Korea Times* reported in its edition from January 28, 2010, about a battle between the smaller and the bigger retail outlets. For instance, in the district of Galsan, within the important port city of Incheon, 30 vegetable dealers had started a nightly unrest, which was aimed at "Samsung Home Express," a joint venture of the Korean Samsung company and the British Tesco Group. Even the ambassador of the UK was brought on the scene, who lamented that about 50 "Homeplus stores" were currently not able to properly start their business in Korea.

The Korean authorities are caught in a dilemma. On the one hand, they have to tally the law, which grants small local retailers the right to oppose the opening of a giant outlet if they can convincingly prove that such a discounter would ruin their business; on the other hand, Korea cannot ignore the general progress and needs to avoid being denounced as a saboteur of the global open market system, which Korea had vehemently protected in the so-called Uruguay Round (1986–1994) of the GATT and the WTO. Indeed, the Korean government interfered quite heavily in the market: partly to protect "mom and pop stores" and partly to serve the interests of particular groups when restricting the sales of radishes or cuts of local beef. The imports of mangos, papayas, and dates are limited, as well as certain types of alcoholic beverages. Consumers have to pay quite high prices for wine, which is an unbelievably cheap item in international trade.

In the public, some believe that the growth of big supermarkets should not be restricted but that the abilities of small shops have to be enhanced. In spring 2012, the district Seongsu in Seoul witnessed how a giant supermarket, E-mart, was closed on its main selling day, namely Sunday. This was the result of huge demonstrations organized by all local shops and dealers in its close vicinity. E-mart and all similar outlets will have to close every second Sunday in the future with no one made responsible to bear the tremendous sales losses. In fact, it is difficult to gain reasonable profits from big chains, and Walmart is not the only supermarket that gave up in Korea. Carrefour, another global retail champion, had to give up as well.

As a result of all these movements, the market structure is always changing. For instance, Shinsegae, a department store group, connected by family relations to Samsung, took over the hypermarkets of the E-mart group from Samsung, thus forming the currently largest retail conglomeration. The Lotte group is ranked second. The Homeplus outlets, which are owned solely by Tesco (Great Britain), occupy the third position in that ranking. Homeplus is very strong in the field of home delivering service. The Hyundai *chaebol* also runs a retail business with some high-class department stores.

All big discounters started a severe price war in 2010. In particular, the "Big Three," namely E-mart, Lotte Mart, and Homeplus, was part of this. When E-mart (dubbed "the Walmart of Korea") reduced its prices by 12 % for a large part of its product range at the beginning of the year, the two major rivals immediately followed its example. The price for the most popular article, belly of pork (*samgyeopsal*), is dropped by 46 %.

As a result, not only small retailers were crumbled, but the manufacturers moan and groan as well in the face of such a severe price despotism of the discounters, which enable such drastic price reductions. Of course, consumers suspect that such falling prices are only possible by reducing the quality of the products. Governmental institutions, in this case the Fair Trade Commission, have meanwhile taken notice of this hustle and bustle. In the interest of the consumers, they want to stop any dirty tricks of the hypermarkets.

Recently, the distribution structure in Korea looks like this (Table 7.1):

Table 7.1 Distribution structure in Korea

Traditional distribution (small stores)	42 %
Internet	15 %
Supermarkets	3 %
Convenience stores	8 %
Department stores	12 %
Hypermarkets	20 %
Total	100 %

For the next years, experts predict a further expansion of the big discounters. From an international view, the segment of "traditional distribution" is still rather big. Furthermore, public authorities of many Korean municipalities would welcome if whole quarters of flying kitchens, ramshackle huts, and mini stores in the city centers would disappear. These shops are all not compatible with the image of a modern and clean place and pose hygienic risks. However, enormous social problems are inflicted on the traders in these shops. Furthermore, many former clients might lament the vanishing of a familiar and eccentric ambience of the nostalgic past.

Qualified specialty stores are still rare in Korea but increasing. Frequently, such specialized stores are organized by chains of franchise shops, and some big companies maintain their own business locations at preferred places as well. The role of specialized trade is conducted by chains of high-class department stores, which are increasing on a middle-class level as well as in the high- and highest-class level. These stores can maintain their business, because they pay attention to individual consumer segments. Thus, next to the terrific Lotte department store in the center of old Seoul, there exists another building with shops for younger consumers, who prefer their own ambiences. Additionally, the *Avenuel*, which is a store that sells very expensive branded articles (textiles, leather ware, jewelry), which cause dizziness to normal clients, is located at the same spot as well.

Many department stores bind their customers not only by various exhibitions but also by offering different classes, ranging from flower arranging, learning a foreign language, learning the Italian art of cooking, packing presents, or swing dance. They either run such classes themselves or sponsor them.

The benefits for the customers are high-quality products that are offered at reasonable prices. The department stores on the other hand are happy to see many of its female customers returning up to three times a week for a class and at subsequently purchasing some items on her way home. Leading department stores such as Shinsegae, Lotte, or Hyundai offer as much as 30 classes every six month, thus attracting middle-class women within an age range from 45 to 65 years, who like to use their free time to acquire interesting skills.

The habit of ordering products via the Internet has increased tremendously. Young as well as old housewives know exactly how to handle this medium. One can order almost everything from the Internet, even fish and vegetables. The purchased products reach the customer freshly within a few hours on an appointed date and time. Fleets of motorbikes and small cars are on their way to deliver ordered goods around the clock, and their drivers carry the ordered goods upstairs, directly to the front doors. Some newspapers reported that many housewives procure two-third of their daily errands utilizing this comfortable system.

The huge majority of the Korean population is living in big apartment buildings, because single family houses are exorbitantly expensive except at the outskirts of the cities—and these houses are not popular, because their maintenance requires high physical as well as financial efforts and is very time-consuming.

Seoul and many other cities have street lines with ultramodern stores, which are still sometimes located close to rather traditional shops, which sell a great variety of basic consumer items such as tools or swimming pants. They usually face the sidewalk, on which they also store part of their products. Sometimes, one can find ten bicycle shops, followed by fifteen outlets for blankets, five stores for television sets, another seven for firewood, and the same number for pets, lamps, or dry cleaning. The latter, for instance, take US$1.7 to clean a shirt, which would cost four times more in a hotel or another qualified place. Among these stores are also repair shops or shops that sell spare parts. They all charge low prices and invite for intensive bargaining. Despite their popularity, these outlets will one by one be absorbed by hypermarkets and department stores.

As in most parts of the world, shopping malls are located next to department stores. Sometimes, they are low-priced, and sometimes they are middle-priced. They can stretch over some hundred yards and are sometimes located underground or on various floors above ground. In Korea, they exist in all towns and cities. For these malls, like for private shops as well, there is no regulation concerning their opening or closing hours. They can open at noon or at midnight, on Sundays, and any public holidays. Everything depends on the consumer needs and the conveniences of the shop owners.

Due to the continuous gap concerning the incomes of the citizens, glittering malls will expand and rather primitive street shops will survive for a long time. Even at exclusive locations such as big arterial roads such as the Namdaemun-no in the center of downtown Seoul, one can find simple stalls or even tent constructions at the roadside from which loud announcements are made on how cheap the offered socks are or commenting on the delicious taste of today's squids. In the district of Yongsan close to Seoul's central station exists an electronic market with more than 500 outlets, which all offer all kinds of electronic devices—a real paradise for fans of electronic articles. Sometimes, one can encounter adventurous dealers who try to sell CDs with the latest K-Pop songs from a trolley bag in the subway.

The COEX Mall, a gigantic shopping mall, where one could spend many days exploring the shops, is located in Gangnam, the posh southern area of Seoul. Hundreds of stores and dozens of reasonably priced restaurants are located within this massive building, and some of the restaurants are partly located below glass roofs. Here, one can buy almost everything, from food, non-durable goods, and appliances to durable commodities. Furthermore, the mall incorporates gambling dens, photographic studios, banks, insurance offices, cinemas, a giant aquarium, and access to a luxury hotel. Of course, everything is connected to the municipal subway system.

Even at low outside temperatures, thousands of predominantly younger people are strolling malls in light attire. Almost 80 % are couples—something absolutely unthinkable only 40 years ago. In a giant bookshop, hundreds of young people are sitting on the carpeted floor and study their desired reading. It is estimated that only three percent of the visitors are over 60 years of age.

Underground shopping arcades are located below many roads. These arcades offer merchandise in the medium price segment and many of them cater especially to tourists. They offer shelter from unpleasant weather. In fact, some of them were originally planned as bunkers, protecting people from air raids. In northeastern Seoul, there exists a weatherproof arcade with multiple floors that stretches nearly for a mile from the old east-gate (Dongdaemun) to the west and offers a broad spectrum of articles in the lower price range. A bizarre mix of these types of arcades can be found close to the south-gate (Namdaemun), which consists of a maze of stores. This notorious south-gate market is an Eldorado for brand pirates. Here, some almost anarchic modes of conduct of Seoul in the 1980s have survived. However, the days are gone when in the catacombs of Namdaemun inconspicuous old little ladies traded with "quilts" (a code word for US dollars) and "underblankets" (a code word for Yen) on an illegal foreign exchange market. This change was brought by the fact that the currency of South Korea has gained tremendous strength.

Besides traditional retail outlets, we find the more modern category of boutiques, particularly in the vicinity of Seoul. These shops offer all of the well-known brands of the world besides local brands, which are increasingly gaining international recognition. The price level is upper middle to high-class, and the apparel is guaranteed to be original. Most prominent for younger customers of the latest fashion trends are the shops of Myeongdong a district in downtown Seoul that is a shopping paradise not only for young Koreans but also for busloads of Chinese fashion hunters.

Members of the young affluent society can find boutiques selling the most recent brands and fashion that has just been released in Milano, Paris, or New York in the southern part of Seoul across the river Han, in the quarters of Cheongdam-dong and Apgujeong-dong (commonly called Gangnam). However, the prices are not modest!

Surprisingly, especially in the northern part of Seoul, primitive stalls that sell cheap knickknacks and, above all, snack carts (*pojangmacha*) offering roasted corncobs, cooked silkworms, rice-cakes, steamed snails, or other popular snacks, can be found in between luxury outlets. Next to some luxury boutiques, one can see a two-story wooden cabin, in which people repair shoes and handbags, surrounded by poisonous fumes from the adhesives. Unassuming young men climb a steep ladder to get into a dusty shed in order to search for materials that stocked there.

On a chilling cold day in January, we saw a little old granny, completely wrapped in warm jackets, almost beyond recognition sitting on a block of wood, and trying to sell some chewing gum. Whereas such pictures have associated almost exclusively with the northern parts of the capital, they can be meanwhile found in the southern parts as well—although the southern part of Seoul frequently tries to maintain its exclusive image.

Because of the population density in South Korea, which is in average ten times larger than in other countries, it is not surprising that precious space is used collectively. This does not indicate the well-known concept of the "shop in a shop," such as a beauty salon or a shoe repair in a department store. Instead, it is the sequential use of a space by different manufacturers, brands, or even trades. A showroom in an exclusive location might be leased out to a famous automobile manufacturer for three months before it is rented to a boat builder for two month, and then to a kitchen designer for four months. A selling room could be used by a cosmetic brand for four weeks and afterward serve as a space to sell fashionable hats.

Hourly rent systems are being tested as well, for example, using a space from 7 a.m. to 11 a.m. to sell coffee and buns. Another competitor serves hot snacks to passersby over lunchtime, whereas the next person sells fruits in the afternoon, and later in the evening, a company trains its staff at the same location. One case is known from the densely populated and very expensive south of Seoul, where an automobile repair shop is converted into a barbecue restaurant in the evening. Indeed, Koreans are known to be extremely flexible and very practical people.

All these types of retail trade are found in Busan or Incheon as well, though not always in such a spectacular fashion as in Seoul. The same is true for other multimillion metropolises such as Daegu, Daejeon, Gwangju, and Ulsan, which are all independent administration units beyond the provincial administrations. The city of Daejeon is a curiosity as it is, at the same time, also the capital of the province of Chungcheongnam.

All provincial capitals are remarkable consumer centers. They are as follows: Suwon (Gyeonggi-do) located around Seoul; Chuncheon (Gangwon-do), east of Seoul; Cheongju (Chungcheonbuk-do), southeast of Seoul; Daejeon (Chungcheongnam-do), southwest of Seoul; Gyeongju (Gyeongsangbuk-do), slightly inland from the east coast, north of Busan; Changwon (Gyeoangsangbuk-do), southeast coast; Jeonju (Jeollabuk-do), west coast; Muan (Jeollanam-do), southwest coast; and Jejusi (on the biggest island, 50 miles south of the Korean peninsula, Jeju-do). Concerning the suffixes, *do* indicates "province," *buk* means "north," and *nam* means "south."

Whereas Seoul obtained its status as an independent administration unit already in 1067 A. D., Busan was elevated to this status only in 1963; Incheon and Daejeon followed in 1981, Gwangju in 1986, and Ulsan was the last in 1997.

Apart from all this more or less traditional places, the district of Itaewon in Seoul has a special position because hundreds of shops target foreigners and tourists. This area (in the Yongsan district) was a popular residential area for foreigners until the end of the nineteenth century—first for Japanese people and later for many other nations. After the Korean War, the main business road served as a shopping and amusement street for the GI's, who were stationed in headquarters in huge park-like areas, right in the center of Seoul. Besides cheap souvenirs for tourists, one can find international restaurants and stores for antiques, textiles, and custom tailors. Here, enthusiast of alcoholic beverages might find brands that are not available anywhere else in Korea.

7.4 Payment Practices in Trade

A common subject of concern with all local customers is the issue of payments; this does not only apply to the working class. In the food retail outlets, bills are normally paid with credit cards or cash. When purchasing expensive consumer durables, often times a deferred payment is requested and installment plans are agreed upon. The dealers usually try to be paid in cash payment by awarding small cash discounts. Koreans are notorious discount hunters and persistent hagglers, which makes sales sometimes very time-consuming. Big department stores and retail chains maintain their own credit card system and tempt their clients by small material benefits or a general awarding point system.

Between industry and trade, payment transactions are tense because money is generally tight. Striving for expansion, many distributors overreach themselves and go insolvent. In this business sector, the industry usually has to calculate with payment periods of 90–180 days. Because of the debt collection, it is important to maintain good personal business relations as this increases inhibition threshold concerning payment. Therefore, it is customary to collect debts around New Year's Eve. At this day, the willingness to settle an invoice is especially high as many Koreans are superstitious.

Furthermore, renowned companies often pay immediately for service or goods for reasons of "face-keeping." Because of the generally scarce of capital, business partners with enough cash have always an advantageous bargaining position. This is very much in favor of the big *chaebol* which usually can generate capital almost on request.

Though generalizations are always problematic, it is a common belief in Korea that when lending money to a private person without any evidence or records, one can usually write it off. At the same token, Korea is a well-known ground for confident tricksters. Therefore, people are generally suspicious toward people who are not close to them.

In Korea, credit cards are omnipresent. Nearly everybody uses a credit card, even for very small amounts. It is convenient and allows everybody to enjoy a little credit. The government supports the use of credit cards for two reasons: It stimulates the consumption and makes it easier to control the liability to pay taxes. Until 2010, the Korean government granted a tax deduction of 20 % when purchasing consumer goods with cards up to an amount of US$4.000 per year, which could be asserted with the annual tax allowance. In the meantime, the allowance has been reduced to annually US$2.500.

In chap. 3.25, it is explained how this general scarcity of capital has created unique rental practices for housing.

7.5 The Consumers

The Korean consumer of today is generally hard to please. He expects little favors such as price reductions, gifts, and many other benefits. At any rate, they expect not only a smile from the sales person but service performances that exceed those in Western countries. In case the customer is disappointed with the quality and scale of service, he might complain at the top of his voice and does not care about discretion or the feelings of people around him. In many shops, squabbling is rather common and guests in restaurants might use their cutlery to make noises on the table or even plates, if no waiter or waitress appears immediately after the customer has pushed the table bell. Even in banks, nasty words are sometimes yelled if the yield of investments did not meet the expectations of the investor. The insulted personnel reacts with admirable patience, though it is usually not directly responsible for the supposed problem.

It is generally assumed by Koreans that 0.5 % of the Korean population is very wealthy and that their fortune continues to increase very quickly. Another 10 % are considered as rather well-to-do and their fortune is increasing slowly. Roughly 70 % consider themselves middle class, and their income situation has stagnated or is even worsening. The considerable rest struggles to make a living. These people are frustrated, knowing very well that they enjoyed substantial wage increases in the past to make up for rising living standards, but that the economy will not permit any significant wage rises in the future. Consequently, the government tries to prepare the other 80 % to pay higher taxes in order to increase its budget for social welfare.

In the decades between 1960 and 1990, the economy made rich people such as *chaebol* families and their favorites even richer. Today, much money is generated by the distribution chains instead of the manufacturing industry; nevertheless, the *chaebol* have quickly turned into the new bonanza. By now, consumers pay rather reasonable prices, but they are still exploited because most of the imported goods are sold at excessive prices since that business is rather monopolized. Increasingly, Foreign Trade Agreements (FTAs) with various countries exercise downward pressure on import prices. As the younger generation changes its eating habits, the local food industry has to adapt its range of goods to their taste. Currently, it seems as if a highly diversified retail business can cope with the different tastes and objectives.

The great majority of Koreans are united in their preference for good food. The Engel Coefficient that was at 52 % in 1953 decreased to below 30 % in recent years. This means that despite increased food prices, the available income for general consumption has significantly increased as well. Yet, the total volume of food consumption will increase for the next years to come, because the population will further rise due to the increasing life expectancy and since more people might turn to a more international cuisine. Afterward, the retail industry might experience painful consumption decline due to the shrinking population.

Currently, 70 % of the population lives in towns with more than half a million inhabitants and the rural population has decreased to below 10 %. This ratio might not change, but people in the countryside will buy more at urban markets due to improved traffic conditions.

Another differentiation will occur between the different age groups of the population; still half of it being younger than 30 years. But an obsession with youth as it can be found in some Western countries does not occur in Korea. Indeed, every age group has its own consumption patterns. This, however, is not valid for electronic devices. When HD television was introduced, most elderly people in Europe continued to use their old appliances for a while, whereas everybody who could afford it bought a new television. However, generally the older population in Korea has a tendency to sit in front of their TV at home and save the money instead of spending it for luxuries.

In general, the younger generation in Korea likes to go out and is satisfied with rather modest apartment flats. Instead, they like to go to concerts, visit exhibitions, and go to eateries or restaurants. They prefer branded products to nameless merchandise. Fortunately, huge book stores as, for example, the Kyobo Book Center at the Sejong-no in Seoul are well frequented by potential customers. This huge store allows customers to choose from unbelievable 2.3 million different publications; among them many written in the English language. Likewise, Kyobo opened a branch of comparable size—a real megastore—in 2003 in Gangnam. In total, it operates eight branches all over the country. This enterprise belongs to the Kyobo Life Insurance group, one of the big three life insurances in Korea. They once started with selling education insurances. But there are some indicators that the new upcoming generation will not buy books anymore but rather rely on electronic devices.

Most of the young and middle-aged consumers are eager to purchase expensive, extravagant, and electronic articles and, even more, buying a trendy automobile. With respect to the latter, the slogan is "the swankier, the more favorable"; and with respect to roadsters "the more expensive, the better." Pseudo-sports cars and convertibles are not very popular. Upper-class families usually keep half a dozen or more cars: Individual cars for each member of the family and special cars to transport the golf equipment.

Playing golf is another important status symbol; the clubs are normally quite luxurious and charge tremendous fees. In particular, bored ladies often play golf as often as five times a week. Visiting professional sport events is quite popular as well. But the majority of Koreans of almost all ages like sports such as hiking, Nordic Walking, gate ball, or skiing. Sport articles are highly demanded. Usually, a trendy outfit of a famous brand is more important than to actually practice the sport. The preference of outdoor activities is further demonstrated by the big sales of camping articles. Even in public parks in the center of Seoul one can see families erect their tents on weekends. Whole clans or groups of friends eat outdoors on Saturdays; they do not only visit eateries but enjoy their food on big mats at a riverside and in parks.

Concerning the interior design, a change from a Korean to a Western style of living is in full swing. The traditional living style required only a few pieces of furniture, whereas an apartment furnished in a Western style requires a lot of furnishing. Big cabinets are popular to showcase the family's glasses, china, and expensive bottles of alcohol. Big leather chair sets and couches are also very popular. Besides many fancy electronic devices, a man often owns an impressive desk that should underline his importance and thus the importance of the whole family.

In a private apartment, only few decorative pieces can be found and antiques are very rare. Generally, the furnishing is rather scanty and carpets are almost never spread out. This permits to clean a flat rather quickly.

A middle-aged Korean expatriate who immigrated to the USA 20 years ago, and now lives in Los Angeles, was flabbergasted by the behavior of young Koreans when he visited Seoul in the spring of 2010. He characterized especially young men in Gangnam as egoistic, demanding, disrespectful, cheeky, and lazy. Thus, he wanted to express in a very generalizing way his uneasiness concerning the development of South Korea, now dominated by a young generation that he thoroughly despised. Yet, for him it is impossible to influence these young people with his opinion as they have long since made their lifestyle a habit. Very likely, they will react with amazement for demanding old values. Being acquainted with many families from various social backgrounds and from different parts of the nation, one has to say that the entire situation is not well reflected in the opinion of the expatriate.

Middle-aged women of the upper class are very fashion-oriented and like solid and expensive jewelry instead of eccentric accessories. They like to meet other women from the same social background and compete with each other when it comes to the question of who wears the most expensive branded outfit. For such occasions, they usually meet in posh restaurants or lounges of first-class hotels. For these places, very well-maintained restrooms are mandatory. Surprisingly, most Koreans in urban areas have turned away from drinking tea, as for example in Japan or China, and have turned to enjoy coffee. An astonishing number of coffee shops line the streets of most towns.

Flowers are not considered very important in the Korean society. There are only few flower shops, and when visiting friends, one gives boxes of sweets and exotic fruits instead of flowers. Only for ceremonial events such as weddings are flowers used to impress the guests. When one visits graveyards, one can see gorgeous flowers that are put on the graves, yet most of them are artificial and made of plastic. In flowerpots, more often than not, people grow herbs.

Official and social relations that necessitate keeping documents are very unpopular. Thus, people do not like to sign insurance contracts as first, Koreans are generally prepared to take risks, and at the same time, they are always optimistic. Second, they hate to keep files and conduct correspondence. This is also true when it comes to the personal laziness of Koreans when it comes to writing letters. Private letters are rarely exchanged, which is also true for season greetings or birthday greeting cards. Even when on vacation, no postcards are sent.

This explains why it is so hard for tourists to buy picture postcards in Korea. If he finally finds postcards, it is very likely that he has to buy a bunch of 20 or 30 cards in a single envelope.

A Korean likes to restrict himself to things he considers essential for him, such as for instance eating, drinking, and talking. Like in China, the taste of the food counts more than the surroundings. Eating or drinking outside the center of Seoul or Busan is accompanied by rather plain customs. In particular at beaches, there are hundreds of stalls which serve simple yet quite delicious meals on cardboard plates. In these regions, it is hard to find a café and one can consider oneself lucky if one is able to purchase a thin brown slop in a paper cup from a hand-drawn cart.

Even in the city center of Seoul there exist simple tent restaurants through which a cold wind blows in winter. Likewise, in many average restaurants, the usually young guests stuff themselves from tables with dirty plastic tablecloths on which the food is carelessly served. As long as the taste is good, nobody complains. In Korea, people are very well informed where to get delicious food. They also tend to prefer crowded restaurants and avoid dining in less-frequented restaurants.

In these restaurants, no matching wines or delicate side dishes are served with tasty fish or lobster. The only side dish that is always served is the notorious *kimchi*. As cutlery, only the compulsory metallic chopsticks and a big metallic spoon are offered. Meat, fish, vegetables, and noodles are usually cut into pieces with stained scissors in front of the guest. Whatever drops besides the plates will be put back with bare fingers. These habits reflect the notion that one should organize his life practically and comfortably. An authentic Japanese restaurant for a Sunday lunch in Korea can offer a completely different experience. There, guests consume small delicacies in an utmost cultivated atmosphere and guests do not flinch when paying the bill.

In the modern southern quarters of Seoul, in Gangnam, there do not only exist noble special shops and luxurious boutiques but also countless restaurants and pubs. Originally build in fine Italian or French design, these places are often run down today. On a mild October evening, an almost Mediterranean atmosphere is created in this part of the city and thousands of fashionably dressed young people push through the narrow quarters, waving to friends and acquaintances, who are sitting in wide-open shops. A good mood prevails and no aggression is felt. Although we might enjoy this scene, one has to remember that maybe in 15 years from now, there will be hardly any young people in Korea.

Koreans can be very diligent if their work is awarded with a material benefit. They are very reluctant when it comes to beauty repairs or anything else that is uncomfortable and nonproductive. In contrast to China or Japan, people in Korea do not like to give tips. A common joke goes: An Indonesian in Jakarta asks: "Who in the world is stingier than a Korean man?" Answer: "A Korean woman."

However, especially young people like to spend money for themselves. In particular, young women attach importance to a trendy international design. At the end of 2009, Seoul declared itself to be the world capital of design and later hosted the third "Seoul Design Fair." The newspaper *Joong Ang Daily* proudly announced in its January 9, 2010, edition: "Forget about Tokyo; design freaks are commuting to Seoul." Therefore, the capital strives for some avant-garde restaurants and cafés, as well as for fashion palaces which might be labeled monumental, and for stylish galleries.

A very special consumer segment is twens of the "Papa Rich" category. The *Korea Times* reported on them in its edition from January 28, 2010. Accordingly, these twens receive a monthly pocket money of over US$7.000, drive expensive imported automobiles, and like to play golf, preferably overseas. At the hotel bar, they order 30-year-old Ballantine whisky and a good lunch might cost nearly US$350 per person.

Their fathers belong to *chaebol* families or have founded their own enterprises. Recently, there might be speculators (so-called investment bankers), medical practitioners, as well as owners of own clinics, real estate entrepreneurs, or less frequently prominent figures of the show business, and professional sports stars among them. Others based their wealth on illegal businesses, corruption, and massive tax evasion. They never attracted attention by donating to the needy, and their sons frequently stayed somewhere overseas when the summons to go to the medical examination for the military service is issued. According to the *Korean Times*, the former great admiration for successful self-made men gives way to hatred and an increasing fury of people. The paper contrasted them with descendants of the old nobility, who acquired their wealth legally over hundreds of years, who would abhor vulgar consumption, keep a tight grip on their children, take responsibility for their home country, and would be ready to help the needy at any time. However, a couple from the show business, Cha In-pyo and Shin Ae-ra, both actors, should be praised as they recently donated US$85,000 for the victims of the earthquake in Haiti.

The conduct of life in Korea is determined in another extreme form by prestige and "face." In this context, relatively heavy fiddles are not unknown. The conversations among neighbors, colleagues, and even friends might sometimes sound like a competition; the statements concerning travel destinations, the ranking of the hotels, or the preferred class in airplanes are often indeed whitewashed. Many families will not admit that their rivals are living above their own level. Similarly, family parties sometimes seem like competitions as one tries very hard to outspend supposed adversaries. The general endeavors for prestigious consumption drive the whole economy to higher levels.

Koreans truly believe that fruits, vegetables, certain types of plants, and meat are very useful for keeping a good health. According to traditional Chinese beliefs, the food determines the physical and also mental well-being of people and extends their life expectation. Particularly, officinal herbs have a high reputation and their effect is not contested. Nevertheless, many legends surround certain herbs and roots, which on closer scrutiny vanish into the realm of mythical hints.

Many people drink a vial of "Bacchus" in the morning before starting a hard workday or after the heavy consumption of alcohol in the evening as a vitalizing effect is ascribed to this liquid. In its brown small glass bottle, it looks quite pharmaceutical. It is offered in the specialized trade (pharmacies and drug stores), but it is mainly offered at all kiosks on the way to work places. People spend a lot of money for anything that promises to be good for body and soul.

At many Korean universities, there exist chairs for natural sciences and for traditionally oriental medicine. The latter essentially embrace the Chinese natural medicine with some Korean additions. It is hoped that in future, a giant Korean market for herbal medicines will develop, similar to treatments such as acupuncture. There is a global trend for alternative medical treatments; nevertheless, this field will be somehow limited as the whole field is restricted to preventive, accompanying, and psychological applications.

The public health care comprises of a wide area. Traditional doctors enjoy a high reputation and have an above-average income. Koreans think that apart from some extremely handicapped people, everybody has to take care of one's own health and should duly pay for it. Many clinics dispose of good medical personnel and competitive equipment and therefore enjoy a high standing overseas. Thus, there already exists a noteworthy medical tourism to Korea, and the government takes a lot of pains to further promote this sector.

Koreans are generally well known for their manual skills, which permits them to produce delicate crafts. This is very advantageous for instance in fields such as invasive surgery. The market segment of cosmetic surgery consequently offers many opportunities to be financially successful. Millions of Koreans (not only women) manipulate their physical appearance and strive to look "Caucasian" instead of "Mongolian." Bigger and narrower noses and the correction of "slanted eyes" are considered more important than other operations. It is assumed that the ordinary patient spends over US$9.000 for a treatment.

Most of the foreign medicine tourists come from other East Asian countries, because the costs of a treatment in the USA or in Japan are twice as high as in Korea. For 2010, the Korean government expected over 140.000 foreign medicine tourists [5].

It has to be kept in mind that the cost of living in Korea is not very high for a family. However, the lion's share of the family budget will not be spent for housing or health, but for the education of the children and grandchildren.

The magic words for most Korean consumers are "bargain" and "discount." By all means and under all circumstances, they want to negotiate with vendors or sales assistants. If they do not achieve to obtain a favor, consumers as well as business people will feel unsatisfied. Many foreign companies selling branded products initially refused to give discounts due to image. Koreans called such companies arrogant or unreasonable and tend to boycott them. Korean manufacturers already plan a reserve within their pricings that permits a variety of price reductions or free-of-charge favors and gifts.

7.6 Modern Distribution Patterns

An overwhelming majority of the population takes part in the progress of electronic media and the present boom in the wireless Internet business. Some enterprises recorded more than 80 % sales increases in 2009. The international platforms Google, Naver, YouTube, Pandora TV, Cyworld, Kakao Talk, My Space, Facebook, Twitter, and others especially from China are enthusiastically frequented. Purchases via the Internet are rapidly growing. Bargain hunting overseas is the latest development in Korea. Formerly, Koreans were only familiar with the domestic market and had to pay too much for imported products. By now, smart consumers visit foreign Web sites and order items directly from overseas; they call themselves *jikgu-jok* and are mainly female.

Though many Korean consumers order from oversea platforms such as amazon or eBay, only few items are purchased by foreigners via the Internet from Korea. The main complaint is that the products come without sufficient instructions for use and poor Chinese or English translations. Another obstacle of ordering from Korean Web sites seems to be insufficient delivery services.

Economic experts generally see great chances in the progressing development of the IT industry for the Korean economy. Time and again, the citizens are reminded that South Korea does not dispose of raw materials and thus depends on the development and application of new technologies.

The *Korean Times* from January 11, 2010, recognized the following consumer trends (Table 7.2):

Such development trends can also be observed in other industrialized countries. Though the Korean society has more male, sometimes even macho characteristics, purchase decisions are made at about 75 % by women, who usually control the family finances. In supermarkets, it might be well over 90 %. These decisions are made after excessively reading the numerous and very informative women's magazines. Consultations with friends, who usually also have read several magazines, are likewise important. The majority of average older middle-class Korean woman is not employed and has sufficient time to inform herself on the various offers of the market. Because the conditions of life become increasingly demanding in Korea, the number of housewives looking for a second job is growing as well.

An interesting center of communication for female upper-class consumers are a kind of club lounges, established by big department stores. If customers pass

Table 7.2 Enumeration of consumer trends in Korea

• Intensification of the use of mobile phones, especially concerning the purchase behavior; here, the rapid distribution of smartphones is of great significance
• Returning to family values
• Reinforcing an environmental consciousness
• Development of products for senior citizens
• Increasing expenditures for personal hobbies and preferences
• Visiting "exotic" restaurants
• Further expansion of fashion items

a certain annual revenue, they are awarded with a prestigious club card. These lounges are equipped with comfortable accommodations, televisions, and music, and offer snacks and beverages, thus offering exhausted shoppers some rest and allowing them to exchange the latest news. On such an occasion, potential rivals observe each other and what one person owns exclusively is desired by the others. These consumers are considered members of the elegant society with an odor of newly rich and are respectfully called *jolbu* by fellow Koreans.

In opposition to this upper price segment of the market, represented by these lofty customers, the average Korean household was indebted in 2015 with 86 % of its annual income; this reduces future purchases because of the burden of repayments and interest. According to the Bank of Korea, many household insolvencies have to be feared in the years to come.

7.7 Structures of Demand

Some local newspapers meanwhile write about a paradigm shift in Korea: the change from a male-oriented society to a female-centered society [6]. It is very hard for a Korean man to be surpassed by a woman. With quite a surprise, we also noticed the headline of the *Korean Times* from February 1, 2010: "Six out of ten Koreans are unsatisfied with their lives-" every day, about 40 Koreans commit suicide (or one person every 36 min). This is the highest rate of all OECD members with 28.5 deaths per 100.000 people. In comparison, the rate was 12.5 for the USA, 1.7 for Turkey, and 20.9 for Japan [*The Korea Herald*, September 9, 2014].

According to a poll of the City group (City Fin-Q), only four out of ten Koreans are satisfied as far as their financial situation is concerned. More than 2 % feel heavily hit by the financial crisis of 2008, which had caused the loss of their retirement provision. Meanwhile, the insecurity of their job forces them to build up financial reserves in case of unemployment. If they had more financial means at their disposal, they would like to invest them into safe financial assets. A surprising 53 %, however, would be ready to invest into risk papers.

In the above-mentioned poll, the average annual income was given with US$34,000 and the capital that was saved for retirement insurances was US$88,000. 77 % of all persons asked owned a credit card. This opinion polling was held in ten other Asian countries (without Japan). Though Korea showed the best data (for instance, 50 % are insured for accident compared to only 23 % of all other countries), still only 53 % of all Koreans looked optimistically into the future, whereas this figure was 69 % in the regional average. This demonstrates that demands on life in Korea are clearly higher than in China, India, Indonesia, or the Philippines.

Already in October 2009, a plan was published by the then president Lee Myung-bak to develop an index, which would enable to measure the quality of life and happiness of people. It was supposed to serve as a kind of barometer for the social development of the nation. President Lee explained that when measuring the feeling of happiness, Korea would be ranked 25th out of the 30 OECD, whereas

Japan for instance would hold the 11th position. According to his opinion, not only the economic progress would be important but also the conversion of it into educational opportunities, the standard of housing, the job situation, and social as well as mental security.

Only two days before this statement, the Korea Institute for Public Finances (KIPF) had released the fact that in 2008, 8.5 % of the population had less than half of the average family income at their disposal and this figure had constantly increased in the course of the last 10 years and has further lead to an undesirable gap between incomes. Within these numbers, 20 % of the population, especially households in which the main breadwinners are between 20 and 25 years or are older than 60 years. It was noticed that the (relative) poverty corresponded directly with the level of education and training as well as the gender of the affected persons. Instant measures were demanded to reduce the gap between the rich and the poor.

It was also revealed that only 11 % of the population, the so-called well-to-do people, owned more than 75 % of the national assets. In Korea, this discrepancy had developed especially fast in the last 10 years when compared to other nations. It will be extremely difficult to correct these imbalances for four reasons: (1) A large part of the population has worked extremely hard for their possessions; (2) many people have studied very hard for a high social standing. These people are unlikely willing to share their wealth with lazy people. (3) A considerable part of the wealthy classes amassed their wealth by more or less dishonest methods, which indicate a character which is not much inclined to altruistic behaviors. (4) More and more people inherit their wealth and are not necessarily used to hard labor. Thus, they are unwilling to share and decrease their standard of living. Stricter laws with respect to corruption and a drastic increase of death duties are possible means for the government to encounter future social unrest.

The day after this chapter was written (September 15, 2014), we attended a garden party of the Walker Hill Hotel in Seoul. When it ended around 9.30 p.m., we went to the queue of taxis waiting for guests of this party. Because the driver was busy with his iPhone, my wife knocked gently at his door. After having driven a hundred yards, the driver started to yell how unfair it was that he had to wait for such a long time to pick up a guest, who in turn had enjoyed delicious wines. While loudly complaining, the taxi driver started to speed down the incline from the hotel complex in a dangerous way. We asked him to stop immediately, paid him, and wanted to look for another taxi. At this moment, the rather young man who did not look like a bad person at first glance started to rant about all the social injustice in Korea. He immediately called the police by phone, which arrived only a few minutes later. He told the policemen that my wife had damaged his car and his self-confidence by knocking at the door of the car and started again to shout wild socialistic slogans. The policemen calmed him down and let him drive away. They explained to us that everybody would occasionally experience a mental blackout. Quite frightened we continued our way home with another taxi. My wife told the story to the new taxi driver, who lamented that nowadays overambitious drivers would be employed, who had high demands without any reasonable qualification. Although this experience was a very rare case, we nevertheless felt that with a new generation, big trouble could lie ahead of the social peace of the nation.

7.8 The Ever-Increasing Importance of Brands

All Korean consumers in general and younger consumers in particular like foreign brands and local brands that are usually successful if they also succeed overseas. Close human relations slowly become obsolete in favor of general brand adoration. Because of this fact, the building of a good image of a company is desirable. At the same time, a perfect appearance and a conscientious care of a brand are mandatory. It is obvious that the Korean lifestyle increasingly adopts Western patterns. Yet, there are exceptions from this general tendency, especially in the food sector, where they survive persistently.

At the beginning of 2010, the Ministry for Health, Welfare, and Family banned commercials between 5 p.m. and 7 p.m. for food items which contain less than 2 grams of proteins and more than 250 cal and 4 g saturated fat or 17 g of sugar per portion since children and teenagers are very likely to watch television during this time slot.

This example demonstrates how much the government takes care of the public health and how meticulously it interprets regulations for the market. The most famous brand name does not protect against such public supervision.

Traditionally, Koreans foster the tradition of exchanging gifts, which sometimes is felt as a nuisance in East Asian countries when perceived from a Western point of view. When making visits or on special occasions, such as special holidays, anniversaries, or specific parties, it is highly recommended to offer small or big presents, respectively.

In particular within the family, it is crucial to select nice, gorgeously wrapped gifts. The same is true within companies and business circles, where generally the exchange of generous presents is customary. Within this realm, the line to corruption is rather blurry. Official efforts to curb this system have not been too successful until recently.

Quite often, the situation in this respect can become very delicate in foreign companies since their audit departments register this supposedly disreputable custom with utmost disconcertment and do not tolerate them. In many US-American companies, presents as well as frequent banquets are considered unethical. However, because the disregard of morally imperative dining and gift-giving practices cause a bad reputation in East Asia, one can imagine how an executive of a foreign company who works within this local market can find himself easily in the dilemma of differing moral concepts.

Special obligations are caused by the big seasonal holidays as, for example, the turn of the year and Thanksgiving (*chuseok*) which is also connected to the remembrance of one's ancestors. In these situations, having to handle local customs, expatriates often refer to "the raging terror of presents."

Both holidays are regarded as the highlights of the year. Yet, the beginning of the New Year is not celebrated at the first of January but according to the traditional Chinese moon calendar. It starts with the appearance of the new moon between the twenty-first of January and the twenty-first of February in a gliding rhythm. For instance, in 2011, the beginning of the New Year was February 3rd. These major holidays are accompanied by an extravagant exchange of presents and indulging in extended feasts. In the retail business, this time of the year culminates in excessive sales, which even surpasses Christmas sales in Western countries.

The favorite product categories for Thanksgiving and New Year's gifts are as follows [7] (Table 7.3):

Here, we can again see that food, health, and good looks are at the center of Koreans desires.

The sale of gift department store vouchers reached a new dimension around New Year 2010. The Lotte offered 50 vouchers with a value of US$40,000 each for sale, but also offered "less expensive" vouchers for US$9.000, respectively, US$5.000 each. The gift voucher of US$40,000 came with golden calendar with the imprint of a tiger, which was the symbol of the approaching year. The competitor, Shinsegae, wanted to sell gift certificates for US$25,000 and US$9.000, while the Hyundai department store was content with selling gift vouchers of US$9.000. If one is given such a voucher, one should only redeem them for expensive branded articles, taking the "face" of the donor into consideration and thus refraining from buying cheap products.

For Korean enterprises, it is not easy to establish famous brands, which also become internationally successful. More recently, this has changed for Korean brands becoming popular in China and Vietnam. First, the local market with only 50 million consumers is too small for a basis to establish a brand. Secondly, despite their generally patriotic attitude, Koreans prefer globally known products to local products. Last but not least, it takes time for Korea to convince international customers that it has meanwhile developed a very successful pop-art scene and remarkable fashion articles. This is partly due to the fact that many people still closely associate Korea with the dark scenario of a ferocious civil war. Furthermore, from time to time, the Northern regime still frightens the international community about all things Korean.

In May 2009, my wife, who was born in Seoul and who holds a regular South Korean passport, was denied entrance on an American cruising ship of the Celebrity X Line in San Francisco. Of course she had a paid ticket; however, the female chief stewardess elaborated that the problem was that my wife was a person of Korean descent. The ship finally left without us, and only after having strongly protested at the shipping company, we were flown to Ketchikan three days later, to board the vessel. We were of course refunded for our additional

Table 7.3 Enumeration of major gifts on thanksgiving and for new year's day

Agricultural products (fruits, etc.)	44.2 %
Daily needs (hygiene, cosmetics)	21.3 %
Processed food (tea, tins)	9.1 %
Vouchers (between 5 and 300 dollar)	7.1 %
Meat products (prime beef, etc.)	7.0 %
Remedies (herbal medicine, vitamins)	5.5 %
Others	5.8 %

expenses. Still, the apology of the responsible management was interesting, as they lamely claimed that the stupid purser had just felt that, no matter if North or South Koreans, all Koreans were the same and thus suspicious anyways.

Nevertheless, while "Korea" sometimes seems to evoke rather negative associations, the products of Samsung Electronics, and LG Electronics as well as the motorcars of Hyundai, for instance, have indeed an excellent image and reputation, not only domestically but also with international clients.

Prof. Sung [8] formulates the qualities, which Koreans expect from a successful brand, as follows: "Reasonable prices, outstanding performances, a magnificent design and always new, creative products. Moreover, the customers will trust those firms with good brands, which keep their promises, react sincerely upon complaints, and also refrain from exaggerations with their advertising and marketing. After all, our daily life depends on trust." For these reasons, people had so far purchased international brand products, and now, consequently similar claims were made concerning the newly established national brands.

The international advertising company Ogilvy Diamonds, which is also active in Korea, makes a drastic statement by telling its employees that they do not work for the client, the company, or themselves, but for a brand!

Recently, big conglomerations such as LG like to diversify their product ranges and supply the market not only with their mainly industrial output, but also with household items. In an actual case, a *chaebol* entered the field of hygienic and cosmetic articles. A Western expert on brands would have severe doubts whether pampered ladies would like to purchase such articles, even if the brand generally stands for high quality. In this range of products, clients do not merely buy the commodities but also their image and supposed aura of a wonderful female world. Of course, if a brand is established from scratch over a long period of time, using a different name, it might succeed in the long run but it is much more recommendable to buy an established company, with the entire image already attached to it.

In particular when it comes to products that are felt to be personal, female customers strive for exclusivity and are prepared to pay a high price for it, as it is about "*my* handbag" and "*my* cleansing lotion." A mass-produced article cannot create the respective intimacy and personal identification. This is why demanding clients in many instances prefer foreign brands, because the world market is full of hundreds of brands and eventually there might be the one brand among them that provides the special aura a customer is looking for.

The USA with its 315 million inhabitants profits in the realm of manufacturing as well as advertising from this huge number. Companies can produce commodities at lower costs and advertise them rather inexpensively at the domestic market as in this matter, and the absolute expenditure counts more than the percentage. Subsequently, a worldwide expansion can be financed relatively easy with the funds that were saved. Korea, however, is not in such a favorable situation.

Likewise, the EU with its approximately 500 million consumers has similar opportunities. In a few years from now, China and India will have similar advantages as well. Japan has missed the chance to develop a comparable economic community, and some neighboring countries are rejecting respective proposals because they have not forgotten their colonial experiences with Japan. Some nations are quite obstinate and try to accomplish everything themselves. Finally, Japan is notoriously self-confident, and this trait prevents the country from accepting a role as an equal among other equals.

Because of the time lead of its economy, the foresighted normalization of relations between nations, and also due to its geographical surrounding, Japanese products and brands were quite successful in Korea. With the global opening of the country—for example, a trade agreement was signed with the EU—Japan was slowly forced out of the Korean market.

With a population of 50 million people, the Korean market is quite attractive for upper segment consumer goods. Yet, domestically, this market with 10.5 million households is hotly disputed. Numerous market segments such as refrigerators, television sets, phones, and computers are already saturated. When attacking this market, technical innovations and a creative procedure are mandatory. In the ideal case, a company enters this market with products which had so far not been available.

German manufacturers of highly priced combined kitchen/living rooms are presently very successful in Korea and have gained a high reputation as well as brand awareness—despite their extraordinary high prices. When entering the market, one has to prepare very quickly for the next improvements because skilled copyists are surprisingly fast with making their own improvements and adapting products to local conditions.

Sometimes, suppliers are surprisingly successful in penetrating the local market with a really new article, but it is very important to defend a position in succession. For this purpose, new products have to be constantly introduced to the market, even when they have only small product improvements or only more trendy packages. The competition is fought with gloves off. The surprised overseas competitor as well as his local rival is often confronted with rather non-orthodox methods from their respective point of view. In many foreign head offices, knowledge and understanding of this supposedly "exotic market" is badly lacking. Nevertheless, the number of foreign companies operating in Korea has increased from 5.900 in 2000 by 63 % to almost 9.600 in 2008 [9].

7.9 Marketing Tools

When entering the Korean market, it is favorable to have a strong local sales partner before one has to establish one's own strong sales force. But these are only necessary conditions and not yet sufficient ones. It is mandatory to utilize the wide range of a strong marketing mix. In this field, the fantasy of a foreign marketing manager is asked for. Of course, local marketing experts are very creative, but the supposedly "exotic" outsider in this market can use different methods and ideas for his specific products. These methods and ideas are alien to his domestic competitors and might not be appropriate for them. Introducing entirely new articles to the market may have the initial advantage that their introduction is not too expensive.

Advertising is generally the ideal solution within the marketing methods. A foreign medium-sized company might initially approach either regional markets or restrict itself to narrow market segments. In that case, it might concentrate its marketing on the region of Busan or, when focusing on golf articles, reduce the advertising to golf magazines. On the contrary, a global player with a wide range of excellent products and huge financial means will take a stake by using classical advertising in the densely populated area around Seoul. Because advertising has already a 100-year-old history in Korea, it is quite a promising instrument of market success.

After the Korean War, it was for a long time prohibited to advertise foreign brands. Later, everything was transcribed into the Korean language and written by using the *hangeul* alphabet. As a result, foreign brands and their slogans lost a lot of their impact. For instance, the Japanese cosmetic giant Shiseido had to adopt the name "Bluebird," which sounds quite meaningless in the Korean language. However, the Japanese wrote the name as a subtitle in Roman letters in such a skillful way that Korean women were able to easily recognize the famous international brand, which already had an excellent image in the country. This example elucidates that by using ones imagination, one can indeed succeed in an awkward market environment with its stumbling blocks.

Nowadays, Korea is almost overwhelmed by national as well as international advertisements. In the evening, neon signs glitter from rooftops and facades in the cities. Most of them are written in *hangeul* and have the advantage that they can be easily attached vertically. Advertising signs are fixed to subways, busses, taxis, and stations of various means of transportation; colorful images and billboards enliven the roads and railways—or depending on one's perception—ruin the entire landscape.

Colored, sometimes full-page advertisements in newspapers, magazines, and numerous trade journals force themselves into the brain of potential customers. Additionally, leaflets, free samples, and minor presents are distributed in stores, in front of public buildings, and alongside the roads. Sometimes they are handed out by strategically well-placed pretty girls with a charming smile.

The television plays an important role in the life of Koreans, and it is turned on everywhere at all times. This is true for public places and bus stations as well as for private flats, where the housewife rushes from one televised room to another and while following her favorite programs. Naturally, she has become indifferent about the messages distributed by this medium and thus advertisements struggle to pass their messages. Maybe this is one reason why many programs turn to hectic actions, roaring, and rather barked announcements.

The television set, for instance in a noodle shop, does not grant even 10 s of silence to the guests, who, however, are surprisingly indifferent about this fact. In particular, newscasters get very excited when announcing the news with a breathless voice, similar to a war correspondent at the front. Only rarely can a relaxed smile be observed. Official news lacks any type of humor or irony in both Koreas; nearly all male adults have gone through a tough time of military training. In the thin-walled apartments that the average Korean inhabits, he is exposed to a nerve-racking cacophony of noises from television sets from other floors and from the streets.

The lion's share of the advertising efforts is allotted to expensive TV commercials that dominate the program loudly, with dazzling colors, full of fantasy, and quite often using comic styles. As there exist countless TV channels, it is not easy to decide which one suits the own message best. Advertising on the radio is much more inexpensive; the audience is usually composed of drivers. Of course, there are also numerous different print media, which makes a choice difficult as well. But there are powerful and competent advertising agencies that give advises concerning an efficient selection of media and that are used by smaller advertisers. Because the market shares are very much disputed in this field, the suppliers often like to assure their clients that they can grant the same quality and the same prices for all. In contrast, a North American supplier might prefer to sometimes offer lower prices; the European will emphasize that he is able to offer a better service in one or another point.

Similar to all highly developed markets, the food business, automobiles, pharmaceuticals, household items, cosmetics, textiles, and tourism offers occupy the top of all advertising costs. A unique field of advertising in Korea is the excessive advertisement for real estates, which often cover a full page or even two pages of a newspaper. For many years, competitors tried to overcome their rivalry by outspending them; this was in many instances an uneconomical way of competition. Since 2000, the big companies started to optimize their advertising and spent increasingly more on market researches.

7.10 The Media

Normally, Koreans like to read. They usually read many newspapers, which usually offer two editions per day. One can choose between six main papers: in the morning between the *Chosum Ilbo*, *Hankook Ilbo*, and *Seoul Shinmun*; in the evening between the *Dong-A Ilbo*, *JoonAng Ilbo*, and *Kyunghyang Shinmun*. Additionally, there exist various national and local papers, which are, for instance, focused on economic matters or sports news and might been published in English or Chinese as well. The variety of the press is enlarged by numerous magazines, which appeal to certain areas of interest (e.g., housewives, young girls, tennis players, animal lovers, and gourmets). Radio and television are not that specialized, but still have a target audience. If a company wants to appeal to all consumers, its campaigns might become very expensive.

For the smaller maker and particularly the foreign markets, it is extremely disadvantageous that the well-spread newspapers usually own their television channels and many of the huge advertising agencies are the property of big *chaebol* such as Samsung or Hyundai. To a large extend, they thus control the advertising scene. This provides them with a clear advantage concerning information, because they know ahead of their competitors about the intentions of other enterprises and

Table 7.4 Major advertising agencies in Korea

1	Cheil worldwide	Samsung group
2	Inocean	Hyundai group
3	HS AD	LG group
4	Daehong communications	Lotte group
5	SK marketing	SK group
6	TBWA Korea	USA
7	L best	Korean group GIIC/LG capital
8	Hancom	Affiliate of British WPP
9	Dentsu media Korea	Japanese competitor
10	Publicis welcome	Member of a British group

consequently, all companies that are related to them, might therefore take advantages concerning placements and expenses.

In order to protect smaller advertisers against such disadvantageous terms of trade, the government has started in 1981 the Kobaco (Korea Broadcast Corporation), which is placed between the advertising agencies and the specific medium (newspaper, radio, television). The advertiser does not participate itself at the conclusions of the contract between Kobaco and the media, but can be sure that Kobaco will take control to his merit and security.

Biggest advertising agencies in South Korea are listed in Table 7.4.

Because four of the seven biggest agencies are owned by giant *chaebol*, one can guess how much of the general public information is controlled by them and that news that might harm their economic interests could be easily suppressed. Because the government tries to exercise sometimes pressure on the media, it can be assumed that Korea enjoys a restricted freedom of press.

7.11 Market Access for Foreign Competitors

One should generally not be afraid of local sales organizations as their main concern is their own profit. If cooperating with a foreign competitor is advantageous for the local company, the foreigner can definitely rely on its support. If substantial material benefits are concerned, the patriotism of the *chaebol* is rather limited.

A successful example for a profitable joint venture is the company Yuhan-Kimberley. It was founded in the 1970s by the Korean Yuhan Corporation and Kimberley Clark from the USA. It produces and sells hygienic articles (baby diapers, toilet paper, plasters, and medical practitioners' outfits) and skin care products. Yuhan-Kimberley has established a marvelous image by being concerned for the well-being of Korean mothers and actively supporting the "Green Korea" campaign. The company has planted more than five million trees since 1984.

Moreover, it cares for the education of its employees and has introduced flexible working hours. Because of all this, college graduates consider the company to be a very attractive employer. In 2009, it achieved a market share of 65 % with baby diapers, a market penetration which is usually reached in developed international markets only by the US industrial giant Procter and Gamble.

The regular long-term target for Korean companies is, nevertheless, to manage things as they please without foreigners. Apart from some exemptions on personal grounds, joint ventures in Korea can be very arduous, unless the type of business requires a permanent input of know-how. Many foreign companies prefer to grant licenses to Korean companies instead of becoming active themselves in this difficult market. In such a case, it is absolutely mandatory to only sign "airtight" contracts. For companies with famous brands, it has to be made sure that its own brand philosophy is by all means closely monitored and not altered by fantasies of Korean marketing managers.

Big foreign competitors usually think globally and want to stabilize their brands on a high level. But many *chaebol* intend to only exploit the precious brand and is not concerned about the brand. Instead, they will try to establish their own brands in the home market in the long run.

For a foreign supplier, it is important to find the right balance between adapting to local requirements and maintaining a homogeneous international brand image. When its scope of the usually high-priced own brands is exhausted, it could try to buy a local brand or even try to establish an own, new brand. Thereby, it is possible to exploit all price segments of the market.

Finally, attention has to be paid to the fact that Korea has a different idea of a free market society than many liberal Western countries. Government authorities always reserve the right to intervene into the markets when they feel that they have to be concerned about problematic developments. The markets that are most affected by this are not the commodity markets but mainly factor markets such as the labor market or the real estate market [10].

The basic idea is not to offer competitors a market that allows them to operate smoothly and comfortably making profits. Instead, local competitors should be able to compete globally, and their strengthening should contribute to the national affluence in order to secure the supply of goods for the citizens and ultimately leads to the well-being of all South Koreans.

The former cozy community of interests between the authorities and the *chaebol* has therefore turned into a tense relationship, in which the people have now a strong partner that helps them to achieve a more balanced distribution of the jointly obtained wealth. Reaching such a height of domestic demand would be ultimately beneficial for both the nation as well as for the *chaebol*.

The original aim of the government was, in addition to ensure a national prosperity, to demonstrate the superiority of its societal model when compared to the North Korean Communist dictatorship. This target has been achieved convincingly. The anachronistic system of the North is no longer a socioeconomic rival.

7.12 Stimulating Seoul

In the USA, there are many stimulating urban centers such as New York, Los Angeles, Chicago, San Francisco, or Washington—just to name a few. The same can be said for Germany, Italy, or China. But in Korea, everything revolves around Seoul. Even North Korea claims that Pyeongyang is only its provisional capital until a reunion is achieved.

Seoul is considered the traditional political center of Korea, though it has only achieved this status in 1394, when general Yi founded a new dynasty and built royal palaces and shrines. Much to the pleasure of even contemporary inhabitants of Seoul, geomantic principles were applied when the layout of the capital was first set up. The city was named Hanyang and later renamed into Hanseong. The modern name "Seoul" was just used from 1946 on.

"This is a city that, in just half a century, pulled itself up from postwar ruins and poverty to become one of Asia's most important financial and trading centers. The streets and markets pulsate with an energy unlike anywhere else in the world, and change is ever present—Seoul could very well be the world's most dynamic city" [11].

This city straddles in east–west direction in the valley of the river Han and is surrounded by mountains. In particular in the north, the mountains are rather rugged and popular with hikers. In the south, they are densely wooded and serve as a holiday retreat. Further to the east, are the mountains, woods, and lakes of the Gangwon Province where many affluent people own a second house. The Yellow Sea with its many islands along the coast side is located twenty to thirty miles west of Seoul. The old fortresses of *Bugaksan* (in the north), *Hwaseong* (in Suwon in the south), and *Namhansanseong* (in Soengnam in the southwest) guard the city. The North Korean border looms only forty miles north of Seoul.

The old capital with its royal palaces and gardens borders the Bugak Mountains in the north and forms almost a four-sided figure with rounded corners. It was surrounded by a wall of eleven miles and bordered Namsan, a forested mountain in a region that today serves as a big recreation area in the center of the city. The Namsan Tower in its center is a landmark, which is widely visible. Later, the city extended until it reached the mountains in the east and west and the river Han in the south. Only 40 years ago, the modern parliament building was erected on an island of the river, and hence, the entire area up to the southern mountains is made accessible by constructing up-to-date roads and buildings with the well-known district of Gangnam in the center. The owners of former orchards and rice paddies became incredibly rich, and later, even parts of the surrounding province of Gyonggi were bought and rounded up the territory. Thus, today, the entire city is bisected by the W-shaped River Han. Numerous bridges and tunnels provide connections to all the quite different parts of this metropolis.

Beyond its natural boundaries, Seoul is part of a huge urban conglomeration. Together with the big cities of Incheon, Suwon, and Soengnam, it is comparable to the areas of Tokyo/ Yokohama, Mexico City, and Sao Paulo and belongs to the four largest urban accumulations of the world. Nearly 25 million people or half of the nation's population lives in this area.

Sitting on the 44th floor of one of the five dozen high-rising sky scrapers, the city looks like an organic being. By day and by night, its arteries of roads and tracks bustle with running cars and trains in almost all directions. Fortunately, the sky above the city is rather quiet and only occasionally crossed by a helicopter. The airports of Gimpo and Incheon are located further to the west. All big industry settlements of the country were either founded in the provinces or later moved to rural areas so that only the trade and smaller industrial settlements remained in the city. The public authorities took great pains to preserve the green lungs of the city, to plant new trees, bushes, and flowers, and to turn former fields into parks and green areas.

Seoul is the center of finance, culture, education, and politics. Almost all *chaebol* and other big companies have erected their headquarters in this city. The elite of the nation regularly meets each other or with international partners in their buildings, buildings of their associates, or in one of the gorgeous international hotels. Apart from their communicative meetings, great national as well as international events and conferences take place in Seoul literally at every hour. For gourmets, almost any type of restaurants is available.

Only in Seoul, it is possible to grasp the current intellectual and economic situation of the country and feel the pulse of the nation. If one wants to be successful in the market, one has to go to Seoul to observe the trends and changes in order to make the right marketing decisions.

Seoul has paid with ever-increasing prices, especially for qualified housing, for this clustering. In mid-January 2015, the local press declared Seoul to be one of the most expensive cities in the world with prices at Starbuck's surpassing Starbuck's prices in Paris. The price for a steak of good beef is just as high as in Tokyo, and the prices for wine are twice as high as in all other cities of the world, with the exception of some Chinese cities.

The city authorities wants to make the city more colorful such as in many northern, Scandinavian cities, where houses are painted in red, green, orange, yellow, or blue. From the top of high-rising buildings, one can observe how this is gradually being realized.

Literature

1. Hart D (2003) From tradition to consumption: Construction of a capitalist culture in South Korea, Seoul
2. Hart D p 70
3. Kim RD (2010) "Self-holiccs" is trend among youngsters. The Korea Times
4. Compare Chang, SM (2006) Markets in traditional Korean society, Seoul
5. Bae JS (2010) Cosmetic surgery emerges as export product. The Korea Times

6. Kim TG (2010) Korea—Neo-Matriarchal society. The Korea Times
7. Lee EJ (2010) Families pinch pennies as holiday approaches. Joong Ang Daily
8. Sung YS (2010) A question of national brand loyalty. Joong Ang Daily
9. (2010) Foreign firms double in decade. Joon Ang Daily
10. Song BN (2003) The rise of the Korean economy, Oxford (NY), p 71
11. Koehler R, Seoul, Sagan-dong (2009) Seoul, p 6

Chapter 8
Final Observations—Future Developments

8.1 Korea in-Between Powerful States

In earlier times, Korea had a certain regional significance in the north (Manchuria). However, in the force-field of powerful nations, it has never played a significant role as an active political power. In the foreseeable future, this might not change. Presently, it provides an important balance between China and the USA, but it might remain a pawn in the wrestling game for influence and peace in the north-eastern Pacific region. Technically and economically, it is a role model for aspiring nations in East- and South Asia and beyond. Korea already challenges its former role model Japan in various fields. After it has just advanced into the circle of the "Big Five" in the construction of automobiles and will surpass the pioneering Ford Company, Hyundai dares to attack the world-market leader Toyota. It is remarkable that this brand has only existed in the market since 1967 [1].

A forecast of the political fate of Korea will remain speculative. The world history of the last quarter of the twentieth century shows how fast political circumstances can change drastically. Some predictions will be risked in the following, several assumptions will be made, and hypothesis advanced—even at the risk of becoming obsolete very soon.

8.2 Reunification: A Far Distant Goal

South Korea will not force any changes on its own. Although the goal for a peaceful reunion with the North is written down in its constitution, and although South Korea has a ministry of reunification, which is obliged to do everything necessary to achieve this goal, its leeway is almost zero. The South Korean population puts up with the present situation and a majority is relatively contented with the

D.K. Schneidewind, *Economic Miracle Market South Korea*,
DOI 10.1007/978-981-10-0615-9_8

situation. Almost everybody longs for a nonviolent reunification, but it is clear that this is not very realistic and cannot be realized in the near-future. Furthermore, a reunion could be accompanied by numerous uncertainties in the medium-run and would probably lead to a subsequent decline of the present standard of living. Thus, it is not considered an urgent matter.

The South Korean *chaebol*, however, are looking covetously at the markets of the North, which would promise sales of investment goods, appliances, commodities, and consumer goods. The cheap labor that could be used in the northern factories or in the service industry of the South, as well as overseas, is also very attractive for the *chaebol*. Furthermore, North Korea's natural resources such as coal, iron, ore, tungsten, manganese, nickel, and copper are interesting as well. It was the new South Korean president Pak Geun-hee, who voiced that a reunion could be an economic bonanza (*taebak*) for her country. Naturally, the owners of *chaebols* will not press for any change in the present sociopolitical patterns of the South.

8.3 The KIC—Project of Gaeseong

The late founder of the Hyundai group, Chung Ju-yung, who was born in North Korea, had the vision to erect an industrial park at his former home ground. In 1998, he selected an area of nearly 100,000 acres close to Gaeseong, only 25 miles north of the demarcation line. He was supported by the South Korean president at that time, Kim Dae-jung [2]. This modern industrial complex (KIC) developed quite promisingly until 2005; 21 South Korean companies had their production site at this place and employed 12,000 North Korean workers, generating products with a value of about 100 million US dollars. Both Korean governments observed this undertaking with mixed feelings.

The new administration under President Lee Myung-baek reacted in 2006 with some restrictions to the continuous North Korean tests with nuclear weapons and long-distance missiles. The KIC projects stagnated after Lee intensified South Korea's relation with the USA. This relationship had cooled down under his predecessors.

North Korean leaders—with the possible exception of Kim Jong-il's children, who were educated in Swiss boarding schools—do not know the world from their own experience and grossly overestimate the importance of their country. Proud as any Korean, they want to be respected and always negotiate with other parties at eye level. For this reason, they developed threatening military capacities, including nuclear weapons. For the political climate at that time it was certainly not helpful that President George W. Bush called the North Korean leader Kim Jong-il a "pygmy" in public.

Except from the governing leadership group of Pyeongyang, nobody really knows what the reclusive country is planning for the future. Possibly it is indeed only trying to survive in a world which it considers hostile toward them. Nevertheless, their frequent attempts to cause unrest in South Korea as well as their attempts to force their way into the country by digging tunnels are a historical fact and have not been forgotten in the South. The North further claims to strive for a reunion of the two states, but it does not indicate what kind of compromises it would be willing to make. The Gaeseong experiment would actually be one way to find this out to a certain extent.

At least, a railway connection between Gaeseong and the South was established. Between 2004 and 2008, not only technicians and business people could visit the city of Gaeseong and the KIC compound, but also a controlled tourism to this area was made possible as well. A similar type of concession was granted for Mount Geumgang, a wooded mountain ridge in the southeast of North Korea, which has been famous for its beauty for a long time. Thousands of South Koreans and foreigners took the chance to travel to this special zone, which is presently closed again. A tourist who carelessly got lost in the forbidden territory was cold-bloodedly shot to death by a North Korean soldier.

Kim Jong-il [3] commented on the idea of joining the two states and suggested that both states could be connected over sea, air, and land. Therefore, the connection between Gaeseong and the international airport of Incheon would need to be realized first. Likewise, a Western railway connection between Seoul, Gaeseong, Pyeongyang, and the Chinese border was planned as well as an eastern railway line via the North Korean cities of Geumgang and Wonsan to the Russian border. [Meanwhile, a test run was performed]. This opened new possibilities of transportations from China to South Korea as well as from Europe to Russia, which both would be very interesting for these non-Korean states. An agreement could also lead to the erection of pipelines for gas and oil from Azerbaijan, Kazakhstan, and Siberia via China, which could supply the peninsula with these important energy sources. A breakthrough could have been achieved by Russia in 2011, when it negotiated with the North Korean leadership. They had agreed on building a pipeline for gas from East Siberia via North Korea to South Korea. Meanwhile, in November 2014, Russia has shipped the first 40,000 tons of coal via North Korea to the South.

South Korea without any primary energy sources has a great interest in a further energy supply chain. In January 2010, South Korea was surprised by an unusual onset of winter and one vulnerable point of the South Korean people became much visible. The government reduced the temperatures in public buildings from 21 to 20 °C and recommended the nation to do the same. Immediately, the Korea Department Store Association (KDSA) declared its attitude of solidarity and announced that all its retail stores would decrease their average temperatures from 22 °C or 21 °C to 20 °C.

However, ever since, no progress of that project or any other project is known. Some people in South Korea believe that the USA has no strategic interests in them.

8.4 North Korea in Isolation

North Korea is the work of a single man: Kim Il-sung, the real father of this nation. Like similar leaders, he had a tremendous ego and believed in his own genius. Like Stalin, Hitler, or Mao though being very intelligent and energetic, he missed a systematic vocational training and did not complete studies at a university. Like the above-mentioned despots, he did not tolerate any other leading figures around him and did not mind to kill enemies and rivals. He had a distinct sense for mass manipulation. Being a self-educated person (like the other three dictators), he lacked well-rounded knowledge and did not like to listen to other authorities. He pledged for an absolute leadership principle and an uncompromising loyalty.

Thus, he produced the incomplete ideologies of *juche* and national self-reliance, which comprised of political sovereignty, military independence, and economic autarky. With respect to the latter, he revealed his total ignorance of economic coherences and since his successors did not have any experiences with economic developments and international relations, they blindly followed dogmas of the almighty leader.

In his unshakable belief in himself, he declined the insights of the vast majority of international authorities and further replaced Marxist-Leninist ideologies with his own ideologies. This led his tiny country into a total seclusion and triggered the desperate attempt to develop nuclear weapons, which could be deadly for the entire world. Because North Korea started to lose even the support of its only mentor, China, the country recently tried to re-establish its relationship to Russia. But Russia has its own economic problems.

The modern world has become in some sense "borderless." The DRPK is proud to be an exemption from this rule. It remains to be seen whether the modern means of wireless communication will penetrate in the long-to-middle-run North Korea's impenetrable borders. For the moment, it looks as if the North itself has learned to successfully hack itself into the computers of the rest of the world.

8.5 Possible Strategic Interests of the USA and China/ International Influences

The KIC project of Gaeseong aroused the suspicion of the USA, which for a long time have been awaiting the collapse of the Northern regime. Therefore, they might not have an interest in an industrial stabilization of North Korea. Railway connections of China and Russia through North Korea would be further detrimental to Western interests. This does not even leave a theoretical chance for the peaceful coexistence of both Koreas. A hypothetical reunification could shake the balance of power in East Asia, if a nation would enter the stage with 75 million industrious people and a high technological standard and on top of this would have nuclear weapons at its disposal. This would be above all a terrifying vision for Japan and the USA could not accept such a scenario as it would have to worry about international peace. This fatal constellation causes the deep hatred of the North Korean leadership toward Americans, who, according to their point of view, undermine all North Korean attempts for development.

During the occasional Six-Power Conference that take place on the invitation of China, five nations are concerned with an improvement of the status quo and are interested in the withdrawal of North Korea from its development of nuclear arms—and with them the whole civilized world. But cementing the current situation is problematic for North Korea because this might lead to an economical and civil collapse of its system. The entire ruling classes and their active supporters—possibly almost 10 % of the population—including high government officers, party bosses, generals, scientists, technicians, artists, and sports people need to be offered a last resort. Without prospects for the future, they will never change sides. The sound of the cannons of Yeonpyeong from November 2010 can be understood as a "saber-rattling," and it is underlined by a grim nuclear threat; theoretically, this could at any time lead to a disaster for both Koreas and the entire world.

The South reacted with unusual reserve to the sinking of its naval ship Cheonan in March 2010, which broke into half by a detonation. During this incident, 46 sailors lost their lives. Most likely, it was struck with great precision by a torpedo of a northern submarine. Because the vessel was hit exactly in the center of its hull, an accidental strike by a mine is almost impossible. Nonetheless, the South Korean government kept remarkably cool and the Northern authorities—or rather its military—were suspected to act irresponsibly and perilous—a ride on the razor's edge.

The key to a digestible solution lies with the mighty neighbor China, yet its long-term targets are also unknown. Currently, a war is certainly not in China's interest but a strong armament is necessary in order to prevent being blackmailed. On the contrary, it will need a strong army to be able to blackmail other nations. Its position is powerful and its country is large enough to grant an unchallenged asylum to the top family of the North Korean Kims and maybe some other top leaders.

Ancient Korea was used to a very mild form of Chinese protecting power, which served China's image and was almost just symbolic. This would possibly not be unpleasant for a reunited country of Korea. Occasionally, a curious jealousy toward Taiwan can be observed in South Korea as Taiwan could invade the world markets if it is annexed by the People's Republic of China, a position that Korea would gladly take itself in the shadow of the giant neighbor. A fair cooperation with the PRC would be the same as gaining access to an enormous market for its highly export-dependent economy. On the other hand, Korea becomes increasingly aware of China as a formidable rival in international markets. The *Korean Herald* issue from December 9, 2014, reported "China outpacing South Korea in the smartphones, cars, shipbuilding and marine plants, petrochemicals, and the steel and refinery sectors." The paper names price competitiveness and technological gains as a reason for this development.

The price of a united Korea, however, would have to be the renunciation of any form of nuclear weapons. The crux of the matter could be to develop a suitable method to allow the concerned states of China, USA, Russia, and Japan to control this process. This is a difficult task as these nations do not trust each other either.

After its total defeat in the World War II, Japan had to renounce any attempt to take a leadership position in East and Southeast Asia. Since its defeat in Tsushima (1906), Russia has not seriously made claims for such a position. By now, it would be a diplomatic matter between the USA and China, to achieve a peaceful definition of their Pacific interests. China's claim to the entire South China Sea with thousands of mainly uninhabited islands and islets—since hundreds of years considered to be international waters—has jolted the neighboring countries from their apathy. Facing this situation, they do not trust the conjured peacefulness of China anymore. China, however, refers to Chinese sailors who at the time of Charles the Great or earlier have supposedly taken shelter on various islands of the archipelago. Most likely, during the vast time span, seafarers from many other nations have done the same.

Far from its own coastline, the Western Pacific is not predominantly American territory but it is obvious that Asian nations welcome the USA as a balancing power to an increasingly frightening China. A disassociation of their zones of interest has to be found, which will require some compromises.

Similarly South and North Korea have to draw closer to each other. Both are extremely concerned with their face and do not dare to provoke the opposite side. The South has frequently made advance concessions to the North, which had not been reciprocated. The population of the North has so far no access to any information from outside their country and has rarely heard about the economic wonder of the South. The northern population very likely believes that capitalism leads to the impoverishment of the common people. A concession of the South to Pyeongyang would therefore not only have to be substantial but must also be recognized necessarily by the entire population of the isolated state. In respect of a denuclearization of North Korea, it has to be remembered that this is the only life insurance for the cadres of the regime. They would have to get some airtight guarantees for their safety in return by China and the USA.

In August 2015, the general mood in Seoul was surprisingly relaxed, whereas the Western press created numerous scenarios of fear. South Koreans put much of their hope on China and trust that it will prevent any attacks from heavily armed North Korea. The Chinese chairman Li Xi Ping has not yet paid any visit to the new North Korean leader Kim Jong-un but already met five times with his South Korean counterpart. It might look as if the military has installed the rather inexperienced young dictator, whereas in reality it determines the fate of the poverty-stricken country. But this is all speculation. At the end of the day, the decisions will be made in Beijing and Washington.

The international community can only hope for the Korean people's strong nerves and for their leadership to be able to distance itself. For Koreans, who have been disturbed for thousands of years by foreign interests, one can only wish that their future path will be a peaceful one. South Korea indeed already follows such a path with its successful lifestyle and existing value system.

Presently, South Koreans feel quite well. Hunger and bitter poverty are forgotten; the country is no longer a nation with a low wage income, and the social welfare system is developing. However, the boom with its ever-increasing wages and real estate prices is over. The considerable innovation capacity of the country must be preserved as well as its delight in technical novelties. Therefore, the high ratio of students of natural sciences and engineering has to be maintained.

Germany and Japan, which are probably fifteen years ahead in their development, can tell that the working morale and determination for development might decrease in a society of relative affluence. The authorities have to strictly control the misuse of social systems and to maintain the commitment of the citizens to work.

The unavoidable increase in the percentage of elderly people will cause problems with the national health system and pensions and the lack of labor will enforce the immigration of more foreign job seekers. The infrastructure requires many more elevators and escalators to be installed in railway and subway stations, safe ground-level pedestrian crossings, and the like. The country does not offer many recreation facilities for elderly people yet. For examples, there are almost no benches in the public that would allow older people to rest and the number of swimming pools for the general public is still quite low.

The government has to take actions like in France, to increase the low birth rate of the present young generation, as this will cause a rapid decrease of the population in just a few years. The fact that 20 % more boys than girls are born further contributes to this development.

Already by now, women from the Philippines, Vietnam, and other parts of Asia, who are willing to marry a Korean man from the rural areas to keep the farms running and to provide them with offspring, are recruited. This will cause enormous problems with the education of children, which is usually taken care of by mothers. Because of the rigorous requirements of performances at schools and colleges in Korea, additional home training is essential.

For more than ten years, numerous schools have been closed nationwide; many of the partly smart buildings are empty and another use for them is much sought after. A small number was converted into schooling centers for young people to make them familiar with the traditional behavior and value systems of Korea.

Differently from the foreign women of the above-described legal relations, numerous Chinese people enter the country illegally; many of them are involved into more or less dubious businesses. In some cases, they are accused of crimes. It has to be assumed that China will in the medium-to-long run exert a considerable migratory pressure on Korea.

The number of Russians visiting Korea is also remarkable. Many of them come for vacation from Vladivostok, which is rather nearby or from far away Moscow. However, many Russians also buy apartments and houses, preferably around Busan. A lot of Russian girls are working in service jobs in large Korean cities and it is not unlikely that they marry a Korean partner. In the renowned Gangnam Severance hospital in Seoul, we did not find CNN or BBC on TV but six Russian channels were on air.

Until the beginning of 2014, the Japanese Yen climbed to ever new heights against any financial logic. In informal conversations, some people reported that Japanese investors had used the chance of incredibly favorable exchange rates to directly or indirectly buy into many local firms and that they have acquired already 5 % of interesting Korean enterprises. If this figure is correct, this could rather stabilize the Korean economy internationally. However, it would weaken it on a national level. Meanwhile, though, the Yen has considerably depreciated and causes headaches for the Korean export industry.

The real challenge for Korea is its great dependence on global markets as well as the structural weakness of its finance sector and the noteworthy volatility of her currency. The generally decreasing demand for real estate might cause deteriorating prices with marked negative repercussions on the entire system of collaterals. Korea will also share the problems of almost all industrialized nations: the lack of skilled labor and, at the same time, lacking job chances for unskilled personnel. Simultaneously, the gap between the very rich, the slowly vanishing middle classes, and the very poor masses will continue to widen.

8.6 Prospects of Further Enhancements of the Republic of Korea

Korea already plays an important role in the international economic context and its influence will further broaden. In the global economy, companies such as Samsung, Hyundai, SK, and LG are already well-known. Korean television screens, refrigerators, and other electronic household devices are bought all over the world. Additionally, many people drive automobiles from this Far Eastern state.

We do hope that apart from businessmen and technicians also many tourists will visit this friendly, often charming and hospitable country. The people from Western countries probably expect that the ugly electrical and telephone wires disappear from the view of the cities and, even more important, that the numerous traffic tunnels are equipped with sufficient facilities for emergency cases. Nevertheless, because most tourists come from China and other Asian countries, this might not be considered to be very urgent matters. But the yellow-brown clouds of smog that hang over Seoul and are euphemistically called "the golden sky over the river Han," should clearly vanish rather quickly in the interest of the health of its inhabitants. In the spring of 2015, there was a media-outcry on air pollution, which lasted for a week and the population suffered from inflammations of the respiratory tracts. It was revealed that only 50 % of the dust clouds stem from the industrial exhaust fumes of Chinese factories alongside dust clouds of the Mongolian deserts. The other 50 % are produced by coal-fired power plants and the millions of motorcars in the capital. It was noticed that the public authorities did not consider any measures to improve this dreadful situation. Additionally, the outskirts of Seoul require a better water supply.

Apart from these deficits, the major subjects for the development of Korea seem to be defined correctly: bio-technology, the energy-industry, health-systems, more efficient agriculture, software, and the development of a so-called soft industry, which consists of folk-art, pop-art, Korean cuisine, and tourism. The government seeks a leading role for the country in the four fields of automobiles, semiconductors, shipbuilding, and nuclear fuel power plants.

In the summer of 2011, the country was awarded with the organization of the Olympic Winter Games in 2018, which will be officially carried out in the small mountain town of Pyeongchang. The major competitions will take place in the neighboring valley of Yongpyong. In the summer of 2012, the World Expo was hosted in the southern port town of Yeosu with great international participation. As a result, the south of the country enjoyed significant improvements of its infrastructure.

An Achilles heel of South Korea is its dependence on energy sources and many kinds of raw materials such as rare metals and earths. The continuous extension of nuclear power plants will serve the energy supply, and the proximity to China could contribute to secure the supply of some raw materials. With respect to the development of renewable energy, Korea occupied with only 1.4 % shares, the last place among all developed nations. Nevertheless, recently the capacity of wind rotors and solar cells was considerably extended. In recent years, the country was worldwide number five at imports of raw materials, far ahead of nations like Italy, France, or India. This results in Korea being among the dictates of the world-market prices of gas and oil as well as that of other important raw materials. Inflation is a hovering ghost in this situation; fortunately, it was only around 2.5 % in recent years and is at present around 0.6 % only (autumn 2015).

The government officially sees itself on the way to a "global energy super power," and launched a mighty program for the erection of new nuclear power plants; it also invests in international oil companies and the development of solar energy. In 2012, 31 % of the electricity of the country was produced by 21 nuclear power stations (*Die Zeit*, March 22, 2012).

The expansion of the economy is accompanied by some enterprises as well as banks generating considerable debts many financial experts observe this without worries. In international comparison (Germany 80 %, USA 100 %, and Japan 230 % of the GNP), South Korea with 40 % does not look too bad; however, recently it was revealed that government-dependent firms and local organizations are highly indebted.

The *Korea Times* [4] named ten challenges for the Korean nation in 2010 and thereafter (Table 8.1).

Generally, progress has been made in most points. Yet, considering points (2), (3), and (7) the progresses were quite small. The situation of the oil prices has temporarily improved; it can only be hoped for that the recent drastic decrease of oil prices is not a nine days' wonder.

The liberalization of the Korean market in recent time is indeed remarkable. The imports—formerly heavily burdened with high custom duties and crafty, invisible trade barriers—have visibly developed. Many overseas companies produce in Korea; most of them are 100 % owned and not bound to joint ventures

Table 8.1 List of the ten major challenges of the Korean business in the future

1	A strategy to give up outmoded portfolios and businesses in due course of time
2	The stimulation of the internal demand
3	The creation of jobs
4	Attacking the "Three Highs," meaning too high oil prices, the won rate, and the interest rate
5	Organizing the market of currencies
6	Stabilization of the real estate market
7	Harmonization of social conflicts
8	Precautions for elderly people of the years with high birth rates
9	Increasing the international image of the G-20 summit (at Seoul 2010)
10	Establishing an infrastructure for an eco-friendly economy

as before. It is interesting that the German giant chemical manufacturer BASF is working exclusively with local personnel.

The domestic industry is increasingly integrated into the global market. In rural areas and among older people, a general suspicion against globalization still persists. Nevertheless, the younger generation awaits joyfully and self-consciously what the internationalization will hold for them. The ideological assertion of Kim Il-sung that Koreans would be the purest race in the world has had some charm for the old generation in the entire country. Some of them have even moved to the North, which appeared to defend the old value systems. This ideology has become totally obsolete for young Koreans and their country is opening up to an intensive mutual exchange with the entire world. South Korea adapts know-how and behavior from Western nations without renouncing some old values and its pride for her independence.

"*Taehanmin-guk* (South Korea) first" is certainly a healthy attitude for leaders of the country. But as a country which has obtained so many favors from numerous members of the international community when it was in need, it should today show as well sympathy for undeveloped nations. Under the headline "The Index for Developing Aid Suggest that Korea is Selfish" the newspaper *JoonAng Daily* from October 23, 2009, elaborates that the country has provided only 0.09 % of her GNP to developing aid, which would be much less than the 0.7 % claimed by the UN. South Korea would be found only on the last rank among the 22 most developed nations in the world. A substantial improvement may probably be not expected because affluent Japan, a country which always served as a model for the economic development of Korea, persists only on rank 21. A program on the television channel Arirang reported that the Brazilian model Gisele Bundchen had donated 1.5 million US dollars for victims of the devastating earthquake on Haiti at the beginning of 2010, whereas the Korean administration had only contributed shameful 1.0 million US dollars.

As pointed out earlier, the level of education will be crucial for Korea. In particular, the quality of technological subjects and natural sciences is indispensable for workers and managers in the factories and decision-makers in bureaucracy and politics. Luckily enough, the entire state was connected by government measures with a fast cable network, which costed the nation 33 billion US dollars. Because the modern broadband technique was used, practically every household has an Internet connection in the high-speed sector. The American *Business Week* [5] already wrote more than a decade ago that no country would make more efforts than Korea in order to improve the level of education and this would explain why this nation had been able to suddenly take a leading position within the cyber world.

As a result, companies like Samsung, SK, or LG for example became leading international competitors in the field of electronics. Whereas these companies had been formerly often charged with international patent infringements, they have by now similar problems as well.

The archabbot Norbert Weber of a Bavarian monastery was heavily engaged in missionary work in Korea prior to WW I. He studied the culture and social conditions in Korea and saw the work of the Japanese who had annexed the country at 1910. When he returned to Germany, he wrote [6]: "As a nation the country will cease to exist and it will hardly recover." Fortunately, this assessment proved to be wrong due to the incredible tenacity of the Koreans. For all developing countries, Korea is at any rate a model of development which should be studied and copied at any rate. The key for a similar success of progress would be to develop, such as Korea, a political and entrepreneurial class which loves its country and proceeds with ratio, pragmatism, open-mindedness, learning ability, willingness to make sacrifices, and subsequently international credibility. The long-term economic and technical guidelines of Pak Chung-hee could be useful blueprints for an upturn of many third-country nations. The population of European countries had to endure severe hardships as well before their grandchildren could enjoy the fruits of their forefathers.

For all those countries that presently strive for democratic government forms a good advice would be to study the bloodless, gradual change of Korea from colonialization through military dictatorships to democratic and pluralistic structures. A shining example in the social advancement of the history of mankind!

8.7 Disappointments and Expectations of Korea

The country has been divided over almost 70 years by now and the desire for reunification of the nation remains unbroken, although the political systems are suspicious of each other. Likewise, the surrounding great powers have different opinions about a Korean future that would serve their own interests best.

A united Korea would have almost 75 million inhabitants. After integrating and adapting the northern part of the country, a powerful economy with a high level of technology and well-trained population could develop. Korea would be on the same level with other middle-sized powers of the world. Geographically and culturally, together with China, it could obtain a favorable access to a gigantic developing market.

Of course, being influenced by a communist ideology for two-thirds of a century might have led North Koreans to forget about the harsh requirements of a market society. It is even thinkable that a unification would negatively influence the entrepreneurial spirits of the southern compatriots.

Nevertheless, a reunited Korea could be an interesting impulse to Asia and the world. The great Indian philosopher Rabindranath Tagore, winner of the Nobel Prize for literature in 1913, who was also an important painter and musician, voiced his optimistic expectation during the earlier, dark period of Korea as follows:

During the golden age of Asia
Korea was one of its lights
And this light is waiting to be ignited again
To illuminate the East.

Literature

1. Focus; Muenchen, edition from July 21, 2011; pp 108–109
2. Lim E (2007) Kaesong industrial complex. Seoul, p 17
3. Lim E cit. above, p 227
4. The Korea Times (2010) Korea faces 10 daunting tasks in 2010, edition from 28 Jan 2010
5. Business Week (2000) Korea's digital quest, edition from 25 Sept 2000
6. Weber N cit. above; p 417

CV Shin Ho Kang

Name	Shin Ho Kang
Date of Birth	May, 13th, 1927
Business Address	252, Yongdu-Dong, Dongdaemun-Gu, Seoul, Korea

Education

Feb. 1952	BS/MS, College of Medicine, Seoul National University (SNU)
Aug. 1958	Ph.D. Internal Medicine, Albert-Ludwigs University of Freiburg

Vocational Career

Dec. 1966–Nov. 1967	National President, Korea Junior Chamber of Commerce
May 1971–Jan. 1989	Director, The Federation of Korean Industries
Feb. 1974–Feb. 1990	President, The Korean Marketing Association
Feb. 1975–June 1881	President, Dong-A Pharmaceutical Co. Ltd.
Apr. 1976	Vice Chairman, The Korea UN—Association
Aug. 1977	Chairman of the Board, Sang-Ju High School Foundation
Mar. 1978–Feb. 1995	Vice-Chairman, Korean Federation of Scientific and Technological Societies
July 1981	Chairman, Dong—A Socio Group
Feb. 1983–Feb. 1995	Vice-Chairman, The Alumni Association of College of Medicine, SNU
Feb. 1983–Jan. 1998	Vice Chairman, Korea Employer's Association
Feb. 1987–Feb. 1991	President, The Korea Pharmaceutical Manufacturers
Feb. 1989–Nov. 2003	Deputy Chairman, The Federation of Korean Industries
Feb. 1992	Chairman, Korea Industrial Technology Association
Aug. 1993	National Representative, Republic of Korea Red Cross
Oct. 1993	Vice-Chairman, The Korea—China Economy Council
Mar. 1994–Mar. 2000	Chairman, The Seoul-Beijing Council for Economic Cooperation

D.K. Schneidewind, *Economic Miracle Market South Korea*,
DOI 10.1007/978-981-10-0615-9

Feb. 1996	Board Member, KIST—Europe Advisory Council
Feb. 2004–Feb. 2007	Chairman, The Federation of Korean Industries
Oct. 2005	Director, Foundation of Sejong Industries
Mar. 2007	Honorary President, The Federation of Korean Industries
Oct. 2008	Advisor, Green Growth Korea
Feb. 2009	Chairman, 2009 Seoul-Tokyo Hanmadang Festival

Prices and Awards

Apr. 2002	Chang-Jo Medal, Order of Science and Technology Merit
Mar. 2005	First Class German National Medal for Distinguished Service (presented by German President Horst Koehler)
Mar. 2007	The Grand Cordon of the Order of the Rising Sun (the Highest Japanese Order, presented personally by the Tenno Heika)
Nov. 2009	Honorary Senator of the Albert-Ludwigs University of Freiburg

Literature on Korea

1. Adami N, Kolatek C (1994) Bibliographische Einfuehrung in die Wirtschaft Japans und Koreas, Muenchen
2. Ambrosius M, Ederer G, Kim H (1988) Korea, geteiltes Land, Berlin
3. Amsden AH (1989) Asia's next giant. Oxford, New York
4. Armstrong CK (ed) (2007) Korean society, 2nd edn. Oxford, New York
5. Beal T (2011) Crisis in Korea. London, New York
6. Beyma R (ed) (1992) Kim Young-sam and the New Korea, Chicago
7. Buzo A (2002) The making of modern Korea. London, New York
8. Chang D (1985) Economic control and political authoritarianism—the role of Japanese corporations in Korean politics 1965–1979, Seoul
9. Chang S (2008) Sony vs. Samsung, New York, Singapore
10. Choi J (1989) Labor and the authoritarian state: labor unions in South Korean manufacturing industries 1961–1980, Seoul
11. Chong SL, Pak CH, Verdes P (Ca) (2012)
12. Chun S (ed) (1982) Korean thought, Seoul
13. Cook, HF (1981) Pioneer American businessman in Korea, Seoul
14. Covell AC (1986) Folk art and magic—shamanism in Korea, Elizabeth (NJ), Seoul
15. Coyner TL, Jang S (2007) Mastering business in Korea, Seoul
16. Deutsch-Koreanische Industrie- und Handelskammer (AHK/ DKIHK) [German Chamber of Industry and Commerce], Seoul 2009
17. Eberstadt N (2009) The North Korean economy, New Brunswick (NJ)
18. Eckert CJ, Lee K, Lew IY, Robinson M, Wagner Edward W (1990) Korea—old and new: a history, Seoul
19. (The) European Union Chamber of Commerce in Korea, Seoul, 1968
20. (The) Federation of Korean Industries (FKI) (1987) Korea's economic policies (1945–1985), Seoul
21. Frank CR, Kim K, Westphal L (1975) Foreign trade regimes and economic development, New York
22. Hahn B, Yamamoto T (eds) (1978) Korea and Japan, Seoul
23. Han W (1969) The history of Korea, Seoul
24. Hopfner J (2010) Living abroad in South Korea, Berkeley
25. Hulbert HR (1969) The passing of Korea, reproduction, Seoul (1st edn, New York, 1906)
26. International Cultural Foundation (ed) (1982) Economic life in Korea, Seoul
27. Jaisohn P (2000) My days in Korea, Seoul, 2nd print
28. Johnson A (2012) The orphan master's son, New York
29. Kang TW (1989) Is Korea the next Japan? New York, London
30. Kendall L, Peterson M (eds) Korean women—view from the inner room, Cushing

D.K. Schneidewind, *Economic Miracle Market South Korea*,
DOI 10.1007/978-981-10-0615-9

31. Kim B, Kim P (1977) Korean public administration, Elizabeth (NJ)
32. Kim B, Vogel E (2011) The Pak Chun Hee Era, Cam Xbridge (Mass), London
33. Kim D, Kim L (1989) Management behind industrialization—readings in Korean business, Seoul
34. Kim H (ed) (1983) Studies on Korea, Honolulu
35. Kim H (1998) Marktbearbeitungsstrategien Koreanischer Unternehmungen im Ausland, Giessen
36. Kim J (1991) The Koreans: their mind and behavior, Seoul
37. Kim K (1986) Man and society in Korea's economic growth: sociological studies, 4th en, Seoul
38. Kim K, The Korea Herald (eds) (2008) Social change in Korea, Paju-si
39. Kim Y, Kim P (1990) If anyone will not work, neither let him eat, Hanam-shi, Seoul
40. Koellner P (1998) Suedkoreas technologische Abhaengigkeit von Japan, Hamburg
41. (The) Korea Herald (ed) (2008) Korean wave, Paju-si
42. Korean National Commission for UNESCO (ed) (1983) Main currents of Korean thought, Seoul
43. Korean National Commission for UNESCO (ed) (2004) Reflections at the New Millenium, Elizabeth (NJ), Seoul
44. Korean National Commission for UNESCO (ed) (2004) Korean philosophy, Elizabeth (NJ), Seoul
45. Lee C, Park C (2012) From poverty to power, Palos Verdes (Ca)
46. Lee J (2000) Historic factors influencing Korean higher education, Seoul
47. Lee K (2005) Training of small and medium-scale enterprises in the knowlege economy—a case study of Korea, Seoul
48. Lee P, Mi Y (2004) Wirtschaftliches Handeln in Suedkorea, Marburg
49. Lee Y (1934) West goes east—Paul von Moellendorff and great power imperialism in late Yi Korea, Honolulu
50. McCune S (1961) Korea's heritage—a regional social geography, 5th edn, Rutland (Vt), Tokyo
51. Oak S, Martin V (2000) American/Korean contrasts, Elizabeth (NJ), Seoul
52. Oberndorfer D (2014) The two Koreas, revised, 3rd edn, New York
53. Odrich P, Odrich B (1994) Korea und seine Unternehmen, Frankfurt/M
54. Park C (ed) (1980) Human resources and social development in Korea, Seoul
55. Park C (ed) (1980) Macroeconomics and industrial development in Korea, Seoul
56. Park E, Park C (eds) (2012) KOREA—from rags to riches, Seoul, 2nd edn
57. Park W (2008) Traditional Korean thought, Incheon
58. Patterson W (1988) The Korean frontier in America—immigration to Hawaii 1896–1919, Honolulu
59. Pfabigan A (1986) Schlaflos in Pjoengjang (Sleepless at Pjoengjang), Wien/Muenchen
60. Rhee ZS, Song B (2003) The rise of the Korean economy, 3rd edn, New York
61. Schneidewind D (1991) Management-Strukturen in der Republic Korea und einige Vergleiche zu Japan. In: Schneidewind D, Toepfer A (eds) Der asiatisch-pazifische Raum, Landsberg
62. Shin E (2004) Energy and environment in the Korean economy, Seoul
63. Spencer RF (1988) Yogong: factory girl, Seoul
64. Sung K (ed) Development experience of the Korean Economy, Seoul
65. Ungson GR, Steers RM, Park S (1997) Korean enterprise—the quest for globalization, Boston
66. Verin M, Morillot J (2004) Korea, Reich der Morgenstille, Muenchen
67. de Ville-Colby J (2001) The expatriate handbook, Seoul, revised edition
68. Woronoff J (1983) Korea's economy: man made miracle, Seoul/Arch (Or)
69. Yu C (1988) Tax aspects of foreign companies doing business in Korea, Seoul
70. Yu S (1986) Uri Dul Ui Simayun, Seoul
71. Yu S, Kyung H (1997) Kyang Young Supil, Seoul

Index

D.K. Schneidewind, *Economic Miracle Market South Korea*,
DOI 10.1007/978-981-10-0615-9

The manufacturer's authorised representative in the EU is Springer Nature Customer Service Centre GmbH, Europaplatz 3, 69115 Heidelberg, Germany. If you have any concerns regarding our products, please contact ProductSafety@springernature.com

Printed and bound by CPI Group (UK) Ltd, Croydon, CR0 4YY
30/09/2026
02225444-0012